Aggression Replacement Training®

Aggression Replacement Training®

A Comprehensive Intervention for Aggressive Youth

Barry Glick
John C. Gibbs

Third Edition–Revised and Expanded

RESEARCH PRESS
PUBLISHERS

Champaign, Illinois ▪ [800] 519-2707 ▪ www.researchpress.com

RESEARCH PRESS
PUBLISHERS

Jim's, Jerry's, Sam's, and Antonio's Problem Situations: From *The EQUIP Program: Teaching Youth to Think and Act Responsibly Through a Peer-Helping Approach,* by J.C. Gibbs, G.B. Potter, and A.P. Goldstein, 1995, Champaign, IL: Research Press. Reprinted by permission.

Mark's and Alonzo's Problem Situations: From *An Analysis of Social Behavioral Skill Deficits in Delinquent and Nondelinquent Adolescent Boys,* by B.J. Freedman, 1974, unpublished doctoral dissertation, University of Wisconsin, Madison. Adapted by permission.

George's Problem Situation: From *Dilemmas for Applied Use,* by A. Colby and B. Speicher, 1973, unpublished manuscript, Harvard University, Cambridge, Massachusetts. Adapted by permission.

Leon's and Reggie's Problem Situations: From *Moral Dilemmas at Scioto Village,* by D.W. Meyers, 1982, unpublished manuscript, Ohio Department of Youth Services, Columbus. Adapted by permission.

Juan's Problem Situation: From *Dilemma Session Intervention with Adult Female Offenders: Behavioral and Attitudinal Correlates,* by H.H. Ahlborn, 1986, unpublished manuscript, Ohio Department of Rehabilitation and Correction, Columbus. Adapted by permission.

The Social Skills Training Session Evaluation Checklist (page 357), Anger Control Training Session Evaluation Checklist (page 358), and Moral Reasoning Session Evaluation Checklist (page 359) have been adapted by permission from materials originally developed in September of 2005 by Christopher J. Hayes, M.Ed., Washington State ART Quality Assurance Specialist, and Robert Barnoski, Ph.D., Washington State Institute for Public Policy, as part of the Washington State Community Juvenile Accountability Act.

> **All handouts and worksheets are available to the purchaser**
> **from the publisher's website at www.researchpress.com/downloads**

Copies of this book may be ordered from Research Press at www.researchpress.com.

Composition by Jeff Helgesen
Cover design by Linda Brown, Positive I.D. Graphic Design, Inc.
Printed by McNaughton & Gunn

ISBN 978-0-87822-637-5
Library of Congress Control Number 2010934451

Contents

Figures and Tables

FIGURES

TABLES

Acknowledgments

Writing acknowledgments for this third edition of *Aggression Replacement Training: A Comprehensive Intervention for Aggressive Youth* is bittersweet. This revised and expanded edition of our program is a result of more than 30 years working with agencies and jurisdictions, helping them to develop policies and programs for their at-risk youth. Many of the ideas and expanded resources herein are a product of training staff, working with youth, and our own implementation experiences.

All of this effort would not be possible without the contributions from the countless young people in the myriad of schools, community-based youth centers, residential treatment systems, and juvenile justice programs who participated in and completed the ART program. From these, we have three young people we wish to distinguish, all of whom were youth at risk but completed the Aggression Replacement Training program, then served as "Junior ART Facilitators" within their youth program, and graduated to become constructive citizens within their communities. They are Eric Svensson, Tarek Al-Mugrabi, and Kadar Zaman.

Our appreciation also goes to the dedicated staffs that have been trained to deliver the program. Without their questions, activities, discussions, and comments, this effort would not have come to fruition. We also recognize with great admiration, affection, and respect a number of trusted colleagues, who are consummate professionals and also happen to be dear, dear friends: Mikael Kalt, Mariusz Hermelin, David Kliba, Jacek and Eva Morawski, and Frans Kassenaar.

We also wish to acknowledge with appreciation and affection our long-standing relationship with Research Press. We have now published under three presidents: Ann Wendel, Russ Pence, and, currently, Gail Salyards, all of whom had the vision and foresight to endorse and support our ideas and efforts. Without their leadership and direction, this product would not be as it is today. However, there is an even more important influence within that organization, without which this volume would not have been possible. With great respect, we honor Karen Steiner, our editor, who provided the discerning eye, asked the difficult questions, and pushed the envelope to insure clarity, without compromising our theory, philosophy, or implementation strategies. She is a genius at what she does.

What is bitter in all this sweetness is that our friend and mentor, Arnold P. Goldstein (1933–2002), has been with us only in spirit. Arnie was first and foremost a university professor and teacher. He also was a distinguished researcher, prolific writer, and tireless advocate for improving methods to help both adults and youth who struggle with issues of emotional and behavioral control. It is impossible to think of the Aggression Replacement Training program without thinking of him.

Introduction

It is almost four decades since Arnold Goldstein and I first sat in his living room, embarking on the journey that would eventually result in the design and development of this program and publication of the first edition of *Aggression Replacement Training* (Goldstein & Glick, 1987). It is more than a decade since we last revised this book, inviting John Gibbs to join us as an expert in the area of moral reasoning applications (Goldstein, Glick, & Gibbs, 1998). Since that time, the field of cognitive-behavioral programs and services has developed into a clinical science with an array of curricula to change cognitions and emotions in a variety of ways.

This third edition of *Aggression Replacement Training* is a rebirth and renewal of the basic principles in the program as initially designed, but it is also more. This volume is for practitioners. It gives both theory and application of theory for group facilitators to use and implement. It provides advanced techniques to further elaborate ART concepts, yet allows for practitioners' individual styles and techniques. This volume, unlike its predecessors, provides techniques based upon 30 years of experience training staff in all kinds of learning situations how to deliver the program while maintaining its original design with integrity and fidelity.

A BRIEF HISTORY OF ART

While our work was formative in many aspects—multimodal, prescriptive, outcome based, well researched, perhaps years before its time—our philosophical and theoretical framework was classical and pragmatic, based on the work of psychologists and behavioral scientists who provided the foundation for our intervention.

In association with Robert Sprafkin and Jane Gershaw, Arnold Goldstein produced the first applications of Albert Bandura's theories of social learning to patients being released from mental institutions (Goldstein, Sprafkin, & Gershaw, 1965). That early effort provided the foundation that enabled them, along with Paul Klein and myself, to adapt the skills and procedures for adolescents, in a social skills learning approach we then called Structured Learning Training (Goldstein, Sprafkin, Gershaw, & Klein, 1980). Ultimately, these pioneering efforts led to Arnold

Goldstein's collaboration with Ellen McGinnis and the advance of these early techniques into the now widely implemented Skillstreaming programs for adolescents (Goldstein & McGinnis, 1997), elementary school children (McGinnis & Goldstein, 1984, 1997), and preschool and kindergarten children (McGinnis & Goldstein, 1990, 2003).

In the same vein, Goldstein and I drew from the work of Donald Meichenbaum, Robert Novaco, Eva Feindler, and Lawrence Kohlberg as we further expanded our ideas about aggressive and violent youth and first piloted Aggression Replacement Training in the early 1980s. We were fortunate to have the aid of many of my staff at Annsville Residential Youth Center in Taberg, New York, to help test those early interventions and ultimately demonstrate how effective ART was as an intervention to change antisocial behaviors.

After our first years of experience, others became interested in applications of ART strategies. Gibbs and Potter, working in Ohio with delinquent adolescents in juvenile institutions, applied ART within a therapeutic community in a positive peer culture. Their program, EQUIP (Gibbs, Potter, & Goldstein, 1995), provided the basis for a major change in the moral reasoning component of ART, described in the second edition of *Aggression Replacement Training* (Goldstein et al., 1998). Briefly, we adapted aspects of the EQUIP group process and simplified the classical Kohlbergian moral reasoning group procedures so practitioners who work with at-risk youth in schools, community agencies, juvenile institutions, and other settings could more easily implement our program.

As is the case for any popular and effective program, over the years ART has attracted a plethora of providers. In the absence of standardized training and a certification process to ensure competency in implementing the program and training individuals to train others, ART has been subject to a degree of what program developers have identified as "program drift"—that is, original standards of design have in some cases been compromised or diluted to suit the needs of the systems using the program. This third edition of *Aggression Replacement Training* is a rebirth and renewal of ART in the sense that it returns to the fundamental principles upon which Arnold Goldstein and I first developed the intervention. As such, one purpose of this volume is to return practitioners to the core concepts and strategies that have been proven effective when implementing ART. We strive to accomplish this goal by doing the following:

- Restating the history, philosophy, and theory by which ART was designed and developed

- Elaborating the techniques and strategies for each of the components, describing actual experiences from practitioners and trainers

- Clarifying the theory for each of the components with illustrative dialogue from actual group sessions

- Refining the implementation processes based on practitioners' experience, program evaluations, and research

- Presenting program procedures and content in the form of sessions, including step-by-step instructions to facilitate each ART group meeting

UNDERSTANDING ANGER AND AGGRESSION IN YOUTH

Aggression among youth is nothing new. Until about 1900, juveniles were treated the same as adults across societies when they behaved aggressively or violently. Usually, they were incarcerated, either in criminal justice systems or "mental hygiene" systems. It was not until 1899 that the first family court was created in Cook County, Illinois, to deal with aggressive and violent children and youth. By the early 1990s, within a mere century of the institution of the family court model, concerns for increased youth violence resulted in a return to harsher laws and incarceration of youth within adult systems. Some family courts have even been dismantled.

We live in an aggressive society, and juvenile delinquency and aggression in youth continue to be huge social problems, expensive both in terms of economic costs and in terms of pain, unhappiness, and unrealized ambition. Unfortunately, aggression is typically a quite difficult behavior to change. For many youths, aggression and antisocial behavior are immediately and richly reinforced, receiving few or no negative consequences. Aggression is not complicated in theory, yet it is a complex human behavior not easily explained in terms of a single dimension. In youth, it takes the form of observable behavior. It is usually initiated when anger grows from cognitive misperceptions of the interpersonal world. Further, aggression and violent behavior typically are given energy and sustenance by the emotional arousal such cognitions generate. In brief, aggression is simultaneously a behavioral, cognitive, and emotional phenomenon. As a result, interventions designed to address it must be multidimensional.

Psychology of the Aggressive Youth

Four primary traits that characterize aggressive youth include verbal and physical aggression, skill deficiency, immaturity, and withdrawal.

Verbal and Physical Aggression

Quay (1965) studied adolescent behaviors using multivariate analysis and developed a classification for aggressive children. He found that aggressive children could be identified by behaviors such as fighting, disruptiveness, profanity, irritability, quarrelsomeness, defiance of authority, irresponsibility, high levels of attention-seeking behavior, and low levels of guilt feelings. Quay also observed active antisocial aggressiveness that resulted in conflict with parents, peers, and social institutions (Quay & Hogan, 1999).

Skill Deficiency

Most behaviorally disordered (i.e., aggressive) adolescents are skill deficient. That is, they have not developed the social skills necessary to negotiate their environments successfully. Indeed, in Glick's own work with delinquent youth in New York state public and private institutions, more than 90 percent presented themselves with serious skill deficits (Glick, 1978, 1979, 1995).

Immaturity

Immature behaviors include short attention span, clumsiness, passivity, incompetence, daydreaming, and preference for younger playmates. These types of behaviors often lead to alienation by peers. By definition, these behaviors represent patterns that may have been age appropriate at earlier stages of development but certainly are not acceptable for the adolescent (American Psychiatric Association, 2000; Bronfenbrenner, 1979).

Withdrawal

In the case of conduct disorders, immaturity leads to attacks on others (aggression); in the case of personality disorders, it results in withdrawal. Withdrawal behaviors have been variously labeled as personality problems, disturbed neuroticism, and overinhibition. These types of conditions have been characterized by depression, feelings of inferiority, self-consciousness, shyness, anxiety, hypersensitivity, reclusiveness, and timidity. While these attributes are not ordinarily associated with aggression, they often co-occur in the aggressive adolescent, as well as in the passive-aggressive adolescent.

Etiology of Adolescent Aggression

Aggression once was viewed as an instinctive human behavior, a combative energy that must be expressed. In more recent years, however, the thinking that catharsis of aggression is helpful has changed, and the idea of an inborn and inevitable aggressive instinct has been shown to be a convenient myth. Although a genetic component may be involved in aggression, fundamentally aggression appears to be a learned behavior.

Bandura (1969, 1973) and others have shown that aggression is learned in one of two ways, directly or vicariously. Direct learning follows from reinforced practice (i.e., the behavior is tried and brings the expected, desired result). Vicarious learning occurs by observing others behaving aggressively and then receiving a reward for doing so.

Family Influences

The first major classroom for the teaching and learning of aggression is the home. In the home, 4 percent of parents seriously physically abuse their children (e.g., burn, fracture bones, shake to the point of concussion), and 90 percent engage in at least occasional physical punishment (e.g., spank, hit, slap; Straus, 1994). What happens when an adult hits a child? The child ceases the behavior that resulted in the punishment, and, thus negatively reinforced, the adult is now more likely to use corporal punishment in response to the child's next transgression. Both adult and child have learned the truth of the adage "might makes right."

The dynamic between siblings is similar, with children learning quickly that aggression pays: Two siblings are watching television in their family room. The older brother wants to watch a sports program, while his younger sister wants to watch cartoons. The older brother screams at his sister, and she leaves. The brother learns that screaming works, and his younger sister learns to submit to avoid further aggression.

School and Community Influences

The school and community are major locations in which aggression is learned. This assertion is supported by the increasingly aggressive nature of many adolescent peer groups (Csikszentmihalyi & Larson, 1984; Goldstein, Apter, & Harootunian, 1984) and also by means directly analogous to those described previously for parents and their children.

However, schools are not the only venue where aggression is learned. Adolescents learn from their peers, and the streets provide the best stage to practice that learning. Gangs have always been available to youth. However, gang activity worldwide is on the increase (Howell & Decker, 1999), and gangs now offer youth the opportunity to act out the violence they see in the media. Gangs have also become substitute families for disadvantaged and disenfranchised youth, thus perpetuating the cycle of violence.

Media and Other Social Influences

Aggression is taught and learned not only in schools and homes. The impact of the mass media on human behavior is difficult to gauge, but many assert that the level of media violence increases the level of violence in our society. The negative effects of this barrage of media violence include an aggression effect (increased copycat violence and self-directed violence), a victim effect (increased fearfulness, mistrust, and self-protectiveness), and a bystander effect (increased desensitization and callousness; Comstock & Paik, 1994; Donnerstein, Slaby, & Eron, 1994; Hoberman, 1990). Young people who watch media violence are more prone to increase their aggression toward others. When they do commit violent acts, they report less remorse, less guilt, greater feelings of virility, and higher intensity of aggression and violence (Comstock & Strasburger, 1990). With the advent of the Internet and cell phones, youth have instant and constant connections with one another in their pursuit of violent activities as well as ready-made strategies to meet their aggressive needs.

Other Factors

Aggression, like many complex behaviors, is most likely the result of both nature and nurture. The following are conditions that promote aggression, as reported and researched in the literature (Zillmann, 1999).

- Weak familial or social bonding

- Being a frequent target of aggression

- Observing successful acts of aggression

- Being frequently positively reinforced for aggressive acts

- Deficiency in information-processing skills (e.g., identifying means-ends relationships, ability to generate alternative solutions and consequences, overattribution of hostile intentions)

- Deficiency in moral reasoning (e.g., inability to take others' perspectives of the world, belief that aggression is legitimate, increases self-worth, and yields positive tangible rewards for self and significant others)

- Deficiency in identifying and using alternative prosocial skills in anger-producing situations

EVOLUTION OF PROSOCIAL AND ANGER MANAGEMENT TECHNOLOGY

Until the early 1970s, psychotherapies to deal with aggressive behaviors were limited to talk. *Psychodynamic/psychoanalytic* therapies attempted to remediate antisocial behaviors by calling forth and interpreting unconscious material that blocked progress and awareness within the client. *Humanistic/client-centered* therapies sought to free the individual's potential by providing a warm, empathic, maximally accepting helping environment. *Behavior modification* attempted to ensure that when latent desirable behaviors or approximations of behavior occurred, the individual received contingent reinforcement. All three of these approaches assumed that the desired behaviors existed within the client's repertoire, to be released by analysis and interpretation, therapeutic climate, or contingent reward.

Cognitive-Behavioral Approaches

As early as the 1970s, beginning with Bandura (1973) and followed by Novaco (1975, 1979), anger was defined as an affective stress reaction to provocative events, and interventions began to address both cognitive and affective domains. Cognitive restructuring and cognitive skills approaches are the basis on which cognitive-behavioral programs have been designed and developed.

Aaron Beck (1976), a psychiatrist working with mentally ill individuals, first introduced the cognitive restructuring approach. Essentially, cognitive restructuring is a process by which individuals are directed to assess their own thoughts, feelings, beliefs, and attitudes in order to identify new thinking that reduces risk behavior. Albert Ellis applied Beck's seminal work in Rational Emotive Therapy, a structured process that helped individuals to deal rationally with problems of living within their affective domain (Ellis, 1962). As a result of that early work, Ellis applied his theory to other areas and introduced Rational Emotive Behavior Therapy (Ellis, 1997), which applied this cognitive process to the behavior of individuals, especially students in school settings.

Yochelson and Samenow (1977) were the first to apply the principles of cognitive restructuring to the criminal population. They designed a process to help staff and offenders identify thinking errors associated with criminal behavior. Yet another program based upon cognitive restructuring principles is Cognitive Self-Change, developed by Bush and Bilodeau (1993). This group program, developed for the most violent criminal offenders, teaches them to replace risk behaviors by substituting new thinking for their risk-related thoughts. The offender in a group situation uses a "thinking report," a structured technique in which offenders identify a problem situation and then write their thoughts about the situation, the feelings they had during their thoughts, and the underlying attitudes and beliefs that culminate as a result of the thoughts and feelings expressed. The process is intense, and the group learns from each situation as it is provided.

Other programs based upon this approach include Rites of Passage, a program of change and transformation for African Americans (Preudhomme & Dunston, 1989; Moral Reconation Therapy (Robinson & Little, 1988); and Reasoning and Rehabilitation (Ross & Fabiano, 1986. Other cognitive skills programs include Problem Solving (Taymans, 1997); Choices (Reno, 1997), and Thinking for a Change–Revised (Glick, Taymans, & Bush, 2010).

Such programs have been implemented in a cross section of systems: schools, community-based programs, juvenile justice programs, adult prisons, and mental hospitals. Their effects upon prosocial behavior have been well documented. In summary, the skills development, habilitation, and clinical impacts produced for individuals involved with these have been analyzed and shown to be significant within the mental health, juvenile justice, and criminal justice systems.

Future Directions

Meaningful progress toward understanding the science of aggression, violence, and criminal behavior has been made through recent meta-analyses of studies on the topic. Donald Andrews and his research group have analyzed thousands of independent studies to explore the relationships that exist between certain variables and criminal behavior (Andrews & Bonta, 2003). He has identified a series of criminogenic factors that are highly related with antisocial behaviors. These factors include companions; interpersonal relationships; personal attitudes, values, and beliefs supportive of crime; behavioral history; psychopathology; social class of family of origin; personal temperament, aptitude, and early behavioral history; early family conditions; school-based risk factors; and personal educational, vocational, and socioeconomic achievement.

Certain programs designed to mitigate against these criminogenic factors include those that do the following:

- Change antisocial attitudes

- Reduce antisocial peer associations

- Promote familial monitoring and supervision

- Promote identification/association with anticriminal role models

- Change antisocial feelings

- Increase self-control, self-management, and problem-solving skills

- Replace the skills of lying, stealing, and aggression with more prosocial alternatives

- Reduce chemical dependencies

In his analysis, Paul Gendreau has identified certain program characteristics that should be present in order to effect change in aggressive and violent offenders (Gendreau, 1996). These characteristics include the inclusion of social learning strategies, behavioral techniques, cognitive methods, educational status, and family-based (structural, systemic) approaches. Programs found not to impact offenders' antisocial, aggressive, or violent nature include nondirective, client-centered counseling; unstructured psychodynamic therapy; approaches that involve intense group interactions without focus on personal responsibility; and variations on themes of official punishment.

Mark Lipsey (1999) has evaluated programs reported to be effective for offenders involved in treatment interventions to help reduce the effects of their antisocial and aggressive personalities. He found as a result of his meta-analysis that the best treatments reduced recidivism by about 30 percent on average. The treatments were structured and focused and had been defined as "appropriate" (i.e., clinically relevant) by professional program staff or clinicians. Milieu therapy provided weak or no treatment effects in serious juvenile offenders.

Edward Latessa (2006) has studied programs throughout the United States and Canada. He has found that programs that effectively impact criminal behavior and reduce aggression and violence as well as the offender's propensity to reoffend are dependent on the extent to which (a) the chief executive of the program was involved in the program's development and implementation; (b) program staff were trained, supervised, and supported in their work; (c) the offender was involved with his or her own program planning and implementation; (d) the program was evaluated and modified, based upon the new knowledge acquired; and (e) the program was developed according to theoretical construct, with internal validity and reliability.

The principles gleaned from these evaluators provide program designers with data to help develop new approaches and techniques. Indeed, many of these tenets and standards are reflected in the ART program.

OVERVIEW OF VOLUME CONTENTS

This book consists of two parts: Part 1 describes ART program content and discusses issues in implementation. Following the present introduction, chapter 1 offers an overview of the three main components of ART: Social Skills Training (the behavioral component), Anger Control Training (the affective component), and Moral Reasoning (the cognitive component). It also describes such concerns as participant and facilitator selection and preparation, scheduling issues, and program maintenance and continuation.

Chapters 2, 3, and 4 examine the three components of ART in detail. Each chapter describes the theoretical foundations of the particular approach and the rationale for including it in ART, then describes session procedures, including sample dialogue and extensive discussion of how ART group facilitators may best apply teaching methods.

Any intervention that involves at-risk youth challenges the practitioner who attempts to implement it. Over the years, staff charged with delivering ART have raised questions about maintaining participant interest and applying tactics to enhance group members' learning and extend that knowledge beyond the group sessions to youths' real-world situations. Toward that end, chapter 5 examines participant motivation and resistance, and chapter 6 describes methods of enhancing generalization of performance.

Chapter 7, describing application models and evaluations of program effectiveness, is especially important. In it, we describe model agencies, systems, and jurisdictions that have successfully implemented ART with fidelity and integrity. These program models are but a sample of the hundreds that currently operate, nationally and internationally, in a variety of conditions.

Chapter 8, on the administration and management of ART, is part of the effort to acknowledge what we have learned from Latessa (2006) and others (Ndrecka, Bechtel, Lowenkamp, & Latessa, 2009): that cognitive-behavioral interventions are most effective when executives are involved with their delivery from their inception and when managers and supervisors seriously monitor, audit, and provide staff with the support they require to be effective practitioners.

Part 2 provides step-by-step guidelines for conducting the 10-week ART program in the form of 30 session outlines. Grouped according to ART component, sessions detail objectives, materials, and procedures for teaching program content and include a number of reproducible handouts and other materials.

Following the session procedures provided in Part 2, a series of useful appendixes completes the volume. These include the complete Skillstreaming curriculum for adolescents, session evaluation checklists for ART components, caregiver/staff materials, alternate moral reasoning problem situations, and other helpful forms.

PART I

ART Program Content and Implementation

CHAPTER 1

ART Components and Program Implementation Concerns

Any and every act of aggression has multiple causes, both within and external to the child or adolescent. With regard to internal causes, aggressive youth frequently possess a series of interlocking and often reciprocally compounding deficiencies. As noted in the introduction, they characteristically are weak or lacking in the intrapersonal, interpersonal, and social-cognitive skills that collectively constitute effective prosocial behavior. Indeed, a major portion of their disruptiveness and overt aggression is a reflection of psychological and social skill deficiencies. Youth with skill deficiencies often lack the knowledge and ability to ask rather than demand, negotiate, compromise, or otherwise respond appropriately to conflict. Instead, they strike out physically and satisfy their desire for immediate gratification rather than exercise self-control. They become highly aroused, agitated, and aggressive. These youth lack the skills necessary to handle frustration; to respond effectively to the complaints, anger, instructions, or accusations of others; and to behave competently in other important personal and interpersonal areas. Their impulsiveness and overreliance on aggressive means for goal attainment often reflect deficiency in anger control. Finally, in the cognitive realm, aggressive youth characteristically reason at a more egocentric, concrete, and primitive level of moral reasoning.

From our theoretical perspective, then, we selected the individual interventions that as a group constitute ART to address these three core deficiencies. While there are more internal and external antecedents of aggressive behavior than those addressed in ART, we predicted that much of the outcome variance associated with efforts to change such behavior would occur in the domains of enhanced prosocial skill proficiency, increased anger control, and advanced levels of moral reasoning.

ART COMPONENTS

Specifically, ART includes three coordinated and integrated components: Social Skills Training, Anger Control Training, and Moral Reasoning.

Social Skills Training

Social Skills Training, the behavioral component of ART, is a systematic psychoeducational intervention to teach prosocial behaviors. In ART, acquiring skills offers participants the chance to substitute prosocial behaviors for their characteristic action of aggression. Sessions involve the following four procedures:

1. Modeling: Showing examples of expert use of behaviors (steps) constituting the skills

2. Role-playing: Providing guided opportunities to try out and rehearse the steps of each skill, using a real-life situation relevant to the group member

3. Performance feedback: Providing praise, reinstruction, and related feedback on how well a youth's role-playing of the skill steps matched the expert model's portrayal of them

4. Transfer training: Encouraging youth to engage in a series of activities designed to increase the chances that the skill learned in the training setting will endure and be available for use when needed in the environment (institution, home, school, community)

The skills employed in ART and related instructional procedures are described in chapter 2. (The complete Skillstreaming curriculum for adolescents, consisting of 50 skills, is reproduced in Appendix A.)

Anger Control Training

Social Skills Training, the behavioral component of ART, teaches youth what to do instead of behaving aggressively. In a complementary manner, Anger Control Training—ART's affective component—teaches participants what *not* to do. In brief, the goal of Anger Control Training is to teach youngsters the inhibition of anger. As sessions progress, participants are required to describe anger-arousing experiences, recording them on a "Hassle Log." They then learn to respond to their hassles with a chain of behaviors that includes the following:

1. Identifying triggers: Attending to those external events and internal self-statements that provoke anger responses

2. Identifying cues: Recognizing individual physical events such as tightened muscles, flushed face, and clenched fists, which let the adolescent know that the emotion he or she is experiencing is anger

3. Using anger reducers: Employing a series of techniques that, like the use of reminders, is designed to lower the individual's level of anger—for example, deep breathing, counting backward, or imagining a peaceful scene

4. Using reminders: Making self-statements such as "Stay calm," "Chill out," and "Cool down," or expressing nonhostile explanations of others' behavior

5. Thinking ahead: Evaluating the likely consequences of one's behavior (*"If* I do this, *then* that may happen")

6. Using self-evaluation: Reflecting on how well the individual responded to the conflict situation (by identifying triggers, identifying cues, using reminders, and using anger reducers), then rewarding oneself for effective performance or coaching oneself to do better

The background of Anger Control Training and its procedures are described in chapter 3.

Moral Reasoning

Participation in Social Skills Training and Anger Control Training helps participants learn what to do and what not to do in circumstances that generally instigate aggression. However, because aggressive behavior is so consistently, immediately, and efficiently rewarded in the real world, youth may still consciously choose to behave aggressively. ART therefore includes Moral Reasoning sessions, the cognitive component of ART. These sessions help raise participants' level of fairness, justice, and concern with the needs and rights of others.

In these sessions, also called *social decision making meetings,* youth thinking at differing levels of moral reasoning discuss problem situations relevant to their lives. This discussion arouses an experience of cognitive conflict, whose resolution will frequently advance participants' reasoning.

Moral Reasoning sessions involve four phases:

1. Introducing the problem situation

2. Cultivating moral maturity

3. Remediating moral development delay

4. Consolidating moral maturity

Chapter 4 includes discussion of the evolution and content of the Moral Reasoning component and details its procedures.

Integration of Components

When used separately, each of these three interventions results in behavior change in those to whom it is directed. Both Social Skills Training and Anger Control Training yield reliable short-term alterations in participant behavior. Moral Reasoning sessions appear to influence perspective taking but less frequently result in short-term changes in behavior. We reasoned that the purposeful combination of these three interventions would yield more reliable and longer term positive outcomes in reducing aggressive and violent behavior than each could individually. This has in fact been the case, as the program evaluations described in chapter 7 have shown.

In the present section, we provide an overview of the 10-week ART program as it is commonly offered in schools, community agencies, and institutions. In this format, group members attend an ART session three times a week, with one session per week devoted to Social Skills Training, Anger Control Training, and Moral Reasoning, respectively. Typically, a single session lasts an hour, with Moral Reasoning sessions sometimes lasting up to an hour and a half.

The 10 social skills included in this program were selected based on three criteria: their effectiveness in reducing aggressive behaviors; their hypothesized value as prosocial inoculations against antisocial impulsivity, and their suitability in meeting program evaluation and research model guidelines. The Anger Control Training component of the ART curriculum is a modified version of that originated by Feindler (Feindler, 1979; Feindler & Ecton, 1986), which was itself based on the earlier work of Meichenbaum and Novaco. The problem situations included in the Moral Reasoning component are those effectively employed by Gibbs et al. (1995) in the EQUIP program, directed toward aggressive youth.

Table 1.1 shows the association of ART components across the 10-week program period. The Social Skills Training and Moral Reasoning sessions involve independent skills or problem situations; the information in Anger Control Training sessions is sequential. It is important to know that each session builds on the next when delivering the program: The skill of the week in Social Skills Training relates to the content of the Anger Control Training session, which in turn is associated with the Moral Reasoning problem situation. As a result, to receive maximum benefit from the program, participants should receive all the sessions in the order listed.

IMPLEMENTATION CONCERNS

The following discussion provides an overview of issues relating to facilities and materials required to run the program, participant and facilitator selection and preparation, scheduling issues, communication with staff and caregivers, and pretesting/posttesting. Staff development, training, and supervision are also discussed, as are issues relating to program adaptation and extension.

TABLE 1.1 Ten-Week ART Curriculum

Week	Social Skills Training	Anger Control Training	Moral Reasoning Training
1	Session 1 *Making a Complaint*	Session 2 *ABCs of Anger*	Session 3 *Jim's (or Emilio's) Problem Situation*
2	Session 4 *Understanding the Feelings of Others*	Session 5 *Hassle Log and Triggers*	Session 6 *Jerry's (or Latoya's) Problem Situation*
3	Session 7 *Getting Ready for a Difficult Conversation*	Session 8 *Cues and Anger Reducers*	Session 9 *Mark's (or Ishan's) Problem Situation*
4	Session 10 *Dealing with Someone Else's Anger*	Session 11 *Reminders*	Session 12 *George's (or Enzio's) Problem Situation*
5	Session 13 *Helping Others*	Session 14 *Thinking Ahead*	Session 15 *Sam's (or Carmen's) Problem Situation*
6	Session 16 *Keeping Out of Fights*	Session 17 *Self-Evaluation*	Session 18 *Leon's (or Cheri's) Problem Situation*
7	Session 19 *Dealing with an Accusation*	Session 20 *Angry Behavior Cycle*	Session 21 *Reggie's (or Big Bear's) Problem Situation*
8	Session 22 *Dealing with Group Pressure*	Session 23 *Using a Social Skill and Rehearsal of Full Anger Control Chain*	Session 24 *Alonzo's (or Tara and Lashonda's) Problem Situation*
9	Session 25 *Expressing Affection*	Session 26 *Rehearsal of Full Anger Control Chain*	Session 27 *Juan's (or Lin's) Problem Situation*
10	Session 28 *Responding to Failure*	Session 29 *Overall Review and Rehearsal of Full Anger Control Chain*	Session 30 *Antonio's (or Emma's) Problem Situation*

Note: Alternate moral problem situations (in parentheses) are provided in Appendix D.

Facilities and Materials

Some general principles should be followed when conducting cognitive-behavioral interventions, including ART. Since ART meets three times a week over 10 weeks, a dedicated space for groups to meet is advantageous. This allows program posters and other group-generated materials introduced each week to remain on the walls for easy reference. The space should be large enough to accommodate 14 people comfortably, along with desks or tables. It should be well ventilated and climate controlled to enhance participant learning and interaction. Finally, the group meetings should be protected from interruptions, except for emergencies.

Figure 1.1 depicts the preferred U-shaped arrangement often used when conducting ART. In this group arrangement, participants can see one another, program posters, and the easel pad or whiteboard on which one facilitator writes related program information. The co-facilitator may sit with the group members or circulate within the room to address any behavioral concerns.

In Social Skills Training and Anger Control Training sessions, participants practice what they learn by role-playing. While role-playing, two group members take a position at the front of the group, where everyone can see them and the facilitator can provide prompting and coaching as necessary.

FIGURE 1.1   Room Arrangement for ART

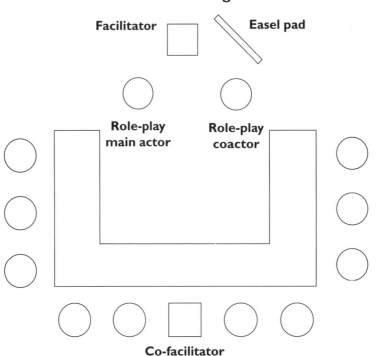

Other materials needed to run the program are readily available and include an easel pad or whiteboard and markers or another form of whole-group display. Access to a photocopy machine or computer and printer is required to generate session handouts and other reproducible materials, included in this text and on the accompanying CD.

A binder or folder for each group member allows group members to keep homework forms and other materials in one place. Giving group members responsibility for bringing necessary materials with them to groups empowers them to take an active part in their own development as they progress through the ART program. If binders are acceptable in the setting, they are preferred because dividers may be used to separate materials for each of the program components, a supply of homework forms can be placed in at the beginning of each section, and youth can easily keep their completed homework in chronological order.

Skill Cards listing the name and steps of the social skills and whole-group displays of specific content for all program components are also required. Skill Cards for each skill are provided in each Social Skills Training session as well as on the CD. Facilitators may reproduce these on card stock, then cut them apart for distribution to individual participants. Pre-printed Skill Cards for all 60 Skillstreaming skills are available from the publisher of this book.

The content for whole-group displays (i.e., posters) is provided in the session text, as well as in an 8½ × 11–inch format on the CD. In addition to using the posters in the training sessions, it is helpful to hang them around the school or institution, both as a means of reminding participants of content and to sensitize school and institutional staff not directly involved in the ART effort to opportunities to observe, reward, and, when necessary, coach. Many facilitators choose to make their own full-size posters, sometimes with the help of participants.

Participant Selection and Preparation

In the majority of school, agency, and residential settings in which ART has been used, youth have been assigned to the program by staff responsible for their education or well-being. Group members who are involuntarily assigned to participate in ART usually come from juvenile justice or mental health settings, or perhaps special education programs. Participation in regular school and community settings more typically has been voluntary or accomplished at the request of teachers or administrators. Regardless of the basis for participation, specific criteria for inclusion in ART are substantial deficiencies in prosocial skills, anger control, and moral reasoning capacity.

Group Composition

We recommend no more than 12 members in an ART group; however, 8 to 10 participants per group is sufficient and allows for some attrition without compromising ART group processes. Sometimes participants drop out of group because they may be involved in a crime that leads to institutional placement, or their families may move from the community. Attrition in institutions often occurs because youth are released or transferred from the facility. Whatever the reason, when participants withdraw from the program, there is a void. If the group falls below seven or eight, the group process in Moral Reasoning and the process by which skills are taught in both Social Skills Training and Anger Control Training may be compromised. Because ART depends heavily on interaction and process, facilitators are challenged to keep participants from abandoning the group. Facilitators may need to reach out to individual participants to assess why they have stopped coming and perhaps use personal influence to coax participants to recommit to the group.

Individual Meetings

Once groups have been formed, the next step is preparing and motivating participants for ART participation. Ideally, basic program information is provided first in an individual meeting, then to the group when it convenes. Purposes, procedures, incentives, and group rules are covered.

The purposes of ART are presented as they relate to the specific youngster with whom one is meeting. For example, the facilitator might say, "Remember last week when you got into a fight with Russell and were suspended for two days? Well, in these meetings you'll be taught new ways of thinking and behaving to help you stay out of that kind of trouble." Note how a statement such as this can serve the goals of both group preparation and motivation.

General procedures for the ART program are next explained. In the case of the standard 10-week curriculum, the facilitator would say that the group will meet three times a week and that meetings will help participants learn skill alternatives to aggression, ways to control their anger, and methods for thinking in more effective ways.

The meeting also includes discussion of basic rules for group participation:

1. Attend and participate.

2. Be respectful (no fighting or put-downs).

3. Be open and honest.

4. What is said in the group stays in the group.

An explanation of any incentives that are available and the specific guidelines that govern how they can be earned or lost is also provided. Rules for group conduct are discussed in greater detail at the first group meeting.

Facilitator Selection and Preparation

Since the inception of ART, hundreds of people with a wide variety of backgrounds and credentials have been effective facilitators. Teachers, counselors, school psychologists, youth care workers, social workers, and correctional officers are primary examples of people who become ART facilitators.

Though sometimes ART groups have been effectively and productively led by one facilitator, we strongly recommend that, whenever possible, two facilitators work together. Aggressive adolescents are often proficient in generating behavior management problems that make learning difficult. If two facilitators are not available, the use of aides, parents, volunteers, or other adults can be effective, under the direction and supervision of a trained ART group facilitator.

Qualities of Effective Facilitators

Three related qualities seem to characterize effective facilitators. First, they are at ease with adolescents, individually and in groups. The concerns participants share are taken seriously, and they are listened to respectfully. Whether dealing with youngsters individually or as a group, skilled facilitators show sensitivity toward the fact that adolescence is a stormy time of life, characterized by unpredictable expressions of both adult and childlike behaviors.

At times, this mix of youth behaviors causes problems manifested in ART groups in a variety of aggressive, resistive, or otherwise difficult behaviors. When these behaviors do occur, the skilled facilitator is able to respond effectively. Effective facilitators can apply the appropriate consequences for the behavior without demeaning the youth and are able to maintain the agenda of the group. Chapter 5 details techniques for moderating, reducing, and eliminating common problem behaviors.

Like many other educational and training approaches, ART's ultimate effectiveness depends not only on its teaching procedures and the content of its curriculum, but also on the core qualities of the group. Is it a safe place, free of put-downs, intimidation, and subtle bullying? Are the facilitators, in addition to being competent teachers or workers, also competent protectors?

The third and final quality of effective facilitators is that they competently deliver the program content. Whether or not their formal credentials are in education, their teaching is alive, energetic, and responsive to different learning abilities and styles. They are able to work with individuals during group sessions without losing the group focus. There is little off-task time, transitions are made smoothly from one activity to another, and, in a variety of ways, they communicate a "can do" attitude.

Cultural Compatibility

Whether culture is defined by geography, ethnicity, nationality, social class, gender, sexual orientation, age, or some combination thereof, for ART to be meaningful it must be viewed in a multicultural context and practiced in a manner responsive to such a context. When facilitators and participants are from different cultural groups, definitions and prescriptions may conflict. Facilitators are challenged to interpret accurately the behaviors of culturally different learners and to employ instructional strategies effective in helping all learners maximize their experiences.

ART is most effective when it is delivered with appreciation for such culturally relevant notions as skill strengths and differences versus skill deficits, the need for differential training strategies and instructional tactics, participant channels of accessibility and communication styles, potential for stereotyping, and culturally associated qualities of participants. Facilitator knowledge, skill, and sensitivity are required in these areas.

Scheduling Issues

Scheduling issues derive from two sources. The first concerns staff; the second concerns group members. As noted, the training schedule for ART involves meeting three times a week, with one session devoted to each of the components. Ideally, sessions meet at the same day and time of the week across the program, with each session separated by one day in between. This schedule is based upon learning principles of consistency (meeting the same day and same time) and transfer training concepts, including stimulus generalization (specifically, one week between sessions of the same type allows participants time to complete their homework assignments, practicing in the real-world setting what they have tried out in group).

Such a rigorous schedule presents a challenge. Staff must devote sufficient time for group sessions (generally, at least three hours each week) in addition to the preparation time to ensure accurate delivery of material and process for each component. Yet another concern is what happens if one of the group facilitators is not available: Can the group still be conducted? While not ideal, it is possible for one confident and competent staff member to conduct a group session or for other people to be enlisted to help, as suggested earlier.

Finally, how can staff arrange for groups to meet at the same time and place each week? While this kind of continuity in part depends on supervisory and administrative support, facilitators ultimately are responsible for determining that the physical space is available and ready.

The issue of scheduling for participants presents yet another set of challenges for staff. First, participants outside the institutional setting usually have time commitments to activities other than attending ART groups (work, school, community service, probation/parole appointments, etc.). Attending groups three times a week sometimes is a burden. In community settings, we have addressed this issue by reducing the number of sessions without reducing the number of contact hours. That is, instead of meeting three times a week for an hour, we have scheduled sessions two times a week, each session two hours in duration. In this case, the first session includes a complete Social Skills Training session, along with 30 minutes of a Moral Reasoning group; the second session starts with the second 30 minutes of the Moral Reasoning group (same problem situation for that week), followed by the complete Anger Control Training session.

Another issue raised by group facilitators is what happens if a participant misses a group session. At the outset, it is important for staff to set the standard of zero tolerance for missing groups. While circumstances sometimes arise when a participant must miss a session, these should be rare. When such situations do occur, it is the staff's responsibility to provide the information missed. This is easier said than done: When group members miss a session, they miss both the information provided and the group process. The group process is important for all components and critical in Moral Reasoning sessions, where the group's analysis of the problem situation is central. In addition, ART sessions build on each other. Anger Control Training especially relies on previous learning, so it is difficult to play catch-up much beyond the second or third week of the program.

Parent and Staff Involvement

Whenever possible, collaboration between group facilitators and group members' parents, teachers, and other significant adults should be sought. Appendix C includes a general description of the ART program, along with a number of other forms designed to help support program learning across the ART components.

In Social Skills Training, each time a new skill is introduced, parents are sent the Staff/Caregiver Social Skills Training Home Note to inform them about the purpose and value of the skill, its steps, and any homework assigned. Parallel forms for Anger Control Training and Moral Reasoning sessions are also included.

Pretesting and Posttesting

Overall program evaluation is usually conducted by independent researchers. However, program administrators and group facilitators can collect data to indicate group member progress and general program efficacy. It is ideal to have program evaluators involved as administrators design and develop their plans for program implementation. In that way, data collection is built into the planning process and group facilitators can take an active role.

Several measures are helpful in collecting information about ART program efficacy. For assessing social skills competencies, the Staff/Caregiver Skillstreaming Checklist, Group Member Skillstreaming Checklist, and Skillstreaming Grouping Chart are useful (see Appendix A).

In the area of anger control, the Multidimensional Anger Inventory (Siegel, 1986) is helpful in assessing five areas: anger arousal, range of anger-eliciting situations, hostile outlook, anger-in, and anger-out. The Novaco Anger Scale and Provocation Inventory (NAS–PI; Novaco, 2004) provides information about how an individual experiences anger and what provokes it.

With regard to moral reasoning, the How I Think (HIT) Questionnaire (Barriga, Gibbs, Potter, & Liau, 2001; Gibbs, Barriga, & Potter, 2001) assesses patterns of self-serving cognitive distortion (i.e., thinking errors). Moral judgment stage scores may be obtained by using the Sociomoral Reflection Measure–Short Form (SRM–SF; Gibbs, Basinger, & Fuller, 1992; Gibbs, Basinger, Grime, & Snarey, 2007).

Finally, the Community Behavior Report and Community Adjustment Rating Scale provide a general measure of youth behavior. These items and the SRM–SF are included in Appendix E.

For quality assurance and evaluation purposes, data should be collected within a week before and after the program is administered. Pretesting on these or other measures can often be accomplished at the individual meeting before sessions begin.

Staff Development, Training, and Supervision

Generally, staff who are effective in working with at-risk, highly aggressive youth must have skill sets that include but are not limited to consistent attendance at work, listening skills, patience, physical ability and experience interacting with the population, positive attitude, and enjoyment working with adolescents. First-line supervisors and managers should possess flexibility, good verbal and written communication skills, patience, and experience. All staff, no matter what their role within the organization, must be competent in decision making, be good communicators, have experience with the target population, and be willing to expand their paradigms to accommodate innovative and creative ideas.

Certainly, all staff should be well informed about adolescent growth and development and able to apply these concepts to practical situations.

Staff Development

Staff development is one of the most important tasks an administrator must manage, for it plays a vital role in the quality of services provided to at-risk youth. As the youth population becomes more antisocial, aggressive, and violent, the competencies of staff to manage behavior in order to provide differential and prescriptive cognitive-behavioral interventions, including ART, must likewise increase.

The area of staff development begins with a well-designed and articulated implementation plan for staff growth and training. Such a plan must take into consideration what qualities the staff should have; what skills they need to sustain the system's vision, mission, goals, and objectives; what areas of competence need to be developed or nurtured; and what content-specific knowledge they need to acquire to implement the program. These and other issues are discussed in more depth in chapter 8.

Staff Training

Staff training is critical for achieving positive program outcomes. Ideally, staff should have preservice training, ongoing continuing training; and individualized outsourced training opportunities. Practical supervised training sessions need to be provided to ensure staff proficiency when applying the theory, strategies and techniques of ART. In addition, training must be supported by a system of supervision and technical assistance that ensures staff continue in their professional and personal development as they provide the ART program to youth.

Comprehensive training ensures that staff are competent and confident in delivering ART groups effectively and efficiently, with program integrity and fidelity. Glick offers offers five-day training sessions for group facilitators, trainers of group facilitators, and master trainers:*

Group Facilitator Training. Practitioner trainees are given a pretest and posttest to assess the knowledge and skill sets they acquire as a result of training. Each trainee is also provided with three months of technical assistance after the initial group facilitator training as they implement the ART program for the first time.

ART Trainers of Group Facilitators Training. Participants attend a seminar providing instruction to prescreened applicants who wish to train ART group facilitators. This seminar combines facilitator skill development sessions and ART facilitator sessions.

---

*For more information on this training, readers may contact G & G Consultants, 106 Acorn Drive–Suite A, Glenville, NY 12302-4702
(Website: http://artgang0.tripod.com/ggconsultantsllc).

ART Master Training. This training provides individualized independent learning for those staff who apply and are accepted to be Master Trainers of ART. Master Trainers are certified to participate in activities relating to program development, curriculum innovation, and independent ART consultation.

Staff Supervision

It is essential to maintain participant motivation as well as to provide orientation to and communication with staff as to what is transpiring within ART groups. Administrative and supervisory support is critical to this effort. Managers must set policy and expectations, supervisors must monitor and account for program delivery, and staff must be held responsible for services. As such, staff are responsible for ensuring that group members attend all ART group sessions and complete assigned homework between sessions. In addition, staff must know what is being taught and discussed each week of the ART groups and deal competently with participants as they gain new skill sets and begin to apply what they learn in ART groups to real-life situations.

The checklists provided in Appendix B are helpful for the purpose of self-evaluation and evaluation by experienced observers.

Program Adaptation and Extension

Reliable program outcomes are a function of the degree to which programs are conducted with fidelity and integrity. Research indicates that when the ART program is not delivered with fidelity and integrity, participant behavior may deteriorate instead of improve (Barnoski, 2004; Latessa, 2006).

In this context, *program fidelity* means staying true to the original program design and development; *program integrity* means that the training must take place in its entirety, with nothing either missing or added. In practice, this means that to assure positive outcomes, the original design of the program must be maintained, including the number and length of sessions and how long participants are involved. Key session content must be retained and covered in the order outlined. Clearly, the theoretical approach upon which ART is based must also be maintained.

However, practitioners know full well that programs must be adapted to meet the specific needs and requirements of an agency or system. Toward that end, what may the practitioner do that is deemed an acceptable adaptation and not a violation of program fidelity? They may certainly modify the vocabulary used so group members better understand the concepts or skills being introduced. They also may modify modeling displays and role-play content to reflect the culture, ethnicity, and gender of participants. Appendix D provides alternate Moral

Reasoning problem situations. Facilitators may use these and adapt any of the problem situations by changing the names or gender of the characters described.

The issue of what to do after the ART program is complete provides both a challenge and an opportunity. The decision to continue programming is associated with but not limited to how long the participant will remain with the agency or organization, what other programs or services are planned for the participant, what staff are available to continue the program, and what needs the participant has.

Once the ART program has been delivered as originally designed and according to standard operating procedures, group facilitators may continue using the techniques employed in the program to sustain group member involvement for an additional period of time (usually an additional 10 weeks). Chapter 7 describes a number of specific program applications and administrative modifications that demonstrate differential programming and prescriptive application of ART to meet group member needs. Using sound adolescent development principles allows the facilitator to empower youth by negotiating additional materials to be learned.

It should be noted that continuing sessions do not constitute a continuation of the ART program per se. Rather, when additional programming is provided, group facilitators are continuing the group process and using the techniques and strategies in each of the components to support and augment participant learning.

To continue the social skill learning process, the facilitator and youth may choose additional social skills to learn and practice. Group members may complete the Group Member Skillstreaming Checklist (in Appendix A). The checklists can then be scored, and items rated as "Almost Never" or "Seldom" can be voted on by the group to become the skills taught in subsequent sessions.

Youth who need additional practice with anger control concepts may be assigned to subsequent groups. If it is determined that a youth is in need of the entire sequence of Anger Control Training, then he or she should be placed in a separate ART group that will meet that goal. Sometimes a youth may need to review only one or two anger control concepts. In that case, the facilitator may wait for that session to be taught in another group or may plan a special group session to assist that youth. Usually, however, youth do not need to repeat specific Anger Control Training group sessions: They either "got it—or not."

Additional Moral Reasoning Problem Situations may be chosen from Appendix D and discussion groups continued as appropriate. Moral Reasoning may also be continued as part of the maintenance of effort with an existing group. In such instances, ongoing groups that contract to learn 10 more social skills may meet a second time each week to discuss a problem situation. The same process used during ART Moral Reasoning sessions is employed for this extended program.

❦

The next three chapters describe each of the ART components in more detail, beginning with a brief theoretical and philosophical overview, followed by specific strategies and techniques.

CHAPTER 2

Social Skills Training: The Behavioral Component of ART

Social Skills Training is a way of teaching interpersonal, aggression management, and related skills to youngsters who are weak or lacking in these competencies. In ART, the emphasis is on skills training with youth who are frequently aggressive, but in schools and elsewhere the program has been used successfully with youth displaying a range of other problematic behaviors—teenagers who are shy or withdrawn, immature, developmentally delayed, or otherwise deficient in their interpersonal skills.

BACKGROUND

Like the other components of ART, the Social Skills Training component stands on the shoulders of its ancestors. Indeed, it was Albert Bandura (1969), the father of cognitive skills within the cognitive-behavioral school of psychology, who first introduced the process by which social skills are taught: modeling, role-playing, and performance feedback. National policy in the late 1960s supporting deinstitutionalization of mental health patients motivated Sprafkin and Gershaw, practicing psychologists at the Veteran's Administration Hospital in Syracuse, New York, to collaborate with Goldstein, then an assistant professor at Syracuse University, to develop a 60-skill curriculum for schizophrenic clients who were scheduled to be released to their communities. This curriculum applied Bandura's theoretical constructs to one of the first cognitive skills curricula available for practitioners (Goldstein, Sprafkin, & Gershaw, 1974).

This work yielded impressive results, in part because of the innovative design of the social skills training process. Goldstein and colleagues included a fourth part to the process, adding to Bandura's original model. They posited that transfer of knowledge from the training setting to the real-world situations clients faced would be enhanced if practitioners paid attention to certain tactics to foster such transfer.

Structured Learning Training

Based upon this early intervention, Goldstein and colleagues developed a more prescriptive, targeted social skills curriculum for emotionally disturbed and at-risk adolescents (Goldstein, Sherman, Gershaw, Sprafkin, & Glick, 1978), calling it Structured Learning Training. The 50 skills in this curriculum were sequential—that is, they built one upon another—with more advanced social competency required by the youth as they progressed through the curriculum.

Over the more than 20 years during which these Structured Learning Training interventions were initiated and applied in a large number of schools, agencies, and institutions, a considerable amount of evaluation research has been reported, both by us and by numerous other investigators (see Goldstein & McGinnis, 1997, for an annotated review). The results have been used not only as overall tests of the training method's efficacy, but also as guidelines for altering and improving its component procedures and materials.

Skillstreaming

Enhancements of procedures and materials are reflected in development of the Skillstreaming programs for adolescents (Goldstein & McGinnis, 1997), elementary school children (McGinnis & Goldstein, 1997), and preschool and kindergarten age children (McGinnis & Goldstein, 2003).

The 50 skills in the Skillstreaming curriculum for adolescents are listed in Table 2.1. (Items in boldface type are the skills taught in the 10-week ART curriculum.) The first group, "Beginning Social Skills," is fundamental to getting along with others and are considered basic because they involve just the individual who is performing the skill. The second group, "Advanced Social Skills," involves accomplishing the skill with another individual or perhaps a group of people and requires knowledge of the skills of the first group. The third group, "Skills for Dealing with Feelings," deals with the affective part of behavior and hence is more complex than those skills that involve less or no emotion. The fourth group in the curriculum, "Skill Alternatives to Aggression," reflects a specialized kind of emotion and as such is considered yet more complex than the previous groups. The fifth group of skills is yet more advanced because these skills require the individual to interact with others and also be aware of his or her environment and surroundings. This group, "Skills for Dealing with Stress," is the basis from which prescriptive cognitive interventions for more aggressive and violent at-risk youth have been developed. The final group, "Planning Skills," reflects the decision-making process and requires involvement with skills training for a longer period of time as well as more sophisticated cognitive processes. The complete

---

TABLE 2.1   Skillstreaming Skills for Adolescents

Group 1: Beginning Social Skills

1. Listening
2. Starting a Conversation
3. Having a Conversation
4. Asking a Question
5. Saying Thank You
6. Introducing Yourself
7. Introducing Other People
8. Giving a Compliment

Group 2: Advanced Social Skills

9. Asking for Help
10. Joining In
11. Giving Instructions
12. Following Instructions
13. Apologizing
14. Convincing Others

Group 3: Skills for Dealing with Feelings

15. Knowing Your Feelings
16. Expressing Your Feelings
17. **Understanding the Feelings of Others**
18. **Dealing with Someone Else's Anger**
19. **Expressing Affection**
20. Dealing with Fear
21. Rewarding Yourself

Group 4: Skill Alternatives to Aggression

22. Asking Permission
23. Sharing Something
24. **Helping Others**

25. Negotiating
26. Using Self-Control
27. Standing Up for Your Rights
28. Responding to Teasing
29. Avoiding Trouble with Others
30. **Keeping Out of Fights**

Group 5: Skills for Dealing with Stress

31. **Making a Complaint**
32. Answering a Complaint
33. Being a Good Sport
34. Dealing with Embarrassment
35. Dealing with Being Left Out
36. Standing Up for a Friend
37. Responding to Persuasion
38. **Responding to Failure**
39. Dealing with Contradictory Messages
40. **Dealing with an Accusation**
41. **Getting Ready for a Difficult Conversation**
42. **Dealing with Group Pressure**

Group 6: Planning Skills

43. Deciding on Something to Do
44. Deciding What Caused a Problem
45. Setting a Goal
46. Deciding on Your Abilities
47. Gathering Information
48. Arranging Problems by Importance
49. Making a Decision
50. Concentrating on a Task

Skillstreaming Curriculum, including skills and skill steps, checklists, and grouping chart, is included as Appendix A.

ART Social Skills Training

For all intents and purposes, the terms *Structured Learning Training* and *Skillstreaming* are synonymous, although the latter term refers to the specific programs developed by McGinnis and her collaborators, while the former references the seminal work of Goldstein et al. (1976), the basis upon which ART was developed. For clarity and simplicity, the term *Social Skills Training* denotes the ART process described in this book.

All Skillstreaming skills, including ART social skills, are composed of skill steps, usually between three and six. The presumption is that if the person performs the steps of the social skill exactly as stated, in their exact order, the person will have accomplished the skill. Skills are composed of "action steps" or "thinking steps." An action step is a step that group members can actually observe. A thinking step is a step that occurs as part of the thought process, which cannot be seen by observers. When a group member role-plays a thinking step, the facilitator instructs the group member to point to his or her head and say aloud what he or she is thinking. Table 2.2 shows the steps in the skill Making a Complaint, the first skill in the 10-session ART program. The first two steps are thinking steps. The last three are action steps.

OVERVIEW OF THE SOCIAL SKILLS TRAINING PROCESS

As previously noted, the four steps of the social skills training process are modeling, role-playing, performance feedback, and transfer training. Let us take a more comprehensive look at each of these processes to understand how they combine to ensure that at-risk youth acquire the skills they are taught.

Modeling

In ART, modeling means demonstrating the behaviors, or skill steps, constituting the skills in which participants are weak or lacking. Defined generally as learning by imitation, modeling has been examined in much research and under many names: copying, empathic learning, observational learning, identification, vicarious learning, matched-dependent behavior, and so forth. In Social Skills Training sessions, modeling is performed by the facilitators, who prepare vignettes that demonstrate how to achieve each step of the skill being taught. It is important that facilitators provide a "picture perfect" representation of the skill because whatever is demonstrated will be repeated by group members as they try to perform each step of the skill.

Several principles are important in modeling a skill. Specifically, facilitators model each skill step in the correct sequence, exactly as written. Modeling displays should depict one skill at a time, and all displays should portray situations that are relevant to group members' real-life situations. This latter detail is critical, especially if we want group members to transfer what is learned in ART sessions to their real-life situations.

Research on modeling has successfully identified a number of modeling enhancers, or circumstances that increase the effectiveness of modeling. These modeling enhancers are characteristics of the model, the modeling

---

TABLE 2.2   Sample Skill—Making a Complaint

Skill Steps

1. Decide what your complaint is.

2. Decide whom to complain to.

3. Tell that person your complaint.

4. Tell that person what you would like done about the problem.

5. Ask how he/she feels about what you've said.

---

display, or the observer that have been shown to affect the degree to which learning by imitation occurs.

Model Characteristics

More effective modeling will occur when the model (the person to be imitated) (a) seems to be highly skilled or expert; (b) is of high status; (c) controls rewards desired by the observer; (d) is of the same sex, approximate age, and social status as the observer; (e) is friendly and helpful; and, of particular importance, (f) is rewarded for the given behaviors. That is, we are all more likely to imitate expert or powerful yet pleasant people who receive rewards for what they are doing, especially when the particular rewards involved are something that we too desire.

Modeling Display Characteristics

More effective modeling will occur when the modeling display shows the behaviors to be imitated (a) in a clear and detailed manner, (b) in the order from least to most difficult behavior, (c) with enough repetition to make overlearning likely, and (d) with as little irrelevant detail as possible. Learning is also enhanced when several different models, rather than a single model, are used.

Observer Characteristics

More effective modeling will occur when the person observing the model is (a) told to imitate the model; (b) similar to the model in background or in attitude toward the skill; (c) friendly toward or likes the model; and, most important, (d) rewarded for performing the modeled behaviors.

⁓⁓

Group members cannot learn from watching a model unless they pay attention to the modeling display and, in particular, to the specific behaviors being modeled. Such attention is maximized by having the co-facilitator point to each step (written on a poster or another whole-group display), eliminating irrelevant detail in the modeling display, minimizing the complexity of the modeled material, making the display vivid, and implementing the modeling enhancers previously described.

Also to help group members attend to the skill enactments, Skill Cards, which present the name of the skill being taught and its behavioral steps, are distributed prior to the modeling displays. (Reproducible Skill Cards for each ART skill are provided after each Social Skills Training session.) Group members are told to watch and listen closely as the models portray the skill and to identify the behavioral steps as they are presented in the context of the modeling vignettes.

Role-Playing

In order for a group member to reproduce the behaviors he or she has observed, the group member must remember or retain them. Memory is aided if the behaviors displayed are classified or coded by the observer. Such coding is facilitated by covert rehearsal (i.e., reviewing in one's mind the performance of the displayed behaviors). An even more important aid to retention is overt, or behavioral, rehearsal. Such practice of the specific behavioral steps, or role-playing, is crucial for learning and is the second major procedure in Social Skills Training.

After the facilitators model the skill steps for the group, they provide several guided opportunities to practice and rehearse these competent interpersonal behaviors. Each group member role-plays the skill, enacting the steps in exactly the way they have been demonstrated. It is important to emphasize that in this context, role-playing is not enacting a skit to dramatize an event. Rather, it is the attempt to repeat what was shown in the modeling of the skill. Simply stated, the facilitators model (show, demonstrate) the steps of the skill, then group members role-play (try, attempt to reenact) the skill steps.

When developing role-plays, we ensure that the situations group members role-play are current and relevant. Group members identify a real situation to role-play, one that they could experience during the upcoming week. Toward that end, the group members must specify when he or she will use the skill, with whom, and where. We also ensure that the person role-playing stays in role—in other words, follows the steps of the skill.

Performance Feedback

Researchers interested in human learning have typically distinguished between learning (acquiring or gaining knowledge about how to do something) and performance (doing it). If a person has paid attention and remembered the behaviors shown in the modeling display, it may be said that the person has learned. The main interest, however, is not so much in whether the person *can* reproduce the behaviors, but whether he or she *does* reproduce them. As with retention, the likelihood that a person will actually perform a learned behavior will depend mostly on the expectation of a reward for doing so.

The crucial nature of reward for performance is further examined in discussion of group member motivation and resistance (see chapter 5). It is important to note here, however, the role of verbal reinforcement in the performance feedback portion of the skills training procedure. After each group member's role-play, the facilitator provides performance feedback in the form of praise, related feedback on how well the youth's role-playing of the skill matched the expert models' portrayal of it, and reinstruction if necessary. Specifically, facilitators provide systematic and objective statements to the person who did the role-play (tried following the steps of the skill) as to how well he or she achieved each step.

Insofar as possible, the feedback is positive in order to reinforce the group member's willingness and ability to perform each step of the skill. Toward that end, reinforcement is provided only after the role-play has been completed, given at the earliest possible opportunity (as soon as the role-play is finished), and consistent with the quality of the role-play. Because adolescents know when the adults who work with them are sincere, reinforcement should always be truthful and direct. The last thing we want to do is appear dishonest to the youth with whom we interact.

Transfer Training

Transfer training enhances the group member's ability to use the newly learned skill in situations outside the learning setting. Many skills instruction interventions incorporate transfer training into their programs by assigning as homework the task of applying the newly learned skill before the next meeting or by setting up practice situations outside of the training setting. Goldstein and others (e.g., Bush, Glick, & Taymans, 1997; Meichenbaum, 1977) have incorporated the transfer training strategies next described in their programs.

Transfer of learning from one situation to another is greatly enhanced when certain principles are observed—in particular, when the material is overlearned (i.e., repeated frequently) and reinforced with identical elements. In the case of ART, repetitive role-plays present the skill several times and identical elements are approximated by role-playing situations in which the skill steps are to be used outside the session. Another way in which transfer is maximized is through stimulus variability, in the form of presentation of skill steps in a variety of forms, such as on posters and Skill Cards that group members can carry with them.

The primary method for promoting transfer of learning in Social Skills Training is the assignment of homework. Participants are asked to practice the skills they learn outside the training session and to record their experiences on a Skill Homework Report like the example shown in Figure 2.1.

Real-life reinforcement, another transfer enhancer, is critically important and takes some effort on the part of the group facilitators. At times, group members are encouraged to use the skill situation outside the session with individuals who will be likely to provide reinforcement and to persist if they do not get what they desire in the first instance. Persons in the group members' real-life environment can also be assisted in providing coaching and reinforcement. Forms included in Appendix C are helpful in this regard.

SOCIAL SKILLS TRAINING SESSION PROCEDURES

The 10 skills included in the basic ART social skills curriculum are as follows:

- Week 1: Making a Complaint
- Week 2: Understanding the Feelings of Others
- Week 3: Getting Ready for a Difficult Conversation
- Week 4: Dealing with Someone Else's Anger
- Week 5: Helping Others
- Week 6: Keeping Out of Fights
- Week 7: Dealing with an Accusation
- Week 8: Dealing with Group Pressure
- Week 9: Expressing Affection
- Week 10: Responding to Failure

One skill is taught per session (assuming a group size between 8 and 12 youth) during each of the 10 weeks of the ART program. The skills are sequenced to complement the content and process of the Anger Control Training and Moral Reasoning components of ART. As noted in chapter 1, it is the combination of the three components each week cumulatively over the 10 weeks that creates a synthesis among these three separate interventions.

When conducting the Social Skills Training portion of ART, group facilitators manage the eight-step process shown in Table 2.3. This process encompasses the four components of social skills training: modeling, role-playing, transfer training, and generalization. The process ensures that group members learn the skill steps and gain confidence to transfer

FIGURE 2.1   Sample Skill Homework Report—Keeping Out of Fights

Name ___Kioka_____ Date ___November 3_____

SKILL STEPS

1. Stop and think about why you want to fight.
2. Decide what you want to happen in the long run.
3. Think about other ways to handle the situation besides fighting.
4. Decide on the best way to handle the situation and do it.

FILL IN DURING THE SESSION

Where will you try the skill?

In the car

With whom will you try the skill?

My boyfriend

When will you try the skill?

When he picks me up after work

FILL IN AFTER YOU PRACTICE THE SKILL

What happened when you tried the skill?

My boyfriend said he would stop bugging me about forgetting his birthday

What skill steps did you really follow?

All of them!

How good a job did you do in using the skill (*check one*)? ☑ excellent   ☐ good   ☐ fair   ☐ poor what they learn in the group to a real-life situation by practicing the newly acquired skill.

Preparing for the Social Skills Training Session

In the context of Social Skills Training, modeling involves showing group members the steps of the skill. Before the session, group facilitators should do as follows:

1. Meet to review the skill being taught, ensuring that they each understand the behavioral steps of the skill. Sometimes this is not as easy as it sounds. In the skill Keeping Out of Fights, for example, each of the four behavioral steps may seem straightforward. However, a closer examination reveals that Step 3 ("Think about other ways to handle the situation besides fighting") requires the modeling display to show a few independent, different ways to avoid fighting. Step 4 ("Decide on the best way to handle the situation and do it") on further inspection reveals that the facilitators enacting the skill must show the group both a thinking step (by pointing to the head while speaking aloud one way from the ways identified in Step 3) and an action step (doing it).

2. Develop a modeling display that accurately depicts the steps of the skill. The extent to which facilitators are able to provide an accurate representation of the behavioral steps of the skill strongly influences the degree to which group members will be able to learn the skill steps and transfer them to a real-life situation outside the group.

3. Rehearse the modeling display. Rehearsal should emphasize demonstrating the behavioral steps of the skill without overdramatizing the situation. Focusing on the behavioral steps alone prevents superfluous processing in the group and helps group members apply the skill steps in a relevant situation.

Each Social Skills Training session includes suggestions for possible role-play content in the following areas: school, home, peer group, and institution. These are just suggestions; role-plays addressing group members' personal experiences and concerns, if they adequately represent the skill, are most effective.

Step 1: Define the Skill

The first step, defining the skill, is actually broader than merely providing a skill definition. The facilitator involves group members in a brief discussion of their understanding of the skill being taught and, using their ideas, helps them develop an operational definition of the skill, along with concrete examples.

TABLE 2.3 Social Skills Training Steps

Step 1: Define the skill

Step 2: Model the skill

Step 3: Establish each group member's need for the skill

Step 4: Select the first role-player and set up the role-play

Step 5: Conduct the role-play

Step 6: Conduct the discussion (performance feedback)

Step 7: Assign the homework (transfer training)

Step 8: Select the next role-player

Facilitator: Today we are going to learn a new skill, one you will find helpful in your everyday lives. The skill we will learn this week is Keeping Out of Fights. Who can tell me what Keeping Out of Fights means to them? *(Pauses.)* Yes, Josh.

Josh: Not smashing someone in the face when they diss you.

Facilitator: Yes. Who else has something to offer? *(Pauses.)* Yes, Tyrone.

Tyrone: Ignoring someone who is putting you down and making fun of you.

Facilitator: Great! Who has another idea? *(Calling on another group member)* Kwame.

Kwame: Not arguing with someone, not yelling and screaming at someone.

Facilitator: Very good, Kwame. That is a bit different because fighting is not always physical . . . sometimes it can be verbal.

Well, group, for our purposes today, we will define Keeping Out of Fights as avoiding hitting, yelling, or otherwise harming another person as a result of a disagreement or misunderstanding with that person.

The co-facilitator writes the skill definition on an easel pad at the front of the group.

Facilitator: We all have at one time or another found ourselves in a predicament where we ended up fighting, either physically or verbally, when we really didn't want to. Who here has ever been in a situation where they could have used this skill, Keeping Out of Fights?

At this point, the facilitator or co-facilitator shows a poster or other whole-class display (overhead, PowerPoint) of the skill and its steps. Individual group members or the entire group reads each step aloud, identifying it as either an action step or a thinking step. (This identification helps participants follow what is happening when facilitators model the skill.)

Step 2: Model the Skill

In this step, facilitators present the vignette they developed and practiced earlier. The modeling display must follow the steps of the skill exactly.

Facilitator: Ms. Eureka *(co-facilitator)* and I are now going to model for you the skill Keeping Out of Fights. We are going to show you how to do each of the steps of the skill so you can get up here and role-play—that is, try it—after we are done. As we show you our little scene, we want you to try to identify each of the steps of the skill. Ms. Eureka will help you by pointing to each of the steps on the poster as we do them.

Here is the situation: I am in the school cafeteria, and one of the older students comes by and pushes in front of me, stepping on my new shoes. You will see Ms. Eureka do that. Watch what I do.

The co-facilitator enacts the first part of the scene, pushing the facilitator, etc. Fists clenched, the facilitator stops from lunging at the co-facilitator and points to his head (indicating thinking aloud).

"Just because that kid is older, she has no right cutting in line and dissing me by stepping on my new shoes (Step 1)."

"I want to get her to apologize and not diss me any more (Step 2)."

"I could walk away; I could go tell the teacher on duty; I could approach the kid and just tell her I didn't appreciate her stepping on my new shoes and cutting in line (Step 3)."

"I think I will approach her when we are alone and tell her I didn't appreciate her stepping on my new shoes and cutting in line (Step 4)."

The facilitator then completes the action phase of Step 4.

"Hey! I don't appreciate your cutting in line on me and stepping on my shoes."

The modeling display ends as soon as the final action step is completed. If a response from the coactor is expected, it must always be brief and prosocial in nature. So when the facilitator expresses concern in this example, the co-facilitator must respond simply and positively: "Oh, I didn't realize I did that" or "I was rushing to my next class and was late." What facilitators show the group is what they will get back in group members' role-plays—nothing more and nothing less. Again, the modeling display is simply a demonstration of the behavioral skill steps and not a full dramatization of a situation.

Step 3: Establish Each Group Member's Need for the Skill

Before group members commence their role-playing of the skill steps they have seen modeled by the group facilitators, it is necessary to identify each group member's current need for the skill. After all, behavioral *rehearsal* is the purpose of the role-play. Enacting the skill as relates to a present or anticipated situation or relationship in the participant's life is far more effective than enacting a fictional situation provided by group facilitators or reenacting a past problem or circumstance that may no longer be relevant.

Before inquiring into each group member's skill need, the facilitator asks the group if they observed the behavioral steps of the skill during the modeling display—for example, "Who saw Step 1, Stop and think about why you want to fight" and "What exactly did you see?" The facilitator follows the same procedure for each behavioral step of the skill, being certain to read the words of each of the steps aloud and have the individual reread the step before responding with an observation. This technique assists in the transfer of learning, previously discussed, increasing the chance that group members will practice the skills they role-play in their lives outside the group.

Skill need generally may have been established earlier in Step 1, when facilitators first introduced the skill. Nonetheless, openly discussing it in the group is part of the sequence necessary to establish relevant and realistic role-plays. Each group member, therefore, is asked in turn briefly to describe where, when, and especially with whom he or she will find it useful to employ the skill. In order to make effective use of such information, it is often valuable for the co-facilitator to list group members' names on the easel pad at the front of the room and to record next to each member's name the name of the target person with whom the skill will be used and the theme of the role-play associated with that person. (Alternatively, the co-facilitator may jot down this information privately, on a sheet of paper.) An ironclad rule is that every group member must perform a role-play for every skill, with no exceptions, and having such information at hand is quite useful if a given member expresses reluctance to participate.

Facilitator: OK, now that you have seen Ms. Eureka and me model the steps of the skill and we have discussed exactly how each of the steps was demonstrated, do you think this is a skill you can use in your own situations, sometime this week before our next Social Skills Training group?

Group members respond: "Hmm," "Maybe," "Yeah," "I gotta think about it."

Facilitator: Who here can share with us a situation where they can use this skill sometime in the upcoming week? Remember, you all will have to identify one. Simply tell the group where, when, and with whom you will use this skill, and give a brief description of the situation.

Maria: My sister who told me she is going to whip my butt for wearing her shirt yesterday to school without asking her. I guess I will have to use this skill this afternoon after school.

Facilitator: Great example to role-play, Maria. Who would like to share next?

Latoya: My friend who is upset that I kissed her boyfriend at the dance last Friday. I will see her this Thursday at work.

Facilitator: That's a good one also. Who would like to follow Latoya? *(Pauses.)* OK, Mike.

Mike: My teacher who yelled at me for cheating on an exam, which I did not do. He said I have to see him Friday after class.

Facilitator: Well, we are not concerned in this group about whether you did or did not cheat on the exam. We are interested in how well you try out the skill Keeping Out of Fights. Next?

Kwame: My dad when he comes home drunk Saturday. This will help me from getting into more trouble with the cops.

Facilitator: Hmmm, OK, this will be an interesting one. However, Kwame, this is so critically important, I would like to chat with you more after group if that is OK with you. Who haven't we heard from? Carla, how about you?

Carla: I, I, I really can't think of anything.

Facilitator: Well, Carla, we all need to participate, so why don't you give it some more thought and I will get back to you. Anyone else?

Tyrone: My coach said that I hogged the ball too much and wasn't being a team player, and he wants to give me some deten-

	tion. That will really piss me off, and I know I am going to take a swing at him.
Facilitator:	Who would like to share next?
Josh:	My girlfriend is going to kill me because I forgot to pick her up at work yesterday. I will have to use this skill tonight when I see her.
Facilitator:	We have two left. Who would like to go next?
Carla:	I guess I should go . . . I will have to use this skill with my dad. He asked me to watch my younger brother while he ran some errands. I told my younger sister to watch him and went to town. So when I visit with my dad this Sunday, I will have to use this skill.
Facilitator:	Thanks, Carla, I am glad you thought of a situation to use the skill, even though it is a tough one. Well, that leaves you, Kioka.
Kioka:	I've got one similar to Josh's. My boyfriend is really pissed at me because I forgot his birthday last week, and he keeps on yelling at me every time we talk. I just want to smack him.
Facilitator:	Well, all of you have very good situations in which you can try the skill Keeping Out of Fights, right here, right now. Once you feel comfortable with the steps of the skill, you will be able to practice the skill in the real situation for homework before our next Social Skills Training meeting.

Step 4: Select the First Role-Player and Set Up the Role-Play

Since all members of the Social Skills Training group will be expected to role-play each skill, in most instances it is not of great concern who does so first. Typically, especially after teaching one or two skills has made clear that all must role-play, the selection process determining the sequence of role-playing can proceed by having facilitators ask for volunteers ("Who wants to role-play first?"). If for any reason there are group members for whom the act of role-playing a particular skill on a particular day seems threatening, it may be helpful not to ask them to role-play first or second. Sometimes having them be the coactor reduces their reluctance to get up in front of their peers or role-play the skill steps. Seeing other group members role-play can be reassuring and help ease them into the activity.

For some, reluctance may turn into outright resistance and refusal. Means for dealing with such problematic behaviors are described at length in chapter 5. For the present, it is useful to indicate that although the "no exceptions" rule holds, we try to involve group members in role-playing by supporting, encouraging, reassuring, and highlighting the usefulness of the skill for their own personal needs, rather than by resorting to penalties, coercion, or authoritarian means. If you have demonstrated that the ART program empowers youth by giving them choices and shown how acquiring skills increases their choices, even shy or reluctant group members are likely to see the value in trying the skill in group before practicing it in their real-life situations.

Once a group member has described a real-life situation in which the skill might be helpful, that person is designated the main actor. He or she chooses a second group member (the coactor) to play the role of the other person (e.g., mother, peer, etc.) involved in the skill situation.

The facilitator urges the group member to pick a coactor who resembles the real-life person in as many ways as possible. The facilitator then elicits from the main actor any additional information needed to set the stage for role-playing. In order to make role-playing as realistic as possible, it is a good idea to obtain a description of the physical setting, events immediately preceding the role-play, the mood or manner the coactor should portray, and any other details of apparent value.

At this point, facilitators give each group member a Skill Card listing the skill name and steps.

Facilitator: OK, group, now it's your turn to try out the skill Keeping Out of Fights. Who would like to use the situation they have just described and role-play the skill steps?

Group members remain silent.

Facilitator: You all now know that everyone will have a chance to role-play. This group will continue until each of us has been the main actor and tried out the new skill we just learned.

Kioka: I guess I'll go and get it over with.

Facilitator: Thanks, Kioka. If I recall, your situation involved your boyfriend.

Kioka: Right! I forgot his birthday, and he is so angry at me that he hasn't stopped yelling at me. I want to hit him.

Facilitator: OK, Kioka, who here reminds you of your boyfriend?

Kioka: Hmmm, let's see . . . Kwame, Kwame does. My boyfriend has dreds just like Kwame.

Facilitator: Kwame, would you please come up here? Now, Kioka, where is this situation likely to happen, and when?

> **Kioka:** Well, I see him every weekend after work, so probably this Saturday after I finish work at about 7:00 P.M. He usually picks me up at work, and we go out for something to eat. Lately, he's been making snide remarks about my forgetting his birthday.

> **Facilitator:** So where will you probably use the skill—at the restaurant?

> **Kioka:** Nah, probably in the car on the way.

> *The co-facilitator takes two chairs and arranges them side by side to help participants imagine the front seat of a car.*

> **Facilitator:** OK, Kwame, you sit here in this chair, driving the car. Kioka, you sit in the other chair . . . and I want you to remember, as we have done each session, that you can look up here at the poster to follow the skill steps. You also have your Skill Card and can choose to look at it at any time.

Step 5: Conduct the Role-Play

Before the role-playing begins, the facilitator reminds the participants of their roles and responsibilities (or explains them, if the session is the first):

1. The main actor follows the behavioral steps of the skill.

2. The coactor stays in the role of the other person.

3. The other participants watch carefully for the enactment of the behavioral steps.

The facilitator assigns one specific behavioral step to each observer and has that participant track the skill step during the role-play. For the first several role-plays, observers can be coached as to what kinds of cues to observe (e.g., posture, tone of voice, content of speech). If there are more group members than skill steps, more than one group member can be assigned to a single step.

Then the actors are instructed to begin. At this point, it is the facilitator's responsibility to provide the main actor with whatever help or coaching is required to keep the role-playing going according to the behavioral steps. Main actors who "break role" and begin to explain their behavior or make other comments should be urged to get back into the role. If the role-play is clearly going astray from the behavioral steps, the facilitator should stop the role-play, provide instruction, then restart the role-play. A useful coaching tool is "PCP," or Praise, Correct, Praise. The group facilitator stops the role-play, praises the main actor for the effort displayed, provides instruction as to what to do better, and then asks the main actor to repeat the role-play, giving praise for trying it again.

While the facilitator provides coaching, the co-facilitator stands near the Skill Poster, pointing in turn to each of the behavioral steps as the role-play unfolds and thus helping the main actor (as well as the other group members) to follow the steps in order.

Facilitator: As Kioka tries out using the skill of Keeping Out of Fights, I want us to pay special attention as to how she follows each step.

Latoya, will you look for Step 1: "Stop and think about why you want to fight."

Would you, Josh and Tyrone, look at Step 2: "Decide what you want to happen in the long run."

Who would like to look for Step 3: "Think about other ways to handle the situation besides fighting"? *(Pauses.)* OK, Maria, thank you for volunteering. You look for Step 3: "Think about other ways to handle the situation besides fighting." Remember to look to see if Kioka actually thinks about more than one way.

And finally, will you, Mike and Carla, look for Step 4: "Decide on the best way to handle the situation and do it."

Note in the preceding dialogue that the facilitator restates the steps verbatim, quickly and without any further explanation or discussion.

OK, Kioka, ready to try this new skill?

Kioka: Sure.

Facilitator: Then let's do it. Remember to try to perform each step of the skill exactly as it is written and as Ms. Eureka and I demonstrated for you. Group, remember the steps of the skill you need to watch for and make sure you can tell us exactly what Kioka did when she tried that step. Be as specific as you can.

Step 6: Conduct the Discussion (Performance Feedback)

A brief feedback period follows each role-play. This helps the main actor find out how well he or she followed or departed from the behavioral steps, examines the psychological impact of the enactment on the coactor, and provides the main actor with encouragement to try out the role-played behaviors in real life. In this process, the facilitator asks the main actor to wait until he or she has heard everyone else's comments before responding to them.

The coactor is asked about his or her reactions first. Next, those group members who were assigned to watch for the various behavioral steps of the skill comment on how well the steps were followed and on other relevant aspects of the role-play. The facilitators then comment on how well the behavioral steps were followed and provide social reinforcement (praise, approval, encouragement) for close following. The main actor shares impressions about following the steps of the skill last. In this way, the main actor can learn to evaluate the effectiveness of his or her skill enactment in light of positive feedback from others. Also, adolescents are greatly influenced by their peers and, as such, are less prone to think poorly of their role-play when their peers report that they followed each of the behavioral steps of the skill.

To use reinforcement most effectively, facilitators should follow these guidelines:

1. Provide reinforcement only after role-plays that follow the behavioral steps.

2. Provide reinforcement at the earliest appropriate opportunity after role-plays that follow the behavioral steps.

3. Always provide reinforcement to the coactor for being helpful, cooperative, and so on.

4. Vary the specific content of the reinforcement offered (e.g., praise particular aspects of the performance, such as tone of voice, posture, phrasing).

5. Provide enough role-playing activity for each group member to have sufficient opportunity to be reinforced.

6. Provide reinforcement in an amount consistent with the quality of the given role-play.

7. Provide no reinforcement when the role-play departs significantly from the behavioral steps (except for "trying" in the first session or two).

8. Provide reinforcement for an individual group member's improvement over previous performances.

In all aspects of feedback, it is crucial that the group facilitators maintain a focus on objective aspects of the role-play. Comments must point to the presence or absence of specific, concrete behaviors and not take the form of broad evaluative generalities. Feedback, of course, may be positive or negative in content. However, as mentioned earlier, negative comments should be minimal. Youth failing to follow the behavioral steps in their role-play may be given another opportunity to role-play these same behavioral steps after coaching by the group facilitators.

Facilitator: OK, now that Kioka has finished her role-play, Kwame, can you tell us how it was to play the part of her boyfriend?

Kwame: It was fun. I like Kioka, so it was cool. And it was great that we didn't get into a big fight.

Facilitator: Latoya, you were assigned to watch for Step 1: "Stop and think about why you want to fight." How did Kioka do with "Stop and think about why you want to fight"?

Latoya: Kioka did Step 1. She stopped and she stated aloud while pointing to her head, showing us she was thinking that she wanted to fight with her boyfriend because he keeps on yelling at her for forgetting his birthday and she is sick of it. She said, "He needs to get over it and get on with his life."

Facilitator: Good, Latoya, you really did a good job watching for Step 1: "Stop and think about why you want to fight." And you gave us specifics about how Kioka did that step.

Facilitator: Josh and Tyrone, you had Step 2: "Decide what you want to happen in the long run." Did Kioka do Step 2: "Decide what you want to happen in the long run"?

Josh: Yes, she did.

Tyrone: Yeah, she actually said that she wanted her boyfriend to stop bitching about her forgetting his birthday—that it wasn't on purpose.

Facilitator: And Step 3: "Think about other ways to handle the situation besides fighting." Who was responsible for looking for that step?

Maria: I was. And Kioka did think about other ways to handle the situation. In fact, she mentioned three different ways. She said she could ignore him, she could yell back, and she could simply tell him that she did not appreciate him always nagging at her about forgetting his birthday—that she did not do it on purpose to hurt his feelings.

Facilitator: Great, Maria. You really paid attention to the role-play and were able to tell us the three things Kioka thought of to handle the situation besides fighting.

Facilitator: Mike, I believe you had Step 4: "Decide on the best way to handle the situation and do it." Did Kioka do that step, "Decide on the best way to handle the situation and do it"?

Mike: Hmmm, I don't remember. I was thinking about something else.

Carla: I had to watch for that step, too. And she did—she decided to tell her boyfriend to cut complaining because she did not mean to do it on purpose to hurt his feelings.

The facilitators summarize and amplify the group's positive comments about Kioka's skill performance.

Facilitator: Kioka, what do you think about your role-play?

Kioka: Well, I didn't think I did that great, that I did the skill at all. But after hearing the group, it was cool. I did the skill, and I didn't even know I did each step—it came so easy.

Facilitator: Do you think you will be able to do this with your boyfriend this weekend when you see him and he starts his complaining to you?

Kioka: Absolutamente!

Step 7: Assign the Homework (Transfer Training)

Following a successful role-play, the group member is instructed to practice in his or her own real-life setting the behaviors tried out during the session. For incarcerated participants, the homework setting is inside the institution but outside the ART group. For participants in the community, homework may be done elsewhere in the facility or school—with peers, at home, or even on the streets.

At this point in the example, the co-facilitator would give Kioka a copy of the Skill Homework Report and ask her to fill out the top part, including the name of the person or persons with whom the group member will try the skill, the day, the place, and so on (see Figure 2.1). The second part of the report requests information about what happened when the group member attempted the homework assignment, how well he or she followed the behavioral steps, and the group member's view of performance quality. Each ART skill session includes a separate Skill Homework Report, reproducing the skill name and steps. (A blank Skill Homework Report is provided in Appendix E.)

Successful experiences at beginning homework attempts are crucial to encourage the group member to make further attempts in real-life situations. If the group member appears to be struggling with the Skill Homework Report, the co-facilitator can quietly offer assistance while the facilitator continues the session. Assistance filling out the form and with the role-play itself can also be provided outside the session.

Step 8: Select the Next Role-Player

The sequence just described is repeated until all members of the group have had an opportunity to participate in the role of main actor. The facilitator asks, "Who would like to go next and try their hand at this skill, Keeping Out of Fights?"

It is important to note that while the framework (behavioral steps) of each role-play in the series remains the same, the actual content can and should change from role-play to role-play. It is the problem as it actually occurs, or could occur, in each youth's own environment that should be the content of the role-play. When the role-play is completed, each group member will thus be better armed to act appropriately in a real-life situation requiring skill use.

Reviewing Skill Homework Reports

The first part of each Social Skills Training session after the first is devoted to discussing participants' experiences completing their homework assignments. When group members have made an effort to complete their homework, facilitators should provide positive social reinforcement. If group members fail to do their homework, facilitators should reiterate the agreements group members made during their individual meetings and/or remind them of the group rule involving participation. If the ART group's functioning is tied to the school's or institution's incentive or behavior modification system, successful homework should be generously rewarded. It is important to stress that without these or a similar attempt to maximize transfer of training, the value of the entire training effort may be in jeopardy.

The following is representative of dialogue that would begin a session in mid-course.

Facilitator: Welcome to our fifth Social Skills Training session. It is hard to believe that after today, we will have completed half of our work in the Social Skills Training part of ART. How have you been since our last session? Is everyone ready to learn a new skill to use?

Group members: "Yeah, we guess so . . ."

Facilitator: Let's first take a look at last week's homework. Will everyone take out their Skill Homework Reports for last week's skill—Dealing with Someone Else's Anger.

Both the facilitator and co-facilitator move around the room to see that everyone has completed a Skill Homework Report.

Facilitator: Latoya, how did you do with your homework last week?

Latoya: *(Reading directly from the bottom of her completed Skill Homework Report)* I approached my mom after dinner last Thursday when she was sitting in her easy chair and confessed I took money from her wallet. I followed each of the four steps of the skill:

1. Listen to the person who is angry.

2. Try to understand what the angry person is saying and feeling.

3. Decide if you can say or do something to deal with the situation.

4. If you can, deal with the other person's anger.

I did a good job because I was able to understand that my mom was angry because I violated her trust, and I just told her I know she was disappointed and was very angry with me.

The facilitator takes about one minute per group member (and ideally less time) to have each group member read the second part of his or her Skill Homework Report. Skill instruction then continues with Step 1 in the Social Skills Training procedure.

Evaluating the Social Skills Training Session

To evaluate how well they conducted the meeting, facilitators should complete the Social Skills Training Session Evaluation Checklist (see Appendix B). They can also make helpful notes concerning the meeting on that form.

CHAPTER 3

Anger Control Training: The Affective Component of ART

We all feel anger at times because anger is a natural human emotion. Anger is a complex human behavior, but its dynamics have been well researched and studied. For most of us, the outlet for our anger is something other than aggression. Sometimes we pout; sometimes we withdraw, perhaps muttering to ourselves; sometimes we allow the anger to spur us to constructive problem solving. Only a small fraction of the time for the majority of people does anger lead to verbal or physical aggression. But for chronically aggressive youth, the opposite is true. Seldom do they merely pout, withdraw, or constructively problem solve. Instead, they often lash out with intent to harm—sometimes with words, commonly with fists, and increasingly with weapons.

Anger Control Training is the affective component of ART, designed to deal with the emotion that most often interferes with participants' use of the prosocial behaviors they acquire in the Social Skills Training sessions. Specifically, Anger Control Training serves two related purposes: to help make the arousal of anger in chronically aggressive youth a less frequent occurrence and to provide youth with the means to learn self-control when their anger is aroused. Whereas Social Skills Training is designed to teach youth what they *should do* in anger-producing situations, Anger Control Training teaches the skills and techniques they require to avoid doing what they *should not do.*

BACKGROUND

Anger control began in what at first may seem to be a setting distant from the study of anger management—the experimental laboratory of the Russian psychologist Alexander Luria. In an extended series of investigations, Luria (1961) explored the manner in which children learn to regulate their external behavior by means of internal speech. Little and Kendall (1979) described the development of verbal control of behavior in children:

> First, the initiation of motor behavior comes under control of adult verbal cues, and then the inhibition of responses is controlled by the speech of adults. Self-control emerges as the

child learns to respond to his own verbal cues, first to initiate responses and then to inhibit them. . . . The 3- or 4-year-old child normally can follow rather complicated instructions given by an adult, and it is at this age that the child is said to begin to regulate his own behavior on the basis of verbal self-instructions. . . . Between the ages of 4½ and 5½, the child's self-verbalizations shift from overt to covert (primarily internal) speech. (p. 101)

As Little and Kendall also noted, considerable evidence exists to support the belief that self-control develops as a function of a child's development of internal language mechanisms. But what of the youngster in whom this sequence fails to fully or correctly unfold? Many youngsters who, deficient in the ability to regulate overt behavior by internal speech, display hyperactivity, impulsivity, poor self-control, and acting-out behaviors. However, impulsive behavior may be reduced by externally imposed interventions that closely replicate the normal developmental sequence described by Luria. This is precisely what Anger Control Training is designed to do.

Self-Instructional Training for Impulsive Youth

Donald Meichenbaum and his research group have been active in the area of anger management and anger impulse control for more than five decades. Their initial investigations sought to further define the relationship between impulsivity and poor verbal control of overt behavior. Meichenbaum and Goodman (1969), using Kagan's (1966) Matching Familiar Figures Test, found that those youngsters who responded on the test quickly and made many errors (impulsive youngsters) exercised diminished verbal control over their overt behavior as compared with youngsters who took their time and made fewer errors (reflective youngsters). But just what do reflective and impulsive youngsters say to themselves, and how does their self-directed speech differ? To answer such questions, Meichenbaum and Goodman (1971) observed and recorded the play behavior and private speech of 16 four-year-olds who were matched for age, intelligence, and socioeconomic status. Half of the children were reflective and half of the children were impulsive, as indicated by performance on the Matching Familiar Figures Test. Results indicated that the private speech of the cognitively impulsive preschoolers was largely composed of the most immature self-stimulatory content. Reflective preschoolers, in comparison, manifested significantly more outer-directed and self-regulatory speech and significantly more inaudible mutterings. The investigators concluded from their observational studies that cognitively reflective preschool children use their private speech in a more mature, instrumental, and self-guiding fashion than impulsive preschoolers do.

These and other findings led Meichenbaum (1977) to duplicate the sequence as a remedial intervention for youngsters deficient in such self-regulatory skills. Specifically, he attempted to systematically train hyperactive, impulsive youngsters to talk to themselves differently in order to alter their problem-solving styles and encourage them to think before they acted. Training involved efforts to teach the children how to comprehend the task, spontaneously produce mediators and strategies, and use such mediators to guide, monitor, and control their performances.

In Meichenbaum's and other research on self-instructional training, the typical sequence of instructional procedures is as follows:

1. The facilitator models task performance and self-instructs aloud while the child observes.

2. The child performs the task, self-instructing aloud as he or she does so.

3. The facilitator models task performance and whispers self-instructions while the child observes.

4. The child performs the task, self-instructing in a whisper while doing so.

5. The facilitator performs the task using covert self-instructions, with pauses and behavioral signs of thinking such as raising the eyes toward the ceiling or stroking the chin.

6. The child performs the task using covert self-instructions.

Meichenbaum and Goodman's (1971) initial use of these procedures yielded decreased impulsivity and enhanced self-reflection (i.e., increased response time and decreased error rate) in samples of hyperactive youngsters in comparison with appropriate controls. The children could indeed learn, as the investigators put it, "to stop, look, and listen." This early research also showed that observing a model using covert self-instructions was insufficient to obtain the desired outcome; the youngsters also had to self-instruct covertly.

Self-Instructional Training for Aggressive Youth

In 1975, Novaco applied the self-instructional training approach to the management of anger. By way of definition, he comments:

> The arousal of anger is here viewed as an affective stress reaction. That is, anger arousal is a response to perceived environmental demands—most commonly, aversive psychosocial events. . . . Anger is thought to consist of a combination of physiological arousal and cognitive labeling of that arousal as anger. . . . Anger arousal results from particular appraisals of

aversive events. External circumstances provoke anger only as mediated by their meaning to the individual. (pp. 252–253)

Novaco also posited that anger is fomented, maintained, and influenced by the self-statements that are made in provocative situations. In Novaco's own research involving people with chronic anger problems, use of self-instructional training was shown to substantially decrease anger arousal levels in comparison with control groups not provided this intervention.

Meichenbaum viewed the remediation of impulsivity in the light of Luria's insights about the normal development of self-regulation, and Novaco needed Meichenbaum's impulsivity research results in order to extend self-instructional training to chronically angry individuals. Similarly, the work of Eva Feindler built upon the extensive foundation provided by Novaco. Feindler and her research group have contributed greatly to the development of anger management, both with important research findings and with significant refinements in technique (Feindler, 1979, 1981; Feindler & Fremouw, 1983; Feindler, Latini, Nape, Romano, & Doyle, 1980; Feindler, Marriott, & Iwata, 1984). A series of investigations by Feindler and colleagues elaborated Novaco's intervention sequence into a chain in which clients learned the following:

1. Triggers—the external events and internal self-statements that serve as provocations to anger arousal

2. Cues—the physiological and kinesthetic sensations that signal to the individual the level of anger arousal

3. Reminders—the self-instructional statements that may function to reduce anger arousal (the converse of internal triggers)

4. Reducers—techniques that in combination with reminders may reduce anger arousal (e.g., deep breathing, backward counting, peaceful imagery, and consideration of long-term consequences)

5. Self-evaluation—the opportunity to self-reinforce and/or self-correct, depending on how well or poorly the previous steps have been implemented

A further refinement of the preceding concepts and methods, our design of Anger Control Training is a multistep sequence in which group members are first helped to understand how they typically perceive and interpret (or, perhaps more accurately, misperceive and misinterpret) the behavior of others in ways that arouse anger. Therefore, attention is given to identifying the outside occurrences (*external triggers*) and inner interpretations (*internal triggers*) that initiate anger.

Though anger is elicited by one's cognitions and self-statements, its main emotional feature is a high level of arousal. Before group members can learn more productive, less provocative, and less arousing ways of interpreting the world and correct their distortions, their arousal levels must be reduced. Attention to *cues and reducers* accomplishes this task.

Impulsive youth frequently confuse the bodily signs or cues that accompany specific emotions such as fear, anxiety, and anger. Accurate interpretation of such signs in the anger control process can signal the need to use one or more techniques to reduce their own levels of anger arousal. Learning to use *reminders* is critical to the anger control outcome.

Once the potential interference of their emotional states has been substantially reduced, participants can proceed to employ more accurate, more benign, and less anger-arousing cognitions and interpretations of the world around them. At this point, it is possible for them to learn the strategy of *thinking ahead* toward consequences.

Chronically aggressive youth are well-practiced in conjuring up anger-arousing perceptions and interpretations (i.e., internal triggers) and often have made poor use of anger-avoiding self-instructions (i.e., reminders). If they do well at this difficult and, for them, often novel task, it is important that they feel the effort is worthwhile. The *self-evaluation* step in the Anger Control Training sequence teaches group members how to praise or coach (correct) themselves for successful accomplishments.

OVERVIEW OF THE ANGER CONTROL TRAINING PROCESS

To teach the anger control techniques and sequence, facilitators use a combination of modeling, role-playing, and performance feedback similar to that employed in Social Skills Training sessions. These same principles and guidelines, discussed in chapter 2, apply. Specifically, participants observe facilitators demonstrating the technique or sequence, try it (with a coactor) while other group members observe how well they perform, then receive constructive commentary on how well they did from both peers and facilitators. Group facilitators assign members of the group to watch for the various steps of the anger control sequence, referred to in the sessions as the Anger Control Chain. In addition to role-playing the techniques in the Anger Control Chain, beginning with Week 8 group members role-play the steps in an ART social skill they choose as being an appropriate response to an anger-provoking situation. In these cases, the modeling, role-playing, and performance feedback procedures are the same as for teaching a single social skill, embedded within the larger anger control role-playing sequence. At this point, group facilitators also assign members of the group to watch for the various skill steps, and similar feedback is provided.

The homework for this component of ART requires group members to complete at least one Hassle Log each week after the second week, when the log is introduced, to record details about conflict situations in which they are involved. (For a sample log, see Figure 3.1.) Group members use the situations they describe in their Hassle Logs when role-playing the anger control techniques and sequence. That way, the next time the situation or a similar one occurs, they will have options to exercise instead of acting on their angry impulses. Of course, because Hassle Logs provide information that increases group members' personal choices and power in decision making, group members are invited to complete as many logs as they wish.

ANGER CONTROL TRAINING SESSION PROCEDURES

Anger control sessions involve teaching both a number of anger control concepts and techniques (e.g., triggers, cues, anger reducers) and the anger control sequence, which builds as the sessions progress (i.e., the Anger Control Chain).

The curriculum for the Anger Control Training component of ART is as follows:

- Week 1: ABCs of Anger

- Week 2: Hassle Log and Triggers

- Week 3: Cues and Anger Reducers

- Week 4: Reminders

- Week 5: Thinking Ahead

- Week 6: Self-Evaluation

- Week 7: Angry Behavior Cycle

- Week 8: Using a Social Skill and Rehearsal of Full Anger Control Chain

- Week 9: Rehearsal of Full Anger Control Chain

- Week 10: Overall Review and Rehearsal of Full Anger Control Chain

Preparing for the Anger Control Training Session

Practitioners are already aware of the value of role-playing in the Social Skills Training component of ART. Facilitators should take the time to develop and rehearse realistic modeling displays that accurately show the entire Anger Control Chain, emphasizing the portion of the sequence taught during the session. Group members then role-play situations from their Hassle Logs that reflect actual stressful situations that caused them to be angry.

FIGURE 3.1   Sample Hassle Log

Name ___Kwame_____ Date ___June 16_____

☐ Morning   ☑ Afternoon   ☐ Evening

1. Where were you?

☑ Classroom/school   ☐ Bathroom   ☐ Community
☐ Dorm   ☐ Office   ☐ Hall
☐ Gym   ☐ Dining room   ☐ On a job
☐ Recreation room   ☐ Outside/grounds   ☐ Other _____

2. What happened?

☑ Somebody teased me.

☐ Somebody took something of mine.

☐ Somebody was doing something I didn't like.

☐ I did something wrong.

☐ Somebody started fighting with me.

☐ Other _____

3. Who was the other person?

☑ Another youth   ☐ Parent/caregiver   ☐ Teacher   ☐ Counselor   ☐ Other _____

4. What did you do?

☐ Hit back   ☐ Ignored it

☐ Ran away   ☐ Talked it out

☐ Yelled   ☑ Used anger control technique *(identify)*

☐ Cried   ___Backward counting_____

☐ Walked away calmly   _____

☐ Broke something   ☐ Used social skill *(identify)*

☐ Told an adult

☐ Told peer   _____

                              ☐ Other _____

5. How angry were you?

☐ Burning   ☐ Really   ☑ Moderately   ☐ Mildly angry   ☐ Not angry
              angry   angry   but still OK   at all

6. How did you handle yourself?

1	2	3	④	5
Poorly	Not so well	OK	Good	Great

Session Summaries and Comments

Week 1: ABCs of Anger

Week 1 introduces the Anger Control Training component and focuses on the ABC formula:

A = Antecedent: What led up to the problem?

B = Behavior: What did you do (your response to A)?

C = Consequence: What were the results of your behavior (B)?

It is important that group facilitators introduce the ABC formula with enthusiasm and concretely because it is the basis upon which all of the anger control concepts are based and is revisited later in training. Facilitators should give sufficient examples for youth to comprehend the importance of the ABCs and should take care to define terms. For example, one group facilitator took the time to drive home the definition of *antecedent,* teaching a vocabulary lesson without taking a great deal of time from the session.

Facilitator: Who here knows what *antecedent* means? It is a big word, isn't it?

Carla: Yeah, it is a big word. I don't like words over four letters. *(Group laughs.)*

Facilitator: Well, Carla, let's see if I can help a bit. Let me tell you all a secret. When you see a big word in English, you can probably break it into a number of little words. Let's take a closer look at our word *antecedent.*

(Writes the word on the easel pad.) I told you that most big words in English are made up of smaller words. Well, *antecedent* is really two words: *ante* and *cedent.*

(Writes the two words under the single word: ante cedent.) Now, I am going to tell you that this word, *ante,* is what we call a prefix, a word that is attached to another word to make it a big word. This prefix, *ante,* means before. Every time you see this word as part of a bigger word, it always means before. What is left in our big word, *antecedent?*

Kwame: Cedent.

Facilitator: That's right, Kwame. And *cedent* means situation. So when you put the two words together—*ante* + *cedent*—what does it mean?

Kwame: What comes before the situation.

Facilitator: Bingo, exactly! It's what happens before the situation. Well, let's move on.

Week 2: Hassle Log and Triggers

Hassle Log

The purposes of the Hassle Log are as follows:

- It provides an accurate picture of conflicts that occurred during the week.

- It helps group members learn about what makes them angry and how they handle these situations so they can work to change behaviors that cause them trouble and leave them feeling bad about themselves.

- It provides ideas for role-playing in future sessions.

Using situations that really happen is much more effective than using made-up situations. While the Hassle Logs may be filled out for situations that group members handle well, they are usually completed for those situations in which they become angry or aggressive.

Participants are given a supply of Hassle Logs and are instructed to fill one out as soon as possible after an anger-provoking incident. Alternatively, various locations for group members to pick up blank Hassle Logs can be specified.

Triggers

The first session also introduces the idea of external and internal triggers:

- *External triggers* are things someone does or things that happen that cause people to react with anger or create stressful situations for them. They may be verbal (e.g., telling someone what to do or calling him or her a name) or nonverbal (e.g., pushing someone or making an obscene gesture).

- *Internal triggers* are things we say to ourselves that increase our angry impulses—for example, "That SOB is making fun of me," "She's making me look like a wimp," or "I'm going to tear that guy's head off." Often, we say these things when we are faced with external triggers.

Negative self-statements are the internal triggers that combine with external triggers to lead to high levels of anger arousal and aggressive behavior. Helping group members identify their internal triggers sets the stage for later sessions, in which they learn how to replace internal triggers that make them angry with positive self-statements or reminders that reduce their anger in conflict situations.

Beginning with Week 2, facilitators begin to create a visual display of the Anger Control Chain, adding new items in the sequence to it as the sessions progress.

Modeling, Role-Playing, and Performance Feedback

Facilitators model *triggers (external/internal),* then have each group member choose a coactor and role-play a situation based on the Hassle Log. Group members then attempt to identify the external and internal triggers. Facilitators ensure that modeling displays and role-plays reflect both internal and external triggers. In all cases, performance feedback follows the same sequence as for Social Skills Training: coactor, observers, and main actor, then facilitators.

Week 3: Cues and Anger Reducers

Cues

The group facilitator gives some personal examples of cues—those physical signs that indicate when we are getting angry—and explains that individuals must know they are angry before they can use the Anger Control Chain to reduce their anger. The facilitator then helps group members identify the personal cues that signal that they are getting angry.

Anger Reducers

Now that the group members are beginning to identify their cues, they can start to make use of anger reduction techniques to lower their arousal levels when they notice themselves getting angry. Any or all of the three anger reducers can be a first step in a sequence of *new* behaviors giving group members greater self-control and more time to decide how to respond effectively. The key sequence here is identification of physical cues of anger (e.g., muscle tension, knot in the stomach, clenched fists) followed by the use of one or more anger reducers.

Anger Reducer 1: Deep breathing. The facilitator instructs group members that appropriate deep breathing requires that we inhale deeply through the nose, holding the breath we take in for two full seconds before we exhale it through the mouth. The facilitator models this technique and performs the display three complete times. The group then tries the technique for three complete breaths. The facilitator reminds the group about their anger cues and explains how deep breathing can help reduce anger by relieving physical symptoms of tension. This constitutes modeling and role-playing for the first anger reducer.

Anger Reducer 2: Backward counting. A second method of reducing anger and increasing personal power in a pressure situation is to count backward silently—for example, from 10 to 1. Counting backward is a way of simultaneously lowering anger arousal levels and gaining time to think about how to respond most effectively. The facilitator again models, demonstrating the correct technique of counting backward by counting one number per second. Group members are instructed that, if possible, it is best to try to turn away from the provoking person or situation while counting. After the facilitator models the counting backward technique, he or she again invites group members to try the technique. This constitutes modeling and role-playing for the second anger reducer.

Anger Reducer 3: Pleasant imagery. A third way to reduce tension in an anger-arousing situation is to imagine being in a peaceful scene (e.g., "You are lying on the beach. The sun is warm, and there is a slight breeze"). Group members are encouraged to think of scenes they find peaceful and relaxing. The facilitator models pleasant imagery by describing a relaxing scene aloud, then has the group close their eyes and think of their own. Alternatively, the facilitator may describe one or two more peaceful scenes while the group members listen. This constitutes modeling and role-playing for the third anger reducer.

Modeling, Role-Playing, and Performance Feedback

Group facilitators model the following sequence:

> *Triggers (external/internal) + cues + anger reducers*
> *(all)*

They encourage each group member to role-play the sequence, using the content from his or her Hassle Log, then lead the group in giving feedback, focusing on the use of cues and anger reducers. Facilitators should demonstrate all three anger reducers in their modeling display; however, when group members role-play, they may choose to try out one, two, or all three anger reducers.

Week 4: Reminders

Reminders are self-instructional statements used to help increase success in pressure situations of all types. In this session, group members generate a list of reminders they have used or could have used in recent anger or conflict situations (drawn from the Hassle Logs). Some reminders are in a sense generic (i.e., they fit almost any anger experience). Examples include such self-instructional statements as "Take it easy," "Relax," "Calm down," "Chill out," and "Cool off." Often, reminders are benign reinterpretations of an anger-arousing internal trigger (e.g., "She didn't bump me on purpose. The hall is really crowded between classes").

As noted previously in this chapter, Luria, Meichenbaum, and Novaco all researched the concept of self-talk as an effective self-regulator of behavior. Novaco (1975) has provided a useful pool of reminders, to be employed before, during, or after an anger-arousing experience (see Table 3.1). Another valuable set of reminders has been provided by Deffenbacher (1996), who has grouped them into cool thoughts (e.g., "Just stay cool," "This battle isn't worth it"); problem-solving thoughts (e.g., "OK, develop a plan," "What's the first thing I want to do?"); control and escape thoughts (e.g., "I can always just walk away," "It's OK to take time out"); and self-rewarding thoughts ("Good, I'm hanging in there," "I feel great—I'm dealing with it and not yelling"). More effective than any selected from a list are those reminders created by group members themselves.

After the list has been created, the facilitator describes and gives several examples of how reminders can be helpful in situations in which group members must try very hard to keep calm (e.g., confrontations with police, arguments with parents or siblings, court appearances).

Modeling, Role-Playing, and Performance Feedback

Group facilitators model the following sequence:

Triggers (external/internal) + cues + anger reducer(s) + reminders

Group members then role-play conflict situations from their Hassle Logs in which the main actors try the sequence and receive feedback on their performance, especially on their use of reminders. If group members have trouble using reminders while role-playing, it may be helpful for the facilitators to quietly give examples at the proper time.

Week 5: Thinking Ahead

In Week 3, participants learned three anger reducers: deep breathing, backward counting, and pleasant imagery. Both Meichenbaum and Novaco classify the thinking ahead strategy as an anger reducer, but in the ART schema it serves as both anger reducer and reminder: As an anger reducer, it decreases arousal by helping participants slow down their responses to judge the likely future consequences of their current behavior. It also functions as a clear reminder that they are at a decision point in the conflict.

Theoretically, the ABC model relates to the anger control sequence in the way shown in Figure 3.2, with internal and external triggers as the A (antecedent); cues, anger reducers, and reminders as the B (behavior); and thinking ahead and self-evaluation as the C (consequence). In this

TABLE 3.1   Self-Instructional Reminders for Use Before, During, and After Provocation

Preparing for Provocation

- This is going to upset me, but I know how to deal with it.
- What is it that I have to do?
- I can work out a plan to handle this.
- I can manage the situation. I know how to control my anger.
- If I find myself getting upset, I'll know what to do.
- There won't be any need for an argument.
- Don't take this too seriously.
- This could be a testy situation, but I believe in myself.
- Time for a few deep breaths of relaxation. Feel comfortable, relaxed, and at ease.
- Easy does it. Remember to keep your sense of humor.

Impact and Confrontation

- Stay calm. Just continue to relax.
- As long as I keep my cool, I'm in control.
- Just roll with the punches; don't get bent out of shape.
- Think of what you want to get out of this.
- You don't need to prove yourself.
- There is no point in getting mad.
- Don't make more out of this than you have to.
- I'm not going to let him get to me.
- Look for the positives. Don't assume the worst or jump to conclusions.
- It's really a shame she has to act like this.
- For someone to be that irritable, he must be awfully unhappy.
- If I start to get mad, I'll just be banging my head against the wall. So I might as well just relax.
- There is no need to doubt myself. What he says doesn't matter.
- I'm on top of this situation, and it's under control.

Coping with Arousal

- My muscles are starting to feel tight. Time to relax and slow things down.
- Getting upset won't help.
- It's just not worth it to get so angry.
- I'll let him make a fool of himself.
- I have a right to be annoyed, but let's keep the lid on.
- Time to take a deep breath.
- Let's take the issue point by point.
- My anger is a signal of what I need to do. Time to instruct myself.
- I'm not going to get pushed around, but I'm not going haywire either.
- Try to reason it out. Treat each other with respect.
- Let's try a cooperative approach. Maybe we are both right.
- Negatives lead to more negatives. Work constructively.
- He'd probably like me to get really angry. Well, I'm going to disappoint him.
- I can't expect people to act the way I want them to.
- Take it easy, don't get pushy.

Reflecting on the Provocation

When conflict is unresolved:

- Forget about the aggravation. Thinking about it only makes you upset.
- These are difficult situations, and they take time to straighten out.
- Try to shake it off. Don't let it interfere with your job.
- I'll get better at this as I get more practice.
- Remember relaxation. It's a lot better than anger.
- Can you laugh about it? It's probably not so serious.
- Don't take it personally.
- Take a deep breath.

When conflict is resolved or coping is successful:

- I handled that one pretty well. It worked!
- That wasn't as hard as I thought.
- It could have been a lot worse.
- I could have gotten more upset than it was worth.
- I actually got through that without getting angry.
- My pride can sure get me into trouble, but when I don't take things too seriously, I'm better off.
- I guess I've been getting upset for too long when it wasn't even necessary.
- I'm getting better at this all the time.

FIGURE 3.2   Anger Control Chain and ABC Model

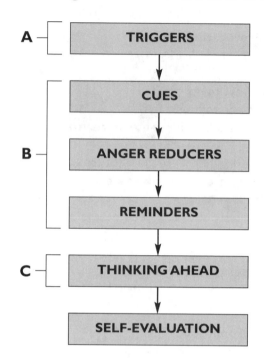

session, the facilitator refers back to the ABC model, presented in Week 1, and explains that thinking ahead helps group members figure out what the C (consequence) will probably be before they decide what to do (i.e., the B step).

To teach thinking ahead, the facilitator instructs the group members in using the "If-then" formula: *"If I do this now, then this will probably happen later."* The facilitator emphasizes that this formula will help guide group members in their decisions to behave in a particular way and identify the consequences, both positive and negative, for their actions.

In the session, the facilitator distinguishes between short- and long-term consequences, encouraging group members to consider the long-term results over the short-term ones (e.g., the short-term "If I slug him now, he'll shut up" versus the long-term "If I slug him now, I'll be put on in-school suspension for a week" or "I will be charged with assault and may be placed in a juvenile institution"). The facilitator explains the difference between the internal and external consequences of being aggressive. For example, external consequences might include going back to court and having to serve a week of in-school suspension, whereas internal consequences might be feeling terrible or losing self-respect. The facilitator also talks about social consequences, such as losing friends or being excluded from a group.

Modeling, Role-Playing, and Performance Feedback

Group facilitators model the entire Anger Control Chain up through this session, emphasizing thinking ahead:

> *Triggers (external/internal) + cues + anger reducer(s) + reminders + thinking ahead*

In this modeling display, facilitators use the "*If* (I act aggressively), *then* (this will probably be the consequence)" formula. After the modeling display, each participant role-plays the sequence, including the "If-then" formula, then receives feedback from peers and facilitators.

Week 6: Self-Evaluation

This session focuses on self-evaluation, a way for group members to do the following:

- Judge for themselves how well they have handled an anger-provoking situation or hassle.

- Reward themselves for handling it well (self-rewarding).

- Help themselves find out how they could have handled the situation better (self-coaching).

Basically, self-evaluation is conducted by using a set of reminders relevant to feelings and thoughts *after* the resolution of a conflict situation. The group discusses statements that group members can use to reward themselves (e.g., "I really kept cool" or "I was really in control") and to coach themselves when they fail to remain in control in a conflict situation (e.g., "I need to pay more attention to my cues"). Table 3.1 lists a number of helpful responses for times conflict is resolved (self-reward) and when it is not (self-coaching).

Now that group members have learned the complete Anger Control Chain, facilitators can help them create individualized self-rewarding and self-coaching statements. Brainstorming, listing self-coaching and self-rewarding statements on an easel pad, and having youth suggest to each other the kinds of statements they use are all useful strategies.

Modeling, Role-Playing, and Performance Feedback

Facilitators model the entire Anger Control Chain:

> *Triggers (external/internal) + cues + anger reducer(s) + reminders + thinking ahead + self-evaluation (self-reward/self-coaching)*

In this modeling display, both self-rewarding and self-coaching statements are emphasized. Group members then role-play conflict situations from their Hassle Logs, trying out the sequence and receiving feedback on their performance, especially on use of self-evaluation statements.

Week 7: Angry Behavior Cycle

This week's session is critical in ART because group members really begin to synthesize the concepts they have been learning in each of the ART components. It is also important for another reason: Until this point in Anger Control Training, the focus has been on what to do when other people make group members angry. This session represents a complete shift in perspective by focusing on what participants do to get *others* angry. It also lays the foundation for what occurs in the next session—that is, choosing a prosocial alternative to being aggressive or violent (i.e., using a social skill).

The facilitator encourages this new perspective by engaging group members in a brief activity: thinking about three things they do to make others angry and listing them on an index card. The facilitator asks group members to identify one thing they could do differently instead of each thing they currently do (usually it is just the opposite) and to commit to doing just one different thing.

The facilitator then introduces the Angry Behavior Cycle to represent the shift in perspective (see Figure 3.3), explaining it in the following way.

Facilitator: Up to this week, we have spent all our time learning how others get us angry—that is, identifying the external and internal triggers that arouse our anger. Then we learned ways to manage our angry impulses so we don't do something stupid. Doing something stupid means doing something that gets us into more trouble and that doesn't get us what we want.

Now I want to show you something, something really important for us all to understand. Here we have all the ideas we have learned about during the last six weeks.

Here is our Anger Control Chain. *(Facilitator indicates a chart like Figure 3.2.)* The chain lists all the concepts we learned in the order we learned them. Now I want you to think about this. Can anyone tell me what a "cycle" is?

Latoya: A cycle is like a circle. It goes round and round and never ends.

Facilitator: Exactly, a cycle is neverending, unless we do something to stop the action. I want to show you something. Now each

FIGURE 3.3   Angry Behavior Cycle

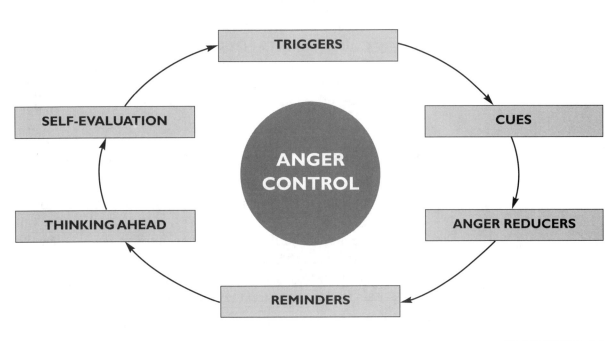

of the steps that we have learned in the Anger Control Chain goes in a circle, which we call the Angry Behavior Cycle.

Facilitator displays a poster of the Angry Behavior Cycle.

Facilitator: So . . . if we're not careful, our Anger Control Chain can turn into an Angry Behavior Cycle. *(Points to triggers.)* Can you see how our triggers cause us to become angry? Our body tells us we are becoming angry by giving us certain cues *(points to cues),* and once we realize we are becoming angry, we can do things to manage our anger impulses. *(Points to anger reducers, reminders, and thinking ahead.)* That is what we have learned so far, including how to reward and coach ourselves through a process we learned called self-evaluation. *(Points to self-evaluation.)*

At this point, the facilitator refers back to the exercise conducted at the beginning of the session.

Facilitator: Now we just finished a little exercise in which we identified three things we do that get others angry. What are those in this chart? Who would like to come up and identify what those things are?

Mike: I will. *(Gets up and points to triggers.)* What I do to get others angry are external triggers.

Facilitator: You are absolutely correct, Mike. Good job. Do you see, group, how what we do to others to get them angry are *their* external triggers? If we do not control our angry impulses, the likelihood that we will use one of the things we do well to get others angry is very high unless . . .

Group: We stop the cycle!

Carla: Unless we, on purpose, don't trigger someone else.

Facilitator: Exactly. If we do not consciously stop the cycle, it will continue. Our triggers will get others angry. If the other person does not manage their angry impulses, then they will use one of the things they do well to get people angry to trigger us, and if we don't purposefully stop ourselves from using our triggers . . . well, the cycle continues. It never, ever stops. Who can stop the Angry Behavior Cycle?

Tyrone: I guess only we ourselves can.

Kioka: That is exactly what happens with our homies. We drive by and shoot them because they drove by and shot at us, and then they retaliate, which is a trigger for us, and the cycle never ends. Wow! We have the power to stop this.

Facilitator: Exactly. We can stop the Angry Behavior Cycle if we want to. As Kioka just said: If we do not break the Angry Behavior Chain, it will become a neverending cycle. And so we want to exit the Angry Behavior Cycle before our actions become someone else's triggers. Like this chart right here.

At this point, the facilitator displays a poster illustrating a point of exit from the Angry Behavior Cycle (see Figure 3.4).

Up until this point, group members have been adding prosocial behaviors to their skill repertoires during Social Skills Training sessions. Most ART facilitators celebrate this seventh week of the program, for it is during this week that youth begin to have "aha" insights and experiences. "They finally get it," most practitioners report.

Modeling, Role-Playing, and Performance Feedback

The facilitators model this sequence, with emphasis on choosing a behavior that will not trigger someone else's anger:

FIGURE 3.4 **Exit the Angry Behavior Cycle: Do Something Different**

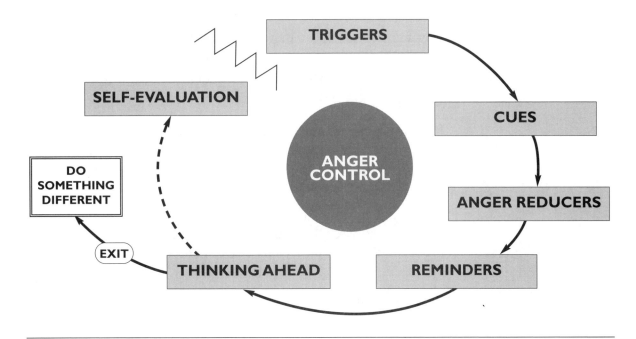

Triggers (external/internal) + cues + anger reducer(s) + reminders + thinking ahead + EXIT (do something different) + self-evaluation (self-reward/self-coaching)

Each member of the group then role-plays the entire Anger Control Chain, demonstrating an alternative behavior to what they usually do to get others angry, thus exiting the Angry Behavior Cycle. Facilitators encourage group members to decide to accomplish this task by using the thinking ahead procedure ("If I do this, then this person may get angry and the situation may get out of hand").

Week 8: Using a Social Skill and Rehearsal of Full Anger Control Chain

By the eighth week of ART, both facilitators and group members generally experience a significant decrease in angry outbursts, and the number of Hassle Logs that need to be completed is dramatically reduced.

In sharing their completed Hassle Logs, group members identify the steps in the Anger Control Chain and describe what they did to exit the Angry Behavior Cycle.

Facilitator: For part of your homework last week, I asked each of you to choose one of the three behaviors you identified as something you do to get others angry and *not* do that behavior. So, who would like to share what happened as a result of not doing the one thing they do well to get someone else angry? How about Kwame—you haven't contributed in a while . . . how did you do?

Kwame: I gotta tell you that I didn't think this crap would work, but I didn't have one hassle last week. I couldn't do my homework and complete a Hassle Log because I didn't have any.

Facilitator: Really?

Kwame: Word! You can ask staff, they were as surprised as I was. I usually get others mad by dissin' their homies and mammas. I didn't do any of that and no one got angry so I was left alone. It was cool.

Maria: I had a similar experience. I usually take my sister's clothes and wear them just to annoy her and I didn't do that so I didn't get hassled by her. But I do have a Hassle Log done because I had trouble elsewhere.

To introduce using a social skill, the facilitator explains that once group members are able to exit the cycle, they can choose one of the skills they have learned in Social Skills Training to get what they want, maximizing positive responses and minimizing negative responses from others. The facilitator refers to the Angry Behavior Cycle again, but this time includes the idea of exiting the cycle by substituting a social skill (see Figure 3.5).

Modeling, Role-Playing, and Performance Feedback

Group facilitators model the entire sequence, this time using a social skill to exit the Angry Behavior Cycle.

> *Triggers (external/internal) + cues + anger reducer(s)*
> *+ reminders + thinking ahead + EXIT (social skill)*
> *+ self-evaluation (self-reward/self-coaching)*

Each group member role-plays the entire sequence, using a selected social skill instead of doing something to trigger others to become angry. Facilitators assign group members to watch for the specific steps in the Anger Control Chain and the social skill used for the role-play.

Week 9: Rehearsal of Full Anger Control Chain

While no new concepts are introduced during this session, the facilitator informs the group that for this and the next session, the group will continue by watching a modeling display and then role-playing the entire anger control sequence, purposely choosing to break the Angry Behavior Cycle by using a skill they learned in Social Skills Training.

The facilitator ensures that the group understands they now have the power to get what they want without being aggressive or violent, maxi-

FIGURE 3.5   Exit the Angry Behavior Cycle: Use a Social Skill

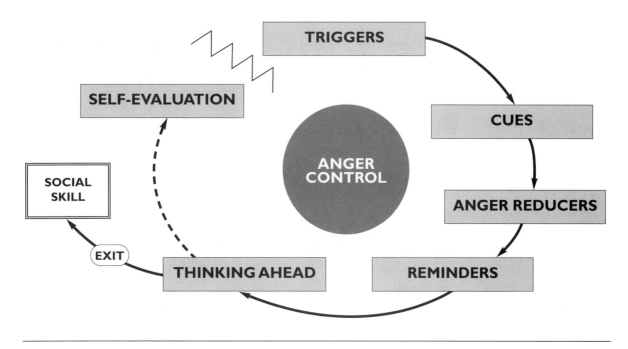

mizing positive results and minimizing negative reactions from others, thus giving them greater power over their own lives.

Modeling, Role-Playing, and Performance Feedback

Group facilitators model the entire sequence, using a social skill to exit the Angry Behavior Cycle.

> *Triggers (external/internal) + cues + anger reducer(s)*
> *+ reminders + thinking ahead + EXIT (social skill)*
> *+ self-evaluation (self-reward/self-coaching)*

Each group member role-plays the entire sequence, using a selected social skill instead of doing something to trigger others to become angry. Facilitators assign group members to watch for the specific steps in the Anger Control Chain and the social skill used for the role-play.

Week 10: Overall Review and Rehearsal of Full Anger Control Chain

By Week 10, a simple comparison of the number of Hassle Logs completed in the first weeks with those completed in the last weeks is a strong indication of how well group members have controlled their angry impulses and reduced the number of angry outbursts they have.

In this last session, the facilitator leads discussion to review all of the concepts and techniques in the Anger Control Chain. The facilitator reminds the group about the Angry Behavior Cycle, the power of managing their angry impulses, and the importance of using an alternative to what they usually do to trigger others to become angry.

Modeling, Role-Playing, and Performance Feedback

Facilitators model the complete sequence, including use of a social skill as a way of exiting the Angry Behavior Cycle:

> *Triggers (external/internal) + cues + anger reducer(s)*
> *+ reminders + thinking ahead + EXIT (social skill)*
> *+ self-evaluation (self-reward/self-coaching)*

Each group member role-plays the entire sequence, using a selected social skill instead of doing something to trigger others to become angry. Facilitators assign group members to watch for the specific steps in both the Anger Control Chain and the social skill used for the role-play.

Reviewing the Hassle Logs

Beginning with Week 3, each Anger Control Training session begins with a review of the Hassle Log filled out as homework for the preceding week. Facilitators briefly discuss participants' conflicts, use of the steps in the Anger Control Chain and social skills (if appropriate), and outcomes, providing positive reinforcement in the form of verbal praise.

Evaluating the Anger Control Training Session

To evaluate how well they conducted the meeting, facilitators may complete the Anger Control Training Session Evaluation Form (see Appendix B). They can also make helpful notes concerning the meeting on that form.

CHAPTER 4

Moral Reasoning: The Cognitive Component of ART

In this chapter, we present the third and final component of ART: Moral Reasoning. In Social Skills Training, participants learn prosocial and balanced skills—that is, they acquire the behaviors needed to deal constructively with anger-provoking or peer pressure situations. In Anger Control Training, they learn to regulate their emotions and thereby manage impulsive tendencies to lash out at others with put-downs, threats, or assaults. But what about those youth who learn prosocial skills in Social Skills Training (what to do) and, in Anger Control Training, how to recognize their anger and modulate their responses (what not to do), yet choose to act aggressively just because they "feel like it?"

In Moral Reasoning sessions, youth engage in discussion of problem situations. They answer questions that challenge them to achieve a more socially and morally mature view of the world. Participants learn how to see the world in a more fair and equitable way and how to take into account perspectives other than their own. Achieving more mature moral understanding means that participants are more likely to make more responsible choices—to use what they learn in the other two components of ART.

In this chapter, we describe the background and procedures for the Moral Reasoning component of ART. The background introduces the cognitive-developmental theory of sociomoral development and delay. Then we describe the ART program's Moral Reasoning training procedures to facilitate this development or remediate the delay.

Facilitating Moral Reasoning groups presents a unique challenge in ART. Unlike Social Skills Training and Anger Control Training, both of which have a prescribed procedure with specific content, these sessions rely on the facilitators to manage several complex processes and functions as they lead the group. Facilitators must be able to guide individual group members' moral development as well as manage the moral and social perspective of the entire group, composed of individual group members' decisions.

BACKGROUND

The stage development of moral reasoning or judgment has been documented in many studies, conducted in many countries. Delays in social perspective taking and moral judgment have been found among delinquents not only in the United States but also in Australia, Bahrain, China, England, Germany, the Netherlands, Sweden, and Taiwan (see review by Gibbs, Basinger, Grime, & Snarey, 2007). This moral judgment delay among antisocial youth has been documented in a meta-analysis (Stams, Brugman, Dekovic, van Rosmalen, van der Laan, & Gibbs, 2006) and is fully discussed elsewhere (Gibbs, 2010).

These findings follow from theoretical work that emphasizes the social and cognitive or "reasoning" aspect of morality. According to Piaget (1932/1965) and Kohlberg (1969, 1973, 1984), in the natural course of interacting with others, children develop more mature social perspective taking and moral reasoning. Whether a youth's moral reasoning is mature or delayed is important because "as you think, so you act." As will be discussed, delay in thought and behavior means two problems: prolonged immaturity in the stage of moral reasoning and persistent and pronounced cognitive distortions. Both of these aspects of delay are remediated in the Moral Reasoning component of ART.

Some historical context is helpful. In our original program design, we adapted Kohlberg's theory of moral development as the basis for this third component of ART. However, Kohlberg's techniques proved challenging for practitioners dealing with our original client base. Gibbs et al. (1995) applied the ART concepts and techniques to their particular youth populations within a therapeutic, positive peer culture environment. Goldstein and Glick adapted and applied these modifications within ART, making the moral reasoning facilitation techniques more effective and easier for practitioners to implement (Goldstein et al., 1998).

We continue to base the Moral Reasoning component on Kohlberg's still influential stages of moral development. Within this cognitive-developmental approach, we use Gibbs' (2010) model of immature or superficial (Stages 1 and 2) and mature or profound (Stages 3 and 4) moral judgment. These four stages are summarized in Table 4.1.

Development and Delay

This section elaborates on the theory behind these stages of sociomoral development, with special attention to the problem of developmental delay. Generally, superficiality is the mark of sociomoral immaturity. Stage 1 is superficial insofar as concrete or physical appeals are made in justifying moral values—for example, "The father's the boss because he's bigger." Saving the life of more than one person is more important because, in the words of one of Kohlberg's (1984) young subjects, "One

TABLE 4.1 Stages of Moral Reasoning

IMMATURE MORALITIES: STAGES 1 AND 2

Stage 1: Power—"Might Makes Right"

- Morality is whatever big or powerful people say that you have to do. If you are big or powerful, whatever you say is right, and whatever you want to do or get is fair.

- If you don't get punished for what you do or no one powerful sees it, whatever you do is OK. It is wrong if you do get punished; the punishment makes it wrong.

- Physical damage or other obvious injury—but not psychological suffering—is noticed and acknowledged to be wrong.

- Individuals tend to spout clichés ("You should never tell a lie") without much understanding of what they mean.

Critique

- A Stage 1 individual doesn't understand the moral reasons for rules, has trouble with reciprocity if it requires taking more than one perspective at a time, and is best at taking the perspective of someone physically powerful.

Stage 2: Deals—"You Scratch My Back, I'll Scratch Yours"

- Morality is an exchange of favors ("I did this for you, so you'd better do that for me") or of blows (misunderstanding of the Golden Rule as "Do it to others before they do it to you" or "Pay them back if they've done it to you").

- You should ask or figure, "What's in it for me?" before you help or obey others.

- The main reason for not stealing, cheating, and so on is that you could get caught.

- Individuals may assert that nobody (even those in legitimate positions of authority) should "boss anybody around," that people should mind their own business, that everybody has his or her own point of view as to what's right, and that everybody should have the right to think and do whatever he or she wants.

- Individuals may suggest that you should "fix things" if somebody gets more than you do.

Critique

- Stage 2 individuals have trouble understanding the ideal of mutuality in a relationship. Also, they tend to be self-centered: better at detecting how others are unfair to or don't do things for them than how they are unfair to or don't do things for others.

MATURE MORALITIES: STAGES 3 AND 4

Stage 3: Mutuality—"Treat Others as You Would Hope They Would Treat You"

- In mutual morality, the relationship itself becomes a value: "Trust" and "mutual caring," although intangible, are real and important.

- People can really care about other people, can have trust in them, and can feel part of a "we."

- You should try to understand if your friend is acting hostile or selfish.

- You should try to make a good impression so others understand that you are a well-intentioned person and so you can think well of yourself.

Table 4.1 (continued)

Critique

• Stage 3 thinking can entail caring about the preciousness of human life. However, Stage 3 thinkers can care so much about what others think of them that they turn into "moral marshmallows" in difficult situations.

Stage 4: Systems—"Are You Contributing to Society?"

• This morality involves interdependence and cooperation for the sake of society: Society can't make it if people don't respect others' rights and follow through on their responsibilities.

• Honoring your commitments is a sign of good character.

• If you are in the position of judge, teacher, or some other social authority, you should uphold consistent and fair standards (but also consider extenuating circumstances).

• In difficult situations, retaining integrity and self-respect may mean becoming unpopular.

Critique

• Stage 4 thinking can entail appeals to moral law and to respect for rights and responsibilities as the basis for society. However, Stage 4 societal morality is more a supplement to than a replacement of Stage 3 interpersonal morality.

---

man has just one house, maybe a lot of furniture, but a whole bunch of people have an awful lot of furniture" (p. 192). Stage 2 is more psychological but is still superficial in a pragmatic way. For example, Stage 2 youth justify keeping promises to ensure that others keep their promises to them and do nice things for them, and to keep others from getting mad at them.

Stages 3 and 4 mark more mature moral judgment, typically emerging in adolescence for children given opportunities to take the perspectives of others. With the advent of Stage 3, moral judgment advances beyond superficiality to a deeper understanding of moral norms, decisions, and values. Stage 3 goes beyond pragmatic thinking to achieve a mutuality of perspectives. Piaget (1932/1965) characterized this transition as one from "reciprocity as a fact" to "reciprocity as an ideal" or "do as you would be done by" (p. 323). As the adolescent interacts in the larger world—school campus, workplace, travel, and so on—the Stage 3 comprehension of the need for mutual understanding expands into an appreciation of the need for commonly accepted, consistent standards and interdependent requirements—in other words, Stage 4. As one of Kohlberg's older adolescent subjects put it, "You've got to have certain understandings in things that everyone is going to abide by or else you could never get anywhere in society, never do anything" (Colby et al., 1987, p. 375).

Mature moral judgment does not always emerge by adolescence, however. Youth who even in the adolescent years show little or no moral judgment beyond Stage 2 are considered developmentally delayed. At home, school, or in the community, they have not had enough opportunity to take on the roles or consider the perspectives of others. Immature moral judgment among adolescents—who, after all, have egos, pubertal desires, still developing frontal cortexes, and access to cars—is a risk factor for delinquent or antisocial behavior. Again, as you think, so you tend to act.

Antisocial youth do have the potential to achieve more mature moral judgment. Most antisocial youth affirm the importance of moral values such as keeping promises, telling the truth, helping others, saving a life, not stealing, and obeying the law (Gregg, Gibbs, & Basinger, 1994; Palmer & Hollin, 1998). Given a choice of possible worlds, they prefer one that is nonviolent and caring (DiBiase, Gibbs, & Potter, 2005), and most can suggest responsible decisions with regard to hypothetical social problem situations (Gibbs et al., 1995).

Yet, as the cited research indicates, when asked *why* moral values such as honesty and property are important, many antisocial youth give reasons that are developmentally delayed or immature. They may even give immature reasons for responsible moral decisions. Studies analyzing moral judgment delay by area of moral value (Gregg et al., 1994; Palmer & Hollin, 1998) have found delay in *every* value area. The area of greatest delay concerns the reasons for not stealing or obeying the law. Nondelinquents generally give Stage 3 reasons—for example, people's mutual expectations of adherence to the law; the selfishness of stealing; and the resulting chaos, insecurity, or loss of trust in the world. By contrast, delinquents generally use reasoning that appeals to the risk of getting caught and going to jail (Stage 2).

We must emphasize that delay in moral judgment refers chiefly to a superficial moral understanding and the use of concrete and egocentric reasons to support responsible moral decisions and values. At a Columbus, Ohio, school for students with aggressive and other behavior problems, 15-year-old Joey was earnest and sincere as he emphatically affirmed the importance of moral values such as helping others, saving a life, honesty, keeping promises, telling the truth, respecting others' property, and obeying the law. Gibbs interviewed Joey.

> **Gibbs:** Joey, in your opinion, why is it so important to obey the law and not steal from or hurt others?
>
> **Joey:** Because, like in a store, you may think no one sees you, but they could have cameras!

Joey's reasons for supporting other moral values were generally similar. Keeping promises or telling the truth was important because if you don't, someone might find out and get even. Helping others, Joey suggested, is important because you may need a favor from the person later on, and so forth. The point here is that "having moral values" or "making responsible decisions" in the mature sense implies a mature understanding of those values and decisions. In the absence of that deeper understanding, antisocial behavior may ensue. The cross-cultural and meta-analytical research noted previously suggests that Joey could not be trusted to live up to his moral values in situations where his fear of observers and surveillance cameras would be less salient than his egocentric desires. Many antisocial juveniles are developmentally delayed, then, in that they do not evidence much grasp of the deeper reasons or bases for moral norms, decisions, or values.

Our combination of Kohlberg's basic approach and Gibbs' theoretical and applied revisions enhances the Moral Reasoning component of ART. We have refined the foundation as well as the techniques in these sessions to ensure the most effective progress for participants and the most efficient implementation for practitioners.

Egocentric Bias and Self-Serving Cognitive Distortions

As Joey's example suggests, delayed moral judgment is not only superficial but also egocentric, or biased toward the immediate desires of the self. That is why Thomas Lickona (1983) called Stage 2 the "What's in it for me?" stage of morality. At-risk youths' egocentric bias typically remains at the pronounced levels characteristic of childhood. Worse, egocentric bias can harden into a system of self-serving cognitive distortions, or inaccurate ways of attending to and interpreting experience. Antisocial youths' levels of these distortions are elevated (e.g., McCrady, Kaufman, Vasey, Barriga, Devlin, & Gibbs, 2008).

The cognitive therapist Stanton Samenow (2004) calls these cognitive distortions *thinking errors*. As measured by the *How I Think Questionnaire* (Barriga et al., 2001; Gibbs et al., 2001), the four thinking errors are as follows:

1. Self-Centered (e.g., If I see something I like, I take it)

2. Assuming the Worst (e.g., You should hurt people first, before they hurt you)

3. Blaming Others (e.g., If people don't cooperate with me, it's not my fault if someone gets hurt)

4. Minimizing/Mislabeling (e.g., Everybody breaks the law—it's no big deal)

Gibbs et al. (1995) define the Self-Centered thinking error as "according status to one's own views, expectations, needs, rights, immediate feelings, and desires to such an extent that the legitimate views, etc., of others are scarcely considered or are disregarded altogether" (p. 108). As such, Self-Centered is a primary thinking error, supported (or protected from empathic distress, guilt, or "bad conscience" over harming others) by the three secondary cognitive distortions: Assuming the Worst, Blaming Others, and Minimizing/Mislabeling.

Illustrating this relationship, one 17-year-old burglar protected his Self-Centered cognitive distortion by blaming his victim (Blaming Others): "If I started feeling bad, I'd say to myself, tough rocks for him; he should have had the house locked better and the alarm on" (Samenow, 1984, p. 115). The cognitive therapist Aaron Beck (1999) is probably correct in his observation that such self-centered and self-servingly distorted thinking is the "eye (I) of the storm of antisocial behavior" (p. 25).

These egocentric distortions are quite common in aggressive youth and are a crucial aspect of sociomoral developmental delay. Facilitators will find an understanding of them to be extremely helpful in gaining insight into participants' thinking and remedying participants' delay through use of the problem situations.

Remedying Delay Through Social Perspective Taking and Decision Making

If ART is to be effective, moral delays must be remediated. The theoretical rationale for this remedy is straightforward: If antisocial or at-risk adolescents' superficial and self-centered reasons stem, at least in part, from their having experienced relatively few social perspective taking opportunities, then Moral Reasoning should provide an enriched, concentrated dose of such opportunities. Through social perspective taking, youth can be stimulated to catch up to an age-appropriate or mature level of moral judgment.

The vehicle for such stimulation is the *social decision making meeting*. In the following section, we discuss this meeting, the concept of training as facilitation, the problem situations used as the basis for discussion in the meetings, and the questions associated with the problem situations.

THE SOCIAL DECISION MAKING MEETING

Antisocial youths' moral reasoning delay is remediated through the social decision making meeting, also referred to as the Moral Reasoning session. In these meetings, group members discuss relevant problem situations and questions and work toward more responsible social decisions supported by mature moral reasons and accurate social perceptions. Generally lasting an hour to an hour and a half, these meetings also help to encourage a mature moral tone or climate for the group. Although these meetings are called social decision making meetings, our concerns go deeper than making decisions per se. Just as "having good moral values" in the mature sense means understanding the deeper reasons for the importance of moral values and taking other perspectives, "making responsible decisions" in the mature sense means basing decisions on those deeper or less superficial reasons. Even if group members converge from the outset on a responsible decision relating to a problem situation, their reasons for those decisions may vary considerably in maturity. For example, deciding not to shoplift is a responsible decision. However, making that decision because you're afraid you'll get caught reflects considerably less developed reasoning than making that same decision because you believe stealing and other forms of lawlessness will harm society. Our fundamental aim is to facilitate the maturity of the *reasoning* used by the group members to support or justify their social decisions and values. Along the way, we reduce the youths' use of self-serving thinking errors, promote the accuracy of their social perceptions, and enhance their tendency to take the perspectives of others.

Role of the Facilitator

In the social decision making meetings, practitioners foster youths' progress toward developing more mature moral understanding. Facilitation can involve teaching, training, modeling, and inculcation. In the main, facilitation means developmental *stimulation*. Group facilitators should ask the group thought-provoking questions, questions that induce group members to consider the perspectives of others. If a group member suggests a Self-Centered decision or value, for example, the facilitator might ask, "What would the world be like if everybody did that?" or "Would you still say that if *you* were the person who gets harmed or wronged?"

In conducting this type of Socratic teaching, the practitioner serves as a guide. The simple rule suggested by Lickona (1983) is "Ask, don't tell." When facilitators do make a constructive criticism, they should make sure to precede and follow the criticism with a supporting comment— the PCP (Praise, Correct, Praise) technique. The following example illustrates.

Facilitator: Latoya, you really are participating well, and I am glad for your contribution *(praise)*. However, one of our rules is to stay on topic when you disagree with someone else. Do you think you could stick to the facts of the problem instead of making up your own scenario *(correct)?*

Latoya: Yeah, I didn't realize I was doing that.

Facilitator: Thank you. I know you can provide us your own perspective about this situation while sticking to the facts at hand (*praise*).

The ability to ask open-ended questions is also important. Open-ended questions do not require a yes/no response or a specific answer involving analysis or justification. "Tell me more," "Can you explain a bit more about what you just said?" and "Help me to understand what you mean?" are examples of open-ended questions.

The fact that practitioners are facilitating progress along a natural developmental trajectory (Gibbs et al., 2007) represents the best defense against the possible objection that group facilitators are imposing their own morals upon vulnerable youth. As the Moral Reasoning sessions progress, participants increasingly catch on to the process. They increasingly consider and challenge one another's perspectives and thereby achieve growth in social development.

Problem Situations

In the social decision making meeting, the group discusses a problem situation and specific related questions. Set in school, on the street, at home, and in other settings, the problem situations pertain to basic moral values such as honesty or responsibility, promise keeping, not stealing or cheating, truthful relationships, resisting drugs, preventing or avoiding violence (against others or self), helping others in various ways, and so forth. Each situation depicts a youth with a problem, typically created by someone *else* with a problem (an effective way to induce a nondefensive discussion of an individual's own problem).

The original ART program (Goldstein & Glick, 1987; Goldstein et al., 1998) included 10 problem situations, specifically written to complement the content of the Social Skills Training and Anger Control Training sessions conducted during that week of the program. Because the initial populations undergoing ART training were exclusively male, these situations involved male protaganists. The original problem situations accompany the Moral Reasoning sessions in Part 2 of this book. To better address the diversity of today's population of ART participants, Appendix D includes 10 additional problem situations, representing both male and female protaganists as well as a wider range of ethnicity. Facilitators should feel free to use these alternate problem situations or to change the names and circumstances of the problem situations to suit their own group membership. Care should be taken not to alter the basic structure of the situations, however, or they may no longer complement the week's associated skill or anger control concept.

It should be emphasized that these are problem situations, not moral dilemmas as defined originally by Kohlberg (1984). Although some of the related questions raise difficult issues, we generally depart from the classic cognitive-developmental practice of using problems that have no clear solutions. In contrast, ART problem situations do have responsible answers—for example, the decision to try to persuade a friend against stealing a car in Alonzo's Problem Situation (see Figure 4.1). For a majority of at-risk group members, the responsible decision or mature reasons for it might not be immediately apparent (hence the need for group facilitation). For many youth with immature moral understanding, resisting a car theft to take a joyride may not be favored if they also have a Minimizing/Mislabeling thinking error that interprets the theft as "having fun with a friend" (*joyride* is already a mislabeling of the offense). Similarly, problem situations in which the responsible answer is to tell on a friend (e.g., if a school friend is talking about plans to shoot people) may be experienced as true dilemmas because the peer norm against "snitching" or "ratting" is so strong. Even when such norms make the group facilitator's job difficult, he or she must still strive to move the group toward maturely supported, responsible decisions.

Discussion Questions

The first question associated with each problem situation solicits a responsible decision with regard to the situation as a whole (e.g., "Should Alonzo try to persuade Rodney not to steal this car?"). Of course, in this case, the responsible response is yes. In the effort to stimulate social perspective taking and accurate thinking, the group facilitator will find the additional probe questions that follow each problem situation to be especially helpful. Some of the probe questions ask group members to imagine that *they* are the prospective victims. Other probe questions ask participants to imagine that the victim of an aggressive or other antisocial act is their sister or another cared-for family member and then to consider whether the act is any *less* wrong if the victim happens to be a stranger. A more open-ended question asks group members to consider the impact of violence (against oneself or another) on others, both near to and far beyond the immediate victim.

In Alonzo's Problem Situation, for example, Question 6 ("Let's say the car is *your* car") directly stimulates group members to take the perspective of the prospective victim. Other questions stimulate group members to consider possible adverse consequences for Alonzo's friend Rodney (Question 8) as well as Rodney's family (Question 5). Still other questions plant cognitive distortions such as Blaming Others (Question 2) and Minimizing/Mislabeling (Questions 3 and 4) for participants to identify and correct.

FIGURE 4.1   Steve's Decisions on Alonzo's Problem Situation

Name _____*Steve*_____ Date _____*April 23*_____

Alonzo is walking along a side street with his friend Rodney. Rodney stops in front of a beautiful new sports car. Rodney looks inside and then says excitedly, "Look! The keys are still in this thing! Let's see what it can do! Come on, let's go!"

What should Alonzo say or do?

1. Should Alonzo try to persuade Rodney not to steal the car?

   ☑ should persuade   ☐ should let steal   ☐ can't decide *(check one)*

2. What if Rodney says to Alonzo that the keys were left in the car, that anyone that careless deserves to get ripped off? Then should Alonzo try to persuade Rodney not to steal the car?

   ☑ should persuade   ☐ should let steal   ☐ can't decide *(check one)*

3. What if Rodney says to Alonzo that the car's owner can probably get insurance money to cover most of the loss? Then should Alonzo try to persuade Rodney not to steal the car?

   ☑ should persuade   ☐ should let steal   ☐ can't decide *(check one)*

4. What if Rodney tells Alonzo that stealing a car is no big deal, that plenty of his friends do it all the time? Then what should Alonzo do?

   ☑ should persuade   ☐ should let steal   ☐ can't decide *(check one)*

5. What if Alonzo knows that Rodney has a wife and child who will suffer if Rodney gets caught, loses his job, and goes to jail? Then should Alonzo try to persuade Rodney not to steal the car?

   ☑ should persuade   ☐ should let steal   ☐ can't decide *(check one)*

6. Let's say the car is your car. Alonzo is Rodney's friend, but Alonzo is also your friend. Alonzo knows it's your car. Then should Alonzo try to persuade Rodney not to steal the car?

   ☑ should persuade   ☐ should let steal   ☐ can't decide *(check one)*

7. In general, how important is it for people not to take things that belong to others?

   ☑ very important   ☐ important   ☐ not important *(check one)*

8. Let's say that Alonzo does try to persuade Rodney not to take the car, but Rodney goes ahead and takes it anyway. Alonzo knows Rodney's in bad shape from being high—he could have a serious accident and someone could get killed. Then what should Alonzo do?

   ☑ should contact the police   ☐ should not contact the police   ☐ can't decide *(check one)*

Problem Situation Analyses

Accompanying each of the original problem situations in the sessions are notes that we call Problem Situation Analyses, intended to alert facilitators to typical trends or patterns in participants' responses. Given the complexity of the process and dynamic nature of the discussion, group members' responses are always unpredictable; however, study of these analyses before conducting a session is particularly helpful. For example, the problem analysis for Alonzo's Problem Situation explains that the majority position tends to be responsible—that is, Alonzo should try to persuade Rodney not to steal the car (Questions 1–6), that it is important not to steal (Question 7), that one tends to hear both pragmatic and mature reasons for the majority decisions, that pragmatic reasons dominate the pro-stealing decisions, and so forth.

MORAL REASONING SESSION PROCEDURES

The problem situations in ART Moral Reasoning represent a variety of circumstances that youth may face in their everyday lives, as well as a wide range of moral concerns. Each week, the facilitators choose one situation, either from the sessions or Appendix D. Sessions include the following problem situations:

- Week 1: Jim's Problem Situation
- Week 2: Jerry's Problem Situation
- Week 3: Mark's Problem Situation
- Week 4: George's Problem Situation
- Week 5: Sam's Problem Situation
- Week 6: Leon's Problem Situation
- Week 7: Reggie's Problem Situation
- Week 8: Alonzo's Problem Situation
- Week 9: Juan's Problem Situation
- Week 10: Antonio's Problem Situation

To facilitate moral reasoning, facilitators guide the social decision making meeting through the four phases listed in Table 4.2. In a well-conducted meeting, these phases flow naturally and seamlessly from one to the next, and there is a certain logic to their flow. Once the group understands clearly what the problem situation is and how it relates to their lives (Phase 1), the facilitator leads discussion to cultivate the group's potential for mature morality (Phase 2). During discussion in these two phases, and on the basis of responses on the problem situation handout group members complete before the session, the facilitator is able to

---

TABLE 4.2   Moral Reasoning Session Phases

Phase 1: Introduce the Problem Situation

Phase 2: Cultivate Mature Morality

Phase 3: Remediate Moral Developmental Delay

Phase 4: Consolidate Mature Morality

---

assess each group member's stage of moral development and any thinking errors. Once the group has voiced some mature, responsibly reasoned positions (Phase 2), the group's more mature (or at least less delayed) members are in a stronger position to challenge other group members' delayed and distorted contributions. The facilitator assists group members in remediating moral delay through further discussion (Phase 3), guiding them toward unanimous support for responsible decisions in relation to the problem situation and mature reasons for making these decisions (Phase 4). Both the individuals and the group as a whole grow through the phases.

With experience, the facilitator's sense of when to transition the group from one phase to the next will become more refined. Throughout the phases, the facilitator must guide, prompt, and ask questions as often as needed to advance the group's thinking. However, he or she should retain a balance that grants some autonomy to the group and must avoid dominating the meeting or entering into one-way communications or dialogue with individual members. As noted previously, the process should involve more asking than telling.

Preparing for the Moral Reasoning Session

Group facilitators must take adequate time to prepare to conduct all ART sessions, but because of the complexity of the process involved in this component, it is even more crucial that they take time to prepare for Moral Reasoning sessions. Facilitators new to the process may require at least an hour for preparation. As facilitators gain more experience, confidence, and competence, preparation will require less time.

Before conducting each session, facilitators first must familiarize themselves with the problem situation to be used in the meeting and its related questions. It is important for facilitators to thoroughly understand the problem situation and the moral positions the problem represents. This preparation is most effective when facilitators meet and prepare together.

Second, they must obtain group members' responses to the problem situation questions. Many facilitators reserve time at the end of the immediately preceding session (an Anger Control Training meeting if you are following the sequence in Table 1.1) to hand out the problem situation, read it aloud, and have participants individually answer the related questions. Group members should not discuss or compare answers, or the tendency to follow negative peer norms may compromise the variety and genuineness of their responses.

Third, facilitators should create a decision chart like the one shown in Figure 4.2. This chart is a matrix showing each participant's responses to each problem situation question. The chart includes a row at the bottom that lists the group's majority decisions, with a question mark next to each such decision (indicating that those majority decisions could become the group's final decisions by the end of the meeting). Reproduced in a size large enough to be seen by the group, the chart forms the basis for group discussion. (Appendix E includes a blank Social Decisions Chart.)

Once the response chart is complete, facilitators are able to analyze group members' responses to the questions, discerning patterns of responsible and irresponsible decision making, as well as instances where group members "can't decide." Group facilitators should also gain an impression of group members' moral reasoning stage (ideally, through prior use of the Sociomoral Reflection Measure–Short Form, included in Appendix E) to help anticipate which group members might provide mature reasons for responsible decisions as well as to help challenge immature reasoners in the group. Although these impressions almost certainly will undergo revision as the actual discussion proceeds, the following specific actions are helpful in reviewing the chart.

Count the Responsible Decisions

Although the responsible decisions relating to the problem situation questions may just reflect group members' desires to "put up a good front," these decisions also can be genuine and in general are a good sign. In the case of Alonzo's Problem Situation, one often finds not only irresponsible but also responsible decisions. Until the group discussion, the *reasons* for these responsible decisions are unknown. Some of the reasons for the responsible decision not to steal may be the result of pragmatic or immature reasoning (e.g., Rodney might get caught, in trouble, shot, killed, etc.), whereas others may be the result of more mature considerations (e.g., Rodney should think about his family, stealing hurts trust, put yourself in the other's position, you'd feel guilty, etc.).

Look Down the Columns

Are there questions on which the responsible decision is unanimous or near-unanimous? For example, everyone discussing Alonzo's Problem Situation decides "Persuade" when Rodney has a family member who

FIGURE 4.2   Preliminary Social Decisions Chart

Question

Name	1	2	3	4	5	6	7	8
Jay	S	S	S	S	P	P	I	CD
Vince	S	S	S	S	P	P	V	CD
Marty	P	P	CD	P	P	P	V	CD
Steve	P	P	P	P	P	P	V	C
Juan	CD	S	S	P	P	P	I	CD
Bill	CD	CD	CD	CD	P	P	I	C
Mike	P	CD	P	P	P	P	I	D
Group decision	P?	S?	S?	P?	P	P	I?	CD?

S = Should let steal   P = Should persuade not to steal   D = Don't contact police
I = Important   V = Very Important   C = Contact police
CD = Can't decide

will suffer (Question 5) and when the car to be stolen is their own car (Question 6). Since one typically hears at least some mature reasons in support of responsible decisions, this is a good sign. It is also a good sign that everyone evaluated not stealing (the property value) as at least "important" (Question 7). "Contact the police" (Question 8), however, looks less promising.

Look Across the Rows

Did some group members consistently make responsible decisions? With regard to Alonzo's Problem Situation, Figure 4.2 shows that a majority of the group made responsible decisions on Questions 5 through 7. These group members are likely allies in the cultivation, remediation, and consolidation phases. Of course, as did Joey in the earlier noted example, it is possible to support a responsible decision or value with immature reasons (respect others' property or don't steal because you might get caught, etc.). However, if from past moral reasoning sessions, or from moral judgment stage assessment, facilitators know that Steve consistently reasons at a Stage 3 level, he could be an uplifting influence. Other possible allies are Marty and Mike. On what rows does one see more negative patterns? We know that mature influences will be needed against more negative deciders such as Jay and Vince. In particular, "let steal" advocate Jay—a strong-willed group member who usually contributes on a Stage 2 level—might try to dominate with irresponsible decisions and pragmatic reasoning. Finally, Bill's responses suggest that he could go either way.

Phase 1: Introduce the Problem Situation

To have an effective social decision-making meeting, all group members must understand clearly what the problem situation is and how it relates to their lives. At the beginning of the session, a group member should read the problem situation aloud. The facilitator then asks the group what the problem situation is, why it is a problem, and whether problems like this actually happen. If a participant has had a problem like it, he or she is invited to describe the experience briefly.

Phase 2: Cultivate Mature Morality

Once the group understands the problem situation and accepts it as relevant, the facilitator transitions to the next phase. The goal in Phase 2 is to cultivate a group atmosphere, climate, or "culture" of mature morality—a morality of responsible decisions supported by mature reasoning.

The facilitator begins the discussion with Question 1 (or with several questions if the group decisions on those quesions cohere). Based on group members' answers to all the questions and past patterns of reasoning, the facilitator is able to make some educated guesses about each group member's likely reasoning. To promote a mature and responsible group moral climate, the facilitator invites responses from the group members most likely to present not only responsible decisions but also the most mature reasons for those decisions.

In the case of Alonzo's Problem Situation, Steve evidences the most consistently responsible position on the questions, followed by Marty and then Mike.

Facilitator: Steve, could you tell the group your reason why you think Alonzo should try to persuade Rodney not to steal the car?

Steve: Well, the owner obviously trusted that people are basically honest and didn't think anyone would take something that did not belong to them. They have their car, they're proud of it, they're trusting that their things are safe, and you steal from them—man, that hurts.

Facilitator: Thank you, Steve. Marty, you also said Alonzo should persuade Rodney not to steal the car. What was your reason for that decision?

Marty: Well, the owner paid good money for the car, and probably worked hard for a long time to save to get it. And if the owner doesn't have insurance, then he may lose his money that he paid for it, especially if the car is damaged. Then the owner has to pay to get it fixed.

Facilitator: Can you tell the group a bit more?

Marty: Well, yeah, if the guy needs the car for work or something, then he's stuck . . . then maybe his family has less to eat or worse.

Facilitator: Thank you for elaborating on that, Marty.

Mike: Yeah, and besides, it's against the Bible and Rodney could wind up in jail.

As one group facilitator is getting responses from group members, the co-facilitator summarizes what each youth states on a sheet of easel pad paper, using the group member's exact words as much as possible.

The discussion process is a dynamic one, and group members may contribute ideas as they occur to them and, quite possibly, out of sequence. Insofar as is possible, the facilitator should try to hold the discussion to responsible decisions, supported at a mature level, and keep to the order of questions as they appear on the problem situation handout. The co-facilitator continues to record group members' reasons. Based on the previous discussion, the co-facilitator could record the following comments under the heading "Persuade" for Questions 1–6. At the same time, he or she could privately note that Steve's and Marty's reasoning appears to be at Stage 3.

Persuade

Hurts trust.

Owner worked hard for it.

Owner's family might suffer.

Against the Bible.

Rodney might go to jail.

Once a mature moral tone has been cultivated through discussion, it is helpful to summarize the reasons for the responsible decision, with emphasis on the mature reasoning for the decision. For example, the facilitator might say, "All right, group, we have a number of good reasons Alonzo should persuade Rodney not to steal the car. For example, we've heard that it hurts trust, the owner worked hard for it, and the owner's family might suffer."

Phase 3: Remediate Moral Developmental Delay

The group facilitator can now transition to Phase 3, Remediate Moral Developmental Delay. The hope is that at this point the group can now prevail against the pragmatic and self-serving influence of some group members—indeed, that more mature members will challenge these suggestions even without being prompted. To some extent, the facilitator has already started to deal with negative influences or developmental delay simply by *not* calling on those with irresponsible decisions and *not* emphasizing the immature reasons for responsible decisions.

These negative group members can't (and shouldn't) be put off forever, however. After all, participants can be easily distracted or bored if they are not involved with the group discussion. Having built up the mature reasons of the responsible deciders, the facilitator invites the negative deciders to explain their reasons. The facilitator solicits reasons from those who made the irresponsible decision that Alonzo should let Rodney steal the car.

Facilitator: Some of the group made the decision that Alonzo should let Rodney steal the car. Let's see, Vince, can you share with us in one or two sentences the reason you answered the way you did?

Vince: Yeah, Alonzo and Rodney want to have some fun and what better way to spend the afternoon?

Facilitator: And, Juan, you also made the same decision as Vince. What was your reason?

Juan: Well, I gotta tell you, that would be great to have that car, see what it can do, like Rodney says. You'd be a big shot, man. You could get money, girls, booze, whatever you want.

Facilitator: What about you, Jay?

Jay: Well, I did answer that Alonzo should let Rodney steal the car, but for a different reason. It says here that Rodney and Alonzo are friends. Friends let friends do what they want. Alonzo doesn't have to go along, but if Rodney wants to take the car, that's his business. Alonzo shouldn't interfere.

As the discussion unfolds, the co-facilitator writes the reasons given for the irresponsible decision.

Let steal

Want to have fun.

Big shot—get money, booze, girls, whatever.

Shouldn't interfere with friend's business.

At this point, the facilitator encourages those who made responsible moral decisions and provided mature reasons for them to discuss their reasons with the less mature moral responders.

Facilitator: What do you think about that, group? Should Alonzo just stay out of Rodney's business?

Mike: Well, I can see the point, Alonzo and Rodney are friends, but how can you argue with what we said so far? We said that Alonzo should try to stop Rodney from stealing the car because the owner worked hard to get the car and without it, his family could suffer and Rodney could go to jail. Rodney could go to jail, dude. Friends don't let friends go to jail and hurt innocent people.

Jay: I see what you mean. I guess Alonzo should try to persuade Rodney not to steal the car.

Facilitator: Jay, it sounds as if you have changed your answer on this question.

Jay: Yeah, I have.

Facilitator: May I change your decision on our chart?

Jay: Yeah.

Vince: You can change my answer while you're at it because it ain't worth going to jail.

Facilitator: OK, sure. And yet you put "Should let steal" for Question 2, Vince. What about Rodney saying that this guy deserves to get ripped off because he was careless, leaving his keys in the car?

Vince: Everyone's careless from time to time. That doesn't mean you deserve to get your car stolen. I want to change that to "Persuade."

Bill: Me, too. I want to change my "Can't decide" to "Persuade."

Facilitator: On Question 2?

Bill: Yeah, and on my other "Can't decides," too. I mean, you got to help your friends, help them stay outta trouble.

When group members change their decisions based on discussion, the co-facilitator crosses out their original decisions and replaces them, as shown in Figure 4.3.

FIGURE 4.3   Final Social Decisions Chart

Question

Name	1	2	3	4	5	6	7	8
Jay	~~S~~ P	~~S~~ P	~~S~~ P	~~S~~ P	P	P	I	CD
Vince	~~S~~ P	~~S~~ P	~~S~~ P	~~S~~ P	P	P	V	CD
Marty	P	P	CD	P	P	P	V	CD
Steve	P	P	P	P	P	P	V	C
Juan	CD	S	S	P	P	P	I	CD
Bill	~~CD~~ P	~~CD~~ P	~~CD~~ P	~~CD~~ P	P	P	I	C
Mike	P	CD	P	P	P	P	I	D
Group decision	(P)	(P)	(P)	(P)	(P)	(P)	(I)	CD

S = Should let steal   P = Should persuade not to steal   D = Don't contact police
I = Important   V = Very Important   C = Contact police
CD = Can't decide

Delayed group members will sometimes argue that their reasons and decisions are more realistic and honest and hence more compelling. For example, Alonzo's joining Rodney to "see what this baby can do" and have fun could be asserted as superior because, after all, that is what Alonzo is actually most *likely* to do. The following exchange illustrates.

> **Steve:** If you let Rodney steal, that's just thinking of you. Like Marty said, you gotta think of the other person.

> **Facilitator:** Yes, and what would the world be like if everyone just thought about themselves, no matter who got hurt?

> **Marty:** Man, that *is* the world! Let's face it. I mean, OK, you shouldn't do it. But, hell, if I was in that situation, I have to say, I'd probably get in the car and go with Alonzo.

In this case, the facilitator can invite members of the majority, especially those who have a more mature moral understanding, to respond to this pragmatic argument. If the group facilitator can find no moral allies in the group to counter the pragmatic "Let's be realistic" attack, then the facilitator will have to do it. The facilitator can relabel or, as Potter (Potter, Gibbs, & Goldstein, 2001) says, "*right*-label" the pragmatic *would* versus the moral *should* appeals. In other words, the facilitator can counter the euphemistic labeling of the antisocial *would* (only realistic, what you'd really do) with a positive, "strong" characterization of the ideal *should*. In the case at hand, the facilitator doesn't even need to intervene—Steve speaks up on his own (after which the facilitator provides support).

Steve: *(To Marty)* But you know that ain't right.

Facilitator: Interesting. It would take real guts for Alonzo not to give in to what he feels like doing and instead do what a lot of people might not be strong enough to do: the right thing.

Juan: Yeah, man, you ain't any big shot if you're dead.

It is crucially important that the majority stand by their responsible decisions and mature reasons. In the successful group process, a participant who attempts to support an irresponsible decision and who usually dominates peers may lose in a challenge from more mature peers in a group where mature moral judgments have set the tone for the group culture (Phase 2). In theoretical terms, the challenged participants may experience an inner conflict or what Piaget called "disequilibration." In moral developmental remediation, participants' self-serving thinking errors tend to give way to more accurate and mature social interpretations and perceptions.

The answers of those who "can't decide" are processed last in this phase. Their uncertainty generally indicates that they are drawn to both sides of the issue—that is, their judgments include arguments for persuading Rodney not to steal the car as well as letting Rodney steal the car. Those who respond with "can't decide" answers are rather fragile in that a strong argument either way may sway them, but they often can be enlisted to support the more morally mature position.

In this discussion, there are two "can't decides" on Question 1: Juan and Bill. As his answers across questions show, Bill seems to have a more responsible moral orientation than Juan, and Bill's contributions in past sessions suggest that his reasoning in support of his responsible decisions tends to be mature. The facilitator continues to remediate moral developmental delay by interacting with Bill first.

Facilitator: Bill, you responded that you can't decide whether Alonzo should persuade Rodney not to steal the car. Now, group, remember that when people state they can't decide in moral reasoning groups, it is not because they really can't make a decision. It is just that they have perspectives on both sides of the question, even though the two sides may not be equal the more they think about it. So, Bill, do you still take the position that you can't decide, given what you have heard discussed thus far?

> **Bill:** Hmmm, well, uh, sorta. I mean I agree with what the group has stated so far, that Alonzo should try to persuade Rodney not to steal the car because the owner worked hard to get the car and without it his family could suffer and Rodney could go to jail. Yet I also believe that friends support each other, and if Rodney wants to take it for a ride, that's cool.

> **Steve:** I don't see how you can agree with the group's reason that the owner will suffer and still let Rodney go ahead and steal the car. Can't you tell him not to and still be friends?

> **Bill:** Well, that's why I'm undecided. I mean, friends should look out for their homies. I guess I wouldn't want my friend to go to jail, and at the same time, I wouldn't want the owner to suffer either. I guess I want to change my answer to Alonzo should try to persuade Rodney not to steal the car.

> **Facilitator:** All right. I'll change your answer from "Let steal" to "Persuade" on our chart.

> **Facilitator:** Juan . . . what do you think? You couldn't decide either.

> **Juan:** I still can't decide.

As the pragmatic group members feel positive pressure and begin to take more responsible positions, they begin to accept and even embrace mature morality. As the discussion continues through the remaining questions and group members change their positions, the co-facilitator continues to indicate the changes on the response chart. Instead of badgering group members like Juan to change their minds in order to force a false consensus, however, it is usually more productive for the facilitator to move on to consolidate the mature morality of the group (Phase 4).

Phase 4: Consolidate Mature Morality

Once mature morality has been sufficiently cultivated and defended, it needs to be consolidated and made as inclusive as possible. Accordingly, the group facilitator transitions the group from Phase 3 to Phase 4. The group's culture becomes more positive and cohesive as the facilitator seeks consensus for responsible decisions and mature reasons. The time is ripe to attempt to convert as many of the positive majority positions, both responsible decisions and mature reasons, as possible into official, even unanimous, group positions.

> **Facilitator:** It looks like the group is already united on Questions 5 and 6, that Alonzo should try to persuade Rodney not to steal the car. Can we circle those *P's* as the group decision?

The group facilitator, co-facilitator, or a responsible group member may circle them.

Facilitator: Is the group all ready to agree that Alonzo should try to persuade Rodney not to steal the car (Question 1)? Does anyone have any objections if someone comes up and crosses out the question mark and circles that as the group's decision?

Some group members (if they haven't already done so) may change their decisions, which the facilitator or group member can indicate on the chart. As shown on Figure 4.3, Jay, Vince, and Bill made changes to responsible decisions, shifting the majority decision in the responsible direction.

Facilitator: With the changes to "Persuade," it looks like we can circle some more group decisions. We already know that "Persuade" is the group decision for Questions 5 and 6, and "Important" is the group decision for Question 7.

What about Questions 2 through 4? Look at the changes. Any big objection if "Persuade" becomes the group decision for those questions as well?

No objections are raised, so the co-facilitator or a responsible group member circles P for Questions 2 through 4 and I for Question 7. However, as Figure 4.3 shows, there is no agreement on Question 8.

As the discussion of Alonzo's Problem Situation continues, the group is able to come up with additional mature reasons for making the responsible decision. Figure 4.4 illustrates what the co-facilitator recorded as the discussion proceeded through the four phases.

At least as important as identifying mature decisions and circling them on the response chart, the group facilitator can identify several mature reasons for those responsible decisions and suggest that, unless there is an objection, the co-facilitator or someone from the group underline those reasons as "the group's best reasons" for their positive decisions.

Facilitator: And what about the best reasons for trying to persuade Rodney not to steal the car? We've got some pretty good reasons on the chart there. We said it is important to put yourself in the other person's place and to remember how much stealing from them hurts their trust, everyone's trust.

Jay: Yeah, and if you remember that, then you don't just feel scared, you feel guilty if you steal from them.

Marty: And the owner's family might suffer.

FIGURE 4.4   Reasons for Decisions on Alonzo's Problem Situation

PERSUADE	IMPORTANT
<u>Hurts trust.</u>	<u>Put yourself in the other's position.</u>
Owner worked hard for it.	You'd get locked up.
<u>Owner's family might suffer.</u>	I've been robbed—it sucks.
Against the Bible.	<u>You'd feel</u> bad, scared, angry, <u>guilty.</u>
Rodney could go to jail.	
Could be your car.	
<u>Help your friend not get in trouble.</u>	

LET STEAL/NOT IMPORTANT

It's not important for people not to steal.

You'd be a big shot.

Lots of fun.

Now you can drive, get money, booze, girls, whatever you want.

Shouldn't interfere in friend's business.

Facilitator: That's true.

Steve: So you have to put yourself in the other guy's position. How would it feel if *your* car got stolen?

Facilitator: OK. Any objections if we underline all those as the group's best reasons for their decisions?

No one objects, so the co-facilitator underlines the "best reasons" listed on Figure 4.4. Alternative selections are acceptable as long as pragmatic or other immature reasons are not underlined as best reasons.

Sometimes a group will reach consensus on responsible decisions and mature reasons. If so, the facilitator can praise the group's work in the following way.

Facilitator: I'm really pleased that the group has been able to come up with so many good, strong decisions and back them up with good, strong reasons. The group has again shown what it can do. You have all worked hard at really listening to each other and making progress.

It is not necessary to force a false group consensus. The benefit of listening to group members debate their reasons for their decisions is sufficient to have group members explore and eventually take perspectives other than their own, thus gaining a deeper understanding as to why they answered the way they did for any given question. A stalemate can be developmentally stimulating, too, and the group can still be praised and encouraged at the conclusion of the social decision making session for its effort.

Facilitator: You have all worked hard at really listening to each other and have made some good progress toward making responsible decisions. I appreciate that.

Regardless of the outcome, at the end of the meeting the group facilitator, co-facilitator, or a responsible group member posts the sheet or sheets showing the list of reasons, with the most mature reasons underlined.

Evaluating the Moral Reasoning Session

To evaluate how well they conducted the meeting, facilitators should complete the Moral Reasoning Session Evaluation Form (see Appendix B) and record any special notes concerning the meeting.

COMMONLY ASKED QUESTIONS

What do I do if I don't have the decision chart prepared before the group meeting?

If group members are unable to answer the problem situation questions before the session, it is possible, though not desirable, for a very experienced facilitator to generate the chart on the spot at the beginning of the session. This option does not allow facilitators much time to assess group members' stages of moral development and general thought patterns, and, as noted, creating the chart in view of group members may compromise their responses.

Can role-playing be a functional part of Moral Reasoning sessions as it is in Social Skills Training and Anger Control Training?

ART assumes average cognitive ability among group members. However, with special populations, role-playing has in some cases been helpful. In a Florida juvenile correctional facility, for example, Gibbs observed as a teacher working with a group of mentally low-functioning, conduct-disordered boys successfully introduced a problem situation by having volunteers from the group act out the situation. Role-plays by younger participants are advocated in a prevention curriculum

(DiBiase et al., 2005). To clarify the problem situation in groups where its meaning may not be understood, then, role-playing can certainly be useful.

Do all the questions for every problem situation have to be processed?

As already stated, the purpose of the questions accompanying the problem situations is to stimulate conversation and debates so group members have every opportunity to take perspectives other than their own. Each question does serve a specific purpose in stimulating the achievement of mature moral understanding and accurate social perception. Ideally, then, for maximum intervention potency and high program integrity, all questions should be discussed. Regrettably, sometimes schedules do not permit that to happen. In that case, questions should be taken in the order they are presented. To expedite, sometimes groups of questions can be presented to the group as a block (Questions 1 through 6 in Alonzo's Problem Situation, for example). If the group agrees on responsible decisions for a series of questions, these questions may be clustered as mature reasons are elicited.

What if the group gets off topic?

In moral reasoning sessions, facilitators have a limited amount of time to accomplish a great deal of work. As such, they must resist allowing the session to become simply another process group or counseling group session. Questions facilitators ask should help identify each participant's stage of moral development and any thinking errors inherent in the reasoning or advance the responsible decisions and mature moral reasoning of group members. Facilitators should take care not to engage in lengthy dialogue with group members and should bring the discussion back to the problem situation as quickly as possible.

What if the group deadlocks and can't reach consensus?

Keep in mind that, in the cognitive-developmental approach, lack of closure is not necessarily such a bad thing. Of course, a group that achieves no consensus *and doesn't care* is a group that has lost the impetus to grow. That should be of some concern. After all, a moral reasoning group, unlike a free-floating process or counseling group, does have a developmental format and aim. Nonetheless, a group *frustrated* by a failure to reach consensus is a different story. Frustration from a lack of closure can be almost as stimulating as closure. If the group is deadlocked on a question, the facilitator might simply say, "Well, I guess the group just wasn't able to come up with a *(group decision, best reason)* for this question," then move on. Or if the group cannot reach overall consensus, "Is the group satisfied with what was accomplished today? I know the group can do better next time because it has succeeded before *(recall positive example, if available)*. What plans can the group make right now so that more good decisions supported by good reasons are accomplished at the next meeting?"

CHAPTER 5

Group Member Motivation and Resistance

Youth who frequently exhibit angry, aggressive, intimidating, bullying, and threatening behaviors toward others in their everyday lives often display the same behaviors in the ART group. Group members may not want to attend, or their attendance may be sporadic. Once in the meeting, they may be unmotivated to participate as requested or as they agreed during their pregroup interview. They may fail to see the relevance of the curriculum to the demands of their everyday lives. In a variety of ways, they may actively resist meaningful group involvement. Their resistive behavior may interfere with their own skill acquisition, anger control, or enhanced moral reasoning and also with the learning of others in the group. Those involved with the juvenile justice system may present additional challenges because their skill deficits are pronounced and their antisocial, aggressive, and violent behaviors are well reinforced. This chapter addresses such matters and offers suggestions to increase group members' motivation and reduce resistance.

INCREASING GROUP MEMBER MOTIVATION

What means do practitioners have at their disposal to increase the likelihood that group members will actually show up for planned ART sessions (attendance motivation), take part as requested in group training procedures (participation motivation), and use what they learn on a continuing basis in their lives (generalization motivation)? Generalization motivation is the topic of chapter 6. Here, focus is on the identification and use of various tactics to motivate regular attendance and enhance active and appropriate participation.

Communicating Behavioral Rules

The first session in the ART program includes the development of behavioral rules to be followed in order to create a safe and effective learning environment in the group. A number of effective "rules for the use of rules" have emerged in the contingency management literature

(Greenwood, Hops, Delquadri, & Guild, 1974; Walker, 1979), including the following:

1. Define and communicate rules for group member behaviors in clear, specific, and, especially, behavioral terms. As Walker (1979) notes, it is better (more concrete and behavioral) to say, "Raise your hand before asking a question" than "Be considerate of others." Similarly, "Listen carefully to instructions" or "Pay attention to the feedback procedure" are statements more likely to serve as rules that actually find expression in student behavior than the more ambiguous statements "Behave in class" or "Do what you are told."

2. Keep in mind that it is more effective to tell group members what to do than what not to do. This accentuation of the positive, for example, finds expression in rules about taking turns, talking over disagreements, or working quietly, rather than in rules directing students not to jump in, not to fight, or not to speak out.

3. Communicate rules in such a manner that group members are assisted in understanding them. Depending on the age of the members and the complexity and difficulty of enacting the rules, such comprehension aids may include keeping rules short and few in number, repeating the rules several times, and posting the rules in written form where they can be seen readily.

4. Provide a chance for group member input. Rule adherence is likely to be more effective when group members have a substantial role in rule development, modification, and implementation. This sense of participation is brought about by explicit involvement in rule development, thorough discussion of rules with the entire group, having selected group members explain to the group the specific meaning of each rule, and group member role-playing of the behaviors identified by the rules.

In addition to the foregoing, further effective rules for the use of rules are that they be developed at the start of the group; that they be fair, reasonable, and within the group members' capacity to follow; that all members of the group understand them; and that they be applied equally and fairly to all group members. ART group rules developed in this manner enhance the likelihood that the group will be a safe and productive place for its members.

Extrinsic and Intrinsic Motivators

The specific use of contingency management principles is discussed in detail later in this chapter. In brief, however, two types of motivational strategies are available: extrinsic and intrinsic. *Extrinsic motivators* are external rewards provided contingent upon performance of desirable behaviors. The use of extrinsic rewards seems especially useful in eliciting initial involvement in ART program activities and is discussed along with other behavior management principles later in this chapter. Briefly, group facilitators can increase motivation to participate in a positive way by conducting a pregroup interview with each potential group member, "selling" the program, and providing external rewards in the form of reinforcers or other extrinsic incentives, perhaps provided within a token economy or level system.

In making decisions about which type of reinforcer to employ with a given youth, the group facilitator must keep in mind that social reinforcement (e.g., attention, praise, approval) is easiest to implement on a continuing basis and is most likely to lead to enduring behavior change. Thus, it is probably the type of reinforcement the group facilitator will wish to use most frequently. Unfortunately, in the initial stages of a behavior change effort—especially when aggressive, disruptive, and other inappropriate behaviors are probably being richly rewarded by the social reinforcement of group facilitator and peer attention as well as by tangible reinforcers—greater reliance on material and activity reinforcers for desirable behaviors may be necessary. Alternatively, a token reinforcement system may prove most effective as the initial reinforcement strategy.

Extrinsic rewards are insufficient to sustain motivation over time, however. There also must be *intrinsic rewards,* or motivation from within the individual. In ART, and particularly in the Social Skills Training and Anger Control Training components, such intrinsic motivators take the form of the social skills and anger impulse control concepts themselves. A group member who has a positive experience actually applying the skill of Dealing with Someone Else's Anger, for example, will be more inclined to try to use the skill again and to want to learn more skills. A participant who avoids punishment by using the technique of thinking ahead, or who as a result of a Moral Reasoning discussion experiences a positive outcome as a result of making a more mature decision, is more likely to be motivated to continue in this vein.

Core Qualities of the Group

The motivational task often is not easy. As noted, many of the youth who are offered the opportunity to participate in ART, which increases *prosocial* behaviors, are highly competent in the regular use of *antisocial* behaviors. Furthermore, this predilection is frequently encouraged, supported, and generously rewarded by many of the significant people in these youths' lives: peers, family members, and other adults.

As is the case for many other educational and training approaches, participants' willingness to participate in a positive way depends not only on teaching procedures and curriculum content, but also on the core qualities of the group. Is it a safe place, free of put-downs, intimidation, and bullying? Are the facilitators, in addition to being competent teachers or workers, also competent protectors? Have members formulated a useful set of group rules, and are members functioning in accordance with them?

Knowing the theory of adolescent development and applying that theory helps facilitators keep group members involved and committed to the program. The bottom line: Adolescents respect those adults who are fair and nonjudgmental yet hold them to account in a respectful way. In facilitator training, we help practitioners learn to confront group members in ways that allow each young person to retain dignity, maintain control over their own decision making (a specific goal of ART), and accomplish the tasks and assignments they have pledged to complete.

The following dialogue provides a glimpse into how a facilitator can deal with conflict around homework completion in a way that reinforces program goals.

Josh: I didn't complete any Hassle Logs and didn't even try using the cues and anger reducers we learned last week.

Facilitator: How come, Josh? Did you have any hassles?

Josh: Oh, yeah, plenty of those. Just didn't do my homework—didn't feel like it.

Facilitator: Well, Josh, you and I will need to discuss this in more detail right after group. However, for now I want to remind the entire group that I had an individual meeting with each of you, including you, Josh (*looking directly at Josh and then turning to others in the group*), during which you all committed to participate in Anger Control Training groups, as well as all of the ART program.

(*Turning back to Josh*) Josh, you and I also had a brief meeting. And refresh my memory. Didn't you state you would participate a full three weeks before we had a follow-up conversation?

Josh: Well, um, ah, hm, yeah, I guess I did.

Facilitator: Can anyone in the group restate what we said participation in group meant?

Latoya: To participate in group activities, do the homework, and follow the group rules.

Facilitator: Exactly. Thank you, Latoya. OK, let's move on, because we have a lot to do today. Josh, I want you to complete a Hassle Log right now, while I continue to review the homework with the group. Do it on a hassle that you had last week, and I will ask you to share it with the group before we introduce the new anger control concepts for today.

It is important for problem behaviors in the group to be dealt with immediately—otherwise, it will be impossible to maintain positive motivation. Group members toward whom these behaviors are aimed may show up for sessions, but their participation will likely be guarded and minimal. Being vigilant in correcting any participant efforts to bully, intimidate, dominate, or otherwise treat others in an inappropriate, aggressive manner serves to protect the one being attacked; it also provides an additional skill lesson for the aggressor.

The next dialogue illustrates this twofold benefit. In this situation, the facilitator has just modeled the new social skill Keeping Out of Fights with the co-facilitator, and the group member, Latoya, has just completed the group's first role-play. Latoya did a fine job in following the skill steps during her role-play, and the group facilitator expects that the group members assigned to watch for specific skill steps will give positive performance feedback.

Facilitator: Carla, you were looking for Step 1: "Stop and think about why you want to fight." Could you tell us what Latoya did to carry out the first skill step: "Stop and think about why you want to fight" and how well you think she did it?

Carla: She did good. She stopped, pointed to her head, and thought aloud. She said, "That girl is dissin' me again by calling my mama names. I want to go and bash her head in."

Facilitator: Thanks, Carla. Josh, you had Step 2: "Decide what you want to happen in the long run." How do you think Latoya did Step 2 of the skill: "Decide what you want to happen in the long run"?

Josh: Pretty good. The step was clear. She did good. Latoya pointed to her head and said, "I don't want that girl to diss my mama no more, and I don't want to get suspended from school for fighting."

Facilitator: Maria, how do you think Latoya performed Step 3: "Think about other ways to handle the situation besides fighting"?

Maria: It was so bad I thought I would puke as she did it.

Maria's statement instantly initiates three problems. The first problem concerns Maria. Maria is exhibiting the type of aggressive behavior that made her a part of the ART group in the first place. Her behavior is threatening to another group member and must be confronted in a manner that is instructive, constructive, and protective to her as well as to

Latoya. The second problem relates to the other group members, who haven't role-played yet. They are likely wondering, "When I get up to role-play, will Maria stick it to me the way she just stuck it to Latoya?" The third problem is Latoya. Latoya is getting the kind of feedback that discourages rather than encourages her to use the skill outside of the group in a real-life situation. The group facilitator's response must address the needs of all participants.

It should be noted that if the proper Social Skills Training and Anger Control Training procedures are followed, the likelihood of this situation happening is minimal. The modeling display shows the "picture perfect" representation of the skill steps and/or anger control concept being taught. The role-play is set up so that each group member charged to observe a particular step is directed to focus on whether the step was accomplished. Finally in the group procedures, if the steps are not being done according to standard, the facilitator stops the role-play, reinstructs the main actor, and continues the group process so that the outcome for the main actor is always positive.

However, in the event that a group member is destructive and disruptive, for whatever reason, the facilitator should first remind the group of the group rule to be respectful. Challenging Maria to respond directly to the question "Did Latoya do the skill step?" should result in a positive response. If that still does not happen, then the facilitator can ask the other group members if they saw Latoya perform the skill step.

In an attempt to protect Maria, the facilitator should avoid challenging her directly on her behavior in public so as not to embarrass her. However, if all the previous actions fail, a direct confrontation might take this form: "Look, Maria, it's good that you gave Latoya frank feedback, but the way you said it is not going to help her. Can you say it in a more constructive way?" If a constructive response is not in Maria's repertoire, the facilitator could stand behind her and whisper in her ear: "Maria, I'm going to say certain things to you, and you say them to Latoya." That teaches Maria about giving constructive feedback and lets her know that threatening comments are not acceptable. Latoya gets the feedback, and the rehearsal of positive behavior encourages real-world skill use. The rest of the group members also get the message that if Maria tries to bully them, the facilitator will come to their aid. In an active manner, the facilitator has provided protection plus instruction to all of the group members.

REDUCING GROUP MEMBER RESISTANCE

The exchanges between the group facilitator and both Josh and Maria, previously presented, were objective and nonaccusatory—and they relied heavily on the facilitator's knowledge of adolescent development principles. Although it is sometimes difficult to avoid negative outcomes, adults who allow adolescents opportunities to have choices, avoid embarrassment (especially in front of their peers), and take responsibility for changing a negative situation will find that they often seize the chance to avoid negative consequences. That said, some youth are highly resistant, even hostile, especially at the second or third week of the program. For those situations, the following discussion will help.

Types of Group Member Resistance

The variety of ways group members seek to thwart, circumvent, object to, or resist participation in the ART group is not infinite, although it may seem that way at times. Table 5.1 lists the more frequently observed types of group member resistance; the following discussion provides a brief description of each. Included with each description are general strategies group facilitators may use to manage these disruptive and counter-productive behaviors.

Inactivity

Minimal participation involves group members who seldom volunteer, provide only brief answers, and in general give group facilitators a feeling that they are "pulling teeth" to keep the group at its various learning tasks.

A more extreme form of minimal participation is *apathy,* in which nearly everything the facilitator does to direct, enliven, or activate the group is met with a lack of interest and spontaneity and little if any progress toward group goals.

While it is rare, *falling asleep* does occur from time to time. Sleepers need to be awakened, and the facilitator should inquire into the cause of the tiredness. Boredom in the group, lack of sleep, and physical illness are all possible reasons, each requiring its own response.

Hyperactivity

Digression is a repetitive, determined, and strongly motivated movement away from the purposes and procedures of ART. The group member feels some emotion strongly (e.g., anger or anxiety or despair) and is determined to express it. Often, the facilitator's brief lecture given on the skill, anger control concept, or problem situation may generate associations with important recent experiences, which the group member feels the need to present and discuss. Digression is also often characterized by "jumping out of role." Rather than merely wandering off track, in digression the group member drives the group off its intended course.

Monopolizing involves subtle and not-so-subtle efforts by a group member to get more than a fair share of time during an ART session. Long monologues sharing a moral reasoning perspective, unnecessary requests to repeat an anger control step, overly elaborate feedback in a

---

TABLE 5.1 Types of Group Member Resistance

Inactivity
- Minimal participation
- Apathy
- Falling asleep

Hyperactivity
- Digression
- Monopolizing
- Interruption
- Excessive restlessness

Active Resistance
- Participation but not as instructed
- Passive-aggressive isolation
- Negativism, refusal
- Disruptiveness

Aggression
- Sarcasm, put-downs
- Bullying, intimidation
- Threats
- Assault

Cognitive Inadequacies and Emotional Disturbances
- Inability to pay attention
- Inability to understand
- Inability to remember
- Bizarre behavior

Social Skills Training session, and other attention-seeking efforts to remain on stage are examples of such monopolizing behaviors.

Similar to monopolizing but more intrusive and insistent, *interruption* is literally breaking into the ongoing flow of a group facilitator's modeling display, role-play or feedback period, or other ART activity with comments, questions, suggestions, observations, or other statements that appear irrelevant to the group content and/or process. Interruption may be overly aggressive or angry, or it may take the pseudo-benevolent form of "help" to the group facilitator. In any event, such interruptions more often than not retard the group's progress toward its goals.

Excessive restlessness is a more extreme, more physical form of hyper-activity. The group member may fidget while sitting; rock chairs; get up and pace; or display other nonverbal, verbal, gestural, or postural signs of restlessness. Excessive restlessness is typically accompanied by digression, monopolizing, or interrupting behavior.

Active Resistance

Group members involved in *participation but not as instructed* are off target. They may be trying to present a moral reasoning perspective, role-play a skill, serve as an anger control co-actor, give feedback, or engage in other required tasks, but their own personal agendas or misperceptions interfere, and they wander off course to irrelevant or semirelevant topics. As such, this problem behavior is related to digression, although digression is perhaps a more intense manifestation of off-task behavior.

Passive-aggressive isolation is not merely apathy, in which group members are simply uninterested in participating. Nor is it participation but not as instructed, in which members actively go off task and raise personal agendas. Passive-aggressive isolation is the purposeful, intentional withholding of appropriate participation, an active shutting down of involvement. It can be thought of as a largely nonverbal "crossing of one's arms" in order to display deliberate nonparticipation.

When displaying *negativism* and *refusal*, group members signal more overtly, by word and deed, the desire to avoid participation. They may openly refuse to be part of a role-play, listen to instructions, or complete homework assignments. Or they may miss sessions, come late to sessions, or walk out in the middle of a session.

Disruptiveness encompasses active resistance behaviors more extreme than negativism and refusal, such as openly and perhaps energetically ridiculing the group facilitator, other group members, or aspects of the ART procedures. Or disruptiveness may be shown by gestures, movements, noises, or other distracting nonverbal behaviors conveying overt criticism and hostility.

Aggression

Sarcasm and *put-downs* are denigrating comments made to ridicule the skill enactment or other behaviors of a fellow group member. The intent of such caustic evaluations is to criticize and diminish the worth of such performances.

Bullying and *intimidation* are common problem behaviors, as they are modes often characteristic of the youth selected for ART participation. We distinguish these problems from the use of sarcasm and put-downs in that the behaviors in this category are more severe in intent and consequences.

Continuing along the severity continuum, the overt use of explicit *threats* is the next category of group management problems. One youth may threaten another with embarrassment, revelation of confidences, or even bodily harm if his or her demands are not met.

Finally, on rare occasions, actual physical *assault* may occur in an ART group. This serious breach of group safety can have long-term negative consequences for group functioning. The negative implications for the group's purposes do not easily dissipate.

Cognitive Inadequacies and Emotional Disturbances

Group members who have severe cognitive inadequacies and emotional disturbances should not be included in ART programs. Developmentally delayed and emotionally disturbed youth are best served by other cognitive-behavioral interventions targeted to meet their specific needs. However, such problems sometimes do manifest in the ART group setting.

Closely related to excessive restlessness, the *inability to pay attention* is often a result of internal or external distractions, daydreaming, or other pressing agendas that command group members' attention. Inability to pay attention, except for brief time spans, may also be due to one or more forms of cognitive impairment.

Cognitive deficits due to developmental disability, intellectual inadequacy, impoverishment of experience, disease processes, or other sources may result in group members' *inability to understand* the ART curriculum. Failure to understand can, of course, also result from lack of instructional clarity or excess complexity.

Material presented in the ART group may be attended to and understood, but not remembered. *Inability to remember* may result not only in problems of transfer, but also in group management problems when what is forgotten includes rules and procedures for participation, homework assignments, and so forth.

Bizarre behavior is uncommon, but when it does occur, it can be especially disruptive to group functioning. This type of group management problem may not only pull other group members off task, it may also frighten them or make them highly anxious. The range of bizarre behaviors possible is quite broad, including talking to oneself or inanimate objects, offering incoherent statements to the group, becoming angry for no apparent reason, hearing and responding to imaginary voices, and exhibiting peculiar mannerisms.

⁓ ⁓

How can such negative behaviors be dealt with constructively and their impact minimized? We provide two answers to this crucial question. First, accurate identification of the resistive behavior will help determine how to remediate it. Second, behavior modification and other specific techniques can be employed successfully to reduce the unwanted behaviors.

Accurate Identification of Resistive Behavior

As a first step in managing resistive behaviors, we urge group facilitators to ask themselves *why?* Why at this moment is this group member engaging in that particular behavior? Facilitators need to make a hypothesis and an assessment. Perhaps one hypothesis is that the group member is displaying the particular resistive behavior at that moment because what is being asked is too complicated (too many steps, too complex a challenge, too demanding a requirement). If so, resistance reduction would take the form of simplifying—decreasing demands on the youth's abilities.

Following are some specific actions facilitators can take during the Social Skills Training or Anger Control Training sessions to simplify when it appears that procedural requests are too complicated:

1. Reward minimal group member accomplishment.

2. Shorten the role-play to include only the steps of the skill or the Anger Control Training concept being taught.

3. Verbally coach the group member by providing cues to follow.

4. Have the group member read a prepared script portraying the behavioral steps.

5. Have the group member play the co-actor role first.

Alternatively, perhaps the group facilitator thinks that because the participant has handled even more difficult demands before, the task is not too complicated, but the participant is feeling intimidated because feedback to the previous role-player was harsh. If this is the case, steps to reduce the threat and make the situation safer must be taken immediately. Following are several suggestions for reducing threat:

1. Employ additional live modeling.

2. Postpone the group member's role-playing until last.

3. Provide reassurance.

4. Provide empathic encouragement.

5. Clarify aspects of the group member's task experienced as threatening.

6. Restructure the aspects of the task the group member experiences as threatening.

Behavior Modification and Other Techniques

The goals in seeking to reduce problematic behaviors are straightforward—first, to maximize the youth's involvement, on-task time, and potential learning and, second, to minimize the time spent in distraction, aggression, or other off-task behaviors. The behavior modification and other techniques next described are helpful in reaching these goals.

Positive Reinforcement

Positive reinforcement is anything that increases the frequency of a behavior when presented following and contingent upon the occurrence of the behavior. *Material reinforcers* (sometimes called *tangible reinforcers*) are actual goods or objects presented to the individual contingent upon enactment of appropriate behaviors. *Activity reinforcers* are those events the youth freely chooses when an opportunity exists to engage in several different activities. *Token reinforcers* are symbolic items or currency (chips, stars, points, etc.) provided to the youth contingent upon the performance of appropriate or desirable behaviors and exchangeable for a wide range of material or activity reinforcers (see Ayllon & Azrin, 1968; Kazdin, 1975). *Social reinforcers*—most often expressed in the form of attention, praise, or approval—are particularly powerful in influencing a broad spectrum of personal and interpersonal behaviors.

Youths' reinforcement preferences change over time, and group facilitators' perspectives of the appropriate reward value of desirable behaviors also change. Given the wide array of potential reinforcers and the fact that almost any event may serve as a reinforcer for one individual but not another, how can the group facilitator decide which reinforcers are best used with a particular youth at a given point in time? Most simply, the group member can be asked which items he or she would like to earn. Often, however, this approach proves insufficient because the youth is not fully aware of the range of reinforcers available or may discount in advance the possibility that the reinforcer will actually be given. When this is the case, other identification procedures must be employed.

First, the group facilitator can often make an accurate determination of whether a given event is in fact functioning as a reinforcer by carefully *observing effects* on the youth. The event probably is reinforcing if the youth asks that the event be repeated, seems happy during the event and unhappy when the event ends, or works in order to earn the event. *Observing choices* can also be helpful. For example, when a youth is free to choose among several equally available activities, which one he or she chooses and how long he or she engages in the chosen activity are readily observed clues to whether an event is reinforcing.

Questionnaires are also useful in identifying positive reinforcers. These may consist of a series of incomplete sentences that the youth must complete by specifying particular reinforcers: for example, "The thing I like to do best with my mother/father is _____" or "I will do almost anything to get _____" (Tharp & Wetzel, 1969). It is important to know who functions as a mediator of reinforcers. Going to a ball game may be a powerful reinforcer if one is accompanied by peers, a weak one if accompanied by one's teacher or mother. Praise from a respected adult may be a potent reinforcing event, whereas the same praise delivered by a peer considered by the youth to be ignorant makes the praise ineffective. Ratings of a youth's perception of just *how* reinforcing a event is are also useful, as are reinforcement menus like the one shown in Table 5.2.

Variety

Reinforcement satiation may occur as a result of an excessive amount of reinforcement. A parallel type of satiation of reinforcement occurs when the group facilitator uses the same approving phrase or other reward over and over again. By varying the content, the facilitator can maintain reinforcer potency. Thus, instead of repeating "Nice job" four or five times, using a mix of comments (e.g., "I'm really proud of you," "You're certainly doing fine," or "Well done") is more likely to yield a sustained effect.

Pairing with Praise

Social reinforcement is most germane to enduring behavioral change, though there are circumstances under which an emphasis upon material, activity, or token reinforcers is at least initially more appropriate. To aid in movement toward social reinforcement, the group facilitator should pair all presentations of material, activity, or token rewards with social reinforcement: an approving comment, a pat on the back, a wink, a smile, and so forth.

⁓⁓

These rules for maximizing positive reinforcement are all essentially remedial in nature—efforts to substitute appropriate prosocial behaviors for existing aggressive, disruptive, antisocial, withdrawal, or asocial behaviors. Positive reinforcement may also be used for preventive purposes. Open attempts to "catch them being good" are strongly recommended for the ART group.

Removing Positive Reinforcers

Increasing the quality and frequency of appropriate, prosocial, or desirable behavior is served primarily by direct teaching in Social Skills Training and by positive reinforcement of desirable behavior. It is impor-

---

TABLE 5.2   Commonly Used Reinforcers

Material
- Favorite snack
- Clothes
- Books
- Gaming system
- Bicycle
- Own room, cell phone, TV
- Watch
- Make-up
- CDs or iPod
- Jewelry
- Musical instrument

Social
- Smiles
- Hugs
- Attention when talking
- Being asked for opinion
- Winks
- Verbal praise
- Head nods
- Thumbs-up sign

Activity
- Having an extended lunch period
- Participating in school trips
- Being in charge of class discussion
- Serving as hall monitor
- Having a homework pass
- Tutoring another student
- Developing a school radio show
- Being on a sports team
- Being dismissed early from class
- Running errands
- Playing a favorite game
- Having time for a hobby
- Watching films or videotapes
- Listening to CDs or iPod
- Playing an instrument
- Playing a video game
- Having free activity time

Token
- Points or coupons (redeemable for other reinforcers)
- Extra money
- Own checking account
- Allowance
- Gift certificate

---

tant for attempts to reduce inappropriate behavior by withdrawing reinforcement to be accompanied by efforts to increase appropriate behavior by providing reinforcement. This combination of efforts succeeds especially well when the appropriate and inappropriate behaviors involved are incompatible with each other (e.g., reward in-seat behavior, ignore out-of-seat behavior; reward talking at a conversational level, ignore yelling).

Extinction

Extinction is the withdrawal or removal of positive reinforcement for aggressive or other undesirable behaviors that have been either deliberately or inadvertently reinforced in the past. This technique is the procedure of choice with milder forms of aggression (e.g., sarcasm, put-downs, or other forms of low-level verbal aggression).

Very often, the reinforcer that youth seek through aggression, disruptiveness, and similar behaviors is attention. Laughing, looking, staring, yelling at, talking to, or turning toward are common facilitator and peer reactions to a youth's aggression. Ignoring such behaviors effects extinction. Ignoring someone who would normally receive one's attention is itself a talent, as the following guidelines for using extinction illustrate:

1. Do not comment that you are ignoring the group member. Long (or even short) explanations provide precisely the type of social reinforcement that extinction is designed to withdraw. Ignoring the behavior simply occurs with no forewarning, introduction, or prior explanation.

2. Do not look away suddenly when the group member behaves aggressively or inappropriately. Behaving abruptly may communicate the message "I really noticed and was impelled to action by your behavior"—the exact opposite of an extinction message.

3. Protect the victims of aggression. If one youth verbally or physically attacks another, the group facilitator must intervene, but the intervention can be accomplished without subverting the extinction effort by providing the victim with attention, concern, and interest and by ignoring the perpetrator.

As is true for the provision of reinforcement, its removal must be consistent. Within a given ART group, this rule of consistency means that the group facilitator and group members must act together and that the facilitator must be consistent across time. When responses are inconsistent and the aggressive behavior is intermittently or partially reinforced, the behavior becomes highly resistant to extinction. Consistency means that, to the degree possible, all group facilitators working with a given youth must strive to ignore the same inappropriate behaviors. Whenever possible, efforts should be made to bring the youth's significant real-world figures into the extinction effort.

Aggressive behaviors often have a long history of positive reinforcement and, especially if much of that history is one of intermittent reinforcement, efforts to undo them must be sustained. Persistence in this regard usually succeeds. There are, however, two types of events to keep in mind when judging the effectiveness of extinction efforts. The first is what is known as the *extinction burst*. When extinction is first introduced, it is not uncommon for the rate or intensity of the aggressive behavior to increase sharply before it begins its more gradual decline toward zero. The meaning of this burst is, in fact, that extinction is beginning to work. In addition, inappropriate behaviors that are successfully extinguished reappear occasionally, for reasons difficult to determine. Like the extinction burst, this *spontaneous recovery* is transitory and disappears if the facilitator persists in the extinction effort.

Time-out

In time-out, a client who engages in aggressive or other inappropriate behaviors is physically removed from all sources of reinforcement for a specified time period. As with extinction, the purpose of time-out is to reduce the undesirable behavior that immediately precedes it. Time-out differs from extinction in that extinction involves removing the individual from reinforcement, whereas time-out usually involves removing the individual from the reinforcing situation.

In school- and facility-based practice, time-out typically takes three forms. *Isolation time-out,* the most common form, requires the youth to be physically removed from the location to a time-out room. *Exclusion time-out* is somewhat less restrictive but also involves physically removing the youth from sources of reinforcement. Here the youth is required to go to a corner of the room and perhaps to sit in a "quiet chair," which is sometimes behind a screen. The youth is not removed from the room but is excluded from ongoing activities for a specified time period. *Nonexclusion time-out* (also called *contingent observation*), the least restrictive time-out variant, requires the youth to sit and observe the appropriate behaviors of other youth. This variant combines time-out with modeling opportunities and is therefore the preferred approach for the ART group.

As is the case for extinction, positive reinforcement for appropriate behaviors accompanies time-out. When possible, the behaviors positively reinforced should be opposite to, or at least incompatible with, those for which the time-out procedure is instituted. Furthermore, there is an additional basis for recommending the combined use of these two techniques: Specifically, extensive use of reinforcers makes staying in the situation more rewarding and time-out all the more aversive.

Extinction is the recommended procedure for those aggressive or otherwise undesirable behaviors that can be safely ignored. Potentially injurious behaviors require a more active response, possibly time-out. Group facilitators should be aware of any established procedures to deal with removing youth from the training environment and apply them as necessary. However, if at all possible, facilitators should avoid excluding youth from ART groups. In the case of many youth, physical removal by the group facilitator may not be wise, appropriate, or even possible. For such youth, procedures other than extinction or time-out, discussed later in this chapter, can be employed.

Response Cost

Extinction and time-out sometimes prove insufficient for severely aggressive adolescents, even when combined with a group facilitator's praise or other reinforcement for appropriate behaviors. In a number of instances, response-cost procedures—especially when combined with positive reinforcement via a token economy for prosocial behaviors—prove effective.

Response cost involves the removal of previously acquired reinforcers contingent upon and in order to reduce future instances of inappropriate behaviors. These reinforcers may be earned, as when the use of response-cost procedures is a component of a token reinforcement system, or they may be provided, as is the case with a freestanding response-cost system. In either instance, reinforcers are removed (the cost) whenever previously targeted undesirable behaviors occur (the response).

Cost setting is a crucial determinant of the success or failure of this approach. For example, Carr (1981) notes that if fines are too large, bankruptcy will ensue and the youth will be unable to purchase any back-up reinforcers. If the fines are too small, the youth will be able to negate the loss by easily performing a variety of appropriate behaviors. Yet other aspects of response-cost implementation make demands on the group facilitator's skills as a creative economist. The relationship of points or other reinforcers to earn to those that can be lost; the relationship of cost to the severity of inappropriate behavior; and a host of similar marketing, pricing, and, ultimately, motivational considerations come into play.

As is true for the other major procedures for the removal of positive reinforcement (extinction and time-out), response-cost procedures require the group facilitator to be *consistent* in the application of procedures across students and across time for each student, *immediate* in delivering contingent costs after the inappropriate behavior occurs, and *impartial* in ensuring that the instance of inappropriate behavior leads to response cost, with an absolute minimum of exceptions.

Punishment and Negative Reinforcement

Punishment and negative reinforcement involve the presentation and removal of aversive stimuli, respectively. These procedures are generally less advisable than procedures for presenting and removing positive reinforcement.

Punishment

Punishment is the presentation of an aversive stimulus contingent upon the performance of a behavior, intended to decrease the likelihood of future occurrences. Two of the major forms that punishment takes are verbal punishment (i.e., reprimands) and corporal punishment (i.e., paddling, spanking, slapping). The effectiveness of these and other forms of punishment in altering inappropriate behaviors such as aggression has been shown to be a function of several factors: likelihood, consistency, immediacy, duration, severity, possibility for escape or avoidance, availability of alternative routes to goal, level of instigation to aggression, level of reward for aggression, and characteristics of the prohibiting agents.

Even assuming an instance in which these determinants yield a substantial impact, what, ideally, can we hope the effect of punishment on aggression or other undesirable behavior will be? If the youth is deficient in the ability to ask rather than take, request rather than command, and negotiate rather than strike out, punishment will not teach the youth desirable alternative behaviors.

The main effect of punishment is a temporary suppression of inappropriate behaviors. Research demonstrates such undesirable side effects of punishment as withdrawal from social contact, counteraggression toward the punisher, modeling of punishing behavior, disruption of social relationships, failure of effects to generalize, selective avoidance (refraining from inappropriate behaviors only when under surveillance), and stigmatizing labeling effects (Azrin & Holz, 1966; Bandura, 1973; Sobsey, 1990). Our own weighing of relevant data and ethical considerations favors selective use of verbal punishment such as reprimands. We reject under all circumstances the use of physical punishment techniques.

We appreciate the potential value of temporary suppression to group facilitators who wish to increase training time; however, it is common for facilitators to punish the same youth over and over again for the same inappropriate behaviors. Therefore, if used at all, punishment must be combined with efforts to teach those behaviors in which the youth is deficient.

Negative Reinforcement

Negative reinforcement is the removal of aversive stimuli contingent upon the occurrence of desirable behaviors. Negative reinforcement is seldom used as a behavior modification approach in classroom or delinquency facility contexts. The exception to this rule occurs when youth are released from time-out (an aversive environment) contingent upon such desirable behaviors as quietness and calmness.

Unfortunately, the dynamics of negative reinforcement are often expressed in classroom and other contexts to less constructive effect. For example, if a student behaves disruptively (shouts, swears, fights), a teacher may respond with an angry reprimand. If the teacher's punishment brings about a temporary suppression of the youth's disruptiveness, the decrease in disruptiveness (i.e., the aversive stimulus) will likely negatively reinforce the immediately preceding teacher behavior (in this case, angry reprimands). The net effect of this sequence is to increase the likelihood of the teacher's use of reprimands. Analogous sequences may occur and function to increase the likelihood of other ineffective or inappropriate behaviors.

Other Behavior Modification Procedures

In addition to the various procedures previously examined for the presentation or removal of positive reinforcement or aversive stimuli, two other behavior modification procedures—overcorrection and contingency contracting—do not rely upon the management of contingencies.

Overcorrection

Overcorrection is a behavior modification approach developed by Foxx and Azrin (1973) for those circumstances when extinction, time-out, and response cost either fail or cannot be used and when few alternative appropriate behaviors are available to reinforce. Overcorrection is a two-part procedure, having both restitution and positive practice components. For instance, if a youth destroys school property and strikes out at classmates, he or she must make restitution by returning the classroom to its original status or better. Broken objects must be repaired, the classmates struck in anger apologized to, scattered papers picked up. The positive practice component of overcorrection would require the youth to repair objects broken by others, apologize to peers who witnessed the classmates being struck, or clean up the rest of the room, including areas not disturbed by the youth. Restitution and positive practice requirements may serve both a punitive and an instructional function.

Contingency Contracting

A contingency contract is a written agreement between a group facilitator and group member. It is a document each signs that specifies, in detailed behavioral terms, desirable behaviors and their positive consequences, as well as undesirable behaviors and their undesirable consequences. Contracts will more reliably lead to desirable behaviors when the contract payoff is immediate; approximations to the desirable behavior are rewarded; the contract rewards accomplishment rather than obedience; accomplishment precedes reward; and the contract is fair, clear, honest, positive, and systematically implemented.

⹾⹿

This chapter has provided practitioners a road map for dealing with the resistant group member while at the same time providing strategies to enhance youth motivation and performance in ART groups. The next chapter addresses ways practitioners can extend group members' knowledge gained from ART groups to their real-world environment.

CHAPTER 6

Enhancing Generalization of Performance

As the cognitive-behavioral interventions movement matures and evidence regarding its effectiveness accumulates, it becomes clear that, whereas the acquisition of new behaviors is a reliable finding across both training methods and populations, generalization is another matter. Both generalization to new settings (transfer) and over time (maintenance) are reported to occur in only a minority of training outcomes. In this chapter, we examine issues in enhancing generalization.

APPROACHES TO ENHANCE GENERALIZATION

Many traditional interventions reflect a core belief in personality change as both target and outcome in treatment. Such interventions express a strong tendency to ignore environmental influences on behavior, viewing successful intervention as a sort of *psychological inoculation.* Positive changes purported to take place within the individual's personality structure are believed to help individuals deal effectively with problem events wherever and whenever they occur. That is, transfer and maintenance are viewed as automatically occurring processes. With reference to the prevailing psychoanalytic view on this matter, Ford and Urban (1963) noted that "no special procedures are necessary to facilitate the transfer from the therapist to other situations if the therapist has successfully resolved the transference pattern of behavior (p. 173)."

The assumption of automatic maintenance and transfer, variously explained, are also characteristic of the therapeutic positions of Adler (1924), Horney (1939), Rank (1945), Rogers (1951), and Sullivan (1953). In each instance, the view put forth is that, when the therapeutic process results in positive intrapsychic changes in the patient, the patient is able to apply these changes where and when needed in the real-life environment. This perspective was widespread among approaches to psychological change throughout the 1950s. No call was made for the development of purposeful means for the enhancement of transfer and maintenance because these outcomes were held to occur automatically as a consequence of within-treatment gains.

Psychotherapy research as a viable enterprise began in the 1950s and grew in both quantity and scope during the 1960s and 1970s. Much of the outcome research conducted during this time included systematic follow-up probes to ascertain whether gains at the termination of formal intervention had generalized across settings and/or time. Stokes and Baer (1977) describe the phase as one of *train and hope.*

The overwhelming result of investigations was that, much more often than not, transfer and maintenance of intervention gains did not occur. Treatment and training did not often serve as an inoculation, gains did not persist automatically, transfer and maintenance did not necessarily follow from the initial training, and the hoped-for generalization of training effects did not occur (Goldstein & Kanfer, 1979; Keeley, Shemberg, & Carbonell, 1976). As a result, observers concluded that transfer and maintenance must be actively sought. In fact, the failure of the inoculation model, as revealed by the evidence accumulated during the train-and-hope phase, led to a third phase of concern with generalization—the development, evaluation, and use of a number of procedures explicitly designed to enhance transfer and maintenance of intervention gains.

A different assumption regarding response maintenance and transfer of therapeutic gains has emerged in the psychotherapy research literature, especially that devoted to the outcome of behavior modification interventions. The position taken is that maintenance-enhancing and transfer-enhancing techniques must be systematically incorporated into the ongoing treatment process. At this point, it is clear that we cannot assume that a behavior acquired in the therapy situation, however well learned, will carry over into other situations. We must understand the rules that determine what responses will be generalized or transferred to other situations and what responses will not.

TRANSFER-ENHANCING PROCEDURES

A variety of useful transfer-enhancing techniques have been developed, evaluated, and put into practice. These procedures, listed in Table 6.1, are examined in detail in the rest of this chapter.

Provision of General Principles

Transfer of training is facilitated by providing group members with the general mediating principles that govern satisfactory performance on both original and transfer tasks. In brief, group members are given the rules, strategies, or organizing principles that lead to successful performance.

No matter how competently the ART group facilitator creates in the role-play setting the "feel" of the real-life setting in which a group member

---

TABLE 6.1   Transfer- and Maintenance-Enhancing Procedures

Transfer
1. Provision of general principles (general case programming)
2. Overlearning (maximizing response availability)
3. Stimulus variability (training sufficient exemplars, training loosely)
4. Identical elements (programming common stimuli)
5. Mediated generalization (self-recording, self-reinforcement, self-punishment, self-instruction)

Maintenance
1. Thinning reinforcement (increased intermittency, unpredictability)
2. Delaying reinforcement
3. Fading prompts
4. Providing booster sessions
5. Preparing for nonreinforcement in the natural environment
    a. Self-reinforcement
    b. Relapse and failure management skills
    c. Graduated homework assignments
6. Programming for reinforcement in the natural environment
7. Using natural reinforcers
    a. Real-life settings
    b. Easily reinforced behaviors
    c. Reinforcement recruitment
    d. Reinforcement recognition

---

will use the skill or anger control concept, and no matter how well the coactor in the given role-play matches the actual qualities and likely response of the real target figure, differences that matter between role-play and real world always exist. Even when the group member role-plays the skill or observes the skill steps a number of times, the demands of the real-world situation will depart from the demands as portrayed in the role-play. And the real parent, peer, teacher, or probation officer is likely to respond to the group member somewhat differently than does his or her role-play partner and peer group members. When the group member has a good grasp of the principles underlying the role-play and real situations he or she is addressing (their demands, expected behaviors, norms, purposes, rules, and the principles underlying the skill or step—why *these* steps, in *this* order, toward *which* ends), transfer becomes more likely.

Overlearning

Transfer of training is enhanced by procedures that maximize overlearning or response availability, and the likelihood that a response will be available is very clearly a function of its prior use. We repeat over and over foreign language phrases we are learning, we insist that our child spend an hour each day in piano practice, or we devote considerable time in practice making a golf swing smooth and automatic. These are simply expressions of the response availability notion—that is, the more we practice responses (especially *correct* ones), the easier it is to use them in other contexts or at later times. All other things being equal, the response made most frequently in the past is more likely to be made on subsequent occasions. However, it is not sheer practice of attempts at effective behaviors that is most beneficial to transfer, but practice of *successful* attempts. Overlearning involves extending learning over more trials than is necessary to produce initial changes in the individual's behavior. In too many situations, one or two successes at a given task are taken as evidence to move on to the next task or the next level of the original task. To maximize transfer through overlearning, the guiding rule is not "practice makes perfect" (implying that one simply practices until one gets it right and then moves on), but "practice of perfect" (implying numerous trials of correct responses after the initial success).

Youth who have successfully role-played a skill or anger control sequence may object to the facilitator's request that every other group member also role-play it. Frequently, in response to this objection we point to the value of repetitive pregame practice (warm-ups, shoot-arounds, batting practice) for professional athletic performance. Such practice makes core skills nearly automatic and frees up the player's attention for strategy or other planning efforts. It is common and appropriate for a Social Skills Training group to observe 8 to 10 role-plays for a single skill. Similarly, in the Anger Control Training sequence, each step is repeated several times as the weeks progress. Given that real-life people and events may work *against* group members' use of prosocial behaviors and anger control techniques, the need for overlearning becomes all the more apparent.

Stimulus Variability

Transfer is enhanced by means of practice and repetition—that is, by the sheer number of correct responses. It is also enhanced by the variability or range of situations to which the individual responds. Training even on two situations is better than training on one. The implication is clear that in order to maximize positive transfer, training should provide for some sampling of the population of stimuli to which the response must ultimately be given. Generalization of new skills or behaviors is also facilitated by training under a wide variety of conditions. Manipulating the numbers of group facilitators, settings, and response classes involved in the intervention promotes generalization by exposing group members to a variety of situations. Thus, if for purposes of overlearning group members are asked to role-play a given social skill correctly many times, each attempt should involve a different coactor, a different constructed setting, and, especially, a different need for the same skill.

We also enhance stimulus variability by providing the steps of skills and anger control steps on Skill Cards and posters in the training setting and, where appropriate, in group members' real-life environment (e.g., schools, community centers, institutional settings).

Identical Elements

In perhaps the earliest experimental work dealing with transfer enhancement, Thorndike and Woodworth (1901) concluded that, when there is a facilitative effect of one habit on another, it is to the extent that and because the habits share identical elements. Ellis (1965) and Osgood (1953) emphasized the importance for transfer of similarity between characteristics of the training and application tasks. In brief, the greater the similarity between practice and test stimuli, the greater the amount of positive transfer. In the context of ART, the principle of identical elements is implemented by procedures that function to increase the correspondence of stimuli within the group (places, people, events, etc.) to real life. Two strategies exist for attaining a high level of correspondence. The first concerns the physical location in which ART takes place. Typically, we remain in the school or institution and by use of props and imagination recreate the physical feel of the real-world context in which the group member plans to use the skill or step. Sometimes we use the actual setting in which the skill will be used (e.g., office, cafeteria, gymnasium). It is critically important to this transfer training principle to approximate the real-life location where the group member will practice the skill after role-playing it in group.

The second principle is to create real-life situations with individuals who remind the group member of the actual person with whom the skill will be used. Toward that end, it is sometimes advantageous to include group members who know each other and who are familiar with the real-life details of the situations being role-played. Live together, play together, go to class together, fight together—get trained together. Therefore, when implementing ART, it is good to draw participants from the same grade, unit, or ward.

Mediated Generalization

The one commonality present in both training and application settings is the individual group member. Generalization mediated by the group member, not by others, is an approach to transfer enhancement that relies on instructing the group member in a series of context-bridging self-regulation competencies. Operationally, it consists of instructing the group member in self-recording, self-reinforcement, self-punishment, and self-instruction. Epps, Thompson, and Lane (1985), working in a token economy in a special education setting, structured these generalization-mediating steps as follows.

Self-Recording

1. The teacher sets up the data collection system—that is, selects a target behavior, defines it in measurable terms, and decides on an appropriate recording technique.

2. The teacher tries out the data collection system.

3. The teacher teaches the group member how to use the data collection system.

4. The teacher reinforces the group member for taking accurate data.

Self-Reinforcement

1. The teacher determines how many points a group member has earned, and the group member simply records these.

2. The teacher tells the group member to decide how many points should be awarded for appropriate behavior.

3. The group member practices self-reinforcement under teacher supervision.

4. The group member employs self-reinforcement without teacher supervision.

Self-Punishment

Self-punishment, illustrated in this example by response cost (taking away points), is taught in a manner directly parallel to that just described for self-reinforcement, in which the teacher employs the technique of fading, or gradually reducing the frequency and intensity of reinforcement.

Self-Instruction

1. The teacher models the appropriate behavior while talking himself or herself through the task aloud so the group member can hear.

2. The group member performs the task with overt instructions from the teacher.

3. The group member performs the task with overt self-instructions.

4. The group member performs the task with covert self-instructions.

As cognitive behavior modification therapies, especially those relying heavily on self-instructional processes, have grown in popularity, the use of self-mediated approaches to generalization has grown correspondingly.

MAINTENANCE-ENHANCING PROCEDURES

The persistence, durability, or maintenance of behaviors developed by skills training approaches is primarily a matter of managing reinforcement during the original training and in the youth's natural environment. Several means exist by which maintenance-enhancing management of reinforcement may proceed. We will examine the following matters first: thinning reinforcement, delaying reinforcement, fading prompts, providing booster sessions, and preparing for nonreinforcement in the natural environment. We will then examine two similar concerns as they occur beyond the ART group setting: programming for reinforcement in the natural environment and using natural reinforcers.

Thinning Reinforcement

A rich, continuous reinforcement schedule is optimal in order to establish new behaviors. Maintenance of such behaviors is enhanced if the reinforcement schedule is gradually thinned. The group facilitator applies thinning of reinforcement by moving from a continuous (every trial) schedule, to an intermittent schedule, to a level of sparse and infrequent reinforcement characteristic of the natural environment. In fact, the maintenance-enhancing goal of such a thinning process is to make the group facilitator's reinforcement schedule indistinguishable from that typically found in real-world contexts.

Delaying Reinforcement

Resistance to extinction is also enhanced by delaying reinforcement. During the early stages of an intervention, reinforcement should be immediate and continous. However, after the behavior becomes firmly established, it is important to introduce a delay in presenting the reinforcement because delayed reinforcement is a closer approximation to reinforcement conditions in the natural environment.

Delay of reinforcement is implemented by (a) increasing the size or complexity of the response required before reinforcement is provided; (b) adding a time delay between the response and the delivery of reinforcement; and (c) in token systems, increasing the time interval between the receipt of tokens and the opportunity to spend them and/or requiring more tokens in exchange for a given reinforcer.

Fading Prompts

Maintenance is enhanced by the gradual removal of suggestions, reminders, prompts, or other similar coaching or instruction. Fading of prompts is a means of moving away from the group facilitator's artificial control to more natural self-control of desirable behaviors. As with all enhancement techniques, fading of prompts must be carefully planned and systematically implemented.

Providing Booster Sessions

Periodically, it is necessary to reinstate instruction in the specifics of appropriate behaviors in order for the group member to continue those behaviors in the natural environment. Booster sessions, either on a preplanned schedule or as needed, often prove valuable in this regard. (See chapter 1 discussion of program adaptation and extension.)

Preparing for Nonreinforcement in the Natural Environment

Group facilitators and group members may take several steps to maximize the likelihood that reinforcement for appropriate behaviors will occur in the natural environment, but on a number of occasions, reinforcement may not be forthcoming. It is important to prepare group members for this eventuality. As described in our earlier examination of mediated generalization, self-reinforcement is one means of responding when desirable behaviors are performed correctly but are unrewarded by external sources.

Research on relapse prevention and failure management in the area of addiction treatment suggests another way to maintain newly learned prosocial behaviors. Appropriate, prosocially directed self-instructional talk and rearrangement of environmental cues toward prosocial patterns (where one goes, with whom one associates, what one does) can help in this regard. Mastery of such social skills as Responding to Failure, Dealing with an Accusation, and Dealing with Group Pressure, to name but a few, may also serve the purpose of relapse and failure management (see Appendix A for these skills and their steps).

A third way in which ART group members are prepared for nonreinforcement in the natural environment is by using graduated homework assignments. In Social Skills Training, for example, it may become clear as the homework is discussed that the real-life figure is too difficult a target—too harsh, too unresponsive, or simply too unlikely to provide reinforcement for competent skill use. In this case, we have recast the homework assignment toward two or three more benevolent and potentially responsive target figures. When the group member finally uses the skill correctly with the original target figure and receives no reinforcement, previously reinforced trials help minimize the likelihood that the behavior will be extinguished.

Programming for Reinforcement in the Natural Environment

The maintenance-enhancing techniques examined thus far are targeted toward the group member. But maintenance of appropriate behaviors is also enhanced by efforts directed toward others, especially those in the natural environment who function as the main providers of reinforcement.

This larger interpersonal world consists of parents, siblings, peers, teachers, neighbors, classmates, and direct care providers, among others. Largely, their responsiveness or unresponsiveness to the group member's newly learned skill behaviors controls the destiny of these behaviors. All of us react to what important people in our lives think or feel about our behavior. What they reward, we are more likely to continue doing. What they are indifferent or hostile to tends to fall into disuse.

As described in detail in chapter 7, one major evaluation of ART, in which the focus was on maintaining group member skill performance, involved the provision of ART sessions to parents as well as youth (Goldstein, Glick, Irwin, McCartney, & Rubama, 1989). Parent training groups met independently of those held for the adolescents three out of every four sessions, the fourth session being a joint meeting. Major ART training programs have also been conducted for group members' peers. In one instance, the peers involved were fellow members of the group members' juvenile gangs (Goldstein & Glick, 1994). In the second, the peers trained were fellow residents in a state facility for juvenile delinquents (Leeman, Gibbs, & Fuller, 1993). In both instances, evaluations demonstrated that enhancing the ART skill levels of the significant people in group members' lives enhances maintenance of group members' skill use. These outcomes reflect the belief long held by many who work with troubled youth: Serious attempts to alter antisocial behaviors for the better must be directed toward youth and toward significant people in their lives.

It is certainly possible to increase the likelihood that school, agency, and institutional staff, as well as parents and peers, will respond to group members' display of newly learned skills with active approval, encouragement, or other social rewards. Materials designed for caregivers of participating youth and staff working with them are included in Appendix C.

Using Natural Reinforcers

A final and especially valuable approach to maintenance enhancement is the use of reinforcers that exist in the real-world environment. It is important to target behaviors for change that are most likely to be seen as desirable and positive by others. Ayllon and Azrin (1968) refer to this as the "Relevance of Behavior Rule." In other words, teach only those behaviors that will continue to be reinforced after training.

Alberto and Troutman (1982) have suggested a four-step process that facilitates effective use of natural reinforcers:

1. Observe which specific behaviors are regularly reinforced and how they are reinforced in the major settings that constitute the group member's natural environment.

2. Instruct the group member in a selected number of such naturally reinforced behaviors (e.g., certain social skills, grooming behaviors).

3. Teach the group member how to recruit or request reinforcement (e.g., by tactfully asking peers or others for approval or recognition).

4. Teach the group member how to recognize reinforcement when it is offered (because its presence in certain gestures or facial expressions may be quite subtle for many group members).

Now that we have discussed how to increase the likelihood that group members will transfer what they learn in group sessions to the real world, we turn our attention to programs that have incorporated many of the principles and strategies described thus far. The next chapter describes programs we consider models to emulate that demonstrate program effectiveness.

CHAPTER 7

Application Models and Evaluations of Program Effectiveness

Aggression Replacement Training has been well researched and evaluated. The program has been identified as evidence based and either a promising or model program by the Office of Juvenile Justice and Delinquency Prevention and the National Institute of Justice (U.S. Department of Justice, 2010; Sherman, Farrington, MacKenzie, & Welsh, 2006), the Office of Safe and Drug-Free Schools (U.S. Department of Education, 2002), and the National Center for Mental Health Promotion and Youth Violence Prevention (2007), among others. ART efficacy studies have provided consistently reliable evidence that the program reduces aggressive, acting out behaviors while increasing prosocial behaviors in high-risk youth.

This chapter describes a wide range of ART program applications and settings and summarizes efficacy evaluations of ART conducted to date. These investigations reveal the impact of ART—its apparent strengths and weaknesses—and serve as examples of the scrutiny we feel all cognitive-behavioral interventions should receive. We begin by describing seminal programs that first implemented ART, then highlight agencies, systems, and jurisdictions at the national level whose adoption of ART as a cognitive-behavioral intervention has been evaluated and judged to be effective and cost efficient. Discussion of international implementations of the ART model follows. We conclude with ART program evaluations conducted by our own research group as well as by independent investigators.

SEMINAL PROGRAMS

The work of ART was greatly enhanced by those who adopted the program early on and who implemented the program with integrity and fidelity, as originally developed and designed. We owe much to these early practitioners.

The New York State Division for Youth

The New York State Division for Youth was the first to implement ART after the initial pilot project was conducted at Annsville Youth Center in central New York State. Many institutions throughout the division incorporated ART into their programming. One example is Taberg Youth

Center, a midlevel residential center for male juvenile delinquents ages 14 to 18 who had committed assaults, robberies, or similar felonies.

Positive Alternative Learning (PAL) Program

The Positive Alternative Learning (PAL) Program at the Ferguson-Florissant School District outside St. Louis incorporated a 10-week ART sequence for elementary and middle school youth. Some youth were assigned to the program preventively, in response to a series of low-level disruptive acts and before major crises occurred. Others were sent for rehabilitation following disciplinary hearings for major infractions. The PAL program is ongoing.

The Boys and Girls Clubs of America

The Boys and Girls Clubs of America implemented ART at four sites throughout its national system to deal with violent gang members and aggressive youth, many of whom were suspended or expelled from school. Initial pilot sites included Mobile, Alabama; Anchorage, Alaska; Little Rock, Arkansas; and Fort Worth, Texas.

Berkshire Farms

Berkshire Farms is a comprehensive, multiservice youth agency with a residential center in Canaan, New York; a statewide aftercare system; and community-based group homes. The large agency incorporated ART within its residential system to mitigate the violent and aggressive behaviors of those youth placed with them.

Children's Village

Children's Village of Dobbs Ferry, New York, is a residential campus agency providing education and mental health services to 300 resident boys—almost all of whom come to the facility with histories of abuse and neglect, current emotional patterns of disturbed functioning, and often serious behavioral and learning problems. ART was included in Children's Village programming in 1996, beginning at the upper elementary level, moving to the secondary level and then to the cottage residences. A substantial facility-wide effort took root and grew.

What We Have Learned

We have learned a great deal from these early interventions. Much of what we gleaned from these initial programs has supported the theoretical and philosophical foundations upon which ART was developed and designed. Some of the more important findings include the following:

- Staff must be trained in the intervention in order to ensure that the delivery of ART is competent and program fidelity is maintained.

- Youth should be screened and assessed to meet the targeted behaviors for which ART was designed (i.e., aggression and violence).

- ART may be delivered in a variety of settings and initially appears to be culturally and gender neutral.

- Program integrity can be maintained even when great distances separate program managers and group facilitators.

- Program monitoring and auditing is essential to ensure program fidelity.

- Administrators and executives must be integrally involved with the program's implementation and maintenance within their systems.

- Program evaluation and research should be associated with ART implementation from its inception.

NATIONAL PROGRAM MODELS

Washington State Juvenile Rehabilitation Administration

In 1997, the state of Washington passed the Community Juvenile Accountability Act (CJAA), monumental legislation that revolutionized how juvenile courts funded programs and provided services to adjudicated youth. Only programs shown to reduce recidivism cost effectively were funded under the CJAA. As far as we know, no other state had attempted to implement research-proven, cost-effective intervention programs for juvenile offenders on a statewide basis at that time. The law called for a coordinated effort between state and local jurisdictions and initially supported five programs to be selected from a review of national research. The programs demonstrated recidivism reductions in small sample studies in other parts of the country. The CJAA also funded the Washington State Institute for Public Policy to evaluate implementation of the law and those programs selected to reduce recidivism within the several jurisdictions. Five programs were originally selected, including ART. Program developers strongly emphasized training and consultation, and Glick was retained to train and develop the system to implement ART in 26 of the 39 counties in the state. Over 100 staff were trained during the first year. The second and third years of the project were devoted to developing organizational systems to support ART implementation and designing a quality assurance program. In order to maintain program fidelity, Glick had weekly telephone contact with program administrators and conducted monthly meetings with program implementers. These meetings were devoted to implementation issues and clinical supervision.

Oregon Youth Authority

The Oregon Youth Authority was among the first state agencies to adopt ART systemwide. In 1996, Oregon committed to implementing ART throughout its institutions, with the vision to expand the program to community services. Training was conducted for 30 staff, who implemented ART throughout the system. From that group, 20 staff were identified to become certified trainers of ART group facilitators. In 1997, Glick and two associates trained trainers while they provided group facilitator training for an additional 60 staff in a learning institute. This ambitious project validated the training model that Glick employed at Annsville Youth Center in 1983 and has refined over the years.

Ramsey County Juvenile Community Corrections

Ramsey County Juvenile Community Corrections in Minnesota is one of the largest community systems in the country. It has its own residential treatment center and probation and parole functions for youth in the community, as well as established cooperative agreements with private community youth service agencies and school districts. The major city within the county, St. Paul, has an active youth census of 600. The county is among the first to implement ART as an evidence-based cognitive-behavioral intervention to serve its youth population. The county initially trained staff as group facilitators, then continued to follow the established training model to train 10 of its staff as certified trainers of ART group facilitators. The county currently continues to train staff and maintain their system as a viable mechanism to deliver ART to its adjudicated juvenile populations. Ramsey County has dedicated a staff person to coordinate ART training and staff development. This practice has proven effective because issues of implementation, training, and quality assurance are coordinated systemwide and reported directly to the chief executive of the youth division.

Alaska Juvenile Justice

Alaska Juvenile Justice implemented ART beginning in 2005, training 80 staff initially, followed by training 8 staff as certified trainers of ART group facilitators. Alaska provides yet another set of issues for cognitive-behavioral intervention practitioners because of its vast geographic size. Although one could fit the state of Texas inside Alaska's borders three and a half times, the population of Alaska is quite small (a couple of million people), 80 percent or more living within Anchorage, Alaska's largest city. Delivering the program and services to youth and their families in regions quite remote is challenging, and this was also the challenge as we trained and implemented ART in that jurisdiction. The implementation was successful because of the executive and administrative support from the highest levels of state government and because a staff member was dedicated to the management of training implementation and quality assurance aspects of program development.

Administrative Office of the Illinois Courts

ART was implemented in 2007 throughout the probation services administered by the Administrative Office of the Illinois Courts (AOIC). Staff from various county courts were trained as ART group facilitators. The courts system represents the first locally funded effort to establish a standardized statewide system, thereby taking a more active role in providing cognitive-behavioral interventions like ART. A Train the Trainers Institute was conducted a year later so the AOIC could maintain their system and program implementation with fidelity and integrity.

Justice Research Center

The Justice Research Center (JRC), based in Tallahassee, Florida, is a woman-owned and operated S corporation with certification as a Florida Minority Business Enterprise since 2001. The JRC has provided research and evaluation services, program and instrument development, and staff training for state and federal agencies, institutions of higher education, and nationally recognized juvenile justice organizations and providers throughout the United States.

In 2007, the JRC was funded by the Florida Department of Juvenile Justice with a two-year community partnership grant to implement ART groups through the Leon County Aggression Replacement Training Initiative. The purpose of the initiative was to provide ART to youth assessed as being at high risk for aggressive behavior and family problems and residing in neighborhoods prone to violence and aggression. The JRC ran multiple mixed-gender groups in second-chance schools in Leon County. Youth were given school credit for the ART groups they attended, and the schools provided group classroom space for the program. The JRC ran multiple groups as an overlay service in a secure residential treatment program that serves adolescent males. The institution provided group classroom space to run the ART groups, as well as additional staff supervision for the youth while in group. The JRC also ran multiple mixed-gender groups for youth ordered by the circuit court into ART as a diversion alternative to state-supervised juvenile probation. Space was provided for the diversion groups in both the Leon County juvenile probation office and the Lincoln Neighborhood Center at no cost to the JRC.

All youth in the three different treatment venues were pretested and posttested on various standardized violence and aggressive behavior measures and administered attitude scales assessing their satisfaction with the group. In all treatment situations, data indicated that youth learned the social skills and anger control concepts taught in the ART program, reduced their aggression and violence, and demonstrated more prosocial behaviors. A final outcome study is pending at the time of this writing.

The program was well received in the community by local law enforcement, who worked with the JRC initially to set up a referral protocol, and by the state's attorney's office, the juvenile circuit court, and the second-chance school administration and teachers, as well as by youth referred to the program and their families.

JRC staff were originally trained by Glick in a JRC-sponsored ART training funded by the Department of Juvenile Justice (DJJ) through federal Juvenile Accountability Block Grant monies in January 2007. Various residential juvenile–contracted provider staff, DJJ program accountability technical assistance staff, and JRC staff were trained. ART was identified by program providers as one cognitive-behavioral intervention in which they wished to be trained, among others identified by the state as model cognitive-behavioral interventions.

Urban Youth Alliance International

Urban Youth Alliance International, in New York, New York, is a faith-based community agency that serves young people from the poorest and most deprived areas throughout the city. The agency offers an alternative-to-incarceration program, an alternative school, and a vocational developmental program, among other services. Glick trained 12 staff to deliver ART to clients in the Bronx and Staten Island. Unique to this approach was the faith-based attribute of the organization; although their policies support nondenominational services, the introduction of this cognitive-behavioral approach presented challenges to some of the staff. Another important aspect that this agency brings to the practitioner is the liaison the agency established with local colleges to provide program evaluation and quality assurance systems (one of the staff trained was a faculty member from a local university).

What We Have Learned

These organizations are but examples of the hundreds at the national level that have adopted ART as an outcome-based, effective, and efficient cognitive-behavioral intervention. As with earlier program applications, we learned much from these various jurisdictions' and agencies' implementation of ART:

- ART is effective across a variety of youth programs and services systems: juvenile justice, education, social services, community-based youth center, public and private, for-profit and not-for-profit organizations.

- ART has been shown to be neutral—that is, effective across gender, culture, and ethnicity.

- Staff who are competently trained and provided technical program support and clinical supervision during their initial implementation of the ART program are better equipped to provide peer consultation and supervision to their colleagues.

- Staff require not only adequate training but also supervisory support to implement the program with integrity. As such, middle managers and administrators must also be familiar with ART in order to reinforce staff implementation and ensure program fidelity.

- Staff are more effective in presenting ART if they are given at least one hour of preparation time for each of the three group sessions each week.

- Jurisdictions that have developed quality assurance systems and designed instruments to monitor and audit ART program integrity have enhanced program effectiveness.

- When staff are poorly trained or the program is not implemented as developed and designed, client behaviors (aggression and violence) may get worse, not better.

INTERNATIONAL PROGRAM MODELS

UngArt (Youth Alternatives)

UngArt (Youth Alternatives) is a comprehensive, private, multiservice community-based youth agency located in Malmö, Sweden. Malmö has over 160 different ethnic groups with a myriad of languages, a large Islamic community, a relatively high rate of social problems, and an active gang population.

UngArt has provided services to youth at risk since 1977 and currently operates a variety of programs and services for youth. One is a program for at-risk youth who are referred by the Ministry of Social Services Authorities in Malmö as well as in other nearby municipalities. Youth may attend this community-based program for up to nine months on average. Although ART is the primary cognitive-behavioral intervention for the program, it is but one of several offered. Youth are placed in ART groups between six and eight weeks after they are referred to UngArt. Before that, they are assessed and provided basic skills to enhance their success in the community and the program.

One innovative strategy developed by UngArt, based on transfer training principles, is that of the youth "transfer coach." These youth have completed ART programs and serve as models and mentors for their peers. They are employed, trained, and supervised by UngArt staff, after which they participate in groups with their assigned mentees, ensuring that they attend groups and helping them complete their ART homework assignments. Working under the supervision of professional staff, the transfer coaches interact with the clients' families, prompt clients to attend group sessions, and aid in the transfer of the learning from ART sessions to the real world. UngArt has captured the essence of the transfer training principles by using its young graduates as models for the clients they serve. By living the way they teach, the transfer coaches embody yet another program concept developed by UngArt: MAGIC, an acronym standing for Motivation (client incentive and inspiration), ART, and Generalization in the Community (taking the program learning from the classroom to real-life situations).

UngArt initiated a second noteworthy program in 2005. They administer an independent elementary special education school (similar to charter schools in the United States) for youth with special needs in the areas of social, emotional, and oppositional defiant behaviors. All youth in this independent school program attend ART groups and, after program completion, continue with additional social skills, anger control booster sessions, and problem-solving classes. The staff to student ratio is about 1:4 and includes four special education teachers, one principal, and two transfer coaches (youth assistants).

UngArt has three certified ART Master Trainers and is one of the few programs in Scandinavia that delivers ART with program fidelity (Kaunitz & Strandberg, 2009). They have trained hundreds of professionals in delivering ART throughout Sweden, Norway, Finland, and Russia.

Amity Institute

Amity Institute is located in Warsaw, Poland, and provides training and consulting services to a wide variety of human service entities. They initially began their work with Goldstein and later continued with Glick to ensure that ART was delivered according to standard, with program integrity. With now more than 10 years experience implementing ART, Amity Institute recently completed a major project to introduce ART into the Warsaw public schools, training about 1,000 ART group facilitators each year according to standards developed in consultation with Glick. Amity Institute has also developed a Train the Trainers Institute, in which experienced ART group facilitators undergo an additional 280 hours of training, including didactic and experiential practicum.

In order to ensure successful implementation throughout the school systems in Poland, particularly Warsaw, Amity Institute also trained the Polish Municipal Guard Officers. The Municipal Guard in Poland is a uniformed law and order unit that has educational and policing responsibilities. A special subgroup of the Municipal Guard was selected to conduct preventive instruction and services in the Warsaw public schools. Eight officers were trained as ART group facilitators to support and augment the public school ART projects.

An extensive evaluation was conducted on students who participated in ART, finding that 78 percent adopted more frequent use of social skills, 91 percent reported reduction in angry behaviors, and teachers and significant adults reported a general reduction of aggressive behaviors and increased prosocial behaviors (Morawski & Morawski, 2009).

Werken med Goldstein (Working with Goldstein)

In the Netherlands, Werken med Goldstein is a foundation in Eindhoven, Holland, that first began its work with Goldstein by publishing social skills in Dutch. It should be noted that Goldstein spent part of his graduate school years in Amsterdam and made Dutch contacts during his formative years working in behavioral psychology. This organization has devoted its time and energy developing materials and training for the Dutch and European markets.

In 2007, Glick was invited to consult with Werken med Goldstein to develop training materials for the U.S. market. That project used students from the American School of Drama in The Hague to produce modeling displays for the social skills in ART. The Goldstein Foundation Group also developed comic strips for the Moral Reasoning Situations and an Anger Control Training cartoon training aide to be used with clients in those group sessions. These group facilitator tools demonstrate the kinds of innovative work now being done throughout the international community.

What We Have Learned

The international ART programs provide us with an experiential base from which we gain further insight into the implementation of ART and the richness of cognitive-behavioral interventions. Some of our insights include the following:

- Youth are the same the world over; they present similar at-risk behaviors, with common aggression and violent reactions to situations.

- Program administrators, managers, and group facilitators should be trained in basic cognitive-behavior therapy principles before they train in any particular intervention, including ART.

- Group facilitators should be matched with target clients to enhance program implementation and maximize participant-staff productivity.

- Certification and credentialing are critically important to the European human services systems, such that ART must be certified to have fidelity and programs are implemented with integrity.

- Staff development is essential to program success. Staff should "live what they teach" so they model for youth what they expect youth to accomplish.

- Adequate resources must be provided to the group facilitators who implement the program, including but not limited to physical space, equipment, supplies and materials, administrative support, and clinical/program technical assistance.

- ART continues to appear to be culturally, gender, and ethnically neutral, as demonstrated by the variety of implementation sites: Sweden, Norway, Russia, Hungary, Poland, Holland, and Belgium, to name but a few.

- The administrator charged with implementing ART should be competent, enthusiastic, and involved in program delivery from its inception.

It should be noted that many of these factors have been reported in North America as well, verifying their validity and reliability as program model issues. Some of these factors have been objectively evaluated and reported as part of effective program design, development, and delivery.

EVALUATIONS OF EFFECTIVENESS: STUDIES BY OUR OWN RESEARCH GROUP

Annsville Youth Center

Our first evaluation of ART was conducted at the New York State Division for Youth facility in central New York State (Goldstein & Glick, 1987), where the program was originally implemented. Sixty youth at Annsville were included, most of them incarcerated at this limited-secure institution for such crimes as burglary, robbery, and various drug offenses. A total of 24 youth received the 10-week ART program outlined in Table 1.1, meeting three times a week. An additional 24 youth were assigned to a no-ART, brief instruction control group. This group controlled for the possibility that any apparent ART-derived gains in skill performance were due not to ART, but to the youths' enhanced motivation to display skills they already possessed but simply were not using. A third group, the no-treatment control group, consisted of 12 youth not participating in either ART or the brief instruction control group.

The overall goal of this evaluation was to examine the effectiveness of ART for the following purposes:

1. Skill acquisition: Do the youth learn the 10 skills in the ART curriculum?

2. Minimal skill transfer: Can the youth perform the skills in response to new situations similar in format to those in which they were trained?

3. Extended skill transfer: Can the youth perform the skills in response to new situations dissimilar in format and more "real-lifelike" than those in which they were trained?

4. Anger control enhancement: Do the youth actually demonstrate fewer altercations or other acting-out behaviors as reflected in weekly behavior incident reports, completed for all participating youth by the center's staff?

5. Impulse reduction: Are the youth rated as less impulsive and more reflective and self-controlled in their interpersonal behaviors?

Analyses of study data revealed, first, that youth undergoing ART, compared with youth in both control groups, significantly acquired and transferred (minimal and extended) four of the ten social skills: Making a Complaint, Getting Ready for a Difficult Conversation, Dealing with Someone Else's Anger, and Dealing with Group Pressure. Similarly, significant ART versus control group comparisons emerged on both the number and intensity of in-facility acting-out behaviors (as measured by the behavior incident reports) as well as on staff-rated impulsiveness.

Following completion of the project's posttesting in Week 11, new ART groups were formed for the 36 youth in the two control groups. As before, these sessions were held three times per week for 10 weeks and duplicated the first-phase ART sessions in all other major respects (curriculum, group size, materials, etc.). Our goal in this second phase was an own-control test of the efficacy of ART, with particular attention to discerning possible reductions in acting-out behaviors by comparing, for these 36 youth, their behavior incident reports during Weeks 11 through 20 (while in ART) with their behavior incident reports from the period when they had served as control group members (Weeks 1 through 10). Both of the statistical comparisons (number and severity) conducted to test for replication effects yielded positive results.

Real-world figures such as family and peers frequently express indifference or even hostility toward trainees' use of newly learned prosocial skills. Our hope was that ART would serve as a sufficiently powerful intervention to effect at least moderate carryover of in-facility ART gains. In order to test for such possible transfer effects, we constructed a global rating measurement of community functioning. During the first-year period following initiation of ART at Annsville, 54 youth were released from this facility. Seventeen had received ART; 37 had not. We contacted the Division for Youth Service team members (analogous to parole officers) around New York State to whom the 54 released youth regularly reported and, without informing the workers as to whether the youth had or had not received ART, asked the workers to complete global rating measurements for each of the Annsville youth. In four of the six areas—namely, home and family, peer, legal, and overall—ART youth were rated significantly higher with regard to in-community functioning than were non-ART youth. In the areas of school and work, no significant differences emerged.

MacCormick Youth Center

Our second evaluation of the efficacy of ART was conducted at MacCormick Youth Center, a New York State Division for Youth maximum-secure facility for male juvenile delinquents between the ages of 13 and 21 (Goldstein & Glick, 1987). In essence, this second evaluation project sought to replicate the exact procedures and findings of the Annsville project and to include youth incarcerated for substantially more serious felonies. A total of 51 youth were in residence at MacCormick at the time of the evaluation. Crimes committed by these youth included murder, manslaughter, rape, sodomy, attempted murder, assault, and armed robbery. In all its procedural and experimental particulars, the MacCormick evaluation project replicated the effort at Annsville. It employed the same preparatory activities, materials, curriculum, testing, staff training, resident training, supervision, and data analysis procedures.

On five of the ten ART social skills, significant acquisition and/or transfer results emerged. These findings essentially replicate the Annsville results. In contrast to the Annsville results, however, the MacCormick data also yielded a significant result on the Sociomoral Reflection Measure (Gibbs, Basinger, & Fuller, 1992). At MacCormick, but not at Annsville, youth participating in Moral Reasoning sessions grew significantly in moral reasoning stages over the 10-week intervention period.

Regarding overt, in-facility behavior, youth receiving ART, compared with those who did not, increased significantly over their base rate levels in their use of constructive prosocial behaviors (e.g., offering or accepting criticism appropriately, employing self-control when provoked) and decreased significantly in their rated levels of impulsiveness. In contrast to the Annsville findings, MacCormick youth who received ART did not differ from controls in either the number or intensity of acting-out behaviors.

Annsville, internally, is not a locked facility. Its 60 youth live in one dormitory, in contrast to the locked, single-room arrangement at MacCormick. MacCormick's staff is twice the size of Annsville's, and the facility operates under a considerably tighter system of sanctions and controls than Annsville. Because of these operational differences, the opportunity for acting-out behaviors is lower across all conditions at MacCormick as compared with Annsville. A "floor effect" therefore seemed to be operating at MacCormick that made a decrease in acting-out at MacCormick less likely to be a direct result of ART participation than at Annsville. At Annsville, such behaviors were contextually more possible at base rate, and they could and did decrease over the intervention period. At MacCormick, all youth started with low base rates and, likely for these same contextual reasons (e.g., sanctions, controls, rich staffing), they remained low. Subjects' use of prosocial behaviors, for which no floor or ceiling influences were relevant, did increase differentially as a function of the ART intervention.

A Community-Based Evaluation

The findings of our first two investigations revealed ART to be a multimodal habilitation intervention of considerable potency with incarcerated juvenile delinquents: It enhanced prosocial skill competency and overt prosocial behavior and reduced levels of impulsiveness. And, in one of the two samples studied, decreases (where possible) in the frequency and intensity of acting-out behaviors and enhancement of participants' levels of moral reasoning were verified.

Furthermore, some evidence provided independently revealed ART to lead to valuable changes in community functioning. In light of the general movement away from residential and toward community-based programming for delinquent youth, this possibility for community change led to our third evaluation of the efficacy of ART. This evaluation sought to discern the value of ART when provided to 84 youth on a post-release basis, while youth were living in the community (Goldstein et al., 1989). We were aware of the potent contribution to effective community functioning that parents and others make in the lives of delinquent youth. This belief led to our attempt to discern the effects of offering ART to the youth, and also to their parents and other family members.

This community-based project was essentially a three-way comparison of ART provided directly to youth, plus ART provided to the youths' parents or other family members (Condition 1), versus ART for youth only (Condition 2), versus a no-ART control group (Condition 3). For the most part, participating youth were assigned to project conditions on a random basis, with departures from randomization necessary on occasion as a function of the five-city, multisite, time-extended nature of the project.

Largely as a result of how long the New York State Division for Youth had aftercare responsibility for youth discharged from their facilities, the ART program offered to project participants was designed to last three months, with sessions meeting twice per week, for a total of approximately 24 sessions. Each session was an hour and a half to two hours long. The first session of each week was spent in a brief discussion of current life events and difficulties and training of a social skill relevant to the life events/difficulties discussed during the first hour of the first session, followed by presentation of a Moral Reasoning problem situation. The second session of the week consisted of Anger Control Training during the first hour, followed by the conclusion of the Moral Reasoning problem situation for that week. The final weekly session provided ART for parents and other family members of a sample of participating youth.

Those parents selected to participate but who did not appear were provided ART in modified form, via a weekly home visit or telephone call.

Since the different ART groups in the project's two treatment conditions chose which of the 50 social skills they wished to learn (see Appendix A), different groups learned different (if overlapping) skills. We did not, therefore, examine in our statistical analyses participant change on individual skills. Instead, analyses focused on total skill change for the youth participating in ART (Conditions 1 and 2) versus each other and non-ART control group youth (Condition 3). Data indicated that, although results for the two ART conditions did not differ significantly, participants in each of these conditions increased significantly in their overall interpersonal skill competence when compared to Condition 3 (no-ART) youth. A similarly significant outcome emerged (both ART groups versus no-ART group) for decrease in self-reported anger levels in response to mild (e.g., minor nuisance, unfair treatment) but not severe (e.g., betrayal of trust, control/coercion, physical abuse) anger-provoking situations.

A particularly important evaluation criterion in delinquency intervention work is recidivism. It is reported that the majority of previously incarcerated youth who recidivate do so within the first six months following their release (Maltz, 1984). Thus, the recidivism criterion employed in this project, rearrest, was tracked during the first three months, in which youth received ART, and during the three subsequent no-ART months. Condition 3 youth, of course, received no ART during the entire tracking period. Analyses examining the frequency of rearrest by condition showed a significant effect for ART participation. Both Condition 1 and Condition 2 youth were rearrested significantly less than were youth not receiving ART. A substantial decrease in rearrest occurred when the youths' families (i.e., parents and siblings) participated simultaneously in their own ART groups.

From this study, it appears that teaching family members interpersonal skills and anger control techniques reciprocal to those delinquent youth are learning may provide the youth with a more responsive and prosocially reinforcing real-world environment—an environment in which prosocial instead of antisocial behaviors are supported, encouraged, and reinforced. Complementing youth ART with group experiences for parents or significant care providers may also enhance youths' ability to resist further antisocial behaviors.

The Gang Intervention Project

Our research group's fourth ART evaluation (Goldstein, Glick, Carthan, & Blancero, 1994), in which ART group members were all gang members, also grew from a systems-oriented perspective. First, we knew from adolescent development theory that peers are one of the most influential forces on youth. In our fourth-year project, we were interested in learning if we could impact the youths' peer group. Our challenge was to find the most influential peer group for antisocial youth. We decided to apply ART with gangs because we believed gangs were powerful and dominant in the lives of antisocial at-risk youth. Our community-based effort focused on delinquent youths' family members with some success. Could we use ART not only to teach youth to behave more prosocially but also to increase the likelihood that their prosocial efforts in real life would be met by acceptance, support, and even praise from fellow gang members?

This project was conducted in two Brooklyn, New York, youth community agencies: the Brownsville Community Neighborhood Action Center and Youth D.A.R.E.S. of Coney Island. Each agency conducted three four-month sequences of ART. Within each sequence, ART group members were all members of the same gang. We constituted a control group for each sequence whose members were also from the same gang but from a gang different from the one to which the ART trainees belonged. Thus, across both agencies, twelve different gangs participated in the program—six receiving ART, six as no-ART controls. All the youth, ART and controls, received the same educational, vocational, and recreational services offered by the two participating agencies.

Repeated measures analysis of variables crossing project conditions (ART versus control) with time of measurement (pre- versus post-study) revealed a significant interaction effect favoring ART participants for each of the seven social skills categories, as well as on a total skills score.

None of the ANOVA comparisons of ART scores with control group scores for the study's measure of anger control yielded significant differences. Of the five community domains, only work adjustment yielded a significant difference. This result accords well with (and no doubt largely reflects) the real-world employment pattern for project participants. For example, in the months immediately following their ART sequence, the majority of the participating Lo-Lives (one of the gangs) left their gang and took jobs in retail businesses. At an analogous point in time, following their own ART participation, a substantial minority of the participating Baby Wolf-Pack members obtained employment in the construction trades and ultimately started their own construction business, refurbishing the very neighborhoods they had previously destroyed.

Arrest data were available for the youth participating in our first two ART gang intervention sequences and their respective control groups. Five of the 38 ART participants (13 percent) and 14 of the 27 control group members (52 percent) were rearrested during the eight-month tracking period. Our favorable outcome verified by rearrest rates implies the possibility that a more harmonious and prosocially supportive post-ART peer environment was created. While it is important for future research to examine this possibility more directly, it is interesting to note that similar rearrest outcomes were obtained in our earlier attempt to create a prosocially reinforcing post-ART environment for delinquent youth and their families. For these youth (ART for self and family), rearrest rates on follow-up were 15 percent; for no-ART control group youth, the comparable figure was 43 percent. These outcomes closely parallel the outcomes for a rather different type of "family"—fellow gang members.

EVALUATIONS OF EFFECTIVENESS: STUDIES BY OTHER RESEARCHERS

Our studies of the effectiveness of ART have yielded several promising findings, both proximal to the ART procedures (i.e., skill acquisition, anger control, enhanced moral reasoning) and distal to ART procedures but central to the program's ultimate purposes (i.e., reduced rearrests, enhanced community functioning). The following discussion highlights research and program evaluations by other investigators who have reported findings independently and separate from our own.

Coleman, Pfeiffer, and Oakland (1991) evaluated the effectiveness of a 10-week ART program for behaviorally disordered adolescents in a Texas residential treatment center. Study results indicated improvement in participant skill knowledge but not in overt skill behaviors. Coleman et al. comment: "The current study thus provides additional support for the contention that although cognitive gains can be demonstrated, the link to actual behavior is tenuous, especially with disturbed populations" (p. 17).

We believe the likelihood of behavioral expression (performance) of newly acquired skills is less a function of the degree of participants' emotional disturbance than it is a matter of their motivation to perform and staff's or other significant persons' perceived receptivity to and reward for such behaviors.

Coleman et al. observed that of the 10 social skills taught, three accounted for the improvement in social skills knowledge: Keeping Out of Fights, Dealing with Group Pressure, and Expressing a Complaint. We also found these same skills to be improved in two separate studies, suggesting that they may be the most responsive to intervention (Goldstein & Glick, 1987). Coleman et al. suggest one plausible explanation is that these three skills may be construed as contributing to self-preservation, especially within the context of residential or institutional living.

Curulla (1990) evaluated (a) a 10-week ART program versus (b) ART without the moral education component versus (c) a no-ART control condition. ART group members were 67 young adult offenders participating in a community intervention setting in Seattle. Curulla reported:

> Tendency toward recidivism and actual recidivism were compared among the three groups. Tendency towards recidivism as measured by the Weekly Activity Record was significantly reduced in the dilemma group. . . . The non-dilemma . . . and control . . . groups showed no significant reduction. The dilemma group also had the lowest frequency of subsequent offense. . . . However, the differences in actual recidivism among the three groups did not reach statistical significance due to the low incidence of recorded changes during the six-month follow-up. (pp. 1–2)

Unlike Coleman et al.'s (1991) result, in Curulla's study, as in our own, overt acting-out behaviors were significantly reduced via ART participation. However, unlike our own results, post-ART recidivism was not reduced.

In a second effort to examine the impact of ART component procedures singly and in combination, Kennedy (1989) assessed the efficacy of structured learning therapy (i.e., Skillstreaming) and Anger Control Training with a sample of 37 adult incarcerated offenders, all of whom had a history of serious anger control difficulties. Outcome comparisons were made of the two procedures used in combination versus either structured learning therapy alone or Anger Control Training alone. Kennedy stated:

> The results of this study demonstrated that anger control training and structured learning therapy are both effective treatment modalities for incarcerated adult male offenders with severe anger and aggressive behavioral problems. Subjects in all four active treatment conditions displayed the following changes. They self-reported less anger to a variety of provocations common to the prison setting. They self-reported decreases in the frequency, intensity, and duration of anger, more appropriate modalities of expression, and fewer consequences of anger reactions. Objective behavioral ratings of their verbal responses to laboratory role-played provocations indicated their responses were more appropriate, as were their self-reported reactions to these provocations. In addition, subjects demonstrated more pro-social attitudes following completion of the program. The overall findings from the follow-up measures provide strong support for the extended maintenance of treatment benefits. Subjects continued to demonstrate lower levels of anger arousal on cognitive indices of anger. (p. 3)

Jones (1990) compared ART to moral education and a no-treatment control using a sample of aggressive male students in a Brisbane, Australia, high school. Her results were consistent and positive:

> When compared to the two control conditions, students completing the ART program: showed a significant decrease in aggressive incidences; a significant increase in coping incidences;

and acquired more social skills. Students in condition 1 [also] improved on . . . self-control and impulsivity. . . . ART appears to be an effective intervention for aggressive youth within a high school setting. (p. 1)

A further investigation, also affirming the efficacy of ART, takes this intervention in a new direction. Gibbs and Potter, in the Ohio Department of Youth Services, have for some years employed and evaluated a positive peer culture approach in their work with delinquent youth. This technique, described as an "adult-guided but youth-run group approach," places major responsibility upon the youth group itself for the management of the living environment as well as for changes in their own behaviors. Believing that youth are sufficiently motivated to conduct much of their own governance and direction but that they too frequently lack the skills and anger control to do so, Gibbs and Potter combined the positive peer culture approach with ART to yield a motivational, skills-oriented intervention they call EQUIP (Gibbs et al., 1995). In EQUIP, moral discussion, anger management, or social skills sessions are designated as "equipment meetings," or meetings in which the group gains equipment for helping group members. These investigators conducted an efficacy evaluation of EQUIP at a medium-secure institution for juvenile felony offenders, the Buckeye Youth Center in Columbus, Ohio. Three conditions were constituted—EQUIP, a motivational control group, and a no-treatment group. Outcome results were significant and supportive of the EQUIP intervention on both proximal and distal criteria. The investigators comment that "institutional conduct improvements were highly significant for the EQUIP relative to the control groups in terms of self-reported misconduct, staff-filed incident reports, and unexcused absences from school" (p. 18).

The investigators also found that, whereas the recidivism rate of EQUIP subjects was low (15 percent) at both six and twelve months following release, the control group rates worsened from six through twelve months (25 to 35 percent for the motivational control, 30 to 40 percent for the simple passage-of-time control). This pattern suggests that the treatment result was maintained as a stable effect.

Another evaluation was conducted by the Michigan Department of Social Services at five sites collectively constituting their Maxey Training School. Glick trained Maxey Training School staff who delivered ART to 44 youth sentenced to Maxey by juvenile court. Again, pre- and post-ART comparisons revealed significant growth in social skills competency. In all but one of the participating sites, there was also a significant decrease in within-institution acting-out behaviors.

Washington State has made a vast contribution to the field of juvenile program interventions at a time when program evaluations and attention to program fidelity was neither popular nor perceived as important. The Institute of Public Policy, under the stewardship of chief investigator Robert Barnoski, developed an ambitious evaluation protocol for the programs under the Community Juvenile Accountability Act (CJAA). Barnoski (1994) published a comprehensive report of the outcome evaluation of Washington's research-based programs for juvenile offenders. Barnoski reported that when competently delivered, ART had positive outcomes, with estimated reductions in 18-month felony recidivism of 24 percent. The cost to deliver ART to youth (including all training costs) was $745 per youth.

The state of Washington established a program committee under CJAA that was responsible for developing criteria for youth participation in cognitive groups, including ART, as well as for reviewing the research design and program models that would be used. For ART, youth had to demonstrate high levels of aggression and lack of prosocial behaviors as measured on state-developed assessment scales.

Research results for ART demonstrated no statistically significant differences in misdemeanor and felony recidivism and violent felony recidivism rates. For ART and control group youth in all courts, five variables had statistically significant differences between the groups: age, social history risk, drug/alcohol risk, employment (protective), and school risk.

A significant finding from the Washington studies reinforced an important principle that also has been reported in the cognitive-behavioral interventions literature (e.g., Andrews & Bonta, 2003; Latessa, 2006). Specifically, when ART is delivered competently, the program reduces felony recidivism and is cost effective. In Washington, for courts rated as competent in delivering ART during 2000, there was a 24 percent reduction in 18-month felony recidivism compared with the control group, a statistically significant finding.

A more recent evaluation conducted by Rudy (2009) in partial fulfillment of dissertation requirements, examined the effectiveness of ART by using an archival data set (113 incarcerated male delinquents with a diagnosis of Conduct Disorder) from a local juvenile detention facility in Southern California. A chi-square analysis was used to determine whether there was a relationship between recidivism for those who successfully completed ART and several variables, including age, ethnicity, number of commitments to that specific facility, and gang membership. Results found that the true population recidivism rate of all participants is between 24 and 41 percent and that ART participants recidivate after an average of 188 days. Since the recidivism range of the true population is between 158 and 217 days, it appears that, although ART makes a positive impact on the lives of more than half its juvenile participants with Conduct Disorder who remain in the community on good behavior, there is minimal benefit from ART when considering the time to recidivate. The trend indicates that ART participants are at the low end of the population in terms of recidivism, as evidenced by a study described by the U.S. Department of Education Office of Safe and Drug Free Schools (2001), in which the results indicated that ART participants had lower recidivism rates than non-ART participants. Given that Katsiyannis et al. (2008) stated that the majority of incarcerated juveniles consist of recidivists, ART appears to be a promising program in reducing both recidivism rates and the costs of incarcerating youth.

Rudy's results suggest that ART participants ages 14 to 16 recidivated more frequently than participants ages 17 and 18. Older participants may be responding to the ART material more efficiently due to greater cognitive development. Specifically, the moral reasoning component of ART utilizes cognitive processes such as abstract thinking that are not fully developed in younger participants. Gathering further information about each participant's Conduct Disorder subtype can also explain this research finding. Compared to those diagnosed with Conduct Disorder Adolescent-Onset Type, research has shown that males diagnosed with Conduct Disorder Childhood-Onset Type are more likely to meet the criteria for Antisocial Personality Disorder as adults (Frances & Ross, 2001; Huebner et al., 2008), making them more vulnerable to recidivate. Another possible explanation for these results is that the juvenile facility in which data were collected houses serious and violent adolescent male offenders. Therefore, the younger offenders with a history of committing serous and violent offenses have a greater likelihood of reincarceration.

Rudy also concluded that there is no statistical significance between recidivism and gang membership, ethnicity, and commitment. ART is equally effective in all aggressive adolescents, regardless of the participants' gang membership status. Gang members are as likely to be treated effectively with ART as non–gang members. ART provides similar benefits to all who participate, appearing to be ethnically and culturally neutral. When holding the variable commitment as a constant, it appears that ART impacts aggressive and violent behavior among participants based on the variables it was designed for—specifically, anger control tasks, skills to manage angry impulses, and the ability to take others' perspectives.

Four one-way ANOVAs were tested among only participants who recidivated, whether the number of days until recidivism varied by age, ethnicity, commitment, or gang membership. Results indicated that the time until recidivism does not vary according to those variables. Therefore, the variables that impact the time it takes for ART participants to recidivate are still unknown. Additionally, it is unknown whether those variables may impact non-ART offenders' time to recidivate.

To summarize, this study demonstrated that ART is an effective and pragmatic option for treatment for incarcerated male juveniles with Conduct Disorder, with the potential to help individual adolescents, families, and the community.

Finally, an evaluation completed by Kaunitz and Strandberg (2009) studied ART in 102 cities and municipalities in Sweden in order to discern ART's effectiveness and the extent to which the program was implemented with integrity. Of the 102 municipalities reviewed, all but two responded to structured interviews. Kaunitz and Strandberg state that only 6 of 67 municipalities/city districts, or 9 percent of the total studied, implemented ART as designed with fidelity and integrity. Further, they report that 90 percent of the ART training is far removed from the structure outlined in the second edition of *Aggression Replacement Training* (Goldstein et al., 1998) and, despite the number of individuals who purportedly have been trained to implement ART, only a few young people within the social services systems participate in ART as originally constructed.

This study was initiated, in part, because many of the municipalities were concerned about the negative outcome behaviors of clients completing ART programs. In effect, this research underscores with additional data what Barnoski (1994) and others have suggested: namely, if ART is not implemented according to design and/or staff are not well trained in its implementation, then participants' behaviors may get worse rather than improve.

⁓⧽⧼⁓

The evaluations described in this chapter combine to suggest that ART is an effective intervention. With considerable reliability, it appears to promote skill acquisition and performance, improve anger control, decrease the frequency of acting-out behaviors, and increase the frequency of constructive prosocial behaviors. Its effects occur when youth are in the controlled institutional environment and beyond institutional walls. These effects are especially pronounced when significant others in the real-world environment are simultaneous recipients of ART. In general, the ART program's potency appears more than adequate to warrant continued program implementation and evaluation with chronically moderately to severely aggressive youth. The next chapter turns attention to what administrators and managers can do to support the successful implementation of ART.

CHAPTER 8

Program Administration and Management

Cognitive-behavioral interventions, including ART, are only as successful as the support they receive from managers, administrators, and executives. A large body of literature attests to the importance of administrative and supervisory involvement with program design, development, and implementation (Gendreau & Andrews, 1992; Glick, 2006, 2009; Latessa, 2006). We are encouraged by the success of ART in a variety of settings: institutions, schools, community-based agencies, public sector and government programs, private for-profit and not-for-profit organizations, mental health systems, educational systems, and social service systems. Across all these entities, programs identified as successful and effective have unconditional support from policy stakeholders, executives, managers, and supervisors. The ideas and concepts in this chapter have been developed over the years as we have provided consultation to help administrators provide support for staff and services to program participants.

ROLES AND RELATIONSHIPS

As noted elsewhere (Glick, 2006), new programs serve as catalysts for organizational change. Any time a new program intervention is introduced into an organization, that program will impact a plethora of functions—including personnel, scheduling, budgets, financing, and clients, to name but a few. Systems that have a well-defined administrative structure are in a better position to accommodate new programs with minimal disruption to their operations. Programs are more effective, demonstrate higher cost efficiency, and better serve clients if they are supported by executives, managers, and supervisors. However, in order for administrators and managers to sustain successful program implementation, well-defined roles and relationships must exist between and among the following types of staff.

Policymakers/Stakeholders

These individuals establish the vision and guiding principles for the organization. They may be members of a board of directors, legislators, or others who have a direct interest in the organization, such as shareholders. Policymakers/stakeholders are not usually involved with the operations of the organization, nor do they supervise personnel or functions. However, they do monitor and audit the operations of the organization to ensure that the program's mission and vision are being targeted.

Executives

Executives are the chief operational officers of the organization. These individuals are charged with implementing the vision, mission, and goals of the system as mandated by the policymakers/stakeholders. They are responsible for the overall implementation of programs and services and have staff to ensure that objectives are met. Executives must know what is going on within their organizations but may not be familiar with the day-to-day operations of specific programs or services. Executives include principals of schools, superintendents of school districts, wardens of correctional facilities, and executive directors of child care agencies, among others.

Managers

Managers are usually directors of large service areas within agencies or division heads within governmental systems. These individuals control budgets within their areas of responsibility; may hire, fire, and discipline staff; and are generally responsible for the implementation of policies and procedures. They may be technical experts within their fields and have a hands-on working knowledge of the organization in general and detailed operational knowledge of their area or responsibility.

Supervisors

Supervisors are directly responsible for program implementation, supervision of line staff, and provision of quality services to clients. These individuals are technically proficient in their areas of expertise and must be able to apply their knowledge in practical ways to ensure that programs are delivered with fidelity. Toward that end, supervisors are charged with the day-to-day operations of programs and services delivered to clients.

Direct Line Staff

These individuals are the practitioners of the system, instrumental to delivering programs and services to clients. Direct line staff have a variety of education, training, and areas of expertise. These individuals fulfill the functions of the organization and are hired by supervisors and administrators to implement the system's goals and objectives. Areas in which they provide service may include education, recreation, clinical (psychology and social work), medical, direct client care, research and program assessment, fiscal, and legal, to name but a few.

In implementing ART, it is essential that all staff know and understand the roles and functions that individuals take on within the organization. Only when staff are knowledgeable about the various tasks that individuals must accomplish can each appreciate the reasons behind certain decisions and actions. For example, direct line staff, newly trained as ART group facilitators, realize how critical it is to prepare for their group sessions, yet that time may not currently be built into the schedule. They may alert their supervisors of the need to provide preparation time. While supervisors may want to accommodate these requests, at the same time they may be informed by their division director that there is a budget shortfall and they may not authorize overtime. The organization's executive has made a commitment to the board that evidence-based cognitive-behavioral programs will be implemented immediately according to the board's policy direction. The complexity of this picture is obvious.

Conflict among the various levels of administration and management can be reinterpreted as different views of the same goal, given the role and function within the organization. Specifically, the direct line staff charged with the responsibility for program implementation must ensure that programs are delivered according to design. They have the expertise to provide the program to clients; they do not have the capacity to set schedules, reassign staff, or offer other problem solutions to accommodate preparation time for program implementation. That is the responsibility of the supervisor who, with some innovation, creativity, and courage, may provide the necessary time for facilitators to prepare. At the same time, it rests with the supervisor, whose primary role is to provide an environment for staff to grow and develop both professionally and personally, to advocate for the staff with the program director. The program director may not necessarily know the details or specifics of program operations, but he or she is charged to implement agency policy. It is incumbent upon the supervisor to advocate for staff. Perhaps that is why supervisors have earned the title within organizations as "middle managers": They are truly caught in the middle between the direct line staff whom they supervise and the managers to whom they report.

PROGRAM PHILOSOPHY AND DESCRIPTION

The philosophical foundation underpinning the design and development of ART encompasses the notion that programs should be differential and prescriptive. The program administrator is responsible for articulating a program philosophy that supports those programs that are included in the differential services to its clients. The agency or organization's program description and statement of philosophy are critical to the implementation of effective and efficient cognitive-behavioral interventions such as ART. Once published, the program philosophy and description is the benchmark from which a myriad of administrative and executive work flows. Program initiatives, budget and finance for program implementation, and staff development are examples of issues that an articulate program description supports. The program description should include at the very least a statement of the philosophy of the agency, its mission, long-term goals, nature of staff, nature of clients served, basic treatment approaches to change client behavior, and fiscal requirements for sound programming. The program description and philosophy are critical to the implementation of ART because they provide a context within which ART functions. Staff, for example, are more likely to embrace the habilitation concepts that underscore the development of the ART curriculum if the agency's program philosophy specifically states what its position is about its clients (e.g., "Our clients are individuals who are skill deficient, and we support an atmosphere for client behavior change that is a learning environment based on sound educational principles"). In addition, with a published program philosophy and program description, staff are apt to take their roles as group facilitators more seriously, ensuring that the ART program is delivered as designed. We have long argued that ART is more likely to be implemented successfully if staff are confident that their roles are well defined and if the task of delivering the ART program is delegated to them with authority, responsibility, and accountability. A well-written program description can help accomplish these objectives.

ADMINISTRATIVE PRINCIPLES

There is little debate that competently delivered cognitive-behavioral interventions depend on a number of well-documented variables. We now know how important it is for the chief executive of a system to be involved with the design and implementation of the program within the system. In the last two decades, we have learned that administrators and managers must be integrally involved with the implementation and day-to-day tactics of program delivery. Responsibility for such functions as monitoring, auditing, and staff supervision (both program and clinical) lies with the supervisory and managerial staff. ART is successful with high-risk aggressive and violent youth when staff are well supervised and managers are able to provide necessary supplies, materials, and support within the work environment.

Thus, principles of effective administration must be responsive to relevant features of the system in which they will be used. The development of such principles must begin with a careful examination of the system. How is the system structured? Who is responsible for what? What are the lines of communication? How are problems identified and resolved? All of these questions are fundamental to the development of effective programs such as ART. The administrator must answer each of these questions decisively, and the answers must be a logical extension of the published statement of philosophy and program description.

Certain system principles are central to the implementation of quality programs and services. Certainly those ART programs that have been found to be effective, cost efficient, and delivered with fidelity and integrity have relied on and complemented a set of administrative doctrines. We offer the following principles as supporting competent program implementation. We have employed all these principles, based upon a philosophical position of participatory management, when implementing ART.

Principle 1: No Pain, No Gain

Simply stated, this principle asserts that there can be no staff growth and development without some staff pain, discomfort, or distress through the process of growth. While this may seem contradictory to all that we already have stated, it really is not. Pain does not imply punishment nor imply malice. In this context, it is an admission that if administrators truly wish to provide an environment for staff to grow and develop and are interested in staff professional advancement, then they must take whatever action is necessary to meet those objectives. For example, many administrators agonize over progressive disciplinary action taken toward staff in the hope of extinguishing inappropriate behavior. Many administrators conduct supervisory meetings or investigatory proceedings to begin to develop the necessary staff attitude or work ethic. And many staff members express frustration with either the system or themselves as they gain new skills and knowledge. It has been our experience that when new programs such as ART are introduced into a system, staff experience the angst of change: environmental, operational, and personal. This experience is often painful because staff may challenge their own values and attitudes toward the new program, work conditions may change and disrupt routine schedules, and staff may be required to learn new skill sets, to name but a few difficulties.

Principle 2: Give Respect to Get Respect

The familiar admonishment to do unto others as you would have them do unto you is a basic administrative principle that mandates that one must treat others with respect. The administrator should show respect for the staff members' job knowledge, skill level, and position. Respect also implies esteem for oneself and one's position, accomplishments, and productivity. The interaction between the administrator's perception of the staff and the staff member's self-perception creates a mutual respect for position and job function. When staff members are able to fully understand their own position and function, no matter what position they have within the organization, then they may freely give and receive feedback with dignity, without fear, and without feeling threatened. When respect is given freely, very often it is reciprocated. We have found as we have trained ART across a myriad of jurisdictions, agencies, and systems that when this principle is not followed, staff morale suffers, staff resistance to training is high, and training is less than productive. All of this leads to unwillingness or inability to deliver ART successfully, with integrity and fidelity.

Principle 3: Acknowledge Effort, Reward Results

One of the most difficult responsibilities of administrators is to evaluate the performance of staff who implement the ART program. Objectivity is obviously essential as staff receive feedback relative to what they do and how well they do it. Administrators often give confusing or unnecessarily negative messages to employees in the area of work performance, including skill development levels, ability, and productivity. A closer look at communication between supervisors and staff often reflects that managers do not adequately differentiate between effort and achievement. How often do employees receive "outstanding" ratings on job evaluations, even though they do only what is expected of them? In addition, it is often the case that the supervisor has rated employees' motivation or willingness rather than actual performance. That case is reflected in such comments as these: "This employee always tries to complete the ART group sessions in an outstanding manner" or "This employee always tries to do the very best job all of the time." These statements reflect effort and ought not to be considered evaluation for work productivity.

Supervisors and middle managers must be able to separate the employee's willingness from the employee's ability. In the same vein, the supervisor needs to be clear about issues that reflect the employee's attitude and affect, as well as issues that are objective work outcomes (i.e., that are observable and measureable). The guideline, then, for the administrator is to reinforce among all supervisory and managerial personnel the need to recognize and acknowledge effort and motivation among staff and positively reinforce and reward employees as they achieve agency goals and objectives. The bottom line is that staff should clearly hear that they are appreciated as they implement ART but be provided positive performance ratings only when they demonstrate competent program implementation.

Principle 4: Bureaucracies Complicate What Staff Make Simple

Every system, every organization, no matter how large or small, creates its own bureaucratic structure. Administrations often have a tendency to complicate things. As one climbs the administrative ladder within an organization, the tendency to complicate often simple matters seems to increase. Add to that the frequently found division of roles and responsibilities, and it is no surprise that many administrations accomplish little or no problem solving. What is crucial is the degree to which the chief executive officer, administrators, managers, and supervisors are able to concretely, simply, and with concise communication take action. For example, most chief executives' primary role is to create vision and set policy. As such, executives should remind staff often that their role requires them always to be thinking at least six months in the future. Thus, middle managers may find it easier to place their superiors' comments into longer term perspective and keep operational, day-to-day goals clear and targeted. Another similar technique is for administrators to restate and clarify the differences between systemwide issues, agendas, and problems, as opposed to concerns of divisions or units. When implemented correctly, this principle usually allows direct line staff to understand that the statements issued from executive offices are often ideals and their role is to simplify the policy directives and apply them effectively to their own work situations. Staff usually can simplify the complicated very well.

Principle 5: Administrative Tolerance for Structured Ambiguity Is Necessary

This principle begins with the premise that one of the primary responsibilities of the executive is planning. The executive, along with the managers of the system, are responsible for formulating goals, directing energy toward the completion of objectives, and ensuring that all staff efforts are on target. In order to do this successfully, the administration must be able to keep in balance a variety of goals and program initiatives, while at the same time directing staff activity toward specific day-to-day outcomes. Many times, the balance between the two needs seems contradictory. This tension often creates a sense of ambiguity for staff within the organization. Often staff want immediate answers to questions they ask or solutions to problems they pose. Managers may know the long-term answer or general direction in which to point staff for problem resolution, but often they must refrain from giving information and purposefully cause ambiguity within the organization. If problem resolution, information, and direction are given too soon, the administration may stifle staff members' creativity, and the participatory management style may be sacrificed. Withholding information or direction does create tension and perpetuate dissonance, but, when done carefully and deliberately, it creates an environment that maximizes staff ability to generate program alternatives and enhance organizational flexibility.

Principle 6: The More the Merrier in Problem Solving, Policy Development, and Program Initiatives

Our bias is for the chief executive to build an administrative model that values broad participation of staff. We have extensive experience in helping systems to implement ART and have found that when staff are involved in program development and implementation, the program is more successful in meeting its original treatment objectives. Further, administrations need to communicate explicitly to staff that there is an open, accessible, responsible team of managers able and willing to listen. The participatory model of administration solicits input from all staff at all levels within the organization and cuts across supervisory lines as well as organizational units. The result, when properly managed, is an environment in which staff morale is high, ownership of task and accomplishment exists, productivity and performance level of staff are above standard, and new ideas and creativity abound. All of these attributes are integral to the implementation of a successful ART program.

The executive who adopts a participatory model of administration must have a tolerance for dialogue and debate of issues, not be threatened by challenges from subordinates, and be nonthreatening to subordinates who desire to participate. Further, the executive must be willing and able to change positions, alter opinions, consider alternatives, and reverse decisions based upon input from staff, without compromising policy or authority.

෯෨

Systems responsive to these philosophical principles can be strong and accountable. In fact, such systems allow greater flexibility for administrators by incorporating features such as standards for successful achievement, criteria for optimal performance, tolerance for error, and value of learning, as well as expectations for continued program growth and personnel development. The chief executive must integrate appropriate management style, supervisory protocol, personnel resources, and administrative principles to guarantee quality service to program participants and an attractive learning environment for staff. While certain basic models of administration have been traditionally used within human services systems, the administration must take great care to develop a model specific to the programs and services that must be managed. One must be vigilant to avoid adopting an administrative model out of convenience because of supervisory or middle management pressures or because of "tradition"—that is, a "We've always done it this way" or "If it ain't broke, don't fix it" mentality. On the contrary, the executive needs to design, develop, or adapt an administrative model and system based on the mission, people, and environment of the particular organization. We leave to the practitioners the task of selecting and modifying these principles to fit their own context and needs.

ADMINISTRATIVE IMPLEMENTATION CONCERNS

The implementation of ART involves a number of concerns at the systems level. Some of the concerns next described have been raised while training staff to become ART group facilitators; others have been identified as we have assisted jurisdictions to design and implement cognitive-behavioral interventions for their clients. Still others have been suggested as possible topics of discussion by our colleagues.

Many of these issues, while having theoretical solutions, are best resolved within individual settings. We often empower those we train by suggesting that they are the best resource to resolve implementation concerns. We believe that, once trained, staff are the "experts" within their systems in ART. Therefore, group facilitators may best serve each other as peer consultants and peer supervisors. We suggest during the implementation and strategic planning section of our training institutes that staff may provide each other with feedback, as they learned to do throughout their training, helping each other become more proficient in the skill sets they acquired as they learned to facilitate ART groups. During the implementation phases of ART, we encourage staff to have each other sit in on groups to observe and provide feedback about technique, process, and skill. Evaluation forms like those included in Appendix B can be used for such a purpose.

From Vision to Action

Once it is decided that ART is to be implemented, considerable action must be taken before the first group session is convened. The executive must convene a planning work group to identify the logistical issues that must be managed. The following are but some of the questions that must be addressed by the planning work group:

- Which staff should be trained to deliver the program?

- Should the program be implemented throughout the entire system or incrementally?

- What schedule should be used to deliver the program?

- Where should groups be held?

- Which individuals should be chosen to participate?

- What budget and finances need to be allocated to ensure there are funds for personnel, equipment (a one-time expenditure), supplies and materials?

We suggest that the planning group identify roles and functions for each of its members. For example, some of the members are "strategists," while others are "visionaries." Still others are "pragmatists," while others are "implementers." It is important to identify roles and assign functions to the planning group members to ensure efficient use of time and resources. The planning group is charged with providing a management and implementation plan to the administration that details the objectives to implement ART. Each objective has a series of tactical steps that articulate how that objective will be met. The basic "Who does what, when, and how" is detailed throughout the plan.

Supervisory Support

Supervisory support is one of the most important issues for systems to address if they are to implement ART with integrity and preserve program fidelity. Supervisory support is manifested in a variety of ways. At the very least, supervisors need to provide staff with direction and instruction for the tasks they perform. Newly trained ART group facilitators require feedback about their performance, consultation about the techniques they use when conducting groups, and resources to further their skill development and program comprehension. Supervisors must be competent to perform these services for their subordinates or know where to acquire the resources to provide the supervision for their staff to grow and develop.

Some systems have required that supervisors be trained as ART group facilitators themselves. Supervisors must also provide support to their staff by creating an environment for their staff to grow and develop professionally and personally. Toward that end, administrators, managers, and supervisors must be skilled problem solvers, for staff will rely on them to resolve implementation issues as they attempt to deliver ART. Practitioners who conduct ART groups have a plethora of issues, some of which they can resolve themselves but most of which require supervisory support. Among others, these issues relate to obtaining supplies and an adequate physical plant, help with disruptive and/or defiant client behavior, staff support to accommodate transfer training (i.e., completion of homework assignments), and scheduling.

Supervisory support also means administrators and supervisors must deal with executives and stakeholders to ensure that ART programs continue. Managers must be vigilant advocates for their staff, defenders of program integrity, competent researchers and program evaluators, resourceful budget makers, and public relations professionals. Each of these areas requires the administrator to be involved in activities that lead to continued sponsorship.

Conflicting Priorities

As has been true in every generation of human services, resources are limited. Money is scarce, and events in the global economy have made programs such as ART even more vulnerable. Executives and administrators struggle with services that are mandated and those that are discretionary. Health and safety are usually priorities, followed by those programs required by statute and policy. After these, administrators must decide which programs and services are most effective and cost efficient in meeting the agency or organization's mission and goals.

Conflicting priorities often arise in the logistical operations of the program. For example, staff in one state complained that it was difficult to conduct ART groups without being disrupted. Staff stated that often program social workers or other clinicians would interrupt the group session to talk with clients, or medical appointments were made during the scheduled group sessions and clients would never show up. When queried as to why that happened, staff merely stated that that was the way it was and they had no power to control it. In this case, an external consultant/trainer can advocate and often succeed in system change. Administrations that are serious about implementing programs will alter the policy or tactically change the system to provide uninterrupted training. Indeed, the chief executive of the state agency in the previous example rewrote policy and amended medical contracts to ensure that clients involved with authorized cognitive-behavioral interventions such as ART were not removed from program.

Finally, conflicting priorities may arise from ART participants themselves. In our third-year project with community aftercare, Goldstein et al. (1989) found that parents often were unable to attend group sessions. Conflicts arose because the social support check did not arrive and there was no gas in the car to get the family to group, younger siblings were sick, one parent had to work late, and so forth. In many cases, creative and innovative group facilitators were able to resolve these logistical problems.

Quality Assurance

Quality assurance is the systematic and deliberate review of a program to ensure that it is delivered with integrity and according to standard. Quality assurance is a function of the agency or system, not the program; although the program (in this case, ART) provides the criteria and tactics by which quality is measured, the administration establishes the benchmarks and measurements to assess effectiveness and efficiency. (Appendix B provides evaluation checklists to use for each of the ART components within a well-managed quality assurance system.)

Quality assurance systems must include two important activities: monitoring and auditing. Monitoring is observing, detecting, and recording the operation of the program with instruments designed to assess its functions for the purpose of supervision and oversight. Auditing is the examination and verification of program implementation to assure correctness according to program design and procedures. Both events should occur on an established schedule that meets staff development objectives and agency or organizational goals.

A number of jurisdictions and organizations have developed quality assurance systems for the purpose of improving outcomes and evidence-based practices and ensuring program fidelity. We have already described some of these in chapter 7), including Juvenile Rehabilitation Administration, Washington; Division of Juvenile Justice, Alaska; Justice Research Center, in cooperation with the Division of Juvenile Justice, Florida; Division of Youth Community Corrections, Ramsey County (St. Paul, Minnesota); Amity Institute, Warsaw, Poland; and UngArt, Malmö, Sweden. Each of these entities has embraced quality outcome-based cognitive-behavioral interventions and has developed a quality assurance system to ensure that ART is delivered to their clients with integrity and fidelity.

≈≈

Programs are successful because of the deliberate interventions and support provided by administrators, not in spite of them. In this chapter, we have provided information for executives, administrators, managers, and supervisors to use as they support the implementation of ART within their systems.

PART 2

ART Sessions

Social Skills Training

Making a Complaint

If you are conducting sessions in an order different from that shown in Table 1.1, follow the procedure for Welcome and Introduction, ART Components, Group Rules, and What Happens in ART Groups before your first session.

OBJECTIVES

- To explain the purpose and content of the ART program and "sell it" to the group

- To establish group rules for behavior

- To introduce the Social Skills Training component of ART and provide a rationale for skill learning

- To introduce the procedures for Social Skills Training sessions and teach the skill of Making a Complaint

- To explain the Skill Homework Report and give participants a chance to practice the skill outside the group

MATERIALS

Easel pad and marker

Making a Complaint Skill Cards

Copies of the Making a Complaint Skill Homework Report

Posters (on CD):

> Aggression Replacement Training (ART)

> Group Rules

> Social Skills

> Making a Complaint

Before the session, discuss and develop the modeling display with your co-facilitator.

PROCEDURE

Welcome and Introduction

Welcome participants to the group and explain that the general purpose of Aggression Replacement Training, or ART, is to learn and use techniques to get along better with other people.

You can use Glick's "pocket analogy" to illustrate the idea of choosing behavior instead of automatically reacting with anger and aggression. (Be sure to have several empty pockets you can turn out as you proceed):

Here is another way to think about the importance of this group. We have all learned how to do one thing very well to survive, haven't we? What is that?

Elicit the response "fight."

That's right, fight. Well, let's pretend that you have the ability to pull out your fist, or a knife, or a gun anytime you want to.

Make a fist and pull it out of one of your pockets.

But what do you have in this pocket? NOTHING! And what do you have in this pocket? NOTHING! And this? NOTHING!

Turn out a pocket each time you ask the question and give a response.

In this program, we will fill up your pockets, so now you can pull out your fist if you want to, but you'll also have other choices—choices that won't get you into trouble. What happens when you have more choices? How do you feel?

Encourage the idea that more choices leads to a greater feeling of empowerment.

ART Components

Display the ART poster and briefly explain that ART includes three main parts: Social Skills Training, Anger Control Training, and Moral Reasoning.

AGGRESSION REPLACEMENT TRAINING (ART)

Social Skills Training: Teaches you social skills that can help you get what you want while getting along with other people.

Anger Control Training: Teaches you to know when you are getting angry and how to calm down so you don't get into trouble.

Moral Reasoning: Teaches you how to think about different situations, understand your own and others' viewpoints, and come up with responsible and morally mature decisions.

Let group members know that they are expected to attend three group sessions each week: one in Social Skills Training, one in Anger Control Training, and one in Moral Reasoning. Inform the members that each session will last an hour to an hour and a half and if they attend all the sessions and complete the entire program, they will have plenty of choices—their pockets will be full.

Group Rules

Explain the group rules, but don't make them complicated. Do make it clear that certain rules are necessary (we can't do the program without them) and therefore not negotiable. Be friendly and matter of fact in communicating your authority.

Present the Group Rules poster. If at all possible, discuss necessary rules with the group and add their ideas to the list to promote ownership.

GROUP RULES

1. Attend and participate.
2. Be respectful (no fighting or put-downs).
3. Be open and honest.
4. What is said in the group stays in the group.

What Happens in ART Groups

Explain that sessions will help group members learn some serious things, but that they will be fun, too, and will involve the following.

- *Discussion:* The group will talk about the skills and ideas we are learning.

- *Modeling:* You and your co-facilitator will *model*—that is, show—how to perform the steps of the skill you are teaching.

- *Role-playing:* Group members will have a chance to try the skill they have seen modeled for them by role-playing it. *Role-playing* means they will choose a real-life situation important to each of them that applies the skill they saw modeled and then perform the steps of the skill just demonstrated for them in that situation.

- *Homework:* Group members will take what they learn and apply it to real life by practicing the skill outside the group, as they described the situation and tried it during each of their own role-plays. Group members will talk about what happens to them, and their experiences become an important part of program.

Introducing Social Skills Training

Explain that each Social Skills Training meeting will be devoted to learning a different social skill. Refer to the poster and define *social skills.*

SOCIAL SKILLS

Social skills are the skills we use when we deal with other people. Good social skills get us what we want. They increase the chance we will get a positive response and decrease the chance we will get a negative response from other people.

Let participants know that the first skill they will be learning is Making a Complaint. They will talk about the skill, then watch you and your co-facilitator model the skill (demonstrate it). Then they will have a chance to role-play (try out) the skill, using the steps themselves.

Skill Teaching

Step 1: Define the Skill

Involve group members in a brief discussion of the skill. Ask, "What does Making a Complaint mean to you?" Elicit several group members' answers. Using participants' ideas, come up with an operational definition of the skill. For example:

> Facilitator: So from what the group has said, Making a Complaint is telling someone something you don't like about a situation. It may be something someone said, did, or decided, and you want to tell them what your gripe or objection is. The person may or may not do something to respond to your complaint.

Ask, "Who has used this skill in the past?" Encourage and acknowledge group members' responses.

Next direct group members' attention to the skill poster and have group members read each step aloud, either individually or as a group. After each step, ask the group whether the step is an "action step" or a "thinking step." (In this skill, Steps 1 and 2 are thinking steps; Steps 3–5 are action steps.)

MAKING A COMPLAINT

SKILL STEPS	FACILITATOR NOTES
1. Decide what your complaint is.	What is your complaint?
2. Decide whom to complain to.	Who is the person causing you an issue?
3. Tell that person your complaint.	Consider alternative ways to complain (e.g., politely, decisively, confidently, privately).
4. Tell that person what you would like done about the problem.	Offer a helpful suggestion about resolving the issue.
5. Ask how he/she feels about what you've said.	

SAMPLE MODELING DISPLAYS

- *School:* Main actor complains to guidance counselor about being assigned to class that is too difficult.
- *Home:* Main actor complains to sibling about unfair division of chores.
- *Peer group:* Main actor complains to friend about spreading a rumor.
- *Institution:* Main actor complains to roommate about stealing canteen items.

Step 2: Model the Skill

With your co-facilitator, model the skill as you prepared and practiced it before the session. The modeling display should be a "picture perfect" representation of the skill steps.

Step 3: Establish Group Members' Need for the Skill

Ask each group member to describe briefly where, when, and with whom he or she would find it useful to employ the skill you have just modeled. If time allows, you can list each participant's name on the easel pad, along with the name of the person with whom the skill will be used and a phrase to indicate the nature of the complaint. If not, the co-facilitator can take notes, either on the easel pad or unobtrusively on a separate page.

Step 4: Select the First Role-Player and Set Up the Role-Play

Ask for a volunteer to conduct the first role-play. Have the main actor briefly describe again the real-life situation in which he or she will use the skill. Encourage the main actor to choose a co-actor who resembles the real-life person in as many ways as possible and elicit from the main actor additional information to set the stage for role-playing: physical setting, events immediately preceding the role-play, mood or manner the co-actor should portray, and so forth.

Next assign group members' tasks:

> *Main actor:* Follow the steps of the skill. (If the step is a "thinking step," the participant should point to his or her head and say the thoughts aloud.)
>
> *Co-actor:* Stay in the role of the other person.
>
> *Other group members:* Watch to see whether the main actor correctly followed the skill steps that you were assigned to observe.

Assign each group member a specific step to observe; if there are more group members than steps, you can assign more than one group member to a step. (More than one step also may be assigned per group member, if necessary.)

Step 5: Conduct the Role-Play

Provide the main actor with whatever help or coaching is required to keep the role-playing going according to the skill steps. Urge actors who "break role" to get back into the role. If the main actor is not doing the skill steps according to standard, stop the role-play, provide instruction, and begin again.

Have the co-facilitator stand near the skill poster and point in turn to the skill steps as the role-play unfolds.

Step 6: Conduct the Discussion (Performance Feedback)

Provide feedback in the following order: coactor, observers, facilitators. Have the main actor wait to hear others' comments before responding about his or her performance or making any general remarks about the role-play.

Step 7: Assign the Homework (Transfer Training)

When the main actor has completed the role-play, provide a Skill Homework Report and instruct him or her to complete the top half. Let group members know that they are to complete the bottom half as soon after they have practiced the skill outside of class in the real-life situation they described and just completed role-playing.

Step 8: Select the Next Role-Player

Invite another group member to serve as the main actor. Repeat the steps until all members of the group have had an opportunity to role-play the skill.

Closing

Congratulate group members on their work during the session and encourage them to practice the skill outside the session. Remind them to fill out the second part of the Skill Homework Report after they have tried out the skill and let them know they will have a chance to share what happens at the next Social Skills Training session.

LEADER NOTES

Some group facilitators prefer to wait until after all group members have completed their role-plays, then assign skill homework at the end of the session. Depending on group members' ability and time available, you can use the blank Skill Homework Report 1 (see Appendix E). Having participants write the skill steps themselves can help reinforce learning.

Skill Cards

MAKING A COMPLAINT

SKILL STEPS

1. Decide what your complaint is.
2. Decide whom to complain to.
3. Tell that person your complaint.
4. Tell that person what you would like done about the problem.
5. Ask how he/she feels about what you've said.

Aggression Replacement Training® (3rd ed.), © 2011 by B. Glick & J.C. Gibbs (www.researchpress.com, 800-519-2707).

MAKING A COMPLAINT

SKILL STEPS

1. Decide what your complaint is.
2. Decide whom to complain to.
3. Tell that person your complaint.
4. Tell that person what you would like done about the problem.
5. Ask how he/she feels about what you've said.

Aggression Replacement Training® (3rd ed.), © 2011 by B. Glick & J.C. Gibbs (www.researchpress.com, 800-519-2707).

MAKING A COMPLAINT

SKILL STEPS

1. Decide what your complaint is.
2. Decide whom to complain to.
3. Tell that person your complaint.
4. Tell that person what you would like done about the problem.
5. Ask how he/she feels about what you've said.

Aggression Replacement Training® (3rd ed.), © 2011 by B. Glick & J.C. Gibbs (www.researchpress.com, 800-519-2707).

MAKING A COMPLAINT

SKILL STEPS

1. Decide what your complaint is.
2. Decide whom to complain to.
3. Tell that person your complaint.
4. Tell that person what you would like done about the problem.
5. Ask how he/she feels about what you've said.

Aggression Replacement Training® (3rd ed.), © 2011 by B. Glick & J.C. Gibbs (www.researchpress.com, 800-519-2707).

Social Skills Training—Skill Homework Report

Making a Complaint

Name _____ Date _____

SKILL STEPS

1. Decide what your complaint is.
2. Decide whom to complain to.
3. Tell that person your complaint.
4. Tell that person what you would like done about the problem.
5. Ask how he/she feels about what you've said.

FILL IN DURING THE SESSION

Where will you try the skill?

With whom will you try the skill?

When will you try the skill?

FILL IN AFTER YOU PRACTICE THE SKILL

What happened when you tried the skill?

What skill steps did you really follow?

How good a job did you do in using the skill *(check one):*   ☐ excellent   ☐ good   ☐ fair   ☐ poor

Understanding the Feelings of Others

OBJECTIVES

- To give group members a chance to process their experiences practicing Making a Complaint outside the group

- To help group members understand the importance of the skill of Understanding the Feelings of Others

- To provide an opportunity for participants to learn and role-play the steps of the skill and encourage skill use outside the group

MATERIALS

Easel pad and marker

Understanding the Feelings of Others Skill Cards

Copies of the Understanding the Feelings of Others Skill Homework Report

Poster (on CD): Understanding the Feelings of Others

Before the session, discuss and develop the modeling display with your co-facilitator.

PROCEDURE

Review

Let the group know that today's session will involve learning a new skill but that first you would like to know about their experiences trying the skill of Making a Complaint. Have group members take out their Making a Complaint Homework Reports and discuss. Ask:

- Who would like to review their homework first?

- OK, _____, please first quickly remind the group about your homework situation—where, when, and with whom?

- What happened when you tried the skill?

- How well do you think you did?

Provide verbal reinforcement to those who completed the homework and have shared their experiences.

Skill Teaching

Step 1: Define the Skill

Briefly discuss and define the skill. Ask, "What does Understanding the Feelings of Others mean to you?" Using participants' ideas, develop an operational definition of the skill. For example:

> Understanding the Feelings of Others means that you are aware what emotions another person may be having as a result of the situation they are in. It also means that you are able to identify how it may feel for yourself.

Ask who has used the skill in the past and acknowledge group members' responses.

Direct group members' attention to the skill poster and have group members read each step aloud, individually or as a group. After each step, ask the group whether the step is an action step or a thinking step. (In this skill, Steps 1 and 2 are action steps, Steps 3 and 4 are thinking steps, and Step 5 is a combination.)

UNDERSTANDING THE FEELINGS OF OTHERS

SKILL STEPS	FACILITATOR NOTES
1. Watch the other person.	Notice tone of voice, posture, and facial expression.
2. Listen to what the other person is saying.	Try to understand the content.
3. Figure out what the person might be feeling.	He/she may be angry, sad, anxious, and so on.
4. Think about ways to show you understand what he/she is feeling.	You might tell the person, touch the person, or leave the person alone.
5. Decide on the best way and do it.	

SAMPLE MODELING DISPLAYS

- *School:* Your friend has been excluded from a party that is going to take place this coming weekend. You have been invited. Your friend may be feeling sad, angry, jealous. *(Pick one.)*

- *Home:* Main actor recognizes parent is preoccupied with financial concerns and decides to leave parent alone.

- *Peer group:* Main actor lets friend know he/she understands friend's discomfort about meeting new people.

- *Institution:* Your friend was just denied a home visit because of behavior. The person is feeling sad, angry, disappointed. *(Choose one)*

Step 2: Model the Skill

With your co-facilitator, model the skill as you practiced it before the session.

Step 3: Establish Group Members' Need for the Skill

Ask each group member to describe briefly where, when, and with whom he or she would find it useful to employ the skill you have just modeled. If time allows, list each participant's name on the easel pad, along with the name of the person with whom the skill will be used and a phrase describing the situation.

Step 4: Select the First Role-Player and Set Up the Role-Play

Ask for a volunteer to conduct the first role-play. Have the main actor briefly describe the real-life situation in which he or she will use the skill and choose a co-actor who resembles the real-life person in as many ways as possible. Elicit additional information to set the stage for role-playing.

Next remind group members of their tasks:

- *Main actor:* Follow the steps of the skill.

- *Co-actor:* Stay in the role of the other person.

- *Other group members:* Observe to see whether the main actor followed the skill steps correctly.

Step 5: Conduct the Role-Play

Coach the main actor as necessary to keep the role-playing going according to the skill steps. Have the co-facilitator stand near the skill poster and point in turn to the steps as the role-play unfolds.

Step 6: Conduct the Discussion (Performance Feedback)

Provide feedback in the following order: coactor, observers, facilitators. Have the main actor wait to hear others' comments before responding about his or her performance or making any general remarks about the role-play.

Provide reinforcement for role-play performance according to the guidelines described in chapter 2.

Step 7: Assign the Homework (Transfer Training)

Provide a Skill Homework Report and encourage the main actor to fill out the top part of the form.

Step 8: Select the Next Role-Player

Invite another group member to serve as main actor. Repeat the steps until all members of the group have had an opportunity to role-play the skill.

Closing

Congratulate group members on the session and encourage them all to practice the skill in the situation outside the session. Remind them to fill out the second part of the Homework Report when they do.

LEADER NOTE

When assigning homework, make sure group members complete the top section of the report accurately and completely. You may help with writing steps of the skill (if using a blank Skill Homework Report form), spelling, and so forth. You may also verify that whatever group members role-played is accurately described as their homework.

Skill Cards

UNDERSTANDING THE FEELINGS OF OTHERS

SKILL STEPS

1. Watch the other person.
2. Listen to what the other person is saying.
3. Figure out what the person might be feeling.
4. Think about ways to show you understand what he/she is feeling.
5. Decide on the best way and do it.

Aggression Replacement Training® (3rd ed.), © 2011 by B. Glick & J.C. Gibbs (www.researchpress.com, 800-519-2707).

UNDERSTANDING THE FEELINGS OF OTHERS

SKILL STEPS

1. Watch the other person.
2. Listen to what the other person is saying.
3. Figure out what the person might be feeling.
4. Think about ways to show you understand what he/she is feeling.
5. Decide on the best way and do it.

Aggression Replacement Training® (3rd ed.), © 2011 by B. Glick & J.C. Gibbs (www.researchpress.com, 800-519-2707).

UNDERSTANDING THE FEELINGS OF OTHERS

SKILL STEPS

1. Watch the other person.
2. Listen to what the other person is saying.
3. Figure out what the person might be feeling.
4. Think about ways to show you understand what he/she is feeling.
5. Decide on the best way and do it.

Aggression Replacement Training® (3rd ed.), © 2011 by B. Glick & J.C. Gibbs (www.researchpress.com, 800-519-2707).

UNDERSTANDING THE FEELINGS OF OTHERS

SKILL STEPS

1. Watch the other person.
2. Listen to what the other person is saying.
3. Figure out what the person might be feeling.
4. Think about ways to show you understand what he/she is feeling.
5. Decide on the best way and do it.

Aggression Replacement Training® (3rd ed.), © 2011 by B. Glick & J.C. Gibbs (www.researchpress.com, 800-519-2707).

Social Skills Training—Skill Homework Report

Understanding the Feelings of Others

Name _____ Date _____

SKILL STEPS

1. Watch the other person.
2. Listen to what the other person is saying.
3. Figure out what the person might be feeling.
4. Think about ways to show you understand what he/she is feeling.
5. Decide on the best way and do it.

FILL IN DURING THE SESSION

Where will you try the skill?

With whom will you try the skill?

When will you try the skill?

FILL IN AFTER YOU PRACTICE THE SKILL

What happened when you tried the skill?

What skill steps did you really follow?

How good a job did you do in using the skill *(check one):* ☐ excellent ☐ good ☐ fair ☐ poor

 From *Aggression Replacement Training®: A Comprehensive Intervention for Aggressive Youth* (3rd ed.), by B. Glick & J. C. Gibbs, © 2011, Champaign, IL: Research Press (800-519-2707, www.researchpress.com).

Getting Ready for a Difficult Conversation

OBJECTIVES

- To give group members a chance to process their experiences practicing Understanding the Feelings of Others outside the group

- To help group members understand the importance of the skill of Getting Ready for a Difficult Conversation

- To provide an opportunity for participants to learn and role-play the steps of the skill and encourage skill use outside the group

MATERIALS

Easel pad and marker

Getting Ready for a Difficult Conversation Skill Cards

Copies of the Getting Ready for a Difficult Conversation Skill Homework Report

Poster (on CD): Getting Ready for a Difficult Conversation

Before the session, discuss and develop the modeling display with your co-facilitator.

PROCEDURE

Review

Have group members take out their Understanding the Feelings of Others Homework Reports and discuss. Ask:

- Who would like to review their homework first?

- OK, _____, please first quickly remind the group about your homework situation—where, when, and with whom?

- What happened when you tried the skill?

- How well do you think you did?

Reinforce those who have completed the homework and shared their experiences.

Skill Teaching

Step 1: Define the Skill

Briefly discuss and define the skill. Ask, "What does Getting Ready for a Difficult Conversation mean to you?" Using participants' ideas, develop an operational definition of the skill. For example:

> Getting Ready for a Difficult Conversation, for our purposes, means preparing to confront someone about something that creates a problem for you. It can be a face-to-face conversation, or over the phone, or even texting or IMing. However, it is best to have the conversation face to face.

Ask who has used the skill in the past and acknowledge group members' responses.

Direct group members' attention to the skill poster and have group members read each step aloud, individually or as a group. After each step, ask the group whether the step is an action step or a thinking step. (In this skill, Steps 1–5 are thinking steps, and Step 6 is a combination.)

GETTING READY FOR A DIFFICULT CONVERSATION

SKILL STEPS	FACILITATOR NOTES
1. Think about how you will feel during the conversation.	You might be tense, anxious, or impatient.
2. Think about how the other person will feel.	He/she may feel anxious, bored, or angry.
3. Think about different ways you could say what you want to say.	
4. Think about what the other person might say back to you.	
5. Think about any other things that might happen during the conversation.	
6. Choose the best approach you can think of and try it.	

Repeat Steps 1–5 at least twice, using different approaches to the situation. For example, you could be directive and friendly and the other person could be accepting, accusatory, conciliatory, or rigid and demanding.

SAMPLE MODELING DISPLAYS

- *School:* Main actor prepares to talk with teacher about dropping subject.
- *Home:* Main actor prepares to tell parent about school failure.
- *Peer group:* Main actor prepares to ask someone to go out with him/her.
- *Institution:* A resident has to tell his roommate he is being transferred to another pod and they will not see each other again.

Step 2: Model the Skill

With your co-facilitator, model the skill as you practiced it before the session.

Step 3: Establish Group Members' Need for the Skill

Ask each group member to describe briefly where, when, and with whom he or she would find it useful to employ the skill you have just modeled. If time allows, list each participant's name on the easel pad, along with the name of the person with whom the skill will be used and a phrase describing the situation.

Step 4: Select the First Role-Player and Set Up the Role-Play

Ask for a volunteer to conduct the first role-play. Have the main actor briefly describe the real-life situation in which he or she will use the skill and choose a co-actor who resembles the real-life person in as many ways as possible. Elicit additional information to set the stage for role-playing.

Next remind group members of their tasks:

- *Main actor:* Follow the steps of the skill.
- *Co-actor:* Stay in the role of the other person.
- *Other group members:* Observe to see whether the main actor followed the skill steps correctly.

Step 5: Conduct the Role-Play

Coach the main actor as necessary to keep the role-playing going according to the behavioral steps. Have the co-facilitator stand near the skill poster and point in turn to the steps as the role-play unfolds.

Step 6: Conduct the Discussion (Performance Feedback)

Provide feedback in the following order: coactor, observers, facilitators. Have the main actor wait to hear everyone's comments before responding about his or her performance or making any general remarks about the role-play.

Provide reinforcement for role-play performance according to the guidelines described in chapter 2.

Step 7: Assign the Homework (Transfer Training)

Provide a Skill Homework Report and encourage the main actor to fill out the top part of the form.

Step 8: Select the Next Role-Player

Invite another group member to serve as main actor. Repeat the steps until all members of the group have had an opportunity to role-play the skill.

Closing

Congratulate group members on the session and encourage them all to practice the skill in the situation outside the session. Remind them to fill out the second part of the Homework Report when they do.

LEADER NOTE

In preparing for difficult or stressful conversations, it is useful for youth to see that the way they approach the situation can influence the final outcome. This skill involves rehearsing a variety of approaches and then reflecting upon which approach produces the best results. Feedback from group members on the effectiveness of each approach can be particularly useful.

Skill Cards

GETTING READY FOR A DIFFICULT CONVERSATION

SKILL STEPS

1. Think about how you will feel during the conversation.
2. Think about how the other person will feel.
3. Think about different ways you could say what you want to say.
4. Think about what the other person might say back to you.
5. Think about any other things that might happen during the conversation.
6. Choose the best approach you can think of and try it.

Aggression Replacement Training® (3rd ed.), © 2011 by B. Glick & J.C. Gibbs (www.researchpress.com, 800-519-2707).

GETTING READY FOR A DIFFICULT CONVERSATION

SKILL STEPS

1. Think about how you will feel during the conversation.
2. Think about how the other person will feel.
3. Think about different ways you could say what you want to say.
4. Think about what the other person might say back to you.
5. Think about any other things that might happen during the conversation.
6. Choose the best approach you can think of and try it.

Aggression Replacement Training® (3rd ed.), © 2011 by B. Glick & J.C. Gibbs (www.researchpress.com, 800-519-2707).

GETTING READY FOR A DIFFICULT CONVERSATION

SKILL STEPS

1. Think about how you will feel during the conversation.
2. Think about how the other person will feel.
3. Think about different ways you could say what you want to say.
4. Think about what the other person might say back to you.
5. Think about any other things that might happen during the conversation.
6. Choose the best approach you can think of and try it.

Aggression Replacement Training® (3rd ed.), © 2011 by B. Glick & J.C. Gibbs (www.researchpress.com, 800-519-2707).

GETTING READY FOR A DIFFICULT CONVERSATION

SKILL STEPS

1. Think about how you will feel during the conversation.
2. Think about how the other person will feel.
3. Think about different ways you could say what you want to say.
4. Think about what the other person might say back to you.
5. Think about any other things that might happen during the conversation.
6. Choose the best approach you can think of and try it.

Aggression Replacement Training® (3rd ed.), © 2011 by B. Glick & J.C. Gibbs (www.researchpress.com, 800-519-2707).

Social Skills Training—Skill Homework Report

Getting Ready for a Difficult Conversation

Name _____ Date _____

SKILL STEPS

1. Think about how you will feel during the conversation.
2. Think about how the other person will feel.
3. Think about different ways you could say what you want to say.
4. Think about what the other person might say back to you.
5. Think about any other things that might happen during the conversation.
6. Choose the best approach you can think of and try it.

FILL IN DURING THE SESSION

Where will you try the skill?

With whom will you try the skill?

When will you try the skill?

FILL IN AFTER YOU PRACTICE THE SKILL

What happened when you tried the skill?

What skill steps did you really follow?

How good a job did you do in using the skill *(check one):* ☐ excellent ☐ good ☐ fair ☐ poor

From *Aggression Replacement Training®: A Comprehensive Intervention for Aggressive Youth* (3rd ed.), by B. Glick & J. C. Gibbs, © 2011, Champaign, IL: Research Press (800-519-2707, www.researchpress.com).

Dealing with Someone Else's Anger

OBJECTIVES

- To give group members a chance to process their experiences practicing Getting Ready for a Difficult Conversation outside the group

- To help group members understand the importance of the skill Dealing with Someone Else's Anger

- To provide an opportunity for participants to learn and role-play the steps of the skill and encourage skill use outside the group

MATERIALS

Easel pad and marker

Dealing with Someone Else's Anger Skill Cards

Copies of the Dealing with Someone Else's Anger Skill Homework Report

Poster (on CD): Dealing with Someone Else's Anger Conversation

Before the session, discuss and develop the modeling display with your co-facilitator.

PROCEDURE

Review

Have group members take out their Getting Ready for a Difficult Conversation Homework Reports and discuss. Ask:

- Who would like to review their homework first?

- OK, _____, please first quickly remind the group about your homework situation—where, when, and with whom?

- What happened when you tried the skill?

- How well do you think you did?

Reinforce those who have completed the homework and shared their experiences.

Skill Teaching

Step 1: Define the Skill

Briefly discuss and define the skill. Ask, "What does Dealing with Someone Else's Anger mean to you?" Using participants' ideas, develop an operational definition of the skill. For example:

> For the purposes of this session, we will define Dealing with Someone Else's Anger as being able to understand when another person is angry and whether you are able to do something about the situation.

Ask who has used the skill in the past and acknowledge group members' responses.

Direct group members' attention to the skill poster and have group members read each step aloud, individually or as a group. After each step, ask the group whether the step is an action step or a thinking step. (In this skill, Steps 1, 2, and 4 are action steps; Step 3 is a thinking step.)

DEALING WITH SOMEONE ELSE'S ANGER

SKILL STEPS	FACILITATOR NOTES
1. Listen to the person who is angry.	Don't interrupt; stay calm.
2. Try to understand what the angry person is saying and feeling.	Ask questions to get explanations of what you don't understand; restate them to yourself.
3. Decide if you can say or do something to deal with the situation.	
4. If you can, deal with the other person's anger.	This may include just listening, being empathic, doing something to correct the problem, ignoring it, or being assertive.

SAMPLE MODELING DISPLAYS

- *School:* Main actor responds to teacher who is angry about disruptive behavior in class by agreeing to cooperate and pay attention.

- *Home:* Main actor responds to parent who is angry about messy house by agreeing to do a fair share of work.

- *Peer group:* Main actor responds to admired older sibling's anger when main actor refuses to go drinking.

- *Institution:* A resident sees a staff member yelling at a group of friends about their poor performance in a game. He approaches his friends to discover why they are angry with the staff member.

Step 2: Model the Skill

With your co-facilitator, model the skill as you practiced it before the session.

Step 3: Establish Group Members' Need for the Skill

Ask each group member to describe briefly where, when, and with whom he or she would find it useful to employ the skill you have just modeled. If time allows, list each participant's name on the easel pad, along with the name of the person with whom the skill will be used and a phrase describing the situation.

Step 4: Select the First Role-Player and Set Up the Role-Play

Ask for a volunteer to conduct the first role-play. Have the main actor briefly describe the real-life situation in which he or she will use the skill and choose a co-actor who resembles the real-life person in as many ways as possible. Elicit additional information to set the stage for role-playing.

Next remind group members of their tasks:

- *Main actor:* Follow the steps of the skill.

- *Co-actor:* Stay in the role of the other person.

- *Other group members:* Observe to see whether the main actor followed the skill steps correctly.

Step 5: Conduct the Role-Play

Coach the main actor as necessary to keep the role-playing going according to the behavioral steps. Have the co-facilitator stand near the skill poster and point in turn to the steps as the role-play unfolds.

Step 6: Conduct the Discussion (Performance Feedback)

Provide feedback in the following order: coactor, observers, facilitators. Have the main actor wait to hear everyone's comments before responding about his or her performance or making any general remarks about the role-play.

Provide reinforcement for role-play performance according to the guidelines described in chapter 2.

Step 7: Assign the Homework (Transfer Training)

Provide a Skill Homework Report and encourage the main actor to fill out the top part of the form.

Step 8: Select the Next Role-Player

Invite another group member to serve as main actor. Repeat the steps until all members of the group have had an opportunity to role-play the skill.

Closing

Congratulate group members on the session and encourage them all to practice the skill in the situation outside the session. Remind them to fill out the second part of the Homework Report when they do. Tell the group that at the next Social Skills Training meeting, they will learn yet another skill they can use to get along better with others and to help them get what they want and need.

LEADER NOTE

This week's skill, Dealing with Someone Else's Anger, is directly dependent upon the previous week's skill, specifically that of Week 2, Understanding the Feelings of Others. Indeed, Step 2 of this skill requires the group members to understand what others are feeling. Connections with other ART components also begin to become apparent at this point.

Skill Cards

DEALING WITH SOMEONE ELSE'S ANGER

SKILL STEPS

1. Listen to the person who is angry.
2. Try to understand what the angry person is saying and feeling.
3. Decide if you can say or do something to deal with the situation.
4. If you can, deal with the other person's anger.

Aggression Replacement Training® (3rd ed.), © 2011 by B. Glick & J.C. Gibbs (www.researchpress.com, 800-519-2707).

DEALING WITH SOMEONE ELSE'S ANGER

SKILL STEPS

1. Listen to the person who is angry.
2. Try to understand what the angry person is saying and feeling.
3. Decide if you can say or do something to deal with the situation.
4. If you can, deal with the other person's anger.

Aggression Replacement Training® (3rd ed.), © 2011 by B. Glick & J.C. Gibbs (www.researchpress.com, 800-519-2707).

DEALING WITH SOMEONE ELSE'S ANGER

SKILL STEPS

1. Listen to the person who is angry.
2. Try to understand what the angry person is saying and feeling.
3. Decide if you can say or do something to deal with the situation.
4. If you can, deal with the other person's anger.

Aggression Replacement Training® (3rd ed.), © 2011 by B. Glick & J.C. Gibbs (www.researchpress.com, 800-519-2707).

DEALING WITH SOMEONE ELSE'S ANGER

SKILL STEPS

1. Listen to the person who is angry.
2. Try to understand what the angry person is saying and feeling.
3. Decide if you can say or do something to deal with the situation.
4. If you can, deal with the other person's anger.

Aggression Replacement Training® (3rd ed.), © 2011 by B. Glick & J.C. Gibbs (www.researchpress.com, 800-519-2707).

Social Skills Training—Skill Homework Report

Dealing with Someone Else's Anger

Name _____ Date _____

SKILL STEPS

1. Listen to the person who is angry.
2. Try to understand what the angry person is saying and feeling.
3. Decide if you can say or do something to deal with the situation.
4. If you can, deal with the other person's anger.

FILL IN DURING THE SESSION

Where will you try the skill?

With whom will you try the skill?

When will you try the skill?

FILL IN AFTER YOU PRACTICE THE SKILL

What happened when you tried the skill?

What skill steps did you really follow?

How good a job did you do in using the skill *(check one):* ☐ excellent ☐ good ☐ fair ☐ poor

 From *Aggression Replacement Training®: A Comprehensive Intervention for Aggressive Youth* (3rd ed.), by B. Glick & J. C. Gibbs, © 2011, Champaign, IL: Research Press (800-519-2707, www.researchpress.com).

Helping Others

OBJECTIVES

- To give group members a chance to process their experiences practicing Dealing with Someone Else's Anger outside the group

- To help group members understand the importance of the skill of Helping Others

- To provide an opportunity for participants to learn and role-play the steps of the skill and encourage skill use outside the group

MATERIALS

Easel pad and marker

Helping Others Skill Cards

Copies of the Helping Others Skill Homework Report

Poster (on CD): Helping Others

Before the session, discuss and develop the modeling display with your co-facilitator.

PROCEDURE

Review

Have group members take out their Dealing with Someone Else's Anger Homework Reports and discuss. Ask:

- Who would like to review their homework first?

- OK, _____, please first quickly remind the group about your homework situation—where, when, and with whom?

- What happened when you tried the skill?

- How well do you think you did?

Reinforce those who have completed the homework and shared their experiences.

Skill Teaching

Step 1: Define the Skill

Briefly discuss and define the skill. Ask, "What does Helping Others mean to you?" Using participants' ideas, develop an operational definition of the skill. For example:

> Helping Others means assisting others in completing a task or doing something to support someone else in getting what they want.

Ask who has used the skill in the past and acknowledge group members' responses.

Direct group members' attention to the skill poster and have group members read each step aloud, individually or as a group. After each step, ask the group whether the step is an action step or a thinking step. (In this skill, Steps 1 and 2 are thinking steps; Steps 3 and 4 are action steps.)

HELPING OTHERS

SKILL STEPS	FACILITATOR NOTES
1. Decide if the other person might need and want your help.	Think about the needs of the other person; observe.
2. Think of ways you could be helpful.	
3. Ask the other person if he/she wants your help.	Make the offer sincere, allowing the other to decline if he/she wishes.
4. Help the other person.	

SAMPLE MODELING DISPLAYS

- *School:* Main actor offers to help teacher arrange chairs in classroom.
- *Home:* Main actor offers to help prepare dinner.
- *Peer group:* Main actor offers to bring class assignments home for sick friend.
- *Institution:* Your roommate just received a call from his girlfriend who told him that she wants to break up with him.

Step 2: Model the Skill

With your co-facilitator, model the skill as you practiced it before the session.

Step 3: Establish Group Members' Need for the Skill

Ask each group member to describe briefly where, when, and with whom he or she would find it useful to employ the skill you have just modeled. If time allows, list each participant's name on the easel pad, along with the name of the person with whom the skill will be used and a phrase describing the situation.

Step 4: Select the First Role-Player and Set Up the Role-Play

Ask for a volunteer to conduct the first role-play. Have the main actor briefly describe the real-life situation in which he or she will use the skill and choose a co-actor who resembles the real-life person in as many ways as possible. Elicit additional information to set the stage for role-playing.

Next remind group members of their tasks:

- *Main actor:* Follow the steps of the skill.

- *Co-actor:* Stay in the role of the other person.

- *Other group members:* Observe to see whether the main actor followed the skill steps correctly.

Step 5: Conduct the Role-Play

Coach the main actor as necessary to keep the role-playing going according to the behavioral steps. Have the co-facilitator stand near the skill poster and point in turn to the steps as the role-play unfolds.

Step 6: Conduct the Discussion (Performance Feedback)

Provide feedback in the following order: coactor, observers, facilitators. Have the main actor wait to hear everyone's comments before responding about his or her performance or making any general remarks about the role-play.

Provide reinforcement for role-play performance according to the guidelines described in chapter 2.

Step 7: Assign the Homework (Transfer Training)

Provide a Skill Homework Report and encourage the main actor to fill out the top part of the form.

Step 8: Select the Next Role-Player

Invite another group member to serve as main actor. Repeat the steps until all members of the group have had an opportunity to role-play the skill.

Closing

Congratulate group members on the session and encourage them all to practice the skill in the situation outside the session. Remind them to fill out the second part of the Homework Report when they do.

Skill Cards

HELPING OTHERS

SKILL STEPS

1. Decide if the other person might need and want your help.

2. Think of ways you could be helpful.

3. Ask the other person if he/she wants your help.

4. Help the other person.

Aggression Replacement Training® (3rd ed.), © 2011 by B. Glick & J.C. Gibbs (www.researchpress.com, 800-519-2707).

HELPING OTHERS

SKILL STEPS

1. Decide if the other person might need and want your help.

2. Think of ways you could be helpful.

3. Ask the other person if he/she wants your help.

4. Help the other person.

Aggression Replacement Training® (3rd ed.), © 2011 by B. Glick & J.C. Gibbs (www.researchpress.com, 800-519-2707).

HELPING OTHERS

SKILL STEPS

1. Decide if the other person might need and want your help.

2. Think of ways you could be helpful.

3. Ask the other person if he/she wants your help.

4. Help the other person.

Aggression Replacement Training® (3rd ed.), © 2011 by B. Glick & J.C. Gibbs (www.researchpress.com, 800-519-2707).

HELPING OTHERS

SKILL STEPS

1. Decide if the other person might need and want your help.

2. Think of ways you could be helpful.

3. Ask the other person if he/she wants your help.

4. Help the other person.

Aggression Replacement Training® (3rd ed.), © 2011 by B. Glick & J.C. Gibbs (www.researchpress.com, 800-519-2707).

Social Skills Training—Skill Homework Report

Helping Others

Name _____ Date _____

SKILL STEPS

1. Decide if the other person might need and want your help.
2. Think of ways you could be helpful.
3. Ask the other person if he/she wants your help.
4. Help the other person.

FILL IN DURING THE SESSION

Where will you try the skill?

With whom will you try the skill?

When will you try the skill?

FILL IN AFTER YOU PRACTICE THE SKILL

What happened when you tried the skill?

What skill steps did you really follow?

How good a job did you do in using the skill *(check one)*: ☐ excellent ☐ good ☐ fair ☐ poor

Keeping Out of Fights

OBJECTIVES

- To give group members a chance to process their experiences practicing Helping Others outside the group

- To help group members understand the importance of the skill Keeping Out of Fights

- To provide an opportunity for participants to learn and role-play the steps of the skill and encourage skill use outside the group

MATERIALS

Easel pad and marker

Keeping Out of Fights Skill Cards

Copies of the Keeping Out of Fights Skill Homework Report

Poster (on CD): Keeping Out of Fights

Before the session, discuss and develop the modeling display with your co-facilitator.

PROCEDURE

Review

Have group members take out their Helping Others Homework Reports and discuss. Ask:

- Who would like to review their homework first?

- OK, _____, please first quickly remind the group about your homework situation—where, when, and with whom?

- What happened when you tried the skill?

- How well do you think you did?

Reinforce those who have completed the homework and shared their experiences.

Skill Teaching

Step 1: Define the Skill

Briefly discuss and define the skill. Ask, "What does Keeping Out of Fights mean to you?" Using participants' ideas, develop an operational definition of the skill. For example:

Keeping Out of Fights means doing something different from escalating a conflict situation. Fighting can be either physical or verbal, so this skill is helpful to keep you from getting into either kind of trouble.

Ask who has used the skill in the past and acknowledge group members' responses.

Direct group members' attention to the skill poster and have group members read each step aloud, individually or as a group. After each step, ask the group whether the step is an action step or a thinking step. (In this skill, Steps 1–3 are thinking steps, and Step 4 is a combination of thinking and action.)

KEEPING OUT OF FIGHTS

SKILL STEPS	FACILITATOR NOTES
1. Stop and think about why you want to fight.	
2. Decide what you want to happen in the long run.	What is the long-term outcome?
3. Think about other ways to handle the situation besides fighting.	You might negotiate, stand up for your rights, ask for help, or pacify the person.
4. Decide the best way to handle the situation and do it.	

SAMPLE MODELING DISPLAYS

- *School:* Main actor tells classmate that he/she wants to talk out their differences instead of being pressured to fight.
- *Home:* Main actor resolves potential fight with older sibling by asking parent to intervene.
- *Peer group:* Main actor sees his friend beginning to fight with another friend and decides to break up the fight after considering alternatives.
- *Institution:* You are waiting on the lunch line when a resident from the next pod cuts in front of you, saying, "What are you going to do about it?"

Step 2: Model the Skill

With your co-facilitator, model the skill as you practiced it before the session.

Step 3: Establish Group Members' Need for the Skill

Ask each group member to describe briefly where, when, and with whom he or she would find it useful to employ the skill you have just modeled. If time allows, list each participant's name on the easel pad, along with the name of the person with whom the skill will be used and a phrase describing the situation.

Step 4: Select the First Role-Player and Set Up the Role-Play

Ask for a volunteer to conduct the first role-play. Have the main actor briefly describe the real-life situation in which he or she will use the skill and choose a co-actor who resembles the real-life person in as many ways as possible. Elicit additional information to set the stage for role-playing.

Next remind group members of their roles:

- *Main actor:* Follow the steps of the skill.

- *Co-actor:* Stay in the role of the other person.

- *Other group members:* Observe to see whether the main actor followed the skill steps correctly.

Step 5: Conduct the Role-Play

Coach the main actor as necessary to keep the role-playing going according to the behavioral steps. Have the co-facilitator stand near the skill poster and point in turn to the steps as the role-play unfolds.

Step 6: Conduct the Discussion (Performance Feedback)

Provide feedback in the following order: coactor, observers, facilitators. Have the main actor wait to hear everyone's comments before responding about his or her performance or making any general remarks about the role-play.

Provide reinforcement for role-play performance according to the guidelines described in chapter 2.

Step 7: Assign the Homework (Transfer Training)

Provide a Skill Homework Report and encourage the main actor to fill out the top part of the form.

Step 8: Select the Next Role-Player

Invite another group member to serve as main actor. Repeat the steps until all members of the group have had an opportunity to role-play the skill.

Closing

Congratulate group members on the session and encourage them all to practice the skill in the situation outside the session. Remind them to fill out the second part of the Homework Report when they do.

LEADER NOTE

When preparing the modeling displays, be sure to develop at least three ways to handle the situation besides fighting (Step 3). It is critical for this skill that there be alternatives from which to choose the best way to handle the situation. If only one way is mentioned in Step 3, then the impact of the Step 4 is diminished in terms of empowering group members.

Skill Cards

KEEPING OUT OF FIGHTS

SKILL STEPS

1. Stop and think about why you want to fight.
2. Decide what you want to happen in the long run.
3. Think about other ways to handle the situation besides fighting.
4. Decide the best way to handle the situation and do it.

Aggression Replacement Training® (3rd ed.), © 2011 by B. Glick & J.C. Gibbs (www.researchpress.com, 800-519-2707).

KEEPING OUT OF FIGHTS

SKILL STEPS

1. Stop and think about why you want to fight.
2. Decide what you want to happen in the long run.
3. Think about other ways to handle the situation besides fighting.
4. Decide the best way to handle the situation and do it.

Aggression Replacement Training® (3rd ed.), © 2011 by B. Glick & J.C. Gibbs (www.researchpress.com, 800-519-2707).

KEEPING OUT OF FIGHTS

SKILL STEPS

1. Stop and think about why you want to fight.
2. Decide what you want to happen in the long run.
3. Think about other ways to handle the situation besides fighting.
4. Decide the best way to handle the situation and do it.

Aggression Replacement Training® (3rd ed.), © 2011 by B. Glick & J.C. Gibbs (www.researchpress.com, 800-519-2707).

KEEPING OUT OF FIGHTS

SKILL STEPS

1. Stop and think about why you want to fight.
2. Decide what you want to happen in the long run.
3. Think about other ways to handle the situation besides fighting.
4. Decide the best way to handle the situation and do it.

Aggression Replacement Training® (3rd ed.), © 2011 by B. Glick & J.C. Gibbs (www.researchpress.com, 800-519-2707).

Social Skills Training—Skill Homework Report

Keeping Out of Fights

Name _____ Date _____

SKILL STEPS

1. Stop and think about why you want to fight.
2. Decide what you want to happen in the long run.
3. Think about other ways to handle the situation besides fighting.
4. Decide on the best way to handle the situation and do it.

FILL IN DURING THE SESSION

Where will you try the skill?

With whom will you try the skill?

When will you try the skill?

FILL IN AFTER YOU PRACTICE THE SKILL

What happened when you tried the skill?

What skill steps did you really follow?

How good a job did you do in using the skill *(check one)*? ☐ excellent ☐ good ☐ fair ☐ poor

Dealing with an Accusation

OBJECTIVES

- To give group members a chance to process their experiences practicing Keeping Out of Fights outside the group.

- To help group members understand the importance of the skill Dealing with an Accusation

- To provide an opportunity for participants to learn and role-play the steps of the skill and to encourage skill use outside the group

MATERIALS

Easel pad and marker

Dealing with an Accusation Skill Cards

Copies of the Dealing with an Accusation Skill Homework Report

Poster (on CD): Dealing with an Accusation

Before the session, discuss and develop the role-play display with your co-facilitator.

PROCEDURE

Review

Have group members take out their Keeping Out of Fights Homework Reports and discuss. Ask:

- Who would like to review their homework first?

- OK, _____, please first quickly remind the group about your homework situation—where, when, and with whom?

- What happened when you tried the skill?

- How well do you think you did?

Reinforce those who have completed the homework and shared their experiences.

Skill Teaching

Step 1: Define the Skill

Briefly discuss and define the skill. Ask, "What does Dealing with an Accusation mean to you?" Using participants' ideas, develop an operational definition of the skill. For example:

> Dealing with an Accusation means responding in a way that doesn't get you in more trouble when someone says you did something. Point out that what you're accused of doing can be good or bad, but it is usually negative and that the person's accusation can be true or false (you might have done it or not).

Ask who has used the skill in the past and acknowledge group members' responses.

Direct group members' attention to the skill poster and have group members read each step aloud, individually or as a group. After each step, ask the group whether the step is an action step or a thinking step. (Steps 1–3 are thinking steps; Step 4 is an action step.)

DEALING WITH AN ACCUSATION

SKILL STEPS	FACILITATOR NOTES
1. Think about what the other person has accused you of.	Is the accusation accurate or inaccurate?
2. Think about why the person might have accused you.	Have you infringed on his/her rights or property? Has a rumor been started by someone else?
3. Think about ways to answer the person's accusation.	
4. Choose the best way and do it.	You might negotiate, stand up for your rights, ask for help, or pacify the person.

SAMPLE MODELING DISPLAYS

- *School:* Teacher accuses main actor of cheating on a test.
- *Home:* Parent accuses main actor of hurting sibling's feelings.
- *Peer group:* Friend accuses main actor of lying.
- *Institution:* Roommate accuses main actor of stealing his canteen.

Step 2: Model the Skill

With your co-facilitator, model the skill as you practiced it before the session.

Step 3: Establish Group Members' Need for the Skill

Ask each group member to describe briefly where, when, and with whom he or she would find it useful to employ the skill you have just modeled. If time allows, list each participant's name on the easel pad, along with the name of the person with whom the skill will be used and a phrase describing the situation.

Step 4: Select the First Role-Player and Set Up the Role-Play

Ask for a volunteer to conduct the first role-play. Have the main actor briefly describe the real-life situation in which he or she will use the skill and choose a co-actor who resembles the real-life person in as many ways as possible. Elicit additional information to set the stage for role-playing.

Next remind group members of their roles:

- *Main actor:* Follow the steps of the skill.

- *Co-actor:* Stay in the role of the other person.

- *Other group members:* Observe to see whether the main actor followed the skill steps correctly.

Step 5: Conduct the Role-Play

Coach the main actor as necessary to keep the role-playing going according to the behavioral steps. Have the co-facilitator stand near the skill poster and point in turn to the steps as the role-play unfolds.

Step 6: Conduct the Discussion (Performance Feedback)

Provide feedback in the following order: coactor, observers, facilitators. Have the main actor wait to hear everyone's comments before responding about his or her performance or making any general remarks about the role-play.

Provide reinforcement for role-play performance according to the guidelines described in chapter 2.

Step 7: Assign the Homework (Transfer Training)

Provide a Skill Homework Report and encourage the main actor to fill out the top part of the form.

Step 8: Select the Next Role-Player

Invite another group member to serve as main actor. Repeat the steps until all members of the group have had an opportunity to role-play the skill.

Closing

Congratulate group members on the session and encourage them all to practice the skill in the situation outside the session. Remind them to fill out the second part of the Homework Report when they do.

LEADER NOTE

It is important for group members to understand that accusations can be valid or false. The response will be different in each case. If the accusation is valid, an apology may be in order.

Skill Cards

DEALING WITH AN ACCUSATION

SKILL STEPS

1. Think about what the other person has accused you of.
2. Think about why the person might have accused you.
3. Think about ways to answer the person's accusation.
4. Choose the best way and do it.

Aggression Replacement Training® (3rd ed.), © 2011 by B. Glick & J.C. Gibbs (www.researchpress.com, 800-519-2707).

DEALING WITH AN ACCUSATION

SKILL STEPS

1. Think about what the other person has accused you of.
2. Think about why the person might have accused you.
3. Think about ways to answer the person's accusation.
4. Choose the best way and do it.

Aggression Replacement Training® (3rd ed.), © 2011 by B. Glick & J.C. Gibbs (www.researchpress.com, 800-519-2707).

DEALING WITH AN ACCUSATION

SKILL STEPS

1. Think about what the other person has accused you of.
2. Think about why the person might have accused you.
3. Think about ways to answer the person's accusation.
4. Choose the best way and do it.

Aggression Replacement Training® (3rd ed.), © 2011 by B. Glick & J.C. Gibbs (www.researchpress.com, 800-519-2707).

DEALING WITH AN ACCUSATION

SKILL STEPS

1. Think about what the other person has accused you of.
2. Think about why the person might have accused you.
3. Think about ways to answer the person's accusation.
4. Choose the best way and do it.

Aggression Replacement Training® (3rd ed.), © 2011 by B. Glick & J.C. Gibbs (www.researchpress.com, 800-519-2707).

Social Skills Training—Skill Homework Report

Dealing with an Accusation

Name _____ Date _____

SKILL STEPS

1. Think about what the other person has accused you of.
2. Think about why the person might have accused you.
3. Think about ways to answer the person's accusation.
4. Choose the best way and do it.

FILL IN DURING THE SESSION

Where will you try the skill?

With whom will you try the skill?

When will you try the skill?

FILL IN AFTER YOU PRACTICE THE SKILL

What happened when you tried the skill?

What skill steps did you really follow?

How good a job did you do in using the skill *(check one):* ☐ excellent ☐ good ☐ fair ☐ poor

Dealing with Group Pressure

OBJECTIVES

- To give group members a chance to process their experiences practicing Dealing with an Accusation outside the group

- To help group members understand the importance of the skill Dealing with Group Pressure

- To provide an opportunity for participants to learn and role-play the steps of the skill and encourage skill use outside the group

MATERIALS

Easel pad and marker

Dealing with Group Pressure Skill Cards

Copies of the Dealing with Group Pressure Skill Homework Report

Poster (on CD): Dealing with Group Pressure

Before the session, discuss and develop the role-play display with your co-facilitator.

PROCEDURE

Review

Have group members take out their Dealing with an Accusation Homework Reports and discuss. Ask:

- Who would like to review their homework first?

- OK, _____, please first quickly remind the group about your homework situation—where, when, and with whom?

- What happened when you tried the skill?

- How well do you think you did?

Reinforce those who have completed the homework and shared their experiences.

Skill Teaching

Step 1: Define the Skill

Briefly discuss and define the skill. Ask, "What does Dealing with Group Pressure mean to you?" Using participants' ideas, develop an operational definition of the skill. For example:

> Dealing with Group Pressure means standing up for yourself when friends or other people in the community, school, or other situations attempt to influence your thoughts or behavior in some way.

Ask who has used the skill in the past and acknowledge group members' responses.

Direct group members' attention to the skill poster and have group members read each step aloud, individually or as a group. After each step, ask the group whether the step is an action step or a thinking step. (In this skill, Steps 1–3 are thinking steps, Step 4 is an action step.)

DEALING WITH GROUP PRESSURE

SKILL STEPS	FACILITATOR NOTES
1. Think about what the group wants you to do and why.	Listen to other people, decide what the real meaning is, try to understand what is being said.
2. Decide what you want to do.	Yield, resist, delay, negotiate.
3. Decide how to tell the group what you want to do.	Give reasons, talk to one person only, delay, assert yourself.
4. Tell the group what you have decided.	

SAMPLE MODELING DISPLAYS

- *School:* Main actor deals with group pressure to vandalize school.
- *Home:* Main actor deals with family pressure to break up friendship.
- *Peer group:* Main actor deals with pressure to fight.
- *Institution:* Main actor's friends want to give a new resident just admitted to the pod and your friends an initiation beatdown when the lights go out tonight.

Step 2: Model the Skill

With your co-facilitator, model the skill as you practiced it before the session.

Step 3: Establish Group Members' Need for the Skill

Ask each group member to describe briefly where, when, and with whom he or she would find it useful to employ the skill you have just modeled. If time allows, list each participant's name on the easel pad, along with the name of the person with whom the skill will be used and a phrase describing the situation.

Step 4: Select the First Role-Player and Set Up the Role-Play

Ask for a volunteer to conduct the first role-play. Have the main actor briefly describe the real-life situation in which he or she will use the skill and choose a co-actor who resembles the real-life person in as many ways as possible. Elicit additional information to set the stage for role-playing.

Next remind group members of their roles:

- *Main actor:* Follow the steps of the skill.

- *Co-actor:* Stay in the role of the other person.

- *Other group members:* Observe to see whether the main actor followed the skill steps correctly.

Step 5: Conduct the Role-Play

Coach the main actor as necessary to keep the role-playing going according to the behavioral steps. Have the co-facilitator stand near the skill poster and point in turn to the steps as the role-play unfolds.

Step 6: Conduct the Discussion (Performance Feedback)

Provide feedback in the following order: coactor, observers, facilitators. Have the main actor wait to hear everyone's comments before responding about his or her performance or making any general remarks about the role-play.

Provide reinforcement for role-play performance according to the guidelines described in chapter 2.

Step 7: Assign the Homework (Transfer Training)

Provide a Skill Homework Report and encourage the main actor to fill out the top part of the form.

Step 8: Select the Next Role-Player

Invite another group member to serve as main actor. Repeat the steps until all members of the group have had an opportunity to role-play the skill.

Closing

Congratulate group members on the session and encourage them all to practice the skill in the situation outside the session. Remind them to fill out the second part of the Homework Report when they do.

Skill Cards

DEALING WITH GROUP PRESSURE

SKILL STEPS

1. Think about what the group wants you to do and why.
2. Decide what you want to do.
3. Decide how to tell the group what you want to do.
4. Tell the group what you have decided.

Aggression Replacement Training® (3rd ed.), © 2011 by B. Glick & J.C. Gibbs (www.researchpress.com, 800-519-2707).

DEALING WITH GROUP PRESSURE

SKILL STEPS

1. Think about what the group wants you to do and why.
2. Decide what you want to do.
3. Decide how to tell the group what you want to do.
4. Tell the group what you have decided.

Aggression Replacement Training® (3rd ed.), © 2011 by B. Glick & J.C. Gibbs (www.researchpress.com, 800-519-2707).

DEALING WITH GROUP PRESSURE

SKILL STEPS

1. Think about what the group wants you to do and why.
2. Decide what you want to do.
3. Decide how to tell the group what you want to do.
4. Tell the group what you have decided.

Aggression Replacement Training® (3rd ed.), © 2011 by B. Glick & J.C. Gibbs (www.researchpress.com, 800-519-2707).

DEALING WITH GROUP PRESSURE

SKILL STEPS

1. Think about what the group wants you to do and why.
2. Decide what you want to do.
3. Decide how to tell the group what you want to do.
4. Tell the group what you have decided.

Aggression Replacement Training® (3rd ed.), © 2011 by B. Glick & J.C. Gibbs (www.researchpress.com, 800-519-2707).

Social Skills Training—Skill Homework Report

Dealing with Group Pressure

Name _____ Date _____

SKILL STEPS

1. Think about what the group wants you to do and why.
2. Decide what you want to do.
3. Decide how to tell the group what you want to do.
4. Tell the group what you have decided.

FILL IN DURING THE SESSION

Where will you try the skill?

With whom will you try the skill?

When will you try the skill?

FILL IN AFTER YOU PRACTICE THE SKILL

What happened when you tried the skill?

What skill steps did you really follow?

How good a job did you do in using the skill *(check one):* ☐ excellent ☐ good ☐ fair ☐ poor

 From *Aggression Replacement Training®: A Comprehensive Intervention for Aggressive Youth* (3rd ed.), by B. Glick & J. C. Gibbs, © 2011, Champaign, IL: Research Press (800-519-2707, www.researchpress.com).

Expressing Affection

OBJECTIVES

- To give group members a chance to process their experiences practicing Dealing with Group Pressure outside the group

- To help group members understand the importance of the skill Expressing Affection

- To provide an opportunity for participants to learn and role-play the steps of the skill and encourage skill use outside the group

MATERIALS

Easel pad and marker

Expressing Affection Skill Cards

Copies of the Expressing Affection Skill Homework Report

Poster (on CD): Expressing Affection

Before the session, discuss and develop the role-play display with your co-facilitator.

PROCEDURE

Review

Have group members take out their Dealing with Group Pressure Homework Reports and discuss. Ask:

- Who would like to review their homework first?

- OK, _____, please first quickly remind the group about your homework situation—where, when, and with whom?

- What happened when you tried the skill?

- How well do you think you did?

Reinforce those who have completed the homework and shared their experiences.

Skill Teaching

Step 1: Define the Skill

Briefly discuss and define the skill. Ask, "What does Expressing Affection mean to you?" Using participants' ideas, develop an operational definition of the skill. For example:

> Expressing Affection means letting another person know you care about them and showing them in some way that they are appreciated.

Ask who has used the skill in the past and acknowledge group members' responses.

Direct group members' attention to the skill poster and have group members read each step aloud, individually or as a group. After each step, ask the group whether the step is an action step or a thinking step. (In this skill, Steps 1–4 are thinking steps; Step 5 is an action step.)

EXPRESSING AFFECTION

SKILL STEPS	FACILITATOR NOTES
1. Decide if you have good feelings about the other person.	
2. Decide if the other person would like to know about your feelings.	Consider the possible consequences (for example, happiness, misinterpretation, embarrassment, encouragement of friendship).
3. Choose the best way to express your feelings.	Do something, say something, give gift, send card, phone or text, offer invitation.
4. Choose the best time and place to express your feelings.	Minimize distractions and possible interruptions.
5. Express your feelings in a friendly way.	

SAMPLE MODELING DISPLAYS

- *School:* Main actor expresses positive feelings toward school counselor after sharing personal problems.
- *Home:* Main actor brings small gift to parents as token of affection.
- *Peer group:* Main actor expresses friendly feelings toward new acquaintance.
- *Institution:* Main actor expresses warm feelings toward roommate, who has been a good friend for two years by sharing snacks, providing protection from bullies, and helping with schoolwork.

Step 2: Model the Skill

With your co-facilitator, model the skill as you practiced it before the session.

Step 3: Establish Group Members' Need for the Skill

Ask each group member to describe briefly where, when, and with whom he or she would find it useful to employ the skill you have just modeled. If time allows, list each participant's name on the easel pad, along with the name of the person with whom the skill will be used and a phrase describing the situation.

Step 4: Select the First Role-Player and Set Up the Role-Play

Ask for a volunteer to conduct the first role-play. Have the main actor briefly describe the real-life situation in which he or she will use the skill and choose a co-actor who resembles the real-life person in as many ways as possible. Elicit additional information to set the stage for role-playing.

Next remind group members of their roles:

- *Main actor:* Follow the steps of the skill.

- *Co-actor:* Stay in the role of the other person.

- *Other group members:* Observe to see whether the main actor followed the skill steps correctly.

Step 5: Conduct the Role-Play

Coach the main actor as necessary to keep the role-playing going according to the behavioral steps. Have the co-facilitator stand near the skill poster and point in turn to the steps as the role-play unfolds.

Step 6: Conduct the Discussion (Performance Feedback)

Provide feedback in the following order: coactor, observers, facilitators. Have the main actor wait to hear everyone's comments before responding about his or her performance or making any general remarks about the role-play.

Provide reinforcement for role-play performance according to the guidelines described in chapter 2.

Step 7: Assign the Homework (Transfer Training)

Provide a Skill Homework Report and encourage the main actor to fill out the top part of the form.

Step 8: Select the Next Role-Player

Invite another group member to serve as main actor. Repeat the steps until all members of the group have had an opportunity to role-play the skill.

Closing

Congratulate group members on the session and encourage them all to practice the skill in the situation outside the session. Remind them to fill out the second part of the Homework Report when they do.

LEADER NOTE

Although group members initially will associate this skill with romantic relationships, they soon grasp the notion that affection and caring can be expressed toward a wide variety of persons in many different ways. Encourage appropriate touch and positive statements expressing appreciation—for example, "I really care about you," "You always make me feel wanted and warm inside," and "You are the kind of person I want to be around."

Skill Cards

EXPRESSING AFFECTION

SKILL STEPS

1. Decide if you have good feelings about the other person.
2. Decide if the other person would like to know about your feelings.
3. Choose the best way to express your feelings.
4. Choose the best time and place to express your feelings.
5. Express your feelings in a friendly way.

Aggression Replacement Training® (3rd ed.), © 2011 by B. Glick & J.C. Gibbs (www.researchpress.com, 800-519-2707).

EXPRESSING AFFECTION

SKILL STEPS

1. Decide if you have good feelings about the other person.
2. Decide if the other person would like to know about your feelings.
3. Choose the best way to express your feelings.
4. Choose the best time and place to express your feelings.
5. Express your feelings in a friendly way.

Aggression Replacement Training® (3rd ed.), © 2011 by B. Glick & J.C. Gibbs (www.researchpress.com, 800-519-2707).

EXPRESSING AFFECTION

SKILL STEPS

1. Decide if you have good feelings about the other person.
2. Decide if the other person would like to know about your feelings.
3. Choose the best way to express your feelings.
4. Choose the best time and place to express your feelings.
5. Express your feelings in a friendly way.

Aggression Replacement Training® (3rd ed.), © 2011 by B. Glick & J.C. Gibbs (www.researchpress.com, 800-519-2707).

EXPRESSING AFFECTION

SKILL STEPS

1. Decide if you have good feelings about the other person.
2. Decide if the other person would like to know about your feelings.
3. Choose the best way to express your feelings.
4. Choose the best time and place to express your feelings.
5. Express your feelings in a friendly way.

Aggression Replacement Training® (3rd ed.), © 2011 by B. Glick & J.C. Gibbs (www.researchpress.com, 800-519-2707).

Social Skills Training—Skill Homework Report

Expressing Affection

Name _____ Date _____

SKILL STEPS

1. Decide if you have good feelings about the other person.
2. Decide if the other person would like to know about your feelings.
3. Choose the best way to express your feelings.
4. Choose the best time and place to express your feelings.
5. Express your feelings in a friendly way.

FILL IN DURING THE SESSION

Where will you try the skill?

With whom will you try the skill?

When will you try the skill?

FILL IN AFTER YOU PRACTICE THE SKILL

What happened when you tried the skill?

What skill steps did you really follow?

How good a job did you do in using the skill *(check one)*: ☐ excellent ☐ good ☐ fair ☐ poor

Responding to Failure

OBJECTIVES

- To give group members a chance to process their experiences practicing Expressing Affection outside the group

- To help group members understand the importance of the skill Responding to Failure

- To provide an opportunity for participants to learn and role-play the steps of the skill and encourage skill use outside the group

MATERIALS

Easel pad and marker

Responding to Failure Skill Cards

Copies of the Responding to Failure Skill Homework Report

Poster (on CD): Responding to Failure

Before the session, discuss and develop the role-play display with your co-facilitator.

PROCEDURE

Review

Have group members take out their Expressing Affection Homework Reports and discuss. Ask:

- Who would like to review their homework first?

- OK, _____, please first quickly remind the group about your homework situation—where, when, and with whom?

- What happened when you tried the skill?

- How well do you think you did?

Reinforce those who have completed the homework and shared their experiences.

Skill Teaching

Step 1: Define the Skill

Briefly discuss and define the skill. Ask, "What does Responding to Failure mean to you?" Using participants' ideas, develop an operational definition of the skill. For example:

> Responding to Failure means dealing in a positive way with not being able to do what you hoped, accomplishing something you wanted, or achieving something.

Ask who has used the skill in the past and acknowledge group members' responses.

Direct group members' attention to the skill poster and have group members read each step aloud, individually or as a group. After each step, ask the group whether the step is an action step or a thinking step. (In this skill, Steps 1–4 are thinking steps, and Step 5 is an action step.)

RESPONDING TO FAILURE

SKILL STEPS	FACILITATOR NOTES
1. Decide if you have failed at something.	The failure may be interpersonal, academic, athletic, or of another nature.
2. Think about why you failed.	It could be due to lack of skill, motivation, or luck. Include personal reasons and circumstances.
3. Think about what you could do to keep from failing another time.	Evaluate what is under your control to \ change: If a skill problem, practice; if motivation, increase effort; if circumstances, think of ways to change them, if possible.
4. Decide if you want to try again.	
5. Try again using your new idea.	

SAMPLE MODELING DISPLAYS

- *School:* Main actor deals with failing grade on exam.
- *Home:* Main actor fails at attempt to help younger sibling with project.
- *Peer group:* Main actor deals with being turned down for date.
- *Institution:* Case manager says main actor did not advance to the next level of the program and will have to wait for the next review, three months later.

Step 2: Model the Skill

With your co-facilitator, model the skill as you practiced it before the session.

Step 3: Establish Group Members' Need for the Skill

Ask each group member to describe briefly where, when, and with whom he or she would find it useful to employ the skill you have just modeled. If time allows, list each participant's name on the easel pad, along with the name of the person with whom the skill will be used and a phrase describing the situation.

Step 4: Select the First Role-Player and Set Up the Role-Play

Ask for a volunteer to conduct the first role-play. Have the main actor briefly describe the real-life situation in which he or she will use the skill and choose a co-actor who resembles the real-life person in as many ways as possible. Elicit additional information to set the stage for role-playing.

Next remind group members of their roles:

- *Main actor:* Follow the steps of the skill.

- *Co-actor:* Stay in the role of the other person.

- *Other group members:* Observe to see whether the main actor followed the skill steps correctly.

Step 5: Conduct the Role-Play

Coach the main actor as necessary to keep the role-playing going according to the behavioral steps. Have the co-facilitator stand near the skill poster and point in turn to the steps as the role-play unfolds.

Step 6: Conduct the Discussion (Performance Feedback)

Provide feedback in the following order: coactor, observers, facilitators. Have the main actor wait to hear everyone's comments before responding about his or her performance or making any general remarks about the role-play.

Provide reinforcement for role-play performance according to the guidelines described in chapter 2.

Step 7: Assign the Homework (Transfer Training)

Provide a Skill Homework Report and encourage the main actor to fill out the top part of the form.

Step 8: Select the Next Role-Player

Invite another group member to serve as main actor. Repeat the steps until all members of the group have had an opportunity to role-play the skill.

Closing

Congratulate group members on the session and encourage them all to practice the skill in the situation outside the session. Remind them to fill out the second part of the Homework Report when they do.

LEADER NOTE

This is the final Social Skills Training session. As time allows, you can review the skills group members have learned and used and discuss ways they are now better able to get what they want without negative consequences.

Skill Cards

RESPONDING TO FAILURE

SKILL STEPS

1. Decide if you have failed at something.
2. Think about why you failed.
3. Think about what you could do to keep from failing another time.
4. Decide if you want to try again.
5. Try again using your new idea.

Aggression Replacement Training® (3rd ed.), © 2011 by B. Glick & J.C. Gibbs (www.researchpress.com, 800-519-2707).

RESPONDING TO FAILURE

SKILL STEPS

1. Decide if you have failed at something.
2. Think about why you failed.
3. Think about what you could do to keep from failing another time.
4. Decide if you want to try again.
5. Try again using your new idea.

Aggression Replacement Training® (3rd ed.), © 2011 by B. Glick & J.C. Gibbs (www.researchpress.com, 800-519-2707).

RESPONDING TO FAILURE

SKILL STEPS

1. Decide if you have failed at something.
2. Think about why you failed.
3. Think about what you could do to keep from failing another time.
4. Decide if you want to try again.
5. Try again using your new idea.

Aggression Replacement Training® (3rd ed.), © 2011 by B. Glick & J.C. Gibbs (www.researchpress.com, 800-519-2707).

RESPONDING TO FAILURE

SKILL STEPS

1. Decide if you have failed at something.
2. Think about why you failed.
3. Think about what you could do to keep from failing another time.
4. Decide if you want to try again.
5. Try again using your new idea.

Aggression Replacement Training® (3rd ed.), © 2011 by B. Glick & J.C. Gibbs (www.researchpress.com, 800-519-2707).

Social Skills Training—Skill Homework Report

Responding to Failure

Name _____ Date _____

SKILL STEPS

1. Decide if you have failed at something.
2. Think about why you failed.
3. Think about what you could do to keep from failing another time.
4. Decide if you want to try again.
5. Try again using your new idea.

FILL IN DURING THE SESSION

Where will you try the skill?

With whom will you try the skill?

When will you try the skill?

FILL IN AFTER YOU PRACTICE THE SKILL

What happened when you tried the skill?

What skill steps did you really follow?

How good a job did you do in using the skill *(check one):* ☐ excellent ☐ good ☐ fair ☐ poor

Anger Control Training

Introducing Anger Control Training/ABCs of Anger

OBJECTIVES

- To explain the goals of the Anger Control Training component and provide a rationale for learning the anger control sequence

- To introduce the procedures for Anger Control Training sessions

- To help group members understand the ABCs of Anger (Antecedent-Behavior-Consequence)

MATERIALS

Easel pad and marker

Optional: Copies of the Anger ABCs Report

Posters (on CD):

Anger Control

ABCs of Anger

PROCEDURE

Review

Briefly review the group rules discussed during the first session and ask if anyone has any questions.

Anger Control Training Procedures

Let group members know that, like Social Skills Training sessions, Anger Control Training sessions will involve discussion, modeling (demonstration), role-playing (trying out what was demonstrated), and homework outside the session.

Anger Control Training Introduction

Ask group members what anger is. Explain that, actually, anger is a very normal feeling and that everyone gets angry. Make the point that anger isn't good or bad: It's what you *do* with your anger that matters. If you become aggressive and hurt others when you are angry, that can lead to trouble with authorities (police, teachers, parents), with peers, and even with regard to how you feel about yourself.

Have a participant read the Anger Control poster aloud.

ANGER CONTROL

Anger control means having more personal power by being able to be in control of your angry reactions despite the attempts of others to hassle you.

Point out that the Anger Control Training part of ART will help group members know when they are getting angry and give them the self-control to keep from losing their temper and getting in trouble.

Ask for examples of people group members admire who have excellent self-control—for example, Jackie Chan and Evander Holyfield. Contrast these individuals' lives with the lives of people like Mike Tyson, who lost his fame and fortune because he was unable to control his angry impulses.

> *Giving real-life examples and stressing that these people would not be successful if they were out of control illustrates that having more self-control empowers you and gives you more choices.*

ABCs of Anger

Refer group members to the ABCs of Anger poster and explain that understanding the ABCs is very important to anger control. Be sure to discuss each part of the ABCs, providing an explanation of each.

ABCs OF ANGER

A = Antecedent

What led up to the problem?

B = Behavior

What did you do (your response to A)?

C = Consequence

What were the results of your behavior (B)?

Give an example of how you handled a personal conflict, being sure to identify the A, B, and C of the anger situation. For example:

- I got cut off on the highway (A), so I got mad and yelled and honked at the guy (B). Then the police pulled me over for reckless driving and gave me a ticket (C).

Next invite group members to give their own examples of actual situations in which they became angry and assist them in identifying the ABCs. For example:

- I got suspended (C) because my homey dissed me in study hall (A), so I punched him in the face (B).

- I cussed my teacher (B) because she was ragging on me (A), and she made me write five extra assignments, so I couldn't go to practice (C).

- I wanted to hang out with my friends at the movies instead of go with my boyfriend (A), but my boyfriend caught me lying to him about it (B), and now we will probably be breaking up (C).

  Have your co-facilitator write group members' ABCs on the easel pad as they are generated.

Closing and Homework

Briefly review the reasons for youth to develop greater self-control, procedures for the Anger Control Training group, and the ABCs of anger control. If you wish, distribute the ABCs of Anger handout, explaining that the homework for next week is to pay attention to times you become angry, when you can, and after you calm down, to apply the ABCs—in other words, identify the Antecedent, Behavior, and Consequences of your action. Explain that while participants don't have to write anything down, the handout can serve as a reminder and a place to make notes.

LEADER NOTE

If you are following the session order specified in Table 1.1, the next session will be a Moral Reasoning session. To give yourself time to compile a response chart (see chapter 4), participants must read the problem situation and answer the questions before the next session. Many group leaders take a moment at the end of Anger Control sessions to introduce the situation.

WEEK 1 MORAL REASONING: JIM'S PROBLEM SITUATION

Reproduce and hand out the Moral Reasoning Situation for the week (see p. 286), then have group members read it and answer the questions. You can paraphrase the following explanation:

> Here's a problem situation that we will discuss at our next session. Every week, I will give you a different problem situation with some questions for you to answer. The questions are quick and easy. Just circle one of the responses to each question. THERE ARE NO RIGHT OR

WRONG ANSWERS—JUST YOUR OPINIONS. I will use your answers to prepare a chart of everyone's responses that we will use to help us discuss the situation. Please put your name on the top of the sheet and read the problem situation to yourselves while I read it aloud. Remember, you are to answer each question based on your own view of the problem. PLEASE DO NOT SHARE YOUR ANSWERS. When you are finished, hand in your paper, and you can leave. Have a great day!

If you wish, you may use Emilio's Problem Situation (see Appendix D).

Anger Control Training—Anger ABCs Report

Name _____   Date _____

Date/time	A = Antecedent (What led up to the problem?)	B = Behavior (What did you do?)	C = Consequence (What were the results?)

From *Aggression Replacement Training®: A Comprehensive Intervention for Aggressive Youth* (3rd ed.), by B. Glick & J. C. Gibbs, © 2011, Champaign, IL: Research Press (800-519-2707, www.researchpress.com).

Hassle Log and Triggers

OBJECTIVES

- To introduce the Hassle Log and explain its use

- To help group members understand internal and external triggers

- To provide an opportunity for group members to role-play their anger *triggers*

MATERIALS

Easel pad and marker

Copies of the Hassle Log

Poster (on CD): Triggers

Before the session, facilitators should choose and practice a conflict situation to serve as a modeling display.

PROCEDURE

Review

Briefly review the group rules and address any questions or concerns. Remind group members that they increase their personal power by having control over their anger and their reactions to others.

Go over the ABC model of anger control, reminding the group of the three parts involved in each conflict. Ask the group members to discuss examples that occurred in their own lives during the past week.

If you assigned the Anger ABCs Report as homework during Week 1, group members may refer to it.

Hassle Log

Distribute copies of the Hassle Log and ask a different group member to read each numbered item aloud. Discuss. Explain the importance of the log:

- It provides an accurate picture of conflicts that occur during the week.

- It helps group members learn about what makes them angry and how they handle these situations so they can work to change behaviors that cause them trouble and leave them feeling bad about themselves.

- It provides ideas for role-playing in future sessions.

At this point, ask each group member to complete the log for a recent hassle. With your co-facilitator, check the logs and correct any misunderstanding of instructions.

Give group members a supply of Hassle Logs. Instruct them to fill out a Hassle Log as soon as possible after an incident in which they became angry or aggressive.

> *If you prefer, you may designate specific locations for group members to pick up blank Hassle Logs as needed.*

Triggers

Referring to the ABCs of Anger poster from Week 1, explain that in this session, the focus is on the A, or antecedent, also known as a *trigger*. The goal of the session is to help group members identify things that trigger, or arouse, their anger.

Explain that identifying triggers is the first link in a series of steps in an Anger Control Chain and the first step in getting control of your anger. Begin building the chain by writing the word *Triggers* on the easel pad.

> *Save this page—you will be adding the rest of the techniques in the sequence to it as sessions progress.*

TRIGGERS

Refer group members to the Triggers poster and define and discuss both external and internal triggers.

TRIGGERS

External triggers are things someone else does or things that happen that cause us to react with anger or become stressed out.

Internal triggers are things we say to ourselves that increase our angry impulses.

External Triggers

Explain that external triggers may be verbal (for instance, someone tells you what to do or calls you a name) or nonverbal (for instance, someone pushes you or makes an obscene gesture).

Help group members identify external triggers (verbal or nonverbal) that have led them to become angry or aggressive within the last week or two. List a number of these on the easel pad. For example:

- Somebody tripped me up on the court.

- I got accused of doing something I didn't do.

- My boyfriend/girlfriend lied to me.

Internal Triggers

Next explain that internal triggers are what people think or say to themselves when faced with an external trigger. Help group members identify negative self-statements that serve as internal triggers. List a number of these on the easel pad. For example:

- That SOB is making fun of me.

- She's making me look like a wimp.

- I'm going to tear that guy's head off.

Point out that these negative self-statements are the internal triggers that combine with external triggers to lead to high levels of anger and aggressive behavior.

Modeling, Role-Playing, and Performance Feedback

1. With your co-facilitator, model the trigger situation you identified earlier. The situation must include both an external trigger and an internal trigger. Ask:

   - What was the external trigger?

   - What was the internal trigger?

2. For participant role-plays, assign half of the group to look for the external trigger and the other half to look for the internal trigger. (For each subsequent role-play, switch the groups observing external and internal triggers.)

3. Have each group member role-play the situation from the Hassle Log completed at the beginning of this session, including external and internal triggers.

4. After each role-play, have the group identify the two types of trigger.

Closing and Homework

Review the use of the Hassle Log and remind group members of the importance of completing it. Point out the part of the form devoted to triggers (Item 2). Let group members know that they can fill out a Hassle Log any time they find themselves in a conflict situation.

Instruct group members to pay special attention to their triggers and to fill out at least one Hassle Log for a real-life conflict situation before the next Anger Control Training session.

LEADER NOTE

Helping group members identify their internal triggers sets the stage for later sessions, in which they learn how to replace internal triggers that make them angry with positive self-statements or reminders that reduce their anger in conflict situations.

WEEK 2 MORAL REASONING: JERRY'S PROBLEM SITUATION

Reproduce and hand out the Moral Reasoning Situation for the week (see p. 291) and read it aloud. Remind the group that there are no right or wrong answers and that they should not share their responses. Have them answer the questions and return the handout to you.

If you wish, you may use Latoya's Problem Situation (see Appendix D).

Anger Control Training—Hassle Log

Name _____ Date _____

☐ Morning ☐ Afternoon ☐ Evening

1. Where were you?

☐ Classroom/school   ☐ Bathroom   ☐ Community

☐ Dorm   ☐ Office   ☐ Hall

☐ Gym   ☐ Dining room   ☐ On a job

☐ Recreation room   ☐ Outside/grounds   ☐ Other _____

2. What happened?

☐ Somebody teased me.

☐ Somebody took something of mine.

☐ Somebody was doing something I didn't like.

☐ I did something wrong.

☐ Somebody started fighting with me.

☐ Other _____

3. Who was the other person?

☐ Another youth   ☐ Parent/caregiver   ☐ Teacher   ☐ Counselor   ☐ Other _____

4. What did you do?

☐ Hit back   ☐ Ignored it

☐ Ran away   ☐ Talked it out

☐ Yelled   ☐ Used anger control technique *(identify)*

☐ Cried   _____

☐ Walked away calmly

☐ Broke something   ☐ Used social skill *(identify)*

☐ Told an adult   _____

☐ Told peer   ☐ Other _____

5. How angry were you?

☐ Burning   ☐ Really angry   ☐ Moderately angry   ☐ Mildly angry but still OK   ☐ Not angry at all

6. How did you handle yourself?

1	2	3	4	5
Poorly	Not so well	OK	Good	Great

Cues and Anger Reducers

OBJECTIVES

- To help group members learn how to recognize the cues that indicate when they are angry

- To provide group members with response options to calm themselves down: deep breathing, counting backward, and pleasant imagery

- To provide an opportunity for group members to role-play the sequence *triggers (external/internal) + cues + anger reducers (all)*

MATERIALS

Easel pad and marker

Optional: Copies of the My Anger Cues handout

Poster (on CD): Anger Reducers

Before the session, facilitators should choose and practice a conflict situation to serve as a modeling display.

PROCEDURE

Review

Briefly review the group rules and address any questions or concerns, then review group members' completed Hassle Logs. Both facilitators can check to be sure the Hassle Logs are filled out properly. Provide positive reinforcement to those who completed logs and successfully identified triggers (both external and internal).

Cues

Explain that recognizing anger cues is the next link in the Anger Control Chain. Add the word *Cues* below *Triggers* on the easel pad.

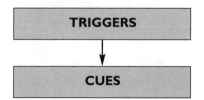

Explain that all people have physical warning signs that let them know they are getting angry—for example, muscle tension, a knot in the stomach, clenched fists, grinding teeth, or a pounding heart. Point out that people must recognize the physical signs that indicate when they are getting angry before they can use self-control to reduce the anger.

Give an example of your anger cues, then encourage group members to identify the cues that signal that they are getting angry. The co-facilitator can write these on the easel pad.

> *If you wish, you may distribute copies of the My Anger Cues handout and ask participants to mark and briefly describe the places in their bodies where they feel these cues. Just be sure you have adequate time for everyone to role-play and finish the group on time.*

Anger Reducers

Explain that using anger reducers is the next link in the Anger Control Chain, and add *Anger Reducers* to the chain.

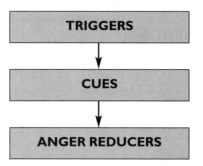

Direct group members' attention to the Anger Reducers poster, then conduct the following procedures.

ANGER REDUCERS

1. Deep breathing: Inhale through your nose, hold for two seconds, exhale through your mouth.
2. Backward counting: Count backward silently from 10 to 1.
3. Pleasant imagery: Imagine a peaceful scene.

Anger Reducer 1: Deep Breathing

Explain that the technique used in deep breathing is taken from the world of exercise and sports—athletes commonly use it to help themselves stay focused. Instruct group members in the appropriate method of deep breathing:

1. Inhale deeply through your nose.

2. Hold the breath you take in for two full seconds.

3. Exhale through your mouth.

Model this technique by performing the deep breathing procedure three complete times. Then invite group members to try (role-play) the technique with you for three more complete breaths.

Let group members know that when they notice cues that they are becoming angry they can use deep breathing to relieve physical tension and reduce their anger.

Anger Reducer 2: Backward Counting

Explain that a second method of reducing anger and increasing personal power in a pressure situation is to count backward silently. Counting backward works because at the same time it calms you down, it gives you time to think about how to respond most effectively.

Demonstrate the correct technique of counting by counting backward, one number per second. After modeling the technique, invite group members to try the technique with you. Let group members know that, if possible, it is best to try to turn away from the provoking person or situation while counting.

Anger Reducer 3: Pleasant Imagery

Explain that a third way to reduce tension in an anger-arousing situation is to imagine being in a peaceful scene, a situation so relaxing that it actually reduces tension and anger.

Model the use of pleasant imagery by closing your eyes, then describing your own relaxing place in detail. For example:

- I'm on a sandy beach. I'm all alone. The sun is hot, but not too hot. There is a slight breeze, and waves are lapping against the shore.

Ask group members to take a moment to think of a scene they find peaceful and relaxing. Have them close their eyes and, in silence, take a minute or two to imagine themselves in this place. For example:

- I am with my girlfriend/boyfriend sitting on the couch in my family room, relaxing and watching a movie. We are talking about things we like to do together, eating some popcorn and just relaxing.

- I am on a lake fishing with my dad and uncle. The water is peaceful, with not a ripple to be seen. The air is cool, and the morning sun is just coming up over the mountains.

Encourage participants to describe their scenes briefly.

Modeling, Role-Playing, and Performance Feedback

1. With your co-facilitator, model the situation you chose earlier to illustrate the following anger control sequence, emphasizing the use of anger reducers:

   Triggers (external/internal) + cues + anger reducers (all)

   Be sure to model all three anger reducers in your role-play.

2. Have each group member choose a conflict situation from a previous Hassle Log to role-play. Give group members the option to try out one, two, or all three anger reducers.

3. Assign specific group members to watch for each step so far in the Anger Control Chain.

4. Conduct the role-play, providing coaching and encouragement as needed.

5. After each role-play, lead the group in giving feedback on the group member's performance, focusing on use of anger reducers. Order of feedback: coactor, observers, facilitators, main actor.

Observer Questions

- Who observed an external trigger? What external trigger did you observe?

- Who observed an internal trigger? What internal trigger did you observe?

- Who observed anger cues? What anger cues did you observe?

- Who observed anger reducers? What anger reducers did you observe?

Closing and Homework

Review each group member's triggers and physical signs of anger (anger cues), along with the three anger reducers. Instruct group members to try out each of the three anger reducers in the coming week in situations in which they notice they are getting angry. They should continue using their Hassle Logs when they find themselves in a conflict situation, filling out at least one before the next Anger Control Training session.

Week 3 Moral Reasoning: Mark's Problem Situation

Reproduce and hand out the Moral Reasoning Situation for the week (see p. 297) and read it aloud. Remind the group that there are no right or wrong answers and that they should not share their responses. Have them answer the questions and return the handout to you.

If you wish, you may use Ishan's Problem Situation (see Appendix D).

Anger Control Training—My Anger Cues

Name _____ Date _____

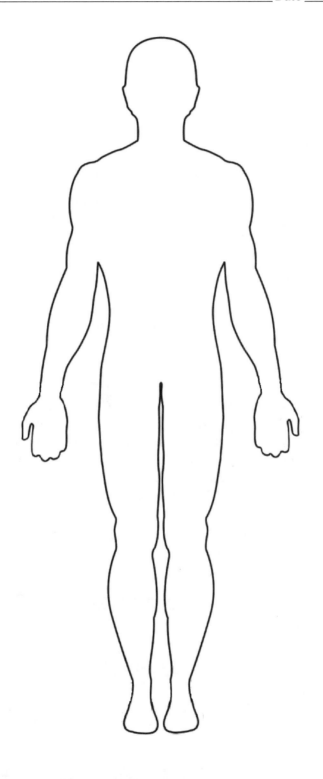

Reminders

OBJECTIVES

- To introduce the concept of reminders

- To provide an opportunity for group members to role-play *triggers (external/internal) + cues + anger reducer(s) + reminders*

MATERIALS

- Easel pad and marker

  Before the session, facilitators should choose and practice a conflict situation to serve as a modeling display.

PROCEDURE

Review

Briefly review the group rules. Discuss anger cues and anger reducers taught during the previous session by going over the Hassle Logs assigned as homework. Provide positive reinforcement to group members who completed logs and attempted to use one or more of the three anger reducers.

Reminders

Let group members know that reminders are self-instructional statements to help increase success in pressure situations of all types. Add *Reminders* to the Anger Control Chain.

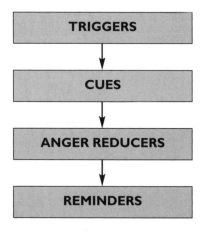

It's helpful to use sports analogies—for example, "Bend your knees and follow through" when making a foul shot in basketball and "Watch out for his left" or "Jab and then hook" in boxing.

Encourage group members to suggest several reminders of this type that they use or could have used in recent anger or conflict situations.

Have the co-facilitator list these reminders on the easel pad as group members generate them. Table 3.2 includes a comprehensive list of reminders for use before, during, and after provocation.

Discuss several examples of how reminders can be helpful in situations in which group members must try very hard to keep calm. For example:

- Cool down.

- Chill out.

- It's not worth it.

- She's my friend and didn't mean it.

Modeling, Role-Playing, and Performance Feedback

1. Model the entire sequence, focusing on the use of reminders:

   Triggers (external/internal) + cues + anger reducer(s) + reminders

2. Have each group member choose a conflict situation from a previous Hassle Log to role-play.

3. Assign group members to watch for each step.

4. Conduct the role-play, providing coaching and encouragement as needed.

5. After each role-play, lead the group in giving feedback on the group member's performance, focusing on use of reminders. Order of feedback: coactor, observers, facilitators, main actor.

Observer Questions

- Who observed an external trigger? What external trigger did you observe?

- Who observed an internal trigger? What internal trigger did you observe?

- Who observed anger cues? What anger cues did you observe?

- Who observed anger reducers? What anger reducers did you observe?

- Who observed reminders? What reminders did you observe?

Closing and Homework

Summarize the use of reminders and the rationale for their use. Point out that using reminders can really help participants take charge of their angry feelings.

Instruct group members to choose the reminders they think would be personally helpful to them and write these on the back of a blank Hassle Log under the heading "My Reminders." They should try using these reminders in the coming week in situations in which they notice they are getting angry. They should continue using their Hassle Logs when they find themselves in a conflict situation, filling out at least one before the next Anger Control Training session.

WEEK 4 MORAL REASONING: GEORGE'S PROBLEM SITUATION

Reproduce and hand out the Moral Reasoning Problem Situation for the week (see p. 302), then read it aloud. Remind the group that there are no right or wrong answers and that they should not share their responses. Have them answer the questions and return the handout to you.

If you wish, you may use Enzio's Problem Situation (see Appendix D).

Thinking Ahead

OBJECTIVES

- To introduce thinking ahead and teach group members the "If-then" formula

- To discuss different types of consequences (short-term/long-term, internal/external)

- To provide group members with a chance to role-play *triggers (external/internal) + cues + anger reducer(s) + reminders + thinking ahead*

MATERIALS

Easel pad and marker

Optional: Copies of the Types of Consequences handout

Poster (on CD): Thinking Ahead

Before the session, facilitators should choose and practice a conflict situation to serve as a modeling display.

PROCEDURE

Review

Briefly remind participants of the group rules. Review the Hassle Logs group members completed since the last session. Ask each group member to evaluate the effect of using reminders on self and others:

- What reminder did you use? ("It's not worth it," "Cool down," "Chill"?)

- Did using a reminder help you gain control of your anger?

- Did using a reminder help you avoid more harmful behaviors—that is, did it keep you from getting into more trouble?

Thinking Ahead

Explain that thinking ahead is a way of controlling anger in a conflict situation by judging the likely future consequences of current behavior. Add *Thinking Ahead* to the Anger Control Chain.

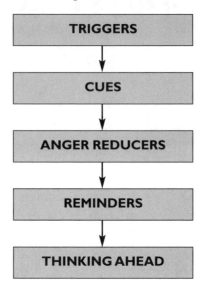

Refer back to the ABCs of Anger poster from Week 1 and explain that thinking ahead helps group members figure out what the C (consequence) will probably be *before* they decide what to do (the B step).

Refer the group to the Thinking Ahead poster, emphasizing that the "If-then" formula will help guide them in their decisions to behave in a particular way by making it easier to identify the C (consequences), both positive and negative, for their actions.

THINKING AHEAD

IF I do this now, THEN this will probably happen later.

- Short-term consequences versus long-term consequences
- External consequences versus internal consequences

Discuss the difference between short- and long-term consequences, encouraging group members to consider long-term results over short-term ones. An example would be the short-term "If I slug him now, he'll shut up" versus the long-term "If I slug him now, I'll be put on in-school suspension for a week" or "I'll be charged with assault and may be placed in a juvenile institution."

Finally, explain the difference between the internal and external consequences of being aggressive. For example, external consequences might include going back to court and having to serve a week of in-school suspension, whereas internal consequences might be feeling terrible about oneself or losing self-respect. Point out that social consequences, such as losing friends or being excluded from a group, are also a kind of external consequence.

It's helpful to point out that negative consequences may serve as additional incentives not to act aggressively.

> *If you wish, you can use the Types of Consequences handout to gauge group members' understanding. Answers: 1 (S, E), 2 (L, E), 3 (S, I), 4 (L, E), 5 (S, E), 6 (S, E), 7 (S or L, I), 8 (S, I), 9 (L, E), 10 (S or L, I).*

Modeling, Role-Playing, and Performance Feedback

1. With your co-facilitator, model the entire anger control sequence, emphasizing your use of the thinking ahead procedure and the "If-then" formula.

   Triggers (external/internal) + cues + anger reducer(s) + reminders + thinking ahead

2. Have each group member choose a conflict situation from a previous Hassle Log to role-play.

3. Assign group members to watch for each step.

4. Conduct the role-play, providing coaching and encouragement as needed.

5. After each role-play, lead the group in giving feedback on the group member's performance, focusing on use of thinking ahead as an anger reducer. Order of feedback: coactor, observers, facilitators, main actor.

Observer Questions

- Who observed an external trigger? What external trigger did you observe?

- Who observed an internal trigger? What internal trigger did you observe?

- Who observed anger cues? What anger cues did you observe?

- Who observed anger reducers? What anger reducers did you observe?

- Who observed reminders? What reminders did you observe?

- Who observed thinking ahead? What "If-then" statement did you observe?

Closing and Homework

Review the reasons to use thinking ahead and "If-then" statements. Remind group members that consequences can be short-term or long-term, internal or external. Instruct group members to complete at least one Hassle Log, using a real situation that occurs during the upcoming week. Have them write "Thinking Ahead" on the back of their logs and instruct them to record an "If-then" statement about the conflict they experience in addition to filling out the log itself.

WEEK 5 MORAL REASONING: SAM'S PROBLEM SITUATION

Reproduce and hand out the Moral Reasoning Situation for the week (see p. 306), then read it aloud. Remind the group that there are no right or wrong answers and that they should not share their responses. Have them answer the questions and return the handout to you.

If you wish, you may use Carmen's Problem Situation (see Appendix D).

Anger Control Training—Types of Consequences

Name _____ Date _____

Circle the letters to show what type of consequence each item is. Consequences may be more than one type.

S = Short term

L = Long term

E = External

I = Internal

CONSEQUENCE		TYPE		
1. Passing a test by cheating	S	L	E	I
2. Getting expelled from school for cheating	S	L	E	I
3. Feeling good when you punch someone.	S	L	E	I
4. Being charged with assault and going to jail	S	L	E	I
5. Getting sanctioned for violating a rule	S	L	E	I
6. Losing canteen for lying about missing curfew	S	L	E	I
7. Feeling guilty for lying	S	L	E	I
8. Feeling powerful when you get over on someone	S	L	E	I
9. Losing someone's friendship	S	L	E	I
10. Feeling lonely	S	L	E	I

From *Aggression Replacement Training®: A Comprehensive Intervention for Aggressive Youth* (3rd ed.), by B. Glick & J. C. Gibbs, © 2011, Champaign, IL: Research Press (800-519-2707, www.researchpress.com).

Self-Evaluation

OBJECTIVES

- To introduce self-evaluation (self-rewarding and self-coaching)

- To provide an opportunity for group members to role-play *triggers (external/internal) + cues + anger reducer(s) + reminders + thinking ahead + self-evaluation (self-reward/self-coaching)*

MATERIALS

- Easel pad and marker

- Poster (on CD): Self-Evaluation

    Before the session, facilitators should choose and practice a conflict situation to serve as a modeling display.

PROCEDURE

Review

Review the Hassle Logs group members completed since the last session. Ask each group member to comment on use of the "If-then" thinking ahead procedure and the effect of using it on self and others:

- What "If-then" statement(s) did you use?

- What kind of consequences did you think about (short-term/long-term, internal/external)?

- How did using thinking ahead help you gain control of your anger?

Self-Evaluation

Refer group members to the Self-Evaluation poster and explain that self-evaluation is a way for group members to judge for themselves how well they handled a conflict situation or hassle and reward themselves for handling it well (self-rewarding)—or help themselves find out how they could have handled it better (self-coaching).

```
┌─────────────────────────────────────────────────────────────┐
│                     SELF-EVALUATION                          │
│                                                              │
│  Self-evaluation means judging how you handled a conflict    │
│  situation or hassle after it is over.                       │
│                                                              │
│  • If you handled it well, reward yourself (self-reward).    │
│                                                              │
│  • If you didn't, figure out how you could have handled it   │
│    better (self-coach).                                      │
└─────────────────────────────────────────────────────────────┘
```

Elicit some statements that group members can use to reward themselves when they handle a situation well (for example, "I really kept cool" or "I was really in control") and to coach themselves when they fail to remain in control in a conflict situation (for example, "I need to pay more attention to my cues" or "I could try counting backward next time").

Have the co-facilitator write these reminders on the easel pad as group members generate them. Table 3.1 lists helpful responses for times conflict is resolved (self-reward) and when it is not (self-coaching).

Modeling, Role-Playing, and Performance Feedback

1. With your co-facilitator, model the entire Anger Control Chain, emphasizing both self-rewarding and self-coaching statements.

   Triggers (external/internal) + cues + anger reducer(s) + reminders + thinking ahead + self-evaluation (self-reward/self-coaching)

2. Have each group member choose a conflict situation from a previous Hassle Log to role-play.

3. Assign group members to watch for each step.

4. Conduct the role-play, providing coaching and encouragement as needed.

5. After each role-play, lead the group in giving feedback on the group member's performance, focusing on use of self-evaluation (self-rewarding and/or self-coaching statements). Order of feedback: coactor, observers, facilitators, main actor.

Observer Questions

- Who observed an external trigger? What external trigger did you observe?

- Who observed an internal trigger? What internal trigger did you observe?

- Who observed anger cues? What anger cues did you observe?

- Who observed anger reducers? What anger reducers did you observe?

- Who observed reminders? What reminders did you observe?

- Who observed thinking ahead? What "If-then" statement did you observe?

- Who observed self-evaluation? What kind of self-evaluation did you observe (self-reward/self-coaching)?

Closing and Homework

Briefly review the two types of self-evaluation (self-reward and self-coaching). Emphasize the idea that evaluating how you did in an anger-provoking situation can help you stay in control in future situations.

Instruct group members to complete at least one Hassle Log, using a real situation that occurs during the upcoming week. Have them write "Self-Evaluation Statements" on the back of their logs and instruct them to record the self-evaluation statements they use in addition to filling out the log itself.

WEEK 6 MORAL REASONING: LEON'S PROBLEM SITUATION

Reproduce and hand out the Moral Reasoning Situation for the week (see p. 310), then read it aloud. Remind the group that there are no right or wrong answers and that they should not share their responses. Have them answer the questions and return the handout to you.

If you wish, you may use Cheri's Problem Situation (see Appendix D).

Angry Behavior Cycle

OBJECTIVES

- To introduce the Angry Behavior Cycle

- To give group members an opportunity to role-play *triggers (external/internal) + cues + anger reducer(s) + reminders + thinking ahead + EXIT (do something different) + self-evaluation (self-reward/self-coaching)*

- To help group members realize that their own behavior can serve as a trigger for others' anger and begin to change their own triggering behaviors by choosing to do something differently

MATERIALS

Easel pad and marker

3- × 5-inch index cards

Posters (on CD):

> Anger Control Chain
>
> Angry Behavior Cycle
>
> Exit the Angry Behavior Cycle: Do Something Different
>
> *Before the session, facilitators should choose and practice a conflict situation to serve as a modeling display.*

PROCEDURE

Review

Review the Hassle Logs group members completed since the last session. Ask each group member to comment on use of self-evaluation statements and the effect of using them on self and others:

- What self-evaluation statement did you use?

- What kind of a self-evaluation statement was it?

- *(If necessary)* Was it a self-reward statement or a self-coaching statement?

• How did using self-evaluation help you gain control of your anger?

Angry Behavior Cycle

Begin by giving personal examples of things someone would do that would be likely to make others angry (for example, calling someone a name, making fun of a person's appearance, dissing an individual's family). Point out that we all have things we "do well" to provoke other people's anger.

Give each group member an index card, and have them think about and list three things they do well to make others angry.

Next ask group members to identify and write down something they could do differently instead of what they currently do to get others angry in each case. Usually it is just the opposite of what they listed—for example, doing an assigned job instead of avoiding it or saying nothing instead of calling someone a name.

Ask the group to put the cards aside for the time being and let them know that they will get back to them at the end of the session. Display the poster of the Anger Control Chain, explaining that the chain lists the concepts in the order the group has learned them.

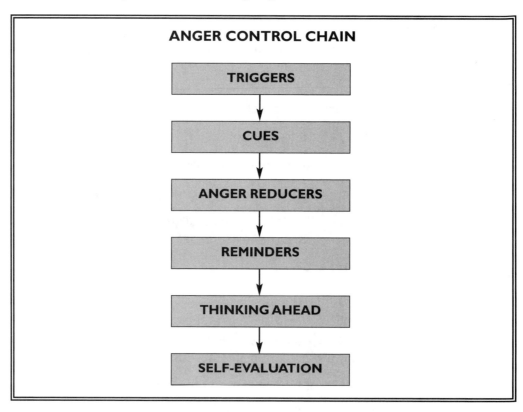

Ask the group what the word *cycle* means, eliciting the idea that a cycle is like a circle—it goes around and around and never ends.

Next display the Angry Behavior Cycle poster and paraphrase the following ideas:

> As you can see, now the Anger Control Chain is an Angry Behavior Cycle. (Point to each concept on the chain and its place in the cycle.) Can you see how our *triggers* cause us to become angry? Our body tells us we are becoming angry by giving us certain *cues,* but once we realize we are becoming angry, we can do things to manage our angry impulses. We can use our *anger reducers.* We can use reminders such as "Keep cool" or "Calm down." We can use *thinking ahead* to the consequences of our actions. Finally, we can use *self-evaluation*—rewarding ourselves if we do well or coaching ourselves to do better if we need to.

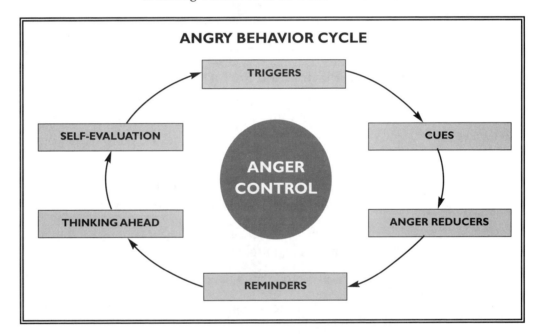

Have the group get out the index cards they filled out earlier, then ask for a volunteer to indicate where on the Angry Behavior Cycle the things they listed that get others angry fall. Point out, if the group does not, that these things are triggers—but they are triggers for *other people* and not for us.

Emphasize that if we do not break the Angry Behavior Cycle somewhere, it will become neverending. Therefore, we want to exit the Angry Behavior Cycle before our actions become someone else's triggers.

Display the Exit the Angry Behavior Cycle: Do Something Different poster and indicate the place where we need to exit the cycle to keep it from continuing.

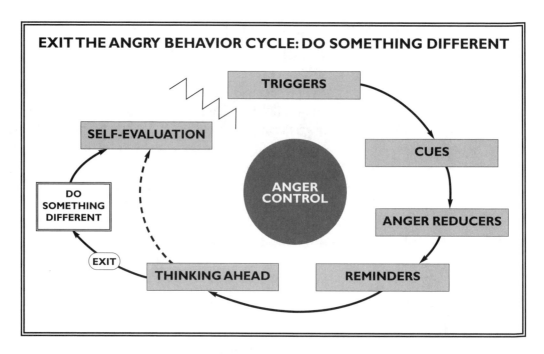

Modeling, Role-Playing, and Performance Feedback

1. With your co-facilitator, model the entire Anger Control Chain again. Be sure to emphasize the change in perspective from what others do to trigger us to what we do to trigger others.

   Triggers (external/internal) + cues + anger reducer(s) + reminders + thinking ahead + EXIT (do something different) + self-evaluation (self-reward/self-coaching)

2. Have each group member choose a conflict situation from a previous Hassle Log to role-play.

3. Assign group members to watch for each step.

4. Conduct the role-play, providing coaching and encouragement as needed.

5. After each role-play, lead the group in giving feedback on the group member's performance, focusing on the change in perspective from what others do to trigger us to what we do to trigger others. Order of feedback: coactor, observers, facilitators, main actor.

Observer Questions

- Who observed an external trigger? What external trigger did you observe?

- Who observed an internal trigger? What internal trigger did you observe?

- Who observed anger cues? What anger cues did you observe?

- Who observed anger reducers? What anger reducers did you observe?

- Who observed reminders? What reminders did you observe?

- Who observed thinking ahead? What "If-then" statement did you observe?

- Who observed doing something different to exit the Angry Behavior Cycle? What did you observe?

- Who observed self-evaluation? What kind of self-evaluation did you observe (self-reward/self-coaching)?

Closing and Homework

Review the Angry Behavior Cycle, emphasizing the importance of using behaviors identified as alternatives to what we usually do to trigger someone else's anger. Stress the importance of changing perspective and focusing on what we do to get others angry in order to exit the Angry Behavior Cycle.

Have group members look at the cards they filled out earlier in the session and choose one of the three behaviors they identified as being something they do that gets someone else angry. Ask them to commit to doing something different from that behavior during the next week. Instruct group members to fill out at least one Hassle Log and to focus on what they did differently.

Week 7 Moral Reasoning: Reggie's Problem Situation

Reproduce and hand out the Moral Reasoning Situation for the week (see p. 314), then read it aloud. Remind the group that there are no right or wrong answers and that they should not share their responses. Have them answer the questions and return the handout to you.

If you wish, you may use Big Bear's Problem Situation (see Appendix D).

LEADER NOTE

This is a critical week in ART, for group members begin to synthesize the concepts they have learned in each of the ART components. Until this point, the focus has been on what to do when other people make group members angry. This session reverses that perspective. It also lays the foundation for what occurs in the next Anger Control Training session—that is, adding a social skill as an alternative to being aggressive or violent.

Using a Social Skill and Rehearsal of Full Anger Control Chain

OBJECTIVES

- To introduce using a social skill in place of aggression to exit the Angry Behavior Cycle

- To give group members an opportunity to role-play *triggers (external/internal) + cues + anger reducer(s) + reminders + thinking ahead + EXIT (social skill) + self-evaluation (self-reward/self-coaching)*

MATERIALS

Easel pad and marker

Skill Cards and Skill Posters (Skills 1–8)

Posters (on CD):

ART Social Skills

Exit the Angry Behavior Cycle: Use a Social Skill

Before the session, facilitators should choose and practice a conflict situation to serve as a modeling display.

Review

Remind group members that last week they learned that things they do may cause others to become angry—in effect, becoming triggers for others. Have group members share their completed Hassle Logs, identifying the Angry Behavior Cycle components and describing what they did to exit it (in other words, the trigger behavior they chose to change of the three they identified in the last session).

Using a Social Skill

Introduce the concept that once group members are able to exit the Angry Behavior Cycle, they can choose one of the social skills they have learned in Social Skills Training to get what they want, maximizing positive responses and minimizing negative responses from others.

Display the ART Social Skills poster. Explain that the group has learned the first eight skills and will learn the last two before the end of the program.

ART SOCIAL SKILLS

1. Making a Complaint
2. Understanding the Feelings of Others
3. Getting Ready for a Difficult Conversation
4. Dealing with Someone Else's Anger
5. Keeping Out of Fights
6. Helping Others
7. Dealing with an Accusation
8. Dealing with Group Pressure
9. Expressing Affection
10. Responding to Failure

Refer to the Exit the Angry Behavior Cycle: Use a Social Skill poster. Explain that now that participants know how to exit the cycle, they can choose one of the social skills they have learned as a way of exiting the cycle. Point out that choosing a skill to get out of the cycle can be a very effective way for them to get what they want without getting into trouble or making others mad. In other words, it can help them stay in control and retain their personal power.

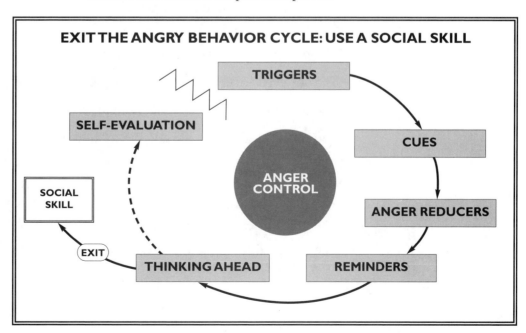

Modeling, Role-Playing, and Performance Feedback

1. With your co-facilitator, model the entire Anger Control Chain, emphasizing exiting the Angry Behavior Cycle by using a social skill. Display the appropriate Skill Poster as you do.

   Triggers (external/internal) + cues + anger reducer(s) + reminders + thinking ahead + EXIT (social skill) + self-evaluation (self-reward/self-coaching)

2. Have each group member choose a conflict situation from a previous Hassle Log to role-play what they will do instead of continuing the cycle and a social skill to use. Provide the appropriate Skill Card and display the related Skill Poster.

3. Assign group members to watch for each step in the Anger Control Chain, as well as each step in the social skill.

4. Conduct the role-play, providing coaching and encouragement as needed.

5. After each role-play, lead the group in giving feedback on the group member's performance, focusing on use of a social skill as a way to exit the Angry Behavior Cycle. Order of feedback: coactor, observers, facilitators, main actor.

Observer Questions

- Who observed an external trigger? What external trigger did you observe?

- Who observed an internal trigger? What internal trigger did you observe?

- Who observed the anger cues? What anger cues did you observe?

- Who observed anger reducers? What anger reducers did you observe?

- Who observed reminders? What reminders did you observe?

- Who observed thinking ahead? What "If-then" statement did you observe?

- Who observed using a social skill to exit the Angry Behavior Cycle? What steps did you observe? (Ask observers of each step for their feedback.)

- Who observed self-evaluation? What kind of self-evaluation did you observe (self-reward/self-coaching)?

Closing and Homework

Remind group members that once they manage their angry impulse and decide not to trigger another person to become angry, they may choose an appropriate social skill instead.

Instruct group members to complete at least one Hassle Log in the upcoming week, using the Anger Control Chain and choosing a social skill to exit the Angry Behavior Cycle.

> *If you wish, you can provide group members with Skill Cards listing the steps for the skill they have chosen to try for homework.*

WEEK 8 MORAL REASONING: ALONZO'S PROBLEM SITUATION

Reproduce and hand out the Moral Reasoning Situation for the week (see p. 319), then read it aloud. Remind the group that there are no right or wrong answers and that they should not share their responses. Have them answer the questions and return the handout to you.

> *If you wish, you may use Tara and Lashonda's Problem Situation (see Appendix D.)*

LEADER NOTE

By this eighth week of ART sessions, both group members and those who work with them generally have experienced a significant decrease in angry outbursts. Also, the number of Hassle Logs that group members need to complete for conflict situations will have been dramatically reduced. Be sure to emphasize that using social skills will help get participants what they want without hurting themselves or others and will maximize positive and minimize negative consequences.

Rehearsal of Full Anger Control Chain

OBJECTIVES

- To provide practice in using a social skill to exit the Angry Behavior Cycle

- To provide group members an opportunity to role-play *triggers (external/internal) + cues + anger reducer(s) + reminders + thinking ahead + EXIT (social skill) + self-evaluation (self-reward/self-coaching)*

MATERIALS

Easel pad and marker

Skill Cards and Skill Posters (Skills 1–9)

Before the session, facilitators should choose and practice a conflict situation to serve as a modeling display.

PROCEDURE

Review

Review the completed Hassle Logs, taking every opportunity to reinforce how well group members have applied the anger control process to manage their angry impulses. Discuss their efforts to exit the Angry Behavior Cycle by using an appropriate social skill.

Modeling, Role-Playing, and Performance Feedback

1. With your co-facilitator, model the entire anger control chain, emphasizing your use of exiting the Angry Behavior Cycle by using a social skill.

   Triggers (external/internal) + cues + anger reducer(s) + reminders + thinking ahead + EXIT (social skill) + self-evaluation (self-reward/self-coaching)

2. Have each group member choose a conflict situation from a previous Hassle Log to role-play. Provide the appropriate Skill Card for reference.

3. Assign group members to watch for each step in the Anger Control Chain, as well as each step in the social skill. Refer them to the appropriate Skill Poster.

4. Conduct the role-play, providing coaching and encouragement as needed.

5. After each role-play, lead the group in giving feedback on the group member's performance, focusing on use of a social skill as a way to exit the Angry Behavior Cycle. Order of feedback: coactor, observers, facilitators, main actor.

Observer Questions

- Who observed an external trigger? What external trigger did you observe?

- Who observed an internal trigger? What internal trigger did you observe?

- Who observed anger cues? What anger cues did you observe?

- Who observed anger reducers? What anger reducers did you observe?

- Who observed reminders? What reminders did you observe?

- Who observed thinking ahead? What "If-then" statement did you observe?

- Who observed using a social skill to exit the Angry Behavior Cycle? What steps did you observe? (Ask observers of each step for their feedback.)

- Who observed self-evaluation? What kind of self-evaluation did you observe (self-reward/self-coaching)?

Closing and Homework

Encourage the group to keep using the social skills they have learned as part of the anger control sequence. Emphasize that doing so and using the other anger control techniques gives them greater power over their own lives.

Instruct group members to complete at least one Hassle Log in the upcoming week, using the steps in the Anger Control Chain and choosing a social skill to use to exit the Angry Behavior Cycle.

If you wish, you can provide group members with Skill Cards listing the steps for the skill they have chosen to try for homework.

WEEK 9 MORAL REASONING: JUAN'S PROBLEM SITUATION

Reproduce and hand out the Moral Reasoning Situation for the week (see p. 323), then read it aloud. Remind the group that there are no right or wrong answers and that they should not share their responses. Have them answer the questions and return the handout to you.

If you wish, you may use Lin's Problem Situation (see Appendix D).

LEADER NOTE

Group facilitators should take every opportunity to reinforce that group members have learned to manage their angry impulses by using the techniques they have learned in Anger Control Training—as a result, they have greater power to get what they want with less hassle.

Overall Review and Rehearsal of Full Anger Control Chain

OBJECTIVES

- To conduct a review of all the techniques in the Anger Control Chain

- To provide additional practice in using a social skill to exit the Angry Behavior Cycle

- To provide group members an opportunity to role-play *triggers (external/internal) + cues + anger reducer(s) + reminders + thinking ahead + EXIT (social skill) + self-evaluation (self-reward/self-coaching)*

MATERIALS

Easel pad and marker

Skill Cards and Skill Posters (Skills 1–10)

Optional: Copies of the Anger Control Chain Review

Before the session, facilitators should choose and practice a conflict situation to serve as a modeling display.

PROCEDURE

Review

Review the completed Hassle Logs to continue reinforcing group members' new ways of handling conflict situations. Celebrate group members' accomplishments, highlighting how well they have learned the Anger Control Chain and applied these techniques to manage their angry impulses. Reinforce how powerful it is to deliberately exit the Angry Behavior Cycle and use an appropriate social skill to get what you want.

Recap of Anger Control Techniques

Review the definitions of and briefly discuss all of the anger control techniques group members have learned so far.

1. Triggers

   • *Internal triggers* are things someone else does or things that happen that cause us to react with anger or become stressed out.

   • *External triggers* are things we say to ourselves that increase our angry impulses.

2. Cues are our physical signs that tell us when we are becoming angry.

3. Anger reducers are techniques we can use to help us calm ourselves down when we realize we are getting angry. We use three: Deep breathing, backward counting, and pleasant imagery.

4. Reminders are statements we say to ourselves to help calm ourselves down even more. They are the opposite of internal triggers because they decrease our angry impulses.

5. Thinking ahead allows us to understand that IF we do something, THEN there will be consequences for ourselves and others.

6. Social skills are things we use to get us what we want, maximizing the positive responses from others and minimizing the negative.

7. Self-evaluation is a way to judge how well we did in managing our angry impulses. We use two kinds: Self-reward is telling ourselves we did a good job, and self-coaching is telling ourselves what we can do better the next time we are in an anger-producing situation.

   If you wish, you can provide copies of the Anger Control Chain Review for discussion and future reference.

Remind the group of the Angry Behavior Cycle, the power of managing their angry impulses, and the effectiveness of using an alternative to what they usually do that triggers others to become angry.

Modeling, Role-Playing, and Performance Feedback

1. With your co-facilitator, model the entire Anger Control Chain, emphasizing exiting the Angry Behavior Cycle by using a social skill.

   Triggers (external/internal) + cues + anger reducer(s) + reminders + thinking ahead + EXIT (social skill) + self-evaluation (self-reward/self-coaching)

2. Have each group member choose a conflict situation from a previous Hassle Log to role-play and a skill to use. Provide the appropriate Skill Card for reference.

3. Assign group members to watch for each step in the anger control sequence as well as each skill step. Refer them to the appropriate Skill Poster.

4. Conduct the role-play, providing coaching and encouragement as needed.

5. After each role-play, lead the group in giving feedback on the group member's performance, focusing on the use of a social skill as a way to exit the Angry Behavior Cycle. Order of feedback: coactor, observers, facilitators, main actor.

Observer Questions

- Who observed an external trigger? What external trigger did you observe?

- Who observed an internal trigger? What internal trigger did you observe?

- Who observed anger cues? What anger cues did you observe?

- Who observed anger reducers? What anger reducers did you observe?

- Who observed reminders? What reminders did you observe?

- Who observed thinking ahead? What "If-then" statement did you observe?

- Who observed using a social skill to exit the Angry Behavior Cycle? What steps did you observe? (Ask observers of each step for their feedback.)

- Who observed self-evaluation? What kind of self-evaluation did you observe (self-reward/self-coaching)?

Closing

As appropriate for your setting, encourage group members to continue using the Hassle Log and following the steps in the Anger Control Chain. Remind them that they now have the ability to get what they want without being aggressive or violent, maximize positive results, and minimize negative reactions from others, thus giving them greater power over their own lives.

WEEK 10 MORAL REASONING: ANTONIO'S PROBLEM SITUATION

Reproduce and hand out the Moral Reasoning Situation for the week (see p. 328), then read it aloud. Remind the group that there are no right or wrong answers and that they should not share their responses. Have them answer the questions and return the handout to you.

If you wish, you may use Emma's Problem Situation (see Appendix D).

LEADER NOTE

If you are following the session order in Table 1.1, at the end of this session let group members know that the next session will be their last. You can discuss any special arrangements and decide how to celebrate their hard work in the program.

Anger Control Training—Anger Control Chain Review

Name _____ Date _____

Write definitions for the following parts of the Anger Control Chain in your own words.

1. **Triggers** _____

   _____

   Internal _____

   External _____

2. **Cues** _____

   _____

3. **Anger Reducers** _____

   _____

   Deep breathing _____

   Backward counting _____

   Pleasant imagery _____

4. **Reminders** _____

   _____

5. **Thinking ahead** _____

   _____

6. **Social skills** _____

   _____

7. **Self-evaluation** _____

   _____

   Self-reward _____

   Self-coaching _____

 From *Aggression Replacement Training®: A Comprehensive Intervention for Aggressive Youth* (3rd ed.), by B. Glick & J. C. Gibbs, © 2011, Champaign, IL: Research Press (800-519-2707, www.researchpress.com).

Moral Reasoning

Introducing Moral Reasoning/Jim's Problem Situation

OBJECTIVES

- To introduce the Moral Reasoning component of ART and explain the procedures for the Moral Reasoning sessions

- To provide a rationale for achieving more mature thinking and facilitate group members' ability to take into account others' perspectives on specific problem situations

- To promote perspective taking, mature moral reasoning, and responsible social decision making on a situation concerning the primary themes of friendship, honesty, and respect for property

MATERIALS

Easel pad and marker

Copies of Jim's Problem Situation (previously completed by group members)

Decision chart for Jim's Problem Situation

> *Before the session, facilitators must familiarize themselves with the problem situation, prepare the decision chart, and analyze group members' responses according to instructions in chapter 4.*

PROCEDURE

Review

Remind participants of group rules; briefly address any issues or concerns.

Introduction to Moral Reasoning

Review the idea that the Moral Reasoning component of ART helps you make responsible decisions that take other people into account. That way you don't do something that either gets you into trouble or that you later regret.

Explain that in this meeting, group members will have a chance to consider how others in the group viewed the problem situation they read earlier and work as a group to come up with a responsible decision supported by morally mature reasoning.

Discussion

Phase 1: Introduce the Problem Situation

Give group members back the problem situation handouts they completed earlier. Ask for a volunteer to read the problem situation aloud, then ask the group:

- Who can tell the group just what _____'s problem is?

- Why is that a problem?

- Do problems like this happen?

- Has anyone had a problem like this?

> *Keep the discussion brief. Once the group understands the problem situation and accepts it as relevant, transition to the next phase.*

Phase 2: Cultivate Mature Morality

1. Refer the group to the decision chart and explain that it shows the answers everyone gave previously to the questions about the situation.

2. Call on all group members who chose the responsible decision to share their reasons for answering the way they did. Have the co-facilitator write down group members' reasons for making the responsible decision on the easel pad.

3. Create discussion first among those group members likely to give mature reasons for their responsible decision.

4. Give less attention to group members who, although they selected the responsible decision, are less likely to support it with mature reasons.

> *Before moving to Phase 3, summarize mature reasons by saying something like "We have a number of good reasons here. For example, the group said (indicate the most mature reasons)."*

Phase 3: Remediate Moral Developmental Delay

1. Bring into the discussion group members who selected the irresponsible decision. Have the co-facilitator write down group members' reasons for making the irresponsible decision on the easel pad.

2. Encourage the more mature moral responders to defend their mature moral positions against less mature suggestions. Ask open-ended questions and provide prompts as necessary to further discussion.

3. Finally, call on participants who "can't decide" to discuss their responses.

Phase 4: Consolidate Mature Morality

1. Ask if anyone would object to declaring the positive majority decision as the group's official decision. Either a facilitator or a responsible group member may circle the majority decision.

2. Continue discussion, attempting to convert as many of the positive majority decisions as possible into official, even unanimous, group decisions.

3. Referring to the reasons listed on the easel pad, orient the group to their most mature reasons for their responsible decisions. Ask the group if those reasons should be underlined as the group's official "best" reasons. Have the co-facilitator underline the reasons.

Closing

If the group reaches consensus on responsible decisions and mature reasons, congratulate them. For example:

> I'm really pleased that this group has been able to come up with so many good, strong decisions and back them up with good, strong reasons. The group has really shown what it can do.

If you are not successful gaining group consensus, you can still praise the group for their effort. For example:

> You have all worked hard at really listening to each other and have made some good progress toward making responsible decisions backed up by good, strong reasons. I really appreciate that. Maybe next time we'll be able to reach a consensus on these decisions and the best reasons for them.

> *At the end of the session, one of the facilitators or a responsible group member may post the easel pad page or pages generated during the discussion, with the most mature reasons for decisions underlined.*

LEADER NOTE

Insofar as possible, all questions for the problem situation should be discussed, beginning with Question 1 and continuing in the order they are presented. Sometimes groups of questions may be presented as a block. If the group agrees on responsible decisions for a series of questions, these questions may be clustered as mature reasons are elicited.

JIM'S PROBLEM SITUATION ANALYSIS

Jim's Problem Situation focuses on the importance of trust in a friendship: How trustworthy is a friend who has a stealing problem? Should you tell on a friend who has stolen in order to give you a gift? Or is stealing all right if it's for a friend? Insofar as this problem situation addresses the value not only of affiliation but also of property, it serves as an excellent introduction to many of the problem situations that follow.

The majority positions tend to be that Jim should tell Scott that the MP3 player is Scott's (Question 1), that Jim would not be able to trust Derek not to steal from him (Question 2), and that it was not all right for Derek to steal the MP3 player even though it was for Jim's birthday (Question 3) or if the MP3 player belonged to a stranger (Question 4). The majority positions tend to be supported by fairly mature reasoning: Jim should tell Scott about the theft because otherwise Jim is letting Derek get away with hurting Scott, because it's the honest thing to do, because Jim would want to be told if he were Scott, and because it would be the way to keep Scott's trust and friendship. Stealing is wrong even if the victim is a stranger because it's against the law and because the stranger is still a person who should be respected instead of hurt. Jim should not consider Derek a good friend because Derek steals things and is untrustworthy: Derek will steal from Jim "the first time Derek thinks he can get away with it." Group members may also suggest that Jim should tell to avoid getting in trouble with Scott.

More pragmatic group members who advocate not telling Scott about the theft may point out that "you'll be out a birthday present" if you tell and that Derek will be angry if he finds out. These group members may also claim that you can trust a friend who steals not to steal from you (Question 2) and, by way of support, claim to have such friends. Because they may be adamant, don't count on achieving a unanimous group decision on Question 2.

The most controversial question, however, is whether Jim should tell on Derek (Question 1). Our groups have often been evenly divided on this question. Group members who favor telling emphasize that Derek took a risk and now has to face up to what he did; if Jim doesn't tell, he becomes involved in Derek's stealing and Derek learns nothing.

Those who favor not telling emphasize that Derek is also a friend (after all, he stole because he wanted to do something nice for Jim), and you should never rat on a friend. They acknowledge the importance of disciplining Derek but caution against getting Scott involved—they will offer lurid descriptions, in fact, of what Scott would do to Derek. Don't expect to persuade the group to reach a unanimous decision on Question 1.

Occasionally, a group member will argue that it would have been all right for Derek to steal an MP3 player for Jim's birthday if only the car hadn't belonged to one of Jim's friends. As noted previously, it is not uncommon for antisocial adolescents to show immature moral judgment, particularly when the persons hurt are strangers. One participant, Joe, explained that if the victim was a stranger, then the theft was "on him"—somehow his fault (i.e., a Blaming Others thinking error).

Moral Reasoning—Week 1: Jim's Problem Situation

Name _____ Date _____

Jim and Derek are high school friends. Jim, whose birthday is coming up, has mentioned to Derek how great it would be to have an MP3 player to listen to music while he goes about his job driving a van. Derek steals an MP3 player from a car in the school parking lot and gives it to Jim for his birthday. Jim is appreciative, not realizing the present is stolen. The next day Jim sees Scott, another friend. Jim mentions that he got an MP3 player for a birthday present. "Great," Scott says with a sigh.

"You look down, Scott. What's wrong?" Jim asks.

"Oh, I was ripped off," Scott says.

"Oh, boy. What did they get?" Jim asks.

"My MP3 player," Scott says. Scott starts describing the stolen MP3 player.

Later, Jim starts thinking about how odd it is that Scott's MP3 player was stolen just at the time Derek gave him one. Jim gets suspicious and calls Derek. Sure enough, Derek confesses that he stole it, and the car he stole it from turns out to be Scott's car!

Scott is on his way over to Jim's to do homework. Scott will probably recognize the MP3 player as his. Scott is at the door, ringing the doorbell.

What should Jim say or do?

1. Should Jim tell Scott that Derek took Scott's MP3 player?

   ☐ should tell   ☐ shouldn't tell   ☐ can't decide *(check one)*

2. How good a friend is Derek? Would Jim be able to trust Derek not to steal from him?

   ☐ yes, could trust   ☐ no, couldn't trust   ☐ can't decide *(check one)*

3. Derek stole the MP3 player for a good cause (Jim's birthday). Does that make it all right for Derek to steal the MP3 player?

   ☐ yes, all right   ☐ no, not all right   ☐ can't decide *(check one)*

4. What if Derek didn't steal the MP3 player from Scott's car? What if instead Derek stole the MP3 player from a stranger's car? Then would it be all right for Derek to steal the MP3 player for Jim's birthday?

   ☐ yes, all right   ☐ no, not all right   ☐ can't decide *(check one)*

From *Aggression Replacement Training®: A Comprehensive Intervention for Aggressive Youth* (3rd ed.), by B. Glick & J. C. Gibbs, © 2011, Champaign, IL: Research Press (800-519-2707, www.researchpress.com).

Jerry's Problem Situation

OBJECTIVE

- To promote perspective taking, mature moral reasoning, and responsible social decision making on a situation concerning the primary themes of relationship and loyalty to friends and to groups

MATERIALS

Easel pad and marker

Copies of Jerry's Problem Situation (previously filled out by group members)

Decision chart for Jerry's Problem Situation

Before the session, facilitators must familiarize themselves with the problem situation, prepare the decision chart, and analyze group members' responses according to instructions in chapter 4.

PROCEDURE

Review

Remind participants of group rules; briefly address any issues or concerns. Note whatever was positive in the group's discussion during the previous Moral Reasoning session.

Discussion

Phase 1: Introduce the Problem Situation

Give group members back the problem situation handouts they completed earlier. Ask for a volunteer to read the problem situation aloud, then ask the group:

- Who can tell the group just what _____'s problem is?

- Why is that a problem?

- Do problems like this happen?

- Has anyone had a problem like this?

*Once the group understands the problem situation and
accepts it as relevant, transition to the next phase.*

Phase 2: Cultivate Mature Morality

1. Refer to the decision chart and remind the group that it shows the answers everyone gave previously to the questions about the situation.

2. Call on all group members who chose the responsible decision to share their reasons for answering the way they did. Have the co-facilitator write down group members' reasons for making the responsible decision on the easel pad.

3. Create discussion first among those group members who are likely to give mature reasons for their responsible decision.

4. Give less attention to group members who, although they selected the responsible decision, are less likely to give mature reasons for it.

   *Before moving to Phase 3, summarize the mature
   reasons.*

Phase 3: Remediate Moral Developmental Delay

1. Bring into the discussion group members who selected irresponsible decisions. Have the co-facilitator write down group members' reasons for making the irresponsible decision on the easel pad.

2. Encourage the more mature moral responders to defend the mature moral position against less mature moral suggestions. Ask open-ended questions and provide prompts as necessary to further discussion.

3. Finally, call on participants who "can't decide" to discuss their responses.

Phase 4: Consolidate Mature Morality

1. Ask if anyone would object to declaring the positive majority decisions as the group's official decisions. Either facilitator or a responsible group member may circle the majority decisions.

2. Continue discussion, attempting to convert as many of the positive majority positions as possible into official, even unanimous, group decisions.

3. On the easel pad, orient the group to their most mature reasons for their responsible decision. Ask the group if those reasons should be underlined as the group's official "best" reasons. Have the co-facilitator underline these reasons.

Closing

If the group reaches consensus on responsible decisions and mature reasons, congratulate them. If you are not successful gaining group consensus, you can still praise the group for their effort.

JERRY'S PROBLEM SITUATION ANALYSIS

Discussion of Jerry's Problem Situation typically promotes a more profound or mature understanding of friendship. Some group members (those who reason at a level no higher than Stage 2) may actually become stimulated to construct Stage 3 moral judgment. For others who already understand and use Stage 3 to some extent, mature reasoning may become more prominent. In either event, at least with respect to the value of friendship or affiliation, this problem situation should facilitate moral judgment development. Also important is the contribution such discussions make to the group itself. Discussion of the value of close friendships seems to promote such friendships in the group and hence contributes to the group's social cohesion.

In our experience, most group members advocate going to Bob's party in response to most questions. The main consideration is that of friendship: Group members point out that Jerry and Bob used to be good friends, and here would be a chance to renew that friendship. An additional consideration is the importance of Jerry's keeping the commitment made to Bob so as to be honest and not let Bob down. After all, in fairness, "Bob was there first when Jerry was lonely, before there was any team for Jerry." Mindful of the friendship, commitment, and/or fairness considerations, group members may suggest that Jerry will feel bad if he goes with the team.

Group members may also make pragmatic points to support going to Bob's party: "Jerry does lots of things with the team, but birthday parties only come once a year" or "Maybe Jerry would like a break from doing things with the team all the time." Pragmatic group members may also suggest that Jerry avoid the problem by attending Bob's party for a while, then catching up with the team. Especially with group leader prompting, pro-Bob group members will counter that leaving early solves nothing: "That's as bad a dump on Bob as not going at all," as one group member once put it.

Group discussion typically reaches the heart of the matter with Question 6; often the choice of "one close friend" is unanimous. Reasons are as follows: "You can tell a close friend anything"; "You need someone you can talk to, who will listen to you"; "You can go to that person with problems"; "Close friends are really friends"; and "A close friend can be trusted not to take advantage of you."

Once a positive peer atmosphere is cultivated through listing and discussion of the reasons for the majority position, attention can turn to the dissenting group members. The few members advocating that Jerry go with the team tend to be unabashed hedonists ("Jerry would have more fun with the team"). They may also try to minimize the harm done to Bob ("Bob won't even notice Jerry didn't come"). These members typically do not care strongly about their positions, however, and will not argue long against majority objections (e.g., that Bob will of course notice). Hence, the choice for going to Bob's party can be made a unanimous group decision on most questions.

The main question on which the majority typically chooses "go with the team" is Question 7, which demotes the relationship between Jerry and Bob from friend to acquaintance. Question 7 makes clear the relevance of Question 6 to the original problem situation, in which Jerry and Bob are friends: Jerry should go to Bob's party because a group of regular buddies just isn't the same as a close friend—and here is a chance to restore such a friendship.

To a lesser extent, the majority may also choose "go with the team" for Question 5, which has Jerry making the first commitment (of sorts) to the team rather than to Bob. Those group members for whom the prior commitment to Bob was the important factor will tend to switch to the "team" response on Question 5.

Moral Reasoning—Week 2: Jerry's Problem Situation

Name _____ Date _____

Jerry just moved to a new school and was feeling pretty lonely until one day a guy named Bob came up and introduced himself. "Hi, Jerry. My name is Bob. I heard one of the teachers say you're new here. If you're not doing anything after school today, how about coming over to shoot some baskets?" Pretty soon Jerry and Bob were good friends.

One day when Jerry was shooting baskets by himself, the basketball coach saw him and invited him to try out for the team. Jerry made the team, and every day after school he would practice with the rest of the team. After practice, Jerry and his teammates would always go out together to get something to eat and sit around and talk about stuff. On weekends they would sometimes take trips together.

As Jerry spends more time with the team, he sees less and less of Bob, his old friend. One day, Jerry gets a call from Bob. "Say, I was wondering," says Bob, "if you're not too busy on Thursday, my family is having a little birthday party for me. Maybe you could come over for dinner that night."

Jerry tells Bob he'll try to come to the party. But during practice on Thursday, everyone tells Jerry about the great place they're all going to after practice.

What should Jerry say or do?

1. Should Jerry go with the team?

   ☐ go with team   ☐ go to Bob's party   ☐ can't decide *(check one)*

2. What if Jerry calls Bob from school and says he's sorry, but something has come up and he can't come over after all? Then would it be all right for Jerry to go with the team?

   ☐ go with team   ☐ go to Bob's party   ☐ can't decide *(check one)*

3. What if Jerry considers that his teammates may be upset if Jerry doesn't come—that they may start to think Jerry's not such a good friend? Then would it be all right for Jerry to go with the team?

   ☐ go with team   ☐ go to Bob's party   ☐ can't decide *(check one)*

4. What if Jerry thinks that, after all, Bob came along and helped Jerry when Jerry was lonely. Then should Jerry go with the team?

   ☐ go with team   ☐ go to Bob's party   ☐ can't decide *(check one)*

5. Let's change the situation a bit. Let's say that before Bob asks Jerry to come over, the teammates ask if Jerry will be coming along on Thursday. Jerry says he thinks so. Then Bob asks Jerry. Then what should Jerry do?

   ☐ go with team   ☐ go to Bob's party   ☐ can't decide *(check one)*

6. Which is more important: to have one close friend or to have a group of regular friends?

   ☐ one close friend   ☐ group of regular friends   ☐ can't decide *(check one)*

7. Let's change the situation a different way. What if Jerry and Bob are not good friends but instead are just acquaintances? Then should Jerry go with the team?

   ☐ go with team   ☐ go to Bob's party   ☐ can't decide *(check one)*

 From *Aggression Replacement Training®: A Comprehensive Intervention for Aggressive Youth* (3rd ed.), by B. Glick & J. C. Gibbs, © 2011, Champaign, IL: Research Press (800-519-2707, www.researchpress.com).

Mark's Problem Situation

OBJECTIVE

- To promote perspective taking, mature moral reasoning, and responsible social decision making on a situation concerning the primary themes of relationship and respect

MATERIALS

Easel pad and marker

Copies of Mark's Problem Situation (previously filled out by group members)

Decision chart for Mark's Problem Situation

Before the session, facilitators must familiarize themselves with the problem situation, prepare the decision chart, and analyze group members' responses according to instructions in chapter 4.

PROCEDURE

Review

Remind participants of group rules; briefly address any issues or concerns. Note whatever was positive in the group's discussion during the previous Moral Reasoning session.

Discussion

Phase 1: Introduce the Problem Situation

Give group members back the problem situation handouts they completed earlier. Ask for a volunteer to read the problem situation aloud, then ask the group:

- Who can tell the group just what _____'s problem is?
- Why is that a problem?
- Do problems like this happen?
- Has anyone had a problem like this?

*Once the group understands the problem situation and
accepts it as relevant, transition to the next phase.*

Phase 2: Cultivate Mature Morality

1. Refer to the decision chart and remind the group that it shows the answers everyone gave previously to the questions about the situation.

2. Call on all group members who chose the responsible decision to share their reasons for answering the way they did. Have the co-facilitator write down group members' reasons for making the responsible decision on the easel pad.

3. Create discussion first among those group members who are likely to give mature reasons for their responsible decision.

4. Give less attention to group members who, although they selected the responsible decision, are less likely to give mature reasons for it.

   *Before moving to Phase 3, summarize the mature
   reasons.*

Phase 3: Remediate Moral Developmental Delay

1. Bring into the discussion group members who selected irresponsible decisions. Have the co-facilitator write down group members' reasons for making the irresponsible decision on the easel pad.

2. Encourage the more mature moral responders to defend the mature moral position against less mature moral suggestions. Ask open-ended questions and provide prompts as necessary to further discussion.

3. Finally, call on participants who "can't decide" to discuss their responses.

Phase 4: Consolidate Mature Morality

1. Ask if anyone would object to declaring the positive majority decisions as the group's official decisions. Either facilitator or a responsible group member may circle the majority decisions.

2. Continue discussion, attempting to convert as many of the positive majority positions as possible into official, even unanimous, group decisions.

3. On the easel pad, orient the group to their most mature reasons for their responsible decision. Ask the group if those reasons should be underlined as the group's official "best" reasons. Have the co-facilitator underline these reasons.

Closing

If the group reaches consensus on responsible decisions and mature reasons, congratulate them. If you are not successful gaining group consensus, you can still praise the group for their effort.

MARK'S PROBLEM SITUATION ANALYSIS

Mark's Problem Situation continues the theme of mature, caring relationships but focuses on the problem of ending a dating relationship that is going nowhere. The main value of this problem situation for moral judgment development arrives with discussion of the last question, which concerns vengeance.

As with most of the problem situations, many group members do choose positive responses. The majority position tends to be that Mark should discuss breaking up (Question 1) rather than making up an excuse (Question 2) or simply starting to date other girls (Question 3).

Accordingly, most of the open-ended suggestions (in response to Question 4) are positive: "Just tell her you'd like to date other girls"; "Be considerate and remember she's human, too"; "Explain how you feel, that you don't want to settle down"; "Listen to what she has to say about it." Of the responses we have heard, our favorite is "I think we should see other people. What do you think?" The group member who gave this response also indicated that he would first try to "work things out" before breaking up with Maria. As to the reasons for bringing the subject up (Question 1), one group member pointed out that Mark "should be man enough to tell her"; if he doesn't, another suggested, "Maria might lose a chance to get another boyfriend" and "would be hurt more in the long run" than by just being told. Speaking more pragmatically (against the idea of simply starting to date other girls), another group member suggested that then those girls could find out how Mark treated Maria and dump him for being a two-timer.

Of course, not all of the responses are positive. On the open-ended question, one group member wrote, "Do things to try to make Maria drop him." Another wrote that he would say, "I'm dumping you, bag!" These group members may also advocate avoiding Maria or making up an excuse. After discussion, however, they are often willing to acquiesce to the majority position and thereby make a positive group decision possible.

An abrupt turnabout occurs on Question 5, in which Mark and Maria are live-in partners with two small children. Then the majority favors not breaking up, on the grounds that Mark has a responsibility to the children (e.g., "The kids should have both a dad and a mom"). If he left "it would hurt the kids, because they would feel it was their fault." One group member suggested, "He loved her once. Why should one argument make him not love her again?" A pragmatic group member pointed out that he might have to pay child support if he leaves.

The majority position continues to be positive on the vengeance questions, 6 and 7. The majority is against either Maria's getting even if Mark breaks up (Question 6) or Mark's getting even if the tables are turned (Question 7). Suggestions are that "Mark should just tell himself that it's her loss"; that "it's no big deal, there are other fish in the sea"; or that Mark or Maria should "let bygones be bygones." Mark "wouldn't want her to get even with him [so he shouldn't do that to her; Stage 3]," and if one of them retaliated "there would just be more trouble." One group member suggested, somewhat ominously, that Mark shouldn't get even because he "might do something really bad and wind up in here."

Count on several group members advocating retaliation, however—especially by Mark against Maria. Reasons have included "Give her a taste of her own medicine" and "He would feel better after he showed her how she hurt him." One group member suggested that Mark should get even because "he'd be mad" and, as further justification, disclosed that he himself had gotten mad and beaten up several girls who had left him for other guys. He remained silent when a peer asked, "Does that make it right?" and asked why he nonetheless thought it was wrong if Maria got even with Mark. Nor would he acquiesce to a group decision against getting even. At least he felt peer group opposition and perhaps for this reason was more accommodating to positive majority positions on subsequent occasions.

It is sometimes helpful to ask the group exactly what is meant by "getting even." Responses range from "showing off [to Maria] with a new girlfriend" to "telling him [the new boyfriend] that she was a good lay for you" to "slashing their tires"—or faces! These responses, once stated for group consideration, will often be branded as immature or destructive by the majority. Nonetheless, many group members will comment that although Mark or Maria—or they—shouldn't get even, they probably would. If the group is still developing, the group leader may need to model relabeling—that is, comment on how much strength and courage it takes not to "give in to childish desires to get even." The degree of positive content may be surprising and should be encouraged. The group leader should comment on the great potential the group has shown for becoming a positive group. Using relabeling, the leader should emphasize that a strong group is one where members care about another's feelings. Bear in mind, however, that the group members expressing more negative sentiments may be speaking more candidly; their words may be consistent with the actual behavior of the majority. After all, consider how common "payback" or vengeance is in the daily life of the troubled school or correctional facility. Similarly, in social skills exercises, the initial absence of caring about another's feelings is striking. Clearly, the group challenge is to accomplish the translation of responsible words into responsible actions.

Moral Reasoning—Week 3: Mark's Problem Situation

Name _____ Date _____

Mark has been in a relationship with a girl named Maria for about two months. It used to be a lot of fun to be with her, but lately it's been sort of a drag. There are some other girls Mark would like to go out with now. Mark sees Maria coming down the school hallway.

What should Mark say or do?

1. Should Mark avoid the subject with Maria so Maria's feelings aren't hurt?

    ☐ should avoid subject   ☐ should bring it up   ☐ can't decide *(check one)*

2. Should Mark make up an excuse, like being too busy to see Maria, as a way of breaking up?

    ☐ excuse   ☐ no excuse   ☐ can't decide *(check one)*

3. Should Mark simply start going out with other girls so that Maria will get the message?

    ☐ yes   ☐ no   ☐ can't decide *(check one)*

4. How should Mark respond to Maria's feelings?

5. Let's change the situation a bit. What if Mark and Maria have been living together for several years and have two small children? Then should Mark still break up with Maria?

    ☐ yes, should break up   ☐ no, shouldn't break up   ☐ can't decide *(check one)*

6. Let's go back to the original situation. This is what happens: Mark does break up with Maria—he lets her know how he feels and starts dating another girl. Maria feels hurt and jealous and thinks about getting even somehow. Should Maria get even?

    ☐ yes, should get even   ☐ no, shouldn't get even   ☐ can't decide *(check one)*

7. What if the tables were turned and Maria did that to Mark?

    ☐ yes, should get even   ☐ no, shouldn't get even   ☐ can't decide *(check one)*

From *Aggression Replacement Training®: A Comprehensive Intervention for Aggressive Youth* (3rd ed.), by B. Glick & J. C. Gibbs, © 2011, Champaign, IL: Research Press (800-519-2707, www.researchpress.com).

George's Problem Situation

OBJECTIVE

- To promote perspective taking, mature moral reasoning, and responsible social decision making on a situation concerning the primary themes of family, loyalty, quality of life, and life itself

MATERIALS

Easel pad and marker

Copies of George's Problem Situation (previously filled out by group members)

Decision chart for George's Problem Situation

Before the session, facilitators must familiarize themselves with the problem situation, prepare the decision chart, and analyze group members' responses according to instructions in chapter 4.

PROCEDURE

Review

Remind participants of group rules; briefly address any issues or concerns. Note whatever was positive in the group's discussion during the previous Moral Reasoning session.

Discussion

Phase 1: Introduce the Problem Situation

Give group members back the problem situation handouts they completed earlier. Ask for a volunteer to read the problem situation aloud, then ask the group:

- Who can tell the group just what _____'s problem is?

- Why is that a problem?

- Do problems like this happen?

- Has anyone had a problem like this?

Once the group understands the problem situation and accepts it as relevant, transition to the next phase.

Phase 2: Cultivate Mature Morality

1. Refer to the decision chart and remind the group that it shows the answers everyone gave previously to the questions about the situation.

2. Call on all group members who chose the responsible decision to share their reasons for answering the way they did. Have the co-facilitator write down group members' reasons for making the responsible decision on the easel pad.

3. Create discussion first among those group members who are likely to give mature reasons for their responsible decision.

4. Give less attention to group members who, although they selected the responsible decision, are less likely to give mature reasons for it.

Before moving to Phase 3, summarize the mature reasons.

Phase 3: Remediate Moral Developmental Delay

1. Bring into the discussion group members who selected irresponsible decisions. Have the co-facilitator write down group members' reasons for making the irresponsible decision on the easel pad.

2. Encourage the more mature moral responders to defend the mature moral position against less mature moral suggestions. Ask open-ended questions and provide prompts as necessary to further discussion.

3. Finally, call on participants who "can't decide" to discuss their responses.

Phase 4: Consolidate Mature Morality

1. Ask if anyone would object to declaring the positive majority decisions as the group's official decisions. Either facilitator or a responsible group member may circle the majority decisions.

2. Continue discussion, attempting to convert as many of the positive majority positions as possible into official, even unanimous, group decisions.

3. On the easel pad, orient the group to their most mature reasons for their responsible decision. Ask the group if those reasons should be underlined as the group's official "best" reasons. Have the co-facilitator underline these reasons.

Closing

If the group reaches consensus on responsible decisions and mature reasons, congratulate them. If you are not successful gaining group consensus, you can still praise the group for their effort.

GEORGE'S PROBLEM SITUATION ANALYSIS

With George's Problem Situation, the stakes are raised with respect to the issue of dealing with an irresponsible friend. Instead of an MP3 player (Jim's Problem Situation), the lives of those who buy drugs from George's brother are at stake.

The majority positions tend to be responsible: George should tell on his brother (Questions 1 through 5), it is sometimes right to tell on someone (Question 6), Jake is to blame in this situation (Question 7), and it is very important for judges to send drug dealers to jail (Question 8).

The reasons for the majority positions tend to be mature. Many of the pro-telling reasons focus on Jake: George would care about Jake; Jake may start taking the drug and die or get messed up himself; Jake could get caught and sent to jail; or Jake could get beaten up or killed in the drug world. Furthermore, Jake is endangering his family because the drug world may get at Jake by killing a member of his family. There is also a concern that Jake is selling a drug that kills, and a particular objection is that he is selling such a drug to kids (Question 3). After reading that Jake actually isn't even helping out the family with his profits (Question 5), some group members may offer the general reason that Jake is self-centered (i.e., is making a Self-Centered thinking error). It is sometimes right to tell on someone (Question 6) when human lives are at stake, as they are with Jake's drug dealing. Jake is the one to blame in this situation (Question 7) because, as the older brother, he should be more responsible and because by selling drugs he has caused the situation (the "Jake" response to Question 7 is often unanimous).

The momentum of responsible reasoning that can be generated through discussion of the earlier questions can be maintained for discussion of the final question (Question 8), concerning the reasons it is "very important" for judges to send drug dealers to jail. Some of the reasoning concerns rehabilitation: "So the dealers will learn a lesson and change"; "So the junkies can get their lives together"; "If they can't find a fix, maybe they'll recover and start using their money to pay their rent." The preponderance of reasoning, however, concerns safety to society: "To make things less violent"; "So people won't die"; "To keep druggies off the streets, protect your family"; "So there won't be so many break-ins"; "To set an example for, send a message to, other drug dealers"; and "To save some kids from being pressured into becoming users and pushers."

George's Problem Situation is controversial, however. After all, many antisocial youths are themselves drug traffickers and identify with Jake. Group members who advocate not telling assert that what Jake does is none of George's business, that George should let Jake learn a lesson, that Jake could be making a lot of money and not be in danger at all, that somebody else will sell the stuff and make money if Jake doesn't, that Jake isn't forcing anybody to buy anything, and that George could get killed if he tells on Jake. Alert majority-position group members can rebut these points: It is George's business if the family is endangered, the "lesson" is too expensive if it's a brother's death, Jake is forcing the drug on 10-year-olds (Question 3) because "they don't know what they're doing," and "Jake is kidding himself if he thinks he's not in any danger—you can't sell drugs and not be in danger." Positive group members may also point out the hypocrisy involved in Jake's not taking the drug himself (Question 4): "He won't hurt himself, but he'll make money off hurting others, dealing death to others."

Some controversy will probably also arise concerning the importance of sending drug dealers to jail (Question 8). Some group members may argue for merely "important" or even "not important" on the grounds that sending drug dealers to jail is "useless" or "hopeless" because you can't send enough of them to make a dent in the problem (an Assuming the Worst thinking error). They may argue that this is exactly how the drug world wants you to think and that avoiding this mistake means doing what you can rather than doing nothing.

Name _____ Date _____

One day George's older brother, Jake, tells him a secret: Jake is selling drugs. George and Jake both know that the kind of drug Jake is selling is highly addictive and causes lung and brain damage. It can even kill people. George asks his brother to stop selling. But the family is poor, and Jake says he is only doing it to help out with the family's money problems. Jake asks his younger brother not to tell anyone.

What should George say or do?

1. Should George promise to keep quiet and not tell on his brother?

   ☐ should keep quiet   ☐ should tell   ☐ can't decide *(check one)*

2. What if Jake tells George that selling drugs is no big deal, that plenty of Jake's friends do it all the time? Then what should George do?

   ☐ should keep quiet   ☐ should tell   ☐ can't decide *(check one)*

3. What if George finds out that Jake is selling the drug to 10-year-olds outside a school? Then what should George do?

   ☐ should keep quiet   ☐ should tell   ☐ can't decide *(check one)*

4. What if Jake himself won't be harmed by the drug—he tells George he knows how addictive and harmful the stuff is and never touches it? Then what should George do?

   ☐ should keep quiet   ☐ should tell   ☐ can't decide *(check one)*

5. What if George finds out that Jake isn't using any of the money at all to "help out the family" but instead is spending it on booze and other things for himself? Then what should George do?

   ☐ should keep quiet   ☐ should tell   ☐ can't decide *(check one)*

6. Is it ever right to tell on someone?

   ☐ sometimes right   ☐ never right   ☐ can't decide *(check one)*

7. Who is to blame in this situation?

   ☐ George   ☐ Jake   ☐ other   ☐ can't decide *(check one)*

8. How important is it for judges to send drug dealers to jail?

   ☐ very important   ☐ important   ☐ not important *(check one)*

Sam's Problem Situation

OBJECTIVE

- To promote perspective taking, mature moral reasoning, and responsible social decision making on a situation concerning the primary themes of honesty and respect for property

MATERIALS

Easel pad and marker

Copies of Sam's Problem Situation (previously filled out by group members)

Decision chart for Sam's Problem Situation

Before the session, facilitators must familiarize themselves with the problem situation, prepare the decision chart, and analyze group members' responses according to instructions in chapter 4.

PROCEDURE

Review

Remind participants of group rules; briefly address any issues or concerns. Note whatever was positive in the group's discussion during the previous Moral Reasoning session.

Discussion

Phase 1: Introduce the Problem Situation

Give group members back the problem situation handouts they completed earlier. Ask for a volunteer to read the problem situation aloud, then ask the group:

- Who can tell the group just what _____'s problem is?

- Why is that a problem?

- Do problems like this happen?

- Has anyone had a problem like this?

Once the group understands the problem situation and accepts it as relevant, transition to the next phase.

Phase 2: Cultivate Mature Morality

1. Refer to the decision chart and remind the group that it shows the answers everyone gave previously to the questions about the situation.

2. Call on all group members who chose the responsible decision to share their reasons for answering the way they did. Have the co-facilitator write down group members' reasons for making the responsible decision on the easel pad.

3. Create discussion first among those group members who are likely to give mature reasons for their responsible decision.

4. Give less attention to group members who, although they selected the responsible decision, are less likely to give mature reasons for it.

   Before moving to Phase 3, summarize the mature reasons.

Phase 3: Remediate Moral Developmental Delay

1. Bring into the discussion group members who selected irresponsible decisions. Have the co-facilitator write down group members' reasons for making the irresponsible decision on the easel pad.

2. Encourage the more mature moral responders to defend the mature moral position against less mature moral suggestions. Ask open-ended questions and provide prompts as necessary to further discussion.

3. Finally, call on participants who "can't decide" to discuss their responses.

Phase 4: Consolidate Mature Morality

1. Ask if anyone would object to declaring the positive majority decisions as the group's official decisions. Either facilitator or a responsible group member may circle the majority decisions.

2. Continue discussion, attempting to convert as many of the positive majority positions as possible into official, even unanimous, group decisions.

3. On the easel pad, orient the group to their most mature reasons for their responsible decision. Ask the group if those reasons should be underlined as the group's official "best" reasons. Have the co-facilitator underline these reasons.

Closing

If the group reaches consensus on responsible decisions and mature reasons, congratulate them. If you are not successful gaining group consensus, you can still praise the group for their effort.

SAM'S PROBLEM SITUATION ANALYSIS

With Sam's Problem Situation, majority positions tend to be responsible: Sam should give the security officer John's name (Questions 1 through 4), it is sometimes right to tell on someone (Question 5), John's to blame in this situation (Question 6), it's very important not to shoplift (Question 7), and it's very important for store owners to prosecute shoplifters (Question 8). The main pragmatic reason in support of telling is that Sam thus protects himself from possible prosecution. Most of the supportive reasons are mature: John was unfair to Sam in getting him into this spot, John's stealing problem will continue until he's stopped and made to think about the consequences, shoplifting makes the prices for everyone go up, the store owner is losing money and will become a popular target if John gets away with it and tells others, the store owner will stop being so nice to kids (Question 3), and John is harming Sam's dad (Question 4). Reasons for the importance of not shoplifting sometimes even reach into Stage 4: "for the sake of order in society" and "because it harms the trust that's needed for society."

Dissenters argue against "ratting on your friend" and suggest that Sam can best stay out of trouble by keeping quiet: "They can't get him—he doesn't have to say anything." These group members may also attribute blame to the store owner (Question 6) on the grounds that the owner should have had customers check things like backpacks before they came in. Note the Blaming Others thinking error in such an attribution.

Name _____ Date _____

Sam and his friend John are shopping in a music store. Sam has driven them to the store. John picks up a CD he really likes and slips it into his backpack. With a little sign for Sam to follow, John then walks out of the store. But Sam doesn't see John. Moments later, the security officer and the store owner come up to Sam. The store owner says to the officer, "That's one of the boys who were stealing CDs!"

The security officer checks Sam's backpack but doesn't find a CD. "OK, you're off the hook, but what's the name of the guy who was with you?" the officer asks Sam.

"I'm almost broke because of shoplifting," the owner says. "I can't let him get away with it."

What should Sam say or do?

1. Should Sam keep quiet and refuse to tell the security officer John's name?

   ☐ should keep quiet   ☐ should tell   ☐ can't decide *(check one)*

2. From the store owner's point of view, what should Sam do?

   ☐ should keep quiet   ☐ should tell   ☐ can't decide *(check one)*

3. What if the store owner is a nice guy who sometimes lets kids buy CDs even if they don't have quite enough money? Then what should Sam do?

   ☐ should keep quiet   ☐ should tell   ☐ can't decide *(check one)*

4. What if the store owner is Sam's father? Then what should Sam do?

   ☐ should keep quiet   ☐ should tell   ☐ can't decide *(check one)*

5. Is it ever right to tell on someone?

   ☐ yes, sometimes   ☐ no, never   ☐ can't decide *(check one)*

6. Who is to blame in this situation?

   ☐ Sam   ☐ John   ☐ he store owner   ☐ other   ☐ can't decide *(check one)*

7. How important is it not to shoplift?

   ☐ very important   ☐ important   ☐ not important *(check one)*

8. How important is it for store owners to prosecute shoplifters?

   ☐ very important   ☐ important   ☐ not important *(check one)*

From *Aggression Replacement Training®: A Comprehensive Intervention for Aggressive Youth* (3rd ed.), by B. Glick & J. C. Gibbs, © 2011, Champaign, IL: Research Press (800-519-2707, www.researchpress.com).

Leon's Problem Situation

OBJECTIVE

- To promote perspective taking, mature moral reasoning, and responsible social decision making on a situation concerning the primary themes of friendship, quality of life, and life itself

MATERIALS

Easel pad and marker

Copies of Leon's Problem Situation (previously filled out by group members)

Decision chart for Leon's Problem Situation

Before the session, facilitators must familiarize themselves with the problem situation, prepare the decision chart, and analyze group members' responses according to instructions in chapter 4.

PROCEDURE

Review

Remind participants of group rules; briefly address any issues or concerns. Note whatever was positive in the group's discussion during the previous Moral Reasoning session.

Discussion

Phase 1: Introduce the Problem Situation

Give group members back the problem situation handouts they completed earlier. Ask for a volunteer to read the problem situation aloud, then ask the group:

- Who can tell the group just what _____'s problem is?

- Why is that a problem?

- Do problems like this happen?

- Has anyone had a problem like this?

Once the group understands the problem situation and accepts it as relevant, transition to the next phase.

Phase 2: Cultivate Mature Morality

1. Refer to the decision chart and remind the group that it shows the answers everyone gave previously to the questions about the situation.

2. Call on all group members who chose the responsible decision to share their reasons for answering the way they did. Have the co-facilitator write down group members' reasons for making the responsible decision on the easel pad.

3. Create discussion first among those group members who are likely to give mature reasons for their responsible decision.

4. Give less attention to group members who, although they selected the responsible decision, are less likely to give mature reasons for it.

   Before moving to Phase 3, summarize the mature reasons.

Phase 3: Remediate Moral Developmental Delay

1. Bring into the discussion group members who selected irresponsible decisions. Have the co-facilitator write down group members' reasons for making the irresponsible decision on the easel pad.

2. Encourage the more mature moral responders to defend the mature moral position against less mature moral suggestions. Ask open-ended questions and provide prompts as necessary to further discussion.

3. Finally, call on participants who "can't decide" to discuss their responses.

Phase 4: Consolidate Mature Morality

1. Ask if anyone would object to declaring the positive majority decisions as the group's official decisions. Either facilitator or a responsible group member may circle the majority decisions.

2. Continue discussion, attempting to convert as many of the positive majority positions as possible into official, even unanimous, group decisions.

3. On the easel pad, orient the group to their most mature reasons for their responsible decision. Ask the group if those reasons should be underlined as the group's official "best" reasons. Have the co-facilitator underline these reasons.

Closing

If the group reaches consensus on responsible decisions and mature reasons, congratulate them. If you are not successful gaining group consensus, you can still praise the group for their effort.

LEON'S PROBLEM SITUATION ANALYSIS

Again, the group faces the problem of dealing with a troublesome friend. Like George, Leon must deal with someone whose actions may be life threatening. Although Leon's friend is not dealing in deadly drugs, he is planning a crime (going AWOL from the institution) in which someone could get killed.

The majority positions with respect to Leon's Problem Situation tend to be responsible. Leon should tell about Raymond's plan (Questions 1 through 3, Questions 6 and 7), it is Leon's business what Raymond does (Question 4), it is sometimes right to "narc" on somebody (as when a life is at stake; Question 5), and what is most important is not letting other people get hurt (Question 8). The majorities are especially strong when the youth leader is Leon's uncle (Question 6) and when Raymond is Leon's brother (Question 7).

Although part of the supportive reasoning for the majority position is pragmatic ("Leon would just get caught and have extra time added"), much of the reasoning is mature: "Leon could prevent someone getting hurt," "It's not worth killing somebody to get out of an institution," "Human life is precious," and "The entire youth group could suffer if Raymond goes AWOL."

A few group members may argue that what Raymond does is none of Leon's business and so Leon shouldn't get involved. After all, Raymond would be knocking off somebody everyone hates (Question 3). Alert majority group members may counter that Raymond has made it Leon's business by telling Leon of his plans, and the youth leader doesn't deserve to get killed.

Moral Reasoning—Week 6: Leon's Problem Situation

Name _____ Date _____

Just after Leon arrived at an institution for boys, he tried to escape. As a result, he was given extra time. It took Leon nearly four months to earn the trust of the staff again. He now thinks it is stupid to try to go AWOL. However, Raymond, a friend of Leon's, tells Leon he is planning to escape that night. "I've got it all figured out," Raymond says. "I'll hit the youth leader on the head with a pipe and take his keys." Raymond asks Leon to come along. Leon tries to talk Raymond out of it, but Raymond won't listen.

What should Leon say or do?

1. Should Leon tell the staff about Raymond's plan to go AWOL?

    ☐ should tell   ☐ should keep quiet   ☐ can't decide *(check one)*

2. What if Raymond is a pretty violent type of guy and Leon thinks that Raymond might seriously injure, maybe even kill, the youth leader? Then what should Leon do?

    ☐ should tell   ☐ should keep quiet   ☐ can't decide *(check one)*

3. What if the youth leader is mean and everyone hates him? Then what should Leon do?

    ☐ should tell   ☐ should keep quiet   ☐ can't decide *(check one)*

4. Is it any of Leon's business what Raymond does?

    ☐ can be Leon's business   ☐ is none of Leon's business   ☐ can't decide *(check one)*

5. Is it ever right to "narc" on somebody?

    ☐ yes, sometimes right   ☐ no, never right   ☐ can't decide *(check one)*

6. Let's change the situation a bit. Let's say the youth leader is Leon's uncle. Then what should Leon do?

    ☐ should tell   ☐ should keep quiet   ☐ can't decide *(check one)*

7. Let's change the situation a different way. Let's say Raymond is Leon's brother. Then what should Leon do?

    ☐ should tell   ☐ should keep quiet   ☐ can't decide *(check one)*

8. Which is the most important?

    ☐ not telling on your friend   ☐ not letting other people get hurt   ☐ minding your own business *(check one)*

From *Aggression Replacement Training®: A Comprehensive Intervention for Aggressive Youth* (3rd ed.), by B. Glick & J. C. Gibbs, © 2011, Champaign, IL: Research Press (800-519-2707, www.researchpress.com).

Reggie's Problem Situation

OBJECTIVE

- To promote perspective taking, mature moral reasoning, and responsible social decision making on a situation concerning the primary themes of family loyalty, honesty, and fairness

MATERIALS

Easel pad and marker

Copies of Reggie's Problem Situation (previously filled out by group members)

Decision chart for Reggie's Problem Situation

Before the session, facilitators must familiarize themselves with the problem situation, prepare the decision chart, and analyze group members' responses according to instructions in chapter 4.

PROCEDURE

Review

Remind participants of group rules; briefly address any issues or concerns. Note whatever was positive in the group's discussion during the previous Moral Reasoning session.

Discussion

Phase 1: Introduce the Problem Situation

Give group members back the problem situation handouts they completed earlier. Ask for a volunteer to read the problem situation aloud, then ask the group:

- Who can tell the group just what _____'s problem is?

- Why is that a problem?

- Do problems like this happen?

- Has anyone had a problem like this?

*Once the group understands the problem situation and
accepts it as relevant, transition to the next phase.*

Phase 2: Cultivate Mature Morality

1. Refer to the decision chart and remind the group that it shows the answers everyone gave previously to the questions about the situation.

2. Call on all group members who chose the responsible decision to share their reasons for answering the way they did. Have the co-facilitator write down group members' reasons for making the responsible decision on the easel pad.

3. Create discussion first among those group members who are likely to give mature reasons for their responsible decision.

4. Give less attention to group members who, although they selected the responsible decision, are less likely to give mature reasons for it.

    *Before moving to Phase 3, summarize the mature
    reasons.*

Phase 3: Remediate Moral Developmental Delay

1. Bring into the discussion group members who selected irresponsible decisions. Have the co-facilitator write down group members' reasons for making the irresponsible decision on the easel pad.

2. Encourage the more mature moral responders to defend the mature moral position against less mature moral suggestions. Ask open-ended questions and provide prompts as necessary to further discussion.

3. Finally, call on participants who "can't decide" to discuss their responses.

Phase 4: Consolidate Mature Morality

1. Ask if anyone would object to declaring the positive majority decisions as the group's official decisions. Either facilitator or a responsible group member may circle the majority decisions.

2. Continue discussion, attempting to convert as many of the positive majority positions as possible into official, even unanimous, group decisions.

3. On the easel pad, orient the group to their most mature reasons for their responsible decision. Ask the group if those reasons should be underlined as the group's official "best" reasons. Have the co-facilitator underline these reasons.

Closing

If the group reaches consensus on responsible decisions and mature reasons, congratulate them. If you are not successful gaining group consensus, you can still praise the group for their effort.

REGGIE'S PROBLEM SITUATION ANALYSIS

Unique among the problem situations, Reggie's Problem Situation concerns parental rather than peer pressure. Furthermore, whereas in peer situations the peer has a negative or irresponsible aim, in Reggie's Problem Situation the mother is at least well intentioned in her questions about the father.

This situation is problematic for groups until Question 3 ("What if Reggie's father drinks a lot when he stops at the bar and then comes home and often beats up on Reggie's mother—sometimes even on Reggie?"); then the majority position tends to be that Reggie should tell his mother what he knows. The majority tend also to choose "what's best for the family" as most important for Reggie's decision (Question 4) and "important" for telling the truth (Question 5). Reasons for telling the truth include the following: By covering, Reggie would be helping his dad become an even worse alcoholic; Reggie should help stop his father's deception and harm to the family; Reggie wouldn't want his mother or himself beaten up (Question 3); the truth will come out sooner or later anyway; someone could get killed by the father's drunk driving. Reasons for the importance of telling the truth are typically mature: You wouldn't want someone to lie to you (otherwise your word would mean nothing), and society is based on truth and trust (an especially mature [Stage 4] reason).

Dissenters emphatically suggest that it was wrong for Reggie's mother to put Reggie on the spot (Question 2) and that getting Reggie involved is too heavy a burden to place on a child—Reggie could feel guilty if his disclosure resulted in a divorce. They may suggest that Reggie could help in a limited way by having a private talk with his dad.

Pragmatically, however, if Reggie tells his mother (Question 1), his dad may beat him up. In response to one group member's minimizing comment ("She shouldn't hassle him just because he had a beer on the way home"), other group members countered that it's rarely just one beer and that they know from their personal experience how often it happens that dad is drunk and violent (Question 3) by the time he gets home.

Name _____ Date _____

"Your father is late again," Reggie's mother tells Reggie one night as he sits down to dinner. Reggie knows why. He passed his father's car on the way home from school. It was parked outside the Midtown Bar and Grill. Reggie's mother and father had argued many times about his father's stopping off at the bar on his way home from work. After their last argument, his father had promised he would never do it again. "I wonder why your father is late," Reggie's mother says. "Do you think I should trust what he said about not drinking anymore? Do you think he stopped off at the bar again?" Reggie's mother asks him.

What should Reggie say or do?

1. Should Reggie cover for his father by lying to his mother?

   ☐ yes, should cover   ☐ no, should tell the truth   ☐ can't decide *(check one)*

2. Was it right for Reggie's mother to put Reggie on the spot by asking him a question about his father?

   ☐ yes, right   ☐ no, wrong   ☐ can't decide *(check one)*

3. What if Reggie's father drinks a lot when he stops at the bar and then comes home and often beats up on Reggie's mother—sometimes even on Reggie? Then what should Reggie do?

   ☐ should cover for him   ☐ should tell the truth   ☐ can't decide *(check one)*

4. Which is most important for Reggie's decision?

   ☐ what's best for himself   ☐ what's best for his mom   ☐ what's best for his dad
   ☐ what's best for the family *(check one)*

5. In general, how important is it to tell the truth?

   ☐ very important   ☐ important   ☐ not important *(check one)*

From *Aggression Replacement Training®: A Comprehensive Intervention for Aggressive Youth* (3rd ed.), by B. Glick & J. C. Gibbs, © 2011, Champaign, IL: Research Press (800-519-2707, www.researchpress.com).

Alonzo's Problem Situation

OBJECTIVE

- To promote perspective taking, mature moral reasoning, and responsible social decision making on a situation concerning the primary themes of honesty and loyalty to friends

MATERIALS

Easel pad and marker

Copies of Alonzo's Problem Situation (previously filled out by group members)

Decision chart for Alonzo's Problem Situation

Before the session, facilitators must familiarize themselves with the problem situation, prepare the decision chart, and analyze group members' responses according to instructions in chapter 4.

PROCEDURE

Review

Remind participants of group rules; briefly address any issues or concerns. Note whatever was positive in the group's discussion during the previous Moral Reasoning session.

Discussion

Phase 1: Introduce the Problem Situation

Give group members back the problem situation handouts they completed earlier. Ask for a volunteer to read the problem situation aloud, then ask the group:

- Who can tell the group just what _____'s problem is?
- Why is that a problem?
- Do problems like this happen?
- Has anyone had a problem like this?

Once the group understands the problem situation and accepts it as relevant, transition to the next phase.

Phase 2: Cultivate Mature Morality

1. Refer to the decision chart and remind the group that it shows the answers everyone gave previously to the questions about the situation.

2. Call on all group members who chose the responsible decision to share their reasons for answering the way they did. Have the co-facilitator write down group members' reasons for making the responsible decision on the easel pad.

3. Create discussion first among those group members who are likely to give mature reasons for their responsible decision.

4. Give less attention to group members who, although they selected the responsible decision, are less likely to give mature reasons for it.

   Before moving to Phase 3, summarize the mature reasons.

Phase 3: Remediate Moral Developmental Delay

1. Bring into the discussion group members who selected irresponsible decisions. Have the co-facilitator write down group members' reasons for making the irresponsible decision on the easel pad.

2. Encourage the more mature moral responders to defend the mature moral position against less mature moral suggestions. Ask open-ended questions and provide prompts as necessary to further discussion.

3. Finally, call on participants who "can't decide" to discuss their responses.

Phase 4: Consolidate Mature Morality

1. Ask if anyone would object to declaring the positive majority decisions as the group's official decisions. Either facilitator or a responsible group member may circle the majority decisions.

2. Continue discussion, attempting to convert as many of the positive majority positions as possible into official, even unanimous, group decisions.

3. On the easel pad, orient the group to their most mature reasons for their responsible decision. Ask the group if those reasons should be underlined as the group's official "best" reasons. Have the co-facilitator underline these reasons.

Closing

If the group reaches consensus on responsible decisions and mature reasons, congratulate them. If you are not successful gaining group consensus, you can still praise the group for their effort.

ALONZO'S PROBLEM SITUATION ANALYSIS

Like Jim in the earlier problem situation, Alonzo must contend with a friend who has a stealing problem. The majority position is that Alonzo should try to persuade Rodney not to steal the car (Questions 1 through 6) and that it is very important not to steal (Question 7).

Mature reasons appeal to the danger and harm to innocent people, including the car owner; to the way one would feel if it were one's own car (a consideration often inspired by Question 6); to the guilt one would feel if one did join Rodney; to the fact that prices have to go up to cover crime; and to the loss of order that would result if everyone stole. In response to the Blaming Others thinking error implied in Question 2, group members may respond, "Everyone's careless at one time or another. That doesn't mean you deserve to get your car stolen." There is concern for what will happen to Rodney's family in Question 5. Pragmatic reasons for not stealing or joining Rodney are also prominent, however: "Alonzo could go to jail, so it's not worth the risk"; "There'd be nothing to do in jail"; "Alonzo could get shot or killed"; "The car owner could get even"; "You wouldn't be able to stop Rodney anyway"; "You'd be drunk and wouldn't care what Rodney did"; "This could even be a set-up against Alonzo"; and "Rodney's a fool and deserves whatever happens to him."

One hears both mature and pragmatic reasons, then, in support of the majority positions. For the opposing positions ("Let Rodney steal it"; "It's not important for people not to steal"), however, pragmatic considerations constitute practically the sum total of reasons—for example, "You'd be a big shot"; "You could have lots of fun"; "It's exciting to steal and get away with it"; "You could get money and booze and girls and do whatever you want"; "If you needed to go somewhere, now you could drive" (a Self-Centered thinking error). Pragmatic group members acknowledge that you could get caught for stealing, but they suggest that that's why it's important for you to "know what you're doing" and "act confident"—so you won't get caught. Thinking errors are plentiful in the pragmatic reasoning: for example, "Everyone steals anyway"; "You'd teach the car owner a good lesson, not to be so careless"; and "The car owner is a dummy, fool, or jerk [for leaving the keys]" (Minimizing/Mislabeling). If group members don't catch and correct these thinking errors, the group leader should intervene to do so.

Question 8 suggests that Rodney goes ahead and—in an intoxicated state—steals the car. Should Alonzo contact the police? Many group members who have persistently advocated trying to persuade Rodney not to steal the car will nonetheless choose against contacting the police because it would mean ratting on a friend and getting him in trouble. They will urge getting Rodney home so he can sleep off his high (alert peers will point out that it's too late for that—Rodney has already stolen the car). Group members who advocate calling the police tend to emphasize the dangers of drunk driving and Rodney's irresponsibility to his family, and they argue that a true friend would contact the police.

Alonzo's Problem Situation is an especially good situation for discussing the gap between moral judgment and moral action. Many group members who proffer superbly mature and compelling reasons for trying to persuade Alonzo against stealing the car will disclose at some point in the discussion that they would probably join Rodney: "I know I shouldn't, but I probably would." The group leader should listen actively but also relabel: "That's right, this is a tough situation to keep your head in. It does take a lot of guts to say no and do the right thing." The group leader can also remind the group of the skill Dealing with Group Pressure, taught during this week.

Moral Reasoning—Week 8: Alonzo's Problem Situation

Name _____ Date _____

Alonzo is walking along a side street with his friend Rodney. Rodney stops in front of a beautiful new sports car. Rodney looks inside and then says excitedly, "Look! The keys are still in this thing! Let's see what it can do! Come on, let's go!"

What should Alonzo say or do?

1. Should Alonzo try to persuade Rodney not to steal the car?

   ☐ should persuade   ☐ should let steal   ☐ can't decide *(check one)*

2. What if Rodney says to Alonzo that the keys were left in the car, that anyone that careless deserves to get ripped off? Then should Alonzo try to persuade Rodney not to steal the car?

   ☐ should persuade   ☐ should let steal   ☐ can't decide *(check one)*

3. What if Rodney says to Alonzo that the car's owner can probably get insurance money to cover most of the loss? Then should Alonzo try to persuade Rodney not to steal the car?

   ☐ should persuade   ☐ should let steal   ☐ can't decide *(check one)*

4. What if Rodney tells Alonzo that stealing a car is no big deal, that plenty of his friends do it all the time? Then what should Alonzo do?

   ☐ should persuade   ☐ should let steal   ☐ can't decide *(check one)*

5. What if Alonzo knows that Rodney has a wife and child who will suffer if Rodney gets caught, loses his job, and goes to jail? Then should Alonzo try to persuade Rodney not to steal the car?

   ☐ should persuade   ☐ should let steal   ☐ can't decide *(check one)*

6. Let's say the car is your car. Alonzo is Rodney's friend, but Alonzo is also your friend. Alonzo knows it's your car. Then should Alonzo try to persuade Rodney not to steal the car?

   ☐ should persuade   ☐ should let steal   ☐ can't decide *(check one)*

7. In general, how important is it for people not to take things that belong to others?

   ☐ very important   ☐ important   ☐ not important *(check one)*

8. Let's say that Alonzo does try to persuade Rodney not to take the car, but Rodney goes ahead and takes it anyway. Alonzo knows Rodney's in bad shape from being high—he could have a serious accident and someone could get killed. Then what should Alonzo do?

   ☐ should contact the police   ☐ should not contact the police   ☐ can't decide *(check one)*

From *Aggression Replacement Training®: A Comprehensive Intervention for Aggressive Youth* (3rd ed.), by B. Glick & J. C. Gibbs, © 2011, Champaign, IL: Research Press (800-519-2707, www.researchpress.com).

Juan's Problem Situation

OBJECTIVE

- To promote perspective taking, mature moral reasoning, and responsible social decision making on a situation concerning the primary themes of loyalty to friends and life itself

MATERIALS

Easel pad and marker

Copies of Juan's Problem Situation (previously filled out by group members)

Decision chart for Juan's Problem Situation

Before the session, facilitators must familiarize themselves with the problem situation, prepare the decision chart, and analyze group members' responses according to instructions in chapter 4.

PROCEDURE

Review

Remind participants of group rules; briefly address any issues or concerns. Note whatever was positive in the group's discussion during the previous Moral Reasoning session.

Discussion

Phase 1: Introduce the Problem Situation

Give group members back the problem situation handouts they completed earlier. Ask for a volunteer to read the problem situation aloud, then ask the group:

- Who can tell the group just what _____'s problem is?

- Why is that a problem?

- Do problems like this happen?

- Has anyone had a problem like this?

Once the group understands the problem situation and accepts it as relevant, transition to the next phase.

Phase 2: Cultivate Mature Morality

1. Refer to the decision chart and remind the group that it shows the answers everyone gave previously to the questions about the situation.

2. Call on all group members who chose the responsible decision to share their reasons for answering the way they did. Have the co-facilitator write down group members' reasons for making the responsible decision on the easel pad.

3. Create discussion first among those group members who are likely to give mature reasons for their responsible decision.

4. Give less attention to group members who, although they selected the responsible decision, are less likely to give mature reasons for it.

   Before moving to Phase 3, summarize the mature reasons.

Phase 3: Remediate Moral Developmental Delay

1. Bring into the discussion group members who selected irresponsible decisions. Have the co-facilitator write down group members' reasons for making the irresponsible decision on the easel pad.

2. Encourage the more mature moral responders to defend the mature moral position against less mature moral suggestions. Ask open-ended questions and provide prompts as necessary to further discussion.

3. Finally, call on participants who "can't decide" to discuss their responses.

Phase 4: Consolidate Mature Morality

1. Ask if anyone would object to declaring the positive majority decisions as the group's official decisions. Either facilitator or a responsible group member may circle the majority decisions.

2. Continue discussion, attempting to convert as many of the positive majority positions as possible into official, even unanimous, group decisions.

3. On the easel pad, orient the group to their most mature reasons for their responsible decision. Ask the group if those reasons should be underlined as the group's official "best" reasons. Have the co-facilitator underline these reasons.

Closing

If the group reaches consensus on responsible decisions and mature reasons, congratulate them. If you are not successful gaining group consensus, you can still praise the group for their effort.

JUAN'S PROBLEM SITUATION ANALYSIS

How to deal with an irresponsible friend is again the problem. With Juan's Problem Situation, however, the life threatened by the friend's activity is not someone else's (as with George's Problem Situation) but instead the friend's own life.

The majority positions tend to be positive: that Juan should tell the youth leader (Questions 1, 2, 4, and 5), that rules against contraband are very important (Question 6), and that it is very important to live even when you don't want to (Question 7). Pragmatic reasons for telling are that you can get in trouble if you don't tell and that you might get hurt—Phil might cut you with a razor blade. Following are some mature reasons we have heard: Juan should care about Phil; telling might enable Phil to get some help before he hurts himself; any life is precious and worth saving; Phil's family and friends will be hurt if Phil kills himself; you wouldn't want to watch someone kill himself; you'd feel guilty if you knew you could have done something and didn't. Living even when you don't want to is very important because things get better and there's a lot to live for; there's a reason you're here; there are things to do and see; committing suicide is selfish—you're thinking only about yourself (note the Self-Centered thinking error); think how your family would feel; consider that you may change your mind. Family—especially parents—are mentioned prominently in response to Question 8, "Who might be affected (in addition to Phil himself) if Phil were to commit suicide?" The majority of the group members may also rate rules against contraband "very important" because some things are dangerous to both oneself and others.

A few group members may advocate covering for Phil on the grounds that Juan should mind his own business and not get involved. One is especially likely to see "cover" responses in connection with Question 4 ("What if Phil has been a real pest?"): Then "you couldn't care less what happens to him." These group members may also assert that living even when you don't want to (Question 7) is not important because "it's your life—you can do whatever you want with it." One group member asserted that rules against contraband are not important because "I want to smoke and stuff" (another Self-Centered thinking error).

Moral Reasoning—Week 9: Juan's Problem Situation

Name _____ Date _____

Juan and Phil are roommates at a juvenile institution. They get along well and have become good friends. Phil has confided that he has been getting pretty depressed lately and has managed to get hold of some razor blades. Juan sees where Phil hides the blades. The youth leader, having learned of the razor blades, searches their room but doesn't find them. So the youth leader asks Juan where the razor blades are hidden.

What should Juan say or do?

1. Should Juan cover for Phil, saying he doesn't know anything about any razor blades?

   ☐ should cover for Phil   ☐ should tell the leader   ☐ can't decide *(check one)*

2. What if Phil has told Juan that he plans to cut his wrists with the razor blades that night? Then what should Juan do?

   ☐ should cover for Phil   ☐ should tell the leader   ☐ can't decide *(check one)*

3. Would Phil feel that Juan cared about him if Juan told?

   ☐ yes, would feel Juan cared   ☐ no, would not feel Juan cared   ☐ can't decide *(check one)*

4. What if Juan and Phil actually don't get along well and are not friends? What if Phil has been a real pest? Then what should Juan do?

   ☐ should cover for Phil   ☐ should tell the leader   ☐ can't decide *(check one)*

5. What if Juan isn't Phil's roommate but does know about the razor blades and where they are? The youth leader suspects Juan knows something and asks him about the razor blades. Then what should Juan do?

   ☐ should cover for Phil   ☐ should tell the leader   ☐ can't decide *(check one)*

6. How important is it for a juvenile institution to have rules against contraband?

   ☐ very important   ☐ important   ☐ not important *(check one)*

7. How important is it to live even when you don't want to?

   ☐ very important   ☐ important   ☐ not important *(check one)*

8. Who might be affected (in addition to Phil himself) if Phil were to commit suicide?

Antonio's Problem Situation/Program Conclusion

OBJECTIVE

- To promote perspective taking, mature moral reasoning, and responsible social decision making on a situation concerning the primary themes of honesty, fairness, and negative peer pressure

- To conclude and celebrate the ART group

MATERIALS

Easel pad and marker

Copies of Antonio's Problem Situation (previously filled out by group members)

Decision chart for Antonio's Problem Situation

Copies of the Certificate of ART Completion

> *Before the session, facilitators must familiarize themselves with the problem situation, prepare the decision chart, and analyze group members' responses according to instructions in chapter 4.*

PROCEDURE

Review

Remind participants of group rules; briefly address any issues or concerns. Note whatever was positive in the group's discussion during the previous Moral Reasoning session.

Discussion

Phase 1: Introduce the Problem Situation

Give group members back the problem situation handouts they completed earlier. Ask for a volunteer to read the problem situation aloud, then ask the group:

- Who can tell the group just what _____'s problem is?

- Why is that a problem?

- Do problems like this happen?

- Has anyone had a problem like this?

> *Once the group understands the problem situation and accepts it as relevant, transition to the next phase.*

Phase 2: Cultivate Mature Morality

1. Refer to the decision chart and remind the group that it shows the answers everyone gave previously to the questions about the situation.

2. Call on all group members who chose the responsible decision to share their reasons for answering the way they did. Have the co-facilitator write down group members' reasons for making the responsible decision on the easel pad.

3. Create discussion first among those group members who are likely to give mature reasons for their responsible decision.

4. Give less attention to group members who, although they selected the responsible decision, are less likely to give mature reasons for it.

> *Before moving to Phase 3, summarize the mature reasons.*

Phase 3: Remediate Moral Developmental Delay

1. Bring into the discussion group members who selected irresponsible decisions. Have the co-facilitator write down group members' reasons for making the irresponsible decision on the easel pad.

2. Encourage the more mature moral responders to defend the mature moral position against less mature moral suggestions. Ask open-ended questions and provide prompts as necessary to further discussion.

3. Finally, call on participants who "can't decide" to discuss their responses.

Phase 4: Consolidate Mature Morality

1. Ask if anyone would object to declaring the positive majority decisions as the group's official decisions. Either facilitator or a responsible group member may circle the majority decisions.

2. Continue discussion, attempting to convert as many of the positive majority positions as possible into official, even unanimous, group decisions.

3. On the easel pad, orient the group to their most mature reasons for their responsible decision. Ask the group if those reasons should be underlined as the group's official "best" reasons. Have the co-facilitator underline these reasons.

Closing

If the group reaches consensus on responsible decisions and mature reasons, congratulate them. If you are not successful gaining group consensus, you can still praise the group for their effort.

Celebrating the Program

1. Praise the group for their hard work during the ART sessions. Remind them that what they have learned will help them increase their personal power and be better respected by their peers, teachers, parents, and other significant adults. Emphasize that each group member is now empowered to use appropriate social skills instead of doing the things that got them in trouble, stay in control of their anger, and make good decisions about tough situations.

2. Hand out the Certificates of ART Completion. If you wish, you may have each group member come to the front of the group and congratulate each one individually.

ANTONIO'S PROBLEM SITUATION ANALYSIS

Antonio's Problem Situation returns to the theme of negative peer pressure, in this case from a friend who wants to cheat on a test. Majority positions tend to be that Antonio should not let Ed cheat (Questions 1 through 3, Question 6), that the respondent in the position of the teacher would not want Ed to cheat (Question 4; this position may be unanimous from the outset), that a close relationship with someone who cheats is not possible (Question 5), that it's very important not to cheat (Question 7), and that it is right for teachers to punish cheaters (Question 8). Pragmatic reasons are that the teacher might come back unexpectedly and catch both of you and that if Ed isn't caught he might wind up with a grade higher than yours. Mature reasons are that it's unfair for Ed to get the benefit of Antonio's work, that letting Ed cheat will encourage his attitude that he can let other people do his work for him (a Self-Centered thinking error), that Ed deserves to flunk and needs to learn a lesson, that Ed is hurting himself in the long run by cheating instead of learning, that Ed is also hurting his parents, and that the teacher has placed trust in Ed and you and you are on your honor not to cheat. One cannot have a close relationship with a person who cheats (Question 5) because "you never know when they might be planning to cheat you." Teachers need to punish cheaters (Question 8) because otherwise "there would be no order in the classroom."

Thinking errors are apparent in the arguments of dissenters: "There's nothing wrong with giving a little help to a friend" (a Minimizing/ Mislabeling thinking error); "It's the teacher's fault for leaving the room" (a Blaming Others thinking error).

Moral Reasoning—Week 10: Antonio's Problem Situation

Name _____ Date _____

Antonio is in school taking a math test. Suddenly, the teacher says, "I'm going to leave the room for a few minutes. You are on your honor not to cheat." After the teacher has gone, Ed, Antonio's friend, whispers to him, "Let me see your answers, Antonio."

What should Antonio say or do?

1. Should Antonio let Ed copy his answers?

   ☐ yes, let cheat   ☐ no, don't let cheat   ☐ can't decide *(check one)*

2. What if Ed whispers that cheating is no big deal, that he knows plenty of guys who cheat all the time? Then should Antonio let Ed cheat?

   ☐ yes, let cheat   ☐ no, don't let cheat   ☐ can't decide *(check one)*

3. What if Antonio knows that Ed is flunking because he doesn't study? Then should Antonio let Ed cheat?

   ☐ yes, let cheat   ☐ no, don't let cheat   ☐ can't decide *(check one)*

4. What if you were the teacher? Would you want Antonio to let Ed cheat?

   ☐ yes, let cheat   ☐ no, don't let cheat   ☐ can't decide *(check one)*

5. Is it possible to have a really close, trusting friendship with someone who has a cheating or lying problem?

   ☐ yes, possible   ☐ no, not possible   ☐ can't decide *(check one)*

6. Let's change the situation a little. What if Antonio hardly knows Ed? Then should Antonio let Ed cheat?

   ☐ yes, let cheat   ☐ no, don't let cheat   ☐ can't decide *(check one)*

7. In general, how important is it not to cheat?

   ☐ very important   ☐ important   ☐ not important *(check one)*

8. Is it right for teachers to punish cheaters?

   ☐ yes, right   ☐ no, not right   ☐ can't decide *(check one)*

From *Aggression Replacement Training®: A Comprehensive Intervention for Aggressive Youth* (3rd ed.), by B. Glick & J. C. Gibbs, © 2011, Champaign, IL: Research Press (800-519-2707, www.researchpress.com).

ART

Certificate of Completion

Presented to

_____

Presented by _____

Date _____

From *Aggression Replacement Training®: A Comprehensive Intervention for Aggressive Youth* (3rd ed.), by B. Glick & J. C. Gibbs, © 2011, Champaign, IL: Research Press (800-519-2707, www.researchpress.com).

Skillstreaming Curriculum for Adolescents

Skillstreaming Skills for Adolescents

An asterisk appears before ART social skills.

Group 1: Beginning Social Skills

Skill 1: Listening

SKILL STEPS

1. Look at the person who is talking.

2. Think about what is being said.

3. Wait your turn to talk.

4. Say what you want to say.

Skill 2: Starting a Conversation

SKILL STEPS

1. Greet the other person.

2. Make small talk.

3. Decide if the other person is listening.

4. Bring up the main topic.

Skill 3: Having a Conversation

SKILL STEPS

1. Say what you want to say.

2. Ask the other person what he/she thinks.

3. Listen to what the other person says.

4. Say what you think.

5. Make a closing remark.

Skill 4: Asking a Question

SKILL STEPS

1. Decide what you'd like to know more about.

2. Decide whom to ask.

3. Think about different ways to ask your question and pick one way.

4. Pick the right time and place to ask your question.

5. Ask your question.

Skill 5: Saying Thank You

SKILL STEPS

1. Decide if the other person said or did something that you want to thank him/her for.

2. Choose a good time and place to thank the other person.

3. Thank the other person in a friendly way.

4. Tell the other person why you are thanking him/her.

Skill 6: Introducing Yourself

SKILL STEPS

1. Choose the right time and place to introduce yourself.

2. Greet the other person and tell your name.

3. Ask the other person his/her name if you need to.

4. Tell or ask the other person something to help start your conversation.

Skill 7: Introducing Other People

SKILL STEPS

1. Name the first person and tell him/her the name of the second person.

2. Name the second person and tell him/her the name of the first person.

3. Say something that helps the two people get to know each other.

 From *Aggression Replacement Training®: A Comprehensive Intervention for Aggressive Youth* (3rd ed.), by B. Glick & J. C. Gibbs, © 2011, Champaign, IL: Research Press (800-519-2707, www.researchpress.com).

Skill 8: Giving a Compliment

SKILL STEPS

1. Decide what you want to compliment about the other person.

2. Decide how to give the compliment.

3. Choose the right time and place to say it.

4. Give the compliment.

Group 2: Advanced Social Skills

Skill 9: Asking for Help

SKILL STEPS

1. Decide what the problem is.

2. Decide if you want help for the problem.

3. Think about different people who might help you and pick one.

4. Tell the person about the problem and ask that person to help you.

Skill 10: Joining In

SKILL STEPS

1. Decide if you want to join in an activity others are doing.

2. Decide the best way to join in.

3. Choose the best time to join in.

4. Join in the activity.

Skill 11: Giving Instructions

SKILL STEPS

1. Decide what needs to be done.

2. Think about the different people who could do it and choose one.

3. Ask that person to do what you want done.

4. Ask the other person if he/she understands what to do.

5. Change or repeat your instructions if you need to.

Skill 12: Following Instructions

SKILL STEPS

1. Listen carefully while you are being told what to do.

2. Ask questions about anything you don't understand.

3. Decide if you want to follow the instructions and let the other person know your decision.

4. Repeat the instructions to yourself.

5. Do what you have been asked to do.

Skill 13: Apologizing

SKILL STEPS

1. Decide if it would be best for you to apologize for something you did.

2. Think of the different ways you could apologize.

3. Choose the best time and place to apologize.

4. Make your apology.

Skill 14: Convincing Others

SKILL STEPS

1. Decide if you want to convince someone about something.

2. Tell the other person your idea.

3. Ask the other person what he/she thinks about it.

4. Tell why you think your idea is a good one.

5. Ask the other person to think about what you said before making up his/her mind.

Group 3: Skills for Dealing with Feelings

Skill 15: Knowing Your Feelings

SKILL STEPS

1. Tune in to what is going on in your body that helps you know what you are feeling.

2. Decide what happened to make you feel that way.

3. Decide what you could call the feeling.

Skill 16: Expressing Your Feelings

SKILL STEPS

1. Tune in to what is going on in your body.

2. Decide what happened to make you feel that way.

3. Decide what you are feeling.

4. Think about the different ways to express your feeling and pick one.

5. Express your feeling.

*Skill 17: Understanding the Feelings of Others

SKILL STEPS

1. Watch the other person.

2. Listen to what the other person is saying.

3. Figure out what the person might be feeling.

4. Think about ways to show you understand what he/she is feeling.

5. Decide on the best way and do it.

*Skill 18: Dealing with Someone Else's Anger

SKILL STEPS

1. Listen to the person who is angry.

2. Try to understand what the angry person is saying and feeling.

3. Decide if you can say or do something to deal with the situation.

4. If you can, deal with the other person's anger.

*Skill 19: Expressing Affection

SKILL STEPS

1. Decide if you have good feelings about the other person.

2. Decide if the other person would like to know about your feelings.

3. Choose the best way to express your feelings.

4. Choose the best time and place to express your feelings.

5. Express your feelings in a friendly way.

Skill 20: Dealing with Fear

SKILL STEPS

1. Decide if you are feeling afraid.

2. Think about what you might be afraid of.

3. Figure out if the fear is realistic.

4. Take skill steps to reduce your fear.

Skill 21: Rewarding Yourself

SKILL STEPS

1. Decide if you have done something that deserves a reward.

2. Decide what you could say to reward yourself.

3. Decide what you could do to reward yourself.

4. Reward yourself.

Group 4: Skill Alternatives to Aggression

Skill 22: Asking Permission
SKILL STEPS

1. Decide what you would like to do for which you need permission.

2. Decide whom you have to ask for permission.

3. Decide how to ask for permission.

4. Pick the right time and place.

5. Ask for permission.

Skill 23: Sharing Something
SKILL STEPS

1. Decide if you might like to share some of what you have.

2. Think about how the other person might feel about your sharing.

3. Offer to share in a direct and friendly way.

*Skill 24: Helping Others
SKILL STEPS

1. Decide if the other person might need and want your help.

2. Think of the ways you could be helpful.

3. Ask the other person if he/she needs and wants your help.

4. Help the other person.

Skill 25: Negotiating
SKILL STEPS

1. Decide if you and the other person are having a difference of opinion.

2. Tell the other person what you think about the problem.

3. Ask the other person what he/she thinks about the problem.

4. Listen openly to his/her answer.

5. Think about why the other person might feel this way.

6. Suggest a compromise.

Skill 26: Using Self-Control
SKILL STEPS

1. Tune in to what is going on in your body that helps you know you are about to lose control of yourself.

2. Decide what happened to make you feel this way.

3. Think about ways in which you might control yourself.

4. Choose the best way to control yourself and do it.

Skill 27: Standing Up for Your Rights
SKILL STEPS

1. Pay attention to what is going on in your body that helps you know that you are dissatisfied and would like to stand up for yourself.

2. Decide what happened to make you feel dissatisfied.

3. Think about ways in which you might stand up for yourself and choose one.

4. Stand up for yourself in a direct and reasonable way.

Skill 28: Responding to Teasing
SKILL STEPS

1. Decide if you are being teased.

2. Think about ways to deal with the teasing.

3. Choose the best way and do it.

Skill 29: Avoiding Trouble with Others
SKILL STEPS

1. Decide if you are in a situation that might get you into trouble.

2. Decide if you want to get out of the situation.

3. Tell the other people what you decided and why.

4. Suggest other things you might do.

5. Do what you think is best for you.

*Skill 30: Keeping Out of Fights
SKILL STEPS

1. Stop and think about why you want to fight.

2. Decide what you want to happen in the long run.

3. Think about other ways to handle the situation besides fighting.

4. Decide on the best way to handle the situation and do it.

Group 5: Skills for Dealing with Stress

Skill 31: Making a Complaint
SKILL STEPS

1. Decide what your complaint is.

2. Decide whom to complain to.

3. Tell that person your complaint.

4. Tell that person what you would like done about the problem.

5. Ask how he/she feels about what you've said.

Skill 32: Answering a Complaint
SKILL STEPS

1. Listen to the complaint.

2. Ask the person to explain anything you don't understand.

3. Tell the person that you understand the complaint.

4. State your ideas about the complaint, accepting the blame if appropriate.

5. Suggest what each of you could do about the complaint.

Skill 33: Being a Good Sport
SKILL STEPS

1. Think about how you did and how the other person did in the game you played.

2. Think of a true compliment you could give the other person about his/her game.

3. Think about his/her reactions to what you might say.

4. Choose the compliment you think is best and say it.

Skill 34: Dealing with Embarrassment
SKILL STEPS

1. Decide if you are feeling embarrassed.

2. Decide what happened to make you feel embarrassed.

3. Decide on what will help you feel less embarrassed and do it.

Skill 35: Dealing with Being Left Out
SKILL STEPS

1. Decide if you are being left out.

2. Think about why the other people might be leaving you out of something.

3. Decide how you could deal with the problem.

4. Choose the best way and do it.

Skill 36: Standing Up for a Friend

SKILL STEPS

1. Decide if your friend has not been treated fairly by others.

2. Decide if your friend wants you to stand up for him/her.

3. Decide how to stand up for your friend.

4. Stand up for your friend.

Skill 37: Responding to Persuasion

SKILL STEPS

1. Listen to the other person's ideas on the topic.

2. Decide what you think about the topic.

3. Compare what he/she said with what you think.

4. Decide which idea you like better and tell the other person about it.

*Skill 38: Responding to Failure

SKILL STEPS

1. Decide if you have failed at something.

2. Think about why you failed.

3. Think about what you could do to keep from failing another time.

4. Decide if you want to try again.

5. Try again using your new idea.

Skill 39: Dealing with Contradictory Messages

SKILL STEPS

1. Decide if someone is telling you two opposite things at the same time.

2. Think of ways to tell the other person that you don't understand what he/she means.

3. Choose the best way to tell the person and do it.

*Skill 40: Dealing with an Accusation

SKILL STEPS

1. Think about what the other person has accused you of.

2. Think about why the person might have accused you.

3. Think about ways to answer the person's accusation.

4. Choose the best way and do it.

*Skill 41: Getting Ready for a Difficult Conversation

SKILL STEPS

1. Think about how you will feel during the conversation.

2. Think about how the other person will feel.

3. Think about different ways you could say what you want to say.

4. Think about what the other person might say back to you.

5. Think about any other things that might happen during the conversation.

6. Choose the best approach you can think of and try it.

*Skill 42: Dealing with Group Pressure

SKILL STEPS

1. Think about what the group wants you to do and why.

2. Decide what you want to do.

3. Decide how to tell the group what you want to do.

4. Tell the group what you have decided.

Group 6: Planning Skills

Skill 43: Deciding on Something to Do
SKILL STEPS

1. Decide whether you are feeling bored or dissatisfied with what you are doing.

2. Think of things you have enjoyed doing in the past.

3. Decide which one you might be able to do now.

4. Start the activity.

Skill 44: Deciding What Caused a Problem
SKILL STEPS

1. Define what the problem is.

2. Think about possible causes of the problem.

3. Decide which are the most likely causes of the problem.

4. Check out what really caused the problem.

Skill 45: Setting a Goal
SKILL STEPS

1. Figure out what goal you want to reach.

2. Find out all the information you can about how to reach your goal.

3. Think about the skill steps you will need to take to reach your goal.

4. Take the first step toward your goal.

Skill 46: Deciding on Your Abilities
SKILL STEPS

1. Decide which abilities you might want to use.

2. Think about how you have done in the past when you have tried to use these abilities.

3. Get other people's opinions about your abilities.

4. Think about what you found out and decide how well you use these abilities.

Skill 47: Gathering Information
SKILL STEPS

1. Decide what information you need.

2. Decide how you can get the information.

3. Do things to get the information.

Skill 48: Arranging Problems by Importance
SKILL STEPS

1. Think about the problems that are bothering you.

2. List these problems from most to least important.

3. Do what you can to hold off on your less important problems.

4. Go to work on your most important problems.

Skill 49: Making a Decision
SKILL STEPS

1. Think about the problem that requires you to make a decision.

2. Think about possible decisions you could make.

3. Gather accurate information about these possible decisions.

4. Reconsider your possible decisions, using the information you have gathered.

5. Make the best decision.

Skill 50: Concentrating on a Task

SKILL STEPS

1. Decide what your task is.

2. Decide on a time to work on this task.

3. Gather the materials you need.

4. Decide on a place to work.

5. Decide if you are ready to concentrate.

Staff/Caregiver Skillstreaming Checklist

Group member _____ Group _____

Staff/Caregiver _____ Date _____

INSTRUCTIONS: Listed below you will find a number of skills that youth are more or less proficient in using. This checklist will help you evaluate how well each youth uses the various skills. For each youth, rate his or her use of each skill, based on your observations of the youth's behavior in various situations.

Circle 1 if the youth is almost never good at using the skill.

Circle 2 if the youth is seldom good at using the skill.

Circle 3 if the youth is sometimes good at using the skill.

Circle 4 if the youth is often good at using the skill.

Circle 5 if the youth is almost always good at using the skill.

Please rate the youth on all skills listed. If you know of a situation in which the youth has particular difficulty in using the skill well, please note it briefly in the space marked "Problem situation."

	almost never	seldom	sometimes	often	almost always

1. **Listening:** Does the youth pay attention to someone who is talking and make an effort to understand what is being said?   1   2   3   4   5

   Problem situation:

2. **Starting a Conversation:** Does the youth talk to others about light topics and then lead into more serious topics?   1   2   3   4   5

   Problem situation:

3. **Having a Conversation:** Does the youth talk to others about things of interest to both of them?   1   2   3   4   5

   Problem situation:

 From *Aggression Replacement Training®: A Comprehensive Intervention for Aggressive Youth* (3rd ed.), by B. Glick & J. C. Gibbs, © 2011, Champaign, IL: Research Press (800-519-2707, www.researchpress.com).

	almost never	seldom	sometimes	often	almost always

4. **Asking a Question:** Does the youth decide what information is needed and ask the right person for that information?

   Problem situation:

   1 2 3 4 5

5. **Saying Thank You:** Does the youth let others know that he/she is grateful for favors, etc.?

   Problem situation:

   1 2 3 4 5

6. **Introducing Yourself:** Does the youth become acquainted with new people on his/her own initiative?

   Problem situation:

   1 2 3 4 5

7. **Introducing Other People:** Does the youth help others become acquainted with one another?

   Problem situation:

   1 2 3 4 5

8. **Giving a Compliment:** Does the youth tell others that he/she likes something about them or their activities?

   Problem situation:

   1 2 3 4 5

9. **Asking for Help:** Does the youth request assistance when he/she is having difficulty?

   Problem situation:

   1 2 3 4 5

10. **Joining In:** Does the youth decide on the best way to become part of an ongoing activity or group?

    Problem situation:

    1 2 3 4 5

	almost never	seldom	sometimes	often	almost always

11. **Giving Instructions:** Does the youth clearly explain to others how they are to do a specific task?

    Problem situation:
                                             1 2 3 4 5

12. **Following Instructions:** Does the youth pay attention to instructions, give his/her reactions, and carry the instructions out adequately?   1 2 3 4 5

    Problem situation:

13. **Apologizing:** Does the youth tell others that he/she is sorry after doing something wrong?   1 2 3 4 5

    Problem situation:

14. **Convincing Others:** Does the youth attempt to persuade others that his/her ideas are better and will be more useful than those of the other person?   1 2 3 4 5

    Problem situation:

15. **Knowing Your Feelings:** Does the youth try to recognize which emotions he/she has at different times?   1 2 3 4 5

    Problem situation:

16. **Expressing Your Feelings:** Does the youth let others know which emotions he/she is feeling?   1 2 3 4 5

    Problem situation:

17. **Understanding the Feelings of Others:** Does the youth try to figure out what other people are feeling?   1 2 3 4 5

    Problem situation:

almost never   seldom   sometimes   often   almost always

18. **Dealing with Someone Else's Anger:** Does the youth try to understand other people's angry feelings?

    Problem situation:

    1   2   3   4   5

19. **Expressing Affection:** Does the youth let others know that he/she cares about them?

    Problem situation:

    1   2   3   4   5

20. **Dealing with Fear:** Does the youth figure out why he/she is afraid and do something to reduce the fear?

    Problem situation:

    1   2   3   4   5

21. **Rewarding Yourself:** Does the youth say and do nice things for himself/herself when the reward is deserved?

    Problem situation:

    1   2   3   4   5

22. **Asking Permission:** Does the youth figure out when permission is needed to do something and then ask the right person for permission?

    Problem situation:

    1   2   3   4   5

23. **Sharing Something:** Does the youth offer to share what he/she has with others who might appreciate it?

    Problem situation:

    1   2   3   4   5

24. **Helping Others:** Does the youth give assistance to others who might need or want help?

    Problem situation:

    1   2   3   4   5

	almost never	seldom	sometimes	often	almost always

25. **Negotiating:** Does the youth arrive at a plan that satisfies both him/her and others who have taken different positions?   1   2   3   4   5

Problem situation:

26. **Using Self-Control:** Does the youth control his/her temper so that things do not get out of hand?   1   2   3   4   5

Problem situation:

27. **Standing Up for Your Rights:** Does the youth assert his/her rights by letting people know where he/she stands on an issue?   1   2   3   4   5

Problem situation:

28. **Responding to Teasing:** Does the youth deal with being teased by others in ways that allow him/her to remain in control of himself/herself?   1   2   3   4   5

Problem situation:

29. **Avoiding Trouble with Others:** Does the youth stay out of situations that might get him/her into trouble?   1   2   3   4   5

Problem situation:

30. **Keeping Out of Fights:** Does the youth figure out ways other than fighting to handle difficult situations?   1   2   3   4   5

Problem situation:

31. **Making a Complaint:** Does the youth tell others when they are responsible for creating a particular problem for him/her and then attempt to find a solution for the problem?   1   2   3   4   5

Problem situation:

	almost never	seldom	sometimes	often	almost always

32. **Answering a Complaint:** Does the youth try to arrive at a fair solution to someone's justified complaint?

           1   2   3   4   5

Problem situation:

33. **Being a Good Sport:** Does the youth express an honest compliment to others about how they played a game?

           1   2   3   4   5

Problem situation:

34. **Dealing with Embarrassment:** Does the youth do things that help him/her feel less embarrassed or self-conscious?

           1   2   3   4   5

Problem situation:

35. **Dealing with Being Left Out:** Does the youth decide whether he/she has been left out of some activity and then do things to feel better about the situation?

           1   2   3   4   5

Problem situation:

36. **Standing Up for a Friend:** Does the youth let other people know when a friend has not been treated fairly?

           1   2   3   4   5

Problem situation:

37. **Responding to Persuasion:** Does the youth carefully consider the position of another person, comparing it to his/her own, before deciding what to do?

           1   2   3   4   5

Problem situation:

38. **Responding to Failure:** Does the youth figure out the reason for failing in a particular situation and what he/she can do about it in order to be more successful in the future?

           1   2   3   4   5

Problem situation:

39. **Dealing with Contradictory Messages:** Does the youth recognize and deal with the confusion that results when others tell him/her one thing but say or do things that indicate that they mean something else?

    Problem situation:

    1 2 3 4 5

40. **Dealing with an Accusation:** Does the youth figure out what he/she has been accused of and why, then decide on the best way to deal with the person who made the accusation?

    Problem situation:

    1 2 3 4 5

41. **Getting Ready for a Difficult Conversation:** Does the youth plan on the best way to present his/her point of view prior to a stressful conversation?

    Problem situation:

    1 2 3 4 5

42. **Dealing with Group Pressure:** Does the youth decide what he/she wants to do when others want him/her to do something else?

    Problem situation:

    1 2 3 4 5

43. **Deciding on Something to Do:** Does the youth deal with feeling bored by starting an interesting activity?

    Problem situation:

    1 2 3 4 5

44. **Deciding What Caused a Problem:** Does the youth find out whether an event was caused by something that was within his/her control?

    Problem situation:

    1 2 3 4 5

almost never   *seldom*   *sometimes*   *often*   *almost always*

45. **Setting a Goal:** Does the youth realistically decide on what he/she can accomplish prior to starting a task?

    Problem situation:

    1   2   3   4   5

46. **Deciding on Your Abilities:** Does the youth realistically figure out how well he/she might do at a particular task?

    Problem situation:

    1   2   3   4   5

47. **Gathering Information:** Does the youth decide what he/she needs to know and how to get that information?

    Problem situation:

    1   2   3   4   5

48. **Arranging Problems by Importance:** Does the youth decide realistically which of a number of problems is most important and should be dealt with first?

    Problem situation:

    1   2   3   4   5

49. **Making a Decision:** Does the youth consider possibilities and make choices that he/she feels will be best?

    Problem situation:

    1   2   3   4   5

50. **Concentrating on a Task:** Does the youth make those preparations that will help him/her get a job done?

    Problem situation:

    1   2   3   4   5

Group Member Skillstreaming Checklist

Name _____ Date _____

INSTRUCTIONS: Based on your observations in various situations, rate your use of the following skills.

Circle 1 if you almost never use the skill.
Circle 2 if you seldom use the skill.
Circle 3 if you sometimes use the skill.
Circle 4 if you often use the skill.
Circle 5 if you almost always use the skill.

	almost never	seldom	sometimes	often	almost always
1. Do I listen to someone who is talking to me?	1	2	3	4	5
2. Do I start conversations with other people?	1	2	3	4	5
3. Do I talk with other people about things that interest both of us?	1	2	3	4	5
4. Do I ask questions when I need or want to know something?	1	2	3	4	5
5. Do I say thank you when someone does something for me?	1	2	3	4	5
6. Do I introduce myself to new people?	1	2	3	4	5
7. Do I introduce people who haven't met before to each other?	1	2	3	4	5
8. Do I tell other people when I like how they are or something they have done?	1	2	3	4	5
9. Do I ask for help when I am having difficulty doing something?	1	2	3	4	5
10. Do I try to join in when others are doing something I'd like to be part of?	1	2	3	4	5
11. Do I clearly explain to others how and why they should do something?	1	2	3	4	5
12. Do I carry out instructions from other people quickly and correctly?	1	2	3	4	5
13. Do I apologize to others when I have done something wrong?	1	2	3	4	5
14. Do I try to convince others that my ideas are better than theirs?	1	2	3	4	5
15. Do I recognize the feelings I have at different times?	1	2	3	4	5
16. Do I let others know what I am feeling and do it in a good way?	1	2	3	4	5
17. Do I understand what other people are feeling?	1	2	3	4	5
18. Do I try to understand, and not get angry, when someone else is angry?	1	2	3	4	5
19. Do I let others know when I care about them?	1	2	3	4	5

 From *Aggression Replacement Training®: A Comprehensive Intervention for Aggressive Youth* (3rd ed.), by B. Glick & J. C. Gibbs, © 2011, Champaign, IL: Research Press (800-519-2707, www.researchpress.com).

		almost never	seldom	sometimes	often	almost always
20.	Do I know what makes me afraid and do things so that I don't stay that way?	1	2	3	4	5
21.	Do I say and do nice things for myself when I have earned it?	1	2	3	4	5
22.	Do I understand when permission is needed to do something and ask the right person for it?	1	2	3	4	5
23.	Do I offer to share what I have with others?	1	2	3	4	5
24.	Do I help others who might need or want help?	1	2	3	4	5
25.	Do I try to make both of us satisfied with the result when someone and I disagree?	1	2	3	4	5
26.	Do I control my temper when I feel upset?	1	2	3	4	5
27.	Do I stand up for my rights and let other people know what I think or feel?	1	2	3	4	5
28.	Do I stay in control when someone teases me?	1	2	3	4	5
29.	Do I try to stay out of situations that might get me in trouble?	1	2	3	4	5
30.	Do I figure out ways other than fighting to handle difficult situations?	1	2	3	4	5
31.	Do I make complaints I have about others in a fair way?	1	2	3	4	5
32.	Do I handle complaints made against me in a fair way?	1	2	3	4	5
33.	Do I say nice things to others, after a game, about how they played?	1	2	3	4	5
34.	Do I do things that help me feel less embarrassed when difficulties happen?	1	2	3	4	5
35.	Do I deal positively with being left out of some activity?	1	2	3	4	5
36.	Do I let people know when I feel a friend has not been treated fairly?	1	2	3	4	5
37.	Do I think choices through before answering when someone is trying to convince me about something?	1	2	3	4	5
38.	Do I try to figure out the reasons it happened when I fail at something?	1	2	3	4	5
39.	Do I deal with it well when someone says or does one thing but means something else?	1	2	3	4	5
40.	Do I deal with it well when someone accuses me of doing something?	1	2	3	4	5
41.	Do I plan ahead the best ways to handle it before I have a difficult conversation?	1	2	3	4	5
42.	Do I decide what I want to do when others pressure me to do something else?	1	2	3	4	5
43.	Do I think of good things to do and then do them when I feel bored?	1	2	3	4	5
44.	Do I, when there is a problem, try to find out what caused it?	1	2	3	4	5
45.	Do I think about what I would like to do before I start a new task?	1	2	3	4	5
46.	Do I think about what I am really able to do before I start a new task?	1	2	3	4	5

		almost never	seldom	sometimes	often	almost always
47.	Do I decide, before doing something, what I need to know and how to find out?	1	2	3	4	5
48.	Do I decide which problem is most important and should be handled first?	1	2	3	4	5
49.	Do I think about different possibilities and choose the one that is best?	1	2	3	4	5
50.	Do I pay full attention to whatever I am working on?	1	2	3	4	5

Skillstreaming Grouping Chart

youth names

Group 1: Beginning Social Skills

1. Listening _____

2. Starting a Conversation _____

3. Having a Conversation _____

4. Asking a Question _____

5. Saying Thank You _____

6. Introducing Yourself _____

7. Introducing Other People _____

8. Giving a Compliment _____

Group 2: Advanced Social Skills

9. Asking for Help _____

10. Joining In _____

11. Giving Instructions _____

12. Following Instructions _____

13. Apologizing _____

14. Convincing Others _____

Group 3: Skills for Dealing with Feelings

15. Knowing Your Feelings _____

16. Expressing Your Feelings _____

 From *Aggression Replacement Training®: A Comprehensive Intervention for Aggressive Youth* (3rd ed.), by B. Glick & J. C. Gibbs, © 2011, Champaign, IL: Research Press (800-519-2707, www.researchpress.com).

youth names

17. Understanding the Feelings of Others ____

18. Dealing with Someone Else's Anger ____

19. Expressing Affection ____

20. Dealing with Fear ____

21. Rewarding Yourself ____

Group 4: Skill Alternatives to Aggression

22. Asking Permission ____

23. Sharing Something ____

24. Helping Others ____

25. Negotiating ____

26. Using Self-Control ____

27. Standing Up for Your Rights ____

28. Responding to Teasing ____

29. Avoiding Trouble with Others ____

30. Keeping Out of Fights ____

Group 5: Skills for Dealing with Stress

31. Making a Complaint ____

32. Answering a Complaint ____

33. Being a Good Sport ____

34. Dealing with Embarrassment ____

35. Dealing with Being Left Out ____

youth names

36. Standing Up for a Friend _____

37. Responding to Persuasion _____

38. Responding to Failure _____

39. Dealing with Contradictory Messages _____

40. Dealing with an Accusation _____

41. Getting Ready for a Difficult Conversation_____

42. Dealing with Group Pressure _____

Group 6: Planning Skills

43. Deciding on Something to Do _____

44. Deciding What Caused a Problem _____

45. Setting a Goal _____

46. Deciding on Your Abilities _____

47. Gathering Information _____

48. Arranging Problems by Importance _____

49. Making a Decision _____

50. Concentrating on a Task _____

Session Evaluation Checklists

Social Skills Training Session Evaluation Checklist

Facilitator _____ Group _____

Co-facilitator _____ Week _____

Instructions: Please place a check in the box that best describes what happened in this session.

1. Were students welcomed and a positive climate established? ☐ yes ☐ no
2. Were group norms reviewed and positive participation emphasized? ☐ yes ☐ no
3. Were any issues from the last Social Skills Training session reviewed? ☐ yes ☐ no
4. Did all youth complete a Skill Homework Report? ☐ yes ☐ no
5. Were the Skill Homework Reports used to review last week's skill? ☐ yes ☐ no
6. Were homework efforts genuinely acknowledged and rewarded? ☐ yes ☐ no
7. Were Skill Homework Reports collected or placed in student folders or binders? ☐ yes ☐ no
8. Were visual aids used (Skill Cards distributed and skill posters displayed)? ☐ yes ☐ no
9. Was the new skill correctly introduced, defined, and explained without unnecessary complication? ☐ yes ☐ no
10. Was the new skill perfectly modeled by the facilitator and co-facilitator? ☐ yes ☐ no
11. Did the co-facilitator point to the skill steps during the modeling and role-plays? ☐ yes ☐ no
12. Did the modeling demonstration involve a situation relevant to group members? ☐ yes ☐ no
13. Did each youth express how the skill could be personally useful? ☐ yes ☐ no
14. Did each youth correctly role-play the skill as the main actor? ☐ yes ☐ no
15. Did each youth choose his or her own role-play partner? ☐ yes ☐ no
16. Did each youth provide performance feedback? ☐ yes ☐ no
17. Was the order of performance feedback correct (coactor, group members, facilitators, main actor)? ☐ yes ☐ no
18. Were new Skill Homework Reports provided to each youth and homework assigned? ☐ yes ☐ no
19. Was behavior management an issue during the session? ☐ yes ☐ no
20. Did the session pace keep the group members interested and active? ☐ yes ☐ no
21. Did the group members appear to understand the skill being taught in this session? ☐ yes ☐ no
22. Did the primary facilitator interact effectively with youth? ☐ yes ☐ no
23. Does the co-facilitator interact effectively with the youth? ☐ yes ☐ no
24. Was the session especially well delivered to the group? ☐ yes ☐ no
25. Is any corrective action needed? ☐ yes ☐ no

Comments

_____

_____

_____

Continue on reverse if necessary.

 From *Aggression Replacement Training®: A Comprehensive Intervention for Aggressive Youth* (3rd ed.), by B. Glick & J. C. Gibbs, © 2011, Champaign, IL: Research Press (800-519-2707, www.researchpress.com).

Anger Control Training Session Evaluation Checklist

Facilitator _____ Group _____

Co-facilitator _____ Week _____

Instructions: Please place a check in the box that best describes what happened in this session.

1. Were students welcomed and a positive climate established? ☐ yes ☐ no
2. Were group norms reviewed and positive participation emphasized? ☐ yes ☐ no
3. Were any issues from the last Anger Control Training session reviewed? ☐ yes ☐ no
4. Did all youth complete at least one Hassle Log as homework? ☐ yes ☐ no
5. Were the Hassle Logs used to review the last week's anger control concept(s)? ☐ yes ☐ no
6. Were homework efforts honestly and genuinely acknowledged and rewarded? ☐ yes ☐ no
7. Were Hassle Logs collected or placed in student folders or binders? ☐ yes ☐ no
8. Was the Anger Control Chain correctly reviewed? ☐ yes ☐ no
9. Were visual aids used (posters displayed)? ☐ yes ☐ no
10. Was the new Anger Control Training concept correctly introduced, defined, and explained without unnecessary complication? ☐ yes ☐ no
11. Was the new concept perfectly modeled by the facilitator and co-facilitator? ☐ yes ☐ no
12. Did the co-facilitator point to the Anger Control Chain concepts during the modeling and role-plays? ☐ yes ☐ no
13. Did the modeling demonstration involve a situation relevant to group members? ☐ yes ☐ no
14. Did each youth correctly role-play the concepts as the main actor? ☐ yes ☐ no
15. Did each youth choose his or her own role-play partner? ☐ yes ☐ no
16. Did each youth provide performance feedback? ☐ yes ☐ no
17. Was the order of performance feedback correct (coactor, group members, facilitators, main actor)? ☐ yes ☐ no
18. Were new Hassle Logs given to each youth and homework assigned? ☐ yes ☐ no
19. Was behavior management an issue during the session? ☐ yes ☐ no
20. Did the session pace keep the group members interested and active? ☐ yes ☐ no
21. Did the group members appear to understand the Anger Control Training concept being taught in this session? ☐ yes ☐ no
22. Did the primary facilitator effectively interact with the youth? ☐ yes ☐ no
23. Did the co-facilitator interact effectively with the youth? ☐ yes ☐ no
24. Was the session especially well delivered to the group? ☐ yes ☐ no
25. Is any corrective action needed? ☐ yes ☐ no

Comments

_____

Continue on reverse if necessary.

 From *Aggression Replacement Training®: A Comprehensive Intervention for Aggressive Youth* (3rd ed.), by B. Glick & J. C. Gibbs, © 2011, Champaign, IL: Research Press (800-519-2707, www.researchpress.com).

Moral Reasoning Session Evaluation Checklist

Facilitator(s) _____ Date _____

Week/Problem Situation _____ Group _____

General

1. Did group members follow the ground rules (concerning listening, confidentiality, etc.)?   ☐ yes   ☐ no

2. Were all group members interested and involved?   ☐ yes   ☐ no

   If no, list the names of uninvolved group members:

   _____   _____

   _____   _____

3. Did you find some constructive value in every serious comment made by a group member?   ☐ yes   ☐ no

4. Did you maintain a normal voice volume and speak in a respectful rather than threatening or demanding tone?   ☐ yes   ☐ no

5. Did you maintain a balance between criticism and approval by using the "PCP" style of constructive criticism (in which a critical comment is preceded and followed by supportive ones)?   ☐ yes   ☐ no

6. Did you use the "ask, don't tell" intervention as much as possible?   ☐ yes   ☐ no

Session

In the various phases, did you . . .

Phase 1: Introducing the problem situation

1. Make sure the group understood the problem situation (e.g., "Who can tell the group just what Jerry's problem situation is? Why is that a problem?")?   ☐ yes   ☐ no

2. Relate the problem situation to group members' everyday lives (e.g., "Do problems like this happen? Who has been in a situation like this? Tell the group about it")?   ☐ yes   ☐ no

Phase 2: Cultivating mature morality

3. Establish mature morality as the tone for the rest of the meeting (e.g., eliciting and listing on the easel pad reasons for each positive majority decision)?   ☐ yes   ☐ no

4. Did you support and relabel the "should" as strong (e.g., "Yes, it does take guts to do the right thing")?   ☐ yes   ☐ no

 From *Aggression Replacement Training®: A Comprehensive Intervention for Aggressive Youth* (3rd ed.), by B. Glick & J. C. Gibbs, © 2011, Champaign, IL: Research Press (800-519-2707, www.researchpress.com).

Phase 3: Remediating moral developmental delay

5. Use more mature group members and their reasons (Phase 2) to challenge   ☐ yes   ☐ no
the pragmatic arguments of some group members?

6. Create role-taking opportunities (e.g., "What would the world be like   ☐ yes   ☐ no
if everybody did that?"; "How would you feel if you were Bob?")?

Phase 4: Consolidating mature morality

7. Make positive decisions and mature reasons unanimous for the group (e.g.,   ☐ yes   ☐ no
"Any strong objections if I circle that decision as the group decision/underline
that reason as the group's number one reason?")?

8. Praise the group for its positive decisions and mature reasons (e.g., "I'm really   ☐ yes   ☐ no
pleased that the group was able to make so many good, strong decisions and
back them up with good, strong reasons"; "Would the group like to tape this
sheet onto the wall?")?

Comments

_____

_____

_____

_____

_____

_____

_____

_____

Staff/Caregiver Materials

What Is ART and How Can You Help?

Adolescents who participate in Aggression Replacement Training, or ART, go to three types of sessions. The first type is Social Skills Training, in which a series of useful skills is taught, each one of which is a positive alternative to a destructive or aggressive response an adolescent would usually make. A second type is Anger Control Training, which teaches techniques to reduce and manage feelings of anger in anger-provoking situations. A third type involves Moral Reasoning sessions, designed to have participants understand viewpoints other than their own and develop more mature reasoning abilities, given specific problem situations they discuss during each session.

Becoming a Transfer Coach

Programs like ART that are designed to change the behavior of aggressive adolescents often succeed only at a certain time and in a certain place. That is, the program works, but only at or shortly after the time the program is conducted and only in the same places the program is held. During ART, in addition to instruction in social skills, anger control, and moral reasoning, adolescents receive a great deal of support, enthusiasm, encouragement, and reward for their efforts. After ART, many of them may receive very little support, reward, or other positive responses. So the common failure of transfer of learning isn't surprising.

Research shows that people like you—teachers, facility staff, community workers, parents, friends, peers, employers—are in an ideal position to provide this valuable skill-promoting support and reward. You can be a powerful ART *transfer coach,* helping to make sure that the curriculum of skills and ways of thinking tried in ART turn into long-term or even permanent learning.

Social Skills Training

As a transfer coach, you can help participants when it comes to the use of the social skills taught as a part of ART. When each skill is taught, it is broken down into a few behaviors or steps that actually make up the skill. As the following example shows, the behavioral steps *are* the skill.

MAKING A COMPLAINT

SKILL STEPS

1. Decide what your complaint is.
2. Decide whom to complain to.
3. Tell that person your complaint.
4. Tell that person what you would like done about the problem.
5. Ask how he/she feels about what you've said.

ART teaches 10 social skills. Group members try these skills in their sessions, then practice the skills in real life. After they do so, they complete a Skill Homework Report and talk about how they did. As a transfer coach, you can look for, encourage, and reward these behaviors when they occur. For example, you can see if the individual performs the steps of the skill correctly and provide verbal rewards when they do the steps of the skill, or you can help them complete their Skill Homework Reports.

Anger Control Training

You can respond similarly in Anger Control Training when participants use the techniques they learned in group in situations outside the sessions. You can provide support and encouragement every time a participant identifies things that may cause his or her anger, notices physical signs of anger, or uses other anger control techniques. If you reward and celebrate such behavior, the likelihood of its continuation increases. You can also assist the youth in identifying anger-provoking situations and completing Hassle Logs, the homework for the Anger Control Training component.

Moral Reasoning

Although Moral Reasoning sessions do not have specific homework assignments, participants do gain experience in taking perspectives other than their own and developing more mature reasoning. You can take special care to listen to the youth during conversations outside of group and to take the opportunity to provide encouragement and reward when they demonstrate appreciation and acceptance of different ideas and perspectives.

Specific Coaching Techniques

Specific statements, procedures, and techniques that you may find valuable in your attempts to be an effective ART transfer coach are as follows.

Prompting

Under the pressure of real-life situations both in and out of schools, community agencies, or institutions, individuals may forget all or part of the social skills (or anger-reducing techniques) they learned earlier. If their anxiety isn't too great or they haven't forgotten all that they learned, all that may be needed for them to perform the skill correctly is some prompting. Prompting is reminding the person *what* to do (the skill), *how* to do it (the steps), *when* to do it (now, or the next time the situation occurs), *where* to do it (and where not to), and/or *why* the skill should be used here and now (describing the positive outcomes expected).

Encouraging

Offering support to participants to use a given skill assumes they know it but are reluctant to use it. Encouragement is necessary, therefore, when the problem is lack of motivation rather than lack of knowledge. Encouragement is best given by gently urging the participant to use what he or she knows, showing your enthusiasm for the skill, and communicating optimism about the likely positive outcome of its use.

Reassuring

For particularly anxious individuals, skill transfer attempts are more likely to occur if you are able to reduce the fear of failure. Reassurance is often an effective fear-reduction technique. "You can do it," "I'm here to help you if you need it," and "You've used the other skills (or techniques) well—I think you'll do fine with this one, too" are examples of the kinds of reassuring statements that can help.

Rewarding

The most important contribution by far that you can make for skill transfer is to provide rewards for using a skill correctly. Rewards take the form of approval, praise, or compliments; they may also consist of special privileges, points, tokens, recognition, or other reinforcers built into a school's or facility's behavior management system. All of these rewards increase the likelihood of continued skill use in new settings and at later times.

The most powerful reward, however, is the success of the skill or technique itself. If a youth prepares well for a stressful conversation and the conversation then goes very well, that reward (the successful conversation itself) helps skill transfer more than any other support a transfer coach may give. The same conclusion—that success increases transfer—applies to all of the social skills and all of the Anger Control Training techniques. Thus, whenever possible, create the opportunity to reward a youth's skill use by helping him or her succeed with it.

Staff/Caregiver Social Skills Training Note

The purpose of this note is to tell you what we did in the Social Skills Training group today. Please complete Part 2, then return this form as soon as you can.

Part 1: Staff

Group member _____ Date _____

Skill _____ Week _____

Skill steps

Homework assignment

The group member will use the skill with _____ (who) on _____ (day) at

_____ (time) in/at _____ (where) and will complete a Skill Homework Report.

Part 2: Caregiver

1. Did the group member do his/her homework? ☐ yes ☐ no
2. Did the group member follow the steps of the skill as listed? ☐ yes ☐ no
3. Did you reward the group member for following the skill steps? ☐ yes ☐ no
4. Did you discuss with the group member how he/she did the homework? ☐ yes ☐ no
5. Did the group member refer to a Skill Card during practice? ☐ yes ☐ no
6. Did you assist the group member in filling out the Skill Homework Report? ☐ yes ☐ no

Please rate the group member on how well they practiced the skill steps and completed the homework.

☐ poor ☐ good ☐ very good ☐ outstanding ☐ didn't observe

Additional comments

_____

_____

_____

Caregiver signature _____ Date _____

 From *Aggression Replacement Training®: A Comprehensive Intervention for Aggressive Youth* (3rd ed.), by B. Glick & J. C. Gibbs, © 2011, Champaign, IL: Research Press (800-519-2707, www.researchpress.com).

Staff/Caregiver Anger Control Training Note

The purpose of this note is to tell you what we did in the Anger Control Training group today. Please complete Part 2, then return this form as soon as you can.

Part 1: Staff

Group member _____ Date _____

Skill _____ Week _____

We learned about this anger control concept in group today:

Homework assignment

The group member will complete at least one Hassle Log, paying special attention to the anger control concept identified above.

Part 2: Caregiver

1. Did the group member use the new anger control concept? ☐ yes ☐ no

2. Did you discuss with the group member how he/she did the homework? ☐ yes ☐ no

3. Did the group member complete a Hassle Log? ☐ yes ☐ no

4. Did you assist the group member in completing a Hassle Log? ☐ yes ☐ no

5. Did you reward the group member for completing the homework? ☐ yes ☐ no

Rate the group member on how well he/she practiced the Anger Control Training concepts and completed the homework.

☐ poor ☐ good ☐ very good ☐ outstanding ☐ didn't observe

Additional comments

_____

_____

_____

Caregiver signature _____ Date _____

 From *Aggression Replacement Training®: A Comprehensive Intervention for Aggressive Youth* (3rd ed.), by B. Glick & J. C. Gibbs, © 2011, Champaign, IL: Research Press (800-519-2707, www.researchpress.com).

Staff/Caregiver Moral Reasoning Session Note

The purpose of this note is to tell you what we did in the Moral Reasoning session today. Please complete Part 2, then return this form as soon as you can.

Part 1: Staff

Group member _____ Date _____

Skill _____ Week _____

In the session today, we discussed _____'s Problem. We provided group members opportunities to answer questions about the situation, share their viewpoints, and attempt to take perspectives other than their own.

Please pay careful attention to the group member's behavior during the week, especially discussions with you or others, then answer the questions in Part 2.

Part 2: Caregiver

1. Did the group member have an opportunity to participate in a discussion with you or others that you observed? ☐ yes ☐ no

2. Did the group member listen to what others had to say about the topic and wait his/her turn to respond and share ideas? ☐ yes ☐ no

3. Was the group member able to stay on topic and remain respectful? ☐ yes ☐ no

4. Did the group member change his/her opinion or viewpoint as a result of the discussion or show understanding of another's perspective? ☐ yes ☐ no

5. Did you discuss the group member's experience and offer any reward for respectful listening or understanding another person's perspective? ☐ yes ☐ no

   Please rate the group member on how well he/she was able to participate in a discussion, share ideas, and show understanding of another's point of view.

   ☐ poor ☐ good ☐ very good ☐ outstanding ☐ didn't observe

Additional comments

_____

_____

_____

Caregiver signature _____ Date _____

 From *Aggression Replacement Training®: A Comprehensive Intervention for Aggressive Youth* (3rd ed.), by B. Glick & J. C. Gibbs, © 2011, Champaign, IL: Research Press (800-519-2707, www.researchpress.com).

Alternate Moral Reasoning Problem Situations

Emilio's Problem Situation involves issues of drugs and crime, friendship, and dealing with authority, represented by parents or police. The actions of Emilio's friend Roberto are so troublesome that Emilio expresses a complaint to Roberto about his risky and illegal behavior. The problem is complicated when Emilio's grandfather becomes a victim of a crime that Roberto's friends commit in order to support their drug behaviors.

The typical majority position for the problem situation questions is that authorities should be informed about the antisocial and illegal activities, whether or not they involve a stranger or a family member and even if the stolen property is returned. The point is not just that Roberto will eventually get caught and punished. Mature reasons for the typical majority position appeal to the adverse emotional impact on victims (such as the grandfather) as well as the broader adverse impact on community and society at large.

Moral Reasoning—Week I: Emilio's Problem Situation

Name _____ Date _____

Emilio and Roberto are neighbors. They have known each other since kindergarten and have been best friends ever since then. Roberto often gets involved with some of the neighborhood kids who like to get high and break into people's houses, then sell the stuff they steal so they can support their drug habits. Emilio has never told anyone about Roberto's activities, although frequently he has complained to Roberto about his behavior and told Roberto that he needs to stop hanging around with those kids.

Emilio's grandfather lives in the neighborhood. One day, Emilio overhears his grandfather and mother talking about something upsetting. His grandfather says that around midnight last night, while he was asleep, his house was broken into. Two televisions, a computer, and his grandfather's favorite picture of his deceased wife were stolen. His grandfather has no insurance.

The next day, Emilio is visiting with Roberto. Roberto says he is going to get a new computer and TV from his friends, who stole them last week—in fact, the very night Emilio's grandfather's TVs and computer were stolen.

What should Emilio say or do?

1. Should Emilio tell his mother about Roberto's activities?

   ☐ yes, should tell ☐ no, should not tell ☐ can't decide *(check one)*

2. Should Emilio tell the police about Roberto or his friends?

   ☐ yes, should tell ☐ no, should not tell ☐ can't decide *(check one)*

3. Should Emilio tell Roberto that accepting stolen stuff is wrong and illegal?

   ☐ yes, should tell ☐ no, should not tell ☐ can't decide *(check one)*

4. Should Emilio tell Roberto that the computer and TV were most likely the ones stolen from Emilio's grandfather's house?

   ☐ yes, should tell ☐ no, should not tell ☐ can't decide *(check one)*

5. What if the computer and TV turn out to be the grandfather's but Roberto offers to return them? Does that make a difference in what Roberto should do?

   ☐ yes, makes a difference ☐ no, doesn't make a difference ☐ can't decide *(check one)*

6. What if the neighborhood kids didn't steal the TVs and computer from Emilio's grandfather's house? What if it was a stranger's house? Then would it be all right for them to steal stuff to give to Roberto?

   ☐ yes, all right ☐ no, not all right ☐ can't decide *(check one)*

7. How good a friend is Roberto? Would Emilio be able to trust Roberto not to steal from him?

   ☐ yes, could trust ☐ no, couldn't trust ☐ can't decide *(check one)*

 From *Aggression Replacement Training®: A Comprehensive Intervention for Aggressive Youth* (3rd ed.), by B. Glick & J. C. Gibbs, © 2011, Champaign, IL: Research Press (800-519-2707, www.researchpress.com).

LATOYA'S PROBLEM SITUATION deals with bullying or put-downs and threats (whether face to face or through Internet or cell phone), whether a good relationship is even possible if it includes such behavior, and what a friend can or should do to help. Group members, drawing upon the social skill Understanding the Feelings of Others, may suggest that Latoya must understand what Kioka is feeling and experiencing at the hands of her boyfriend. Their empathic concern may induce a majority group position that Latoya should act to protect her friend, Kioka. The mature position is that Latoya should confront the boyfriend and/or tell authorities, even if the boyfriend threatens Latoya.

Moral Reasoning—Week 2: Latoya's Problem Situation

Name _____ Date _____

Latoya and Kioka are friends. While walking in the mall, Kioka gets a text message from her boyfriend. She becomes very quiet and goes to sit down at a nearby bench. Then she starts texting and mumbling to herself. Kioka begins to cry and shake her head.

Later, Kioka tells Latoya that Kioka's boyfriend, Jamal, often uses the cell phone to give her "bad" messages. Latoya asks her what kind of bad messages. Kioka tells Latoya that Jamal is nice and shows people that he is a gentleman but then texts her all kinds of put-downs and threats. He makes her do stuff for his friends, and sometimes he makes her stay at his house against her will.

Kioka explains that while at the mall Jamal texted her that he was watching her walk with Latoya. He told Kioka not to hang out with Latoya. He then texted that Kioka now has to be punished and that he will pick her up after work. Kioka says she knows what that means, but not to tell anyone or do anything.

What should Latoya say or do?

1. Should Latoya do what Kioka asks and not tell anyone that Jamal is threatening her?

   ☐ no, should tell ☐ yes, should not tell ☐ can't decide *(check one)*

2. Should Latoya tell Jamal to back off and leave Kioka alone?

   ☐ yes, should tell ☐ no, should not tell ☐ can't decide *(check one)*

3. Should Latoya tell some authority like a parent, a teacher, or the police?

   ☐ yes, should tell some authority ☐ no, should not tell some authority ☐ can't decide *(check one)*

4. What if Jamal starts texting Latoya and threatening her, too? Then should Latoya tell some authority?

   ☐ yes, should tell some authority ☐ no, should not tell some authority ☐ can't decide *(check one)*

5. Is it ever possible to have a good relationship with someone who, although sometimes nice, also bullies or threatens you?

   ☐ yes, sometimes possible ☐ no, never possible ☐ can't decide *(check one)*

From *Aggression Replacement Training®: A Comprehensive Intervention for Aggressive Youth* (3rd ed.), by B. Glick & J. C. Gibbs, © 2011, Champaign, IL: Research Press (800-519-2707, www.researchpress.com).

ISHAN'S PROBLEM SITUATION presents a difficult set of circumstances for group members to understand and process. The situation deals with cultural expectations and standards, domestic violence, date abuse, and issues of obedience to family versus protection of a sibling from harm. In this situation, Ishan must get ready for a difficult conversation with his sister if he is to protect her, both from her boyfriend and their father. The majority group position for Question 1 is often that Ishan should confront his sister and talk with her about what he saw rather than involve the parents, despite parental expectations (Question 2). More morally mature group members may point out that extenuating circumstances will not matter to the father or that severe harm could come to Isabelle (Question 3), or even that the 18-year-old boyfriend is predatory since Isabelle is still a minor (Question 4).

Name _____ Date _____

Ishan and Isabelle are 16-year-old twins, a boy and a girl. They come from a strict conservative family. Their father is bossy and has been known to beat their mother and them for not following his instructions.

Ishan comes home late from school one day. His parents are not home. Ishan finds his sister and her 18-year-old boyfriend in their father's home office making out. Her blouse is unbuttoned. They don't know that Ishan sees them. Ishan knows that if their father finds out about what Isabelle did, she will be beaten, perhaps severely.

What should Ishan say or do?

1. Should Ishan confront his sister and talk with her about what he saw? Or should he just keep quiet?

   ☐ yes, should confront   ☐ no, should keep quiet   ☐ can't decide *(check one)*

2. What if Ishan considers that he is expected to be obedient and helpful to his parents? Then should he tell his father (or his mother, who would tell his father) what he saw?

   ☐ yes, should tell   ☐ no, shouldn't tell   ☐ can't decide *(check one)*

3. What if Ishan's sister says that she was being pressured to do what Ishan saw in their father's office? Then should Ishan tell his parents, knowing that his father will punish his sister anyway?

   ☐ yes, should tell   ☐ no, should keep quiet   ☐ can't decide *(check one)*

4. What if Ishan considers that the older boyfriend is taking advantage of a minor, his sister? Should he confront the boyfriend or seek help outside the family?

   ☐ yes, should confront/seek help   ☐ no, should not confront/seek help   ☐ can't decide *(check one)*

ENZIO'S PROBLEM SITUATION raises issues relating to gang behaviors, intimidation, and loyalty, both to a friend as well as to groups. The mature moral position is that Enzio will confront Sal about the retaliation on the rival gang members and will tell the authorities what he knows, even if he is threatened and intimidated by Sal. In confronting Sal, Enzio will find it helpful to use the skill Dealing with Someone Else's Anger. Those with more mature reasoning will accede to the importance of the relationship between Sal and Enzio as critically more important than the issues of punishment, power, and control. They will also express the notion that society, even gang society, will not benefit from vigilante justice.

Moral Reasoning—Week 4: Enzio's Problem Situation

Name _____ Date _____

Enzio and Sal are members of a local street gang. Last week, while coming out of school, they were attacked by two guys in ski masks. Enzio and Sal believe the attackers were members of a rival gang from a different neighborhood; however, they couldn't see their attackers' faces. Sal is usually a hothead—sure enough, he wants to get even by going to the other gang's hood and randomly shooting some people. Enzio tells Sal to chill and calm down—that if they are patient, they will find out who their attackers were.

Enzio does find out who attacked Sal and him, and they were in fact rival gang members. That very same day, Enzio reads in the newspaper that four people were shot in the rival gang's hood. Enzio is sure that Sal was the one who shot them.

What should Enzio say or do?

1. Should Enzio find Sal and confront him about the neighborhood shootings?

    ☐ yes, should confront ☐ no, should mind his own business ☐ can't decide *(check one)*

2. Should Enzio tell the authorities what he knows?

    ☐ yes, should tell ☐ no, should keep quiet ☐ can't decide *(check one)*

3. What if Sal tells Enzio that "those people got what they deserved" and warns Enzio to mind his own business? Then should Enzio tell the authorities what he knows?

    ☐ yes, should tell ☐ no, should keep quiet ☐ can't decide *(check one)*

4. What if Sal reminds Enzio of his obligation of loyalty to the gang? Then should Enzio tell the authorities what he knows?

    ☐ yes, should tell ☐ no, should keep quiet ☐ can't decide *(check one)*

5. Is it ever right to tell on someone?

    ☐ sometimes right ☐ never right ☐ can't decide *(check one)*

From *Aggression Replacement Training®: A Comprehensive Intervention for Aggressive Youth* (3rd ed.), by B. Glick & J. C. Gibbs, © 2011, Champaign, IL: Research Press (800-519-2707, www.researchpress.com).

Carmen's Problem Situation deals with authority, bullying, and retaliation among teammates, who are working together toward a shared goal. Of particular concern is how Carmen manages a situation where she is the victim of a teammate's bullying behavior. Group members who themselves have a tendency to be aggressive or violent may at least initially endorse tit-for-tat retaliation (Question 1). A group discussion that consolidates mature morality, however, will be one that does not tolerate excuses for bullying but instead moves toward dealing with the situation more constructively. The remaining questions, all of which deal with varying degrees of authority, require that Carmen tell what is happening so as to safeguard herself and the group, as well as the bully.

Moral Reasoning—Week 5: Carmen's Problem Situation

Name _____ Date _____

Carmen is on the cheerleading squad for the soccer team at school. She is quite popular and usually doesn't have problems meeting new people. About three weeks into the season, she and her teammates are at an away game.

During one of the squad's routines, one of the team members, a new girl in school, steps on Carmen's foot quite hard and then apologizes. After the third time this happens, Carmen decides that her teammate is doing it deliberately. The next time the girl tries to step on Carmen's foot, Carmen steps back just in time. The girl stomps on the ground instead, hurting her own ankle. The girl gets up and shoves Carmen to the ground.

Carmen feels like hitting the girl but thinks about what she should do. She asks her squad mate what is going on. Her squad mate tells her the new girl considers herself "queen of the hill" and likes to hurt others that she thinks are weaker.

What should Carmen say or do?

1. Should Carmen have gotten back at the girl by stepping hard on her foot?

   ☐ yes, should have gotten back   ☐ no, should not have gotten back   ☐ can't decide *(check one)*

2. Should Carmen tell the coach what is happening and get the girl kicked off the squad?

   ☐ yes, should tell   ☐ no, should not tell   ☐ can't decide *(check one)*

3. What if Carmen finds out that the girl comes from a very poor family and needs to control others to feel good about herself? Should Carmen then tell the coach what is happening?

   ☐ yes, should tell   ☐ no, should not tell   ☐ can't decide *(check one)*

4. What if the girl has been bullied herself and is only doing what she has seen others do? Now should Carmen tell the coach?

   ☐ yes, should tell   ☐ no, should not tell   ☐ can't decide *(check one)*

5. Is doing back to someone else what they did to you the right or best thing to do?

   ☐ yes, the right or best thing   ☐ no, not the right or best thing   ☐ can't decide *(check one)*

From *Aggression Replacement Training®: A Comprehensive Intervention for Aggressive Youth* (3rd ed.), by B. Glick & J. C. Gibbs, © 2011, Champaign, IL: Research Press (800-519-2707, www.researchpress.com).

CHERI'S PROBLEM SITUATION deals with animal cruelty and what responsibilities neighbors and society in general have in dealing with the problem. The first three questions deal with the individual responsibility to preserve the good and welfare of animals as well as people. The mature moral position is that Cheri should tell the veterinarian the truth, even if she is pressured not to interfere. The mature reasoning for this position appeals to the responsibility of the community and society to protect animals as well as people. The last question deals with social justice and how much those who have guardianship should be held to account for their ward's behavior. Since during this week group members learn the social skill Helping Others, this problem presents tremendous opportunity for group members to begin to integrate their learning.

Name _____ Date _____

Cheri works after school at a local veterinarian's office. She enjoys helping with the animals and caring for them in their kennels and cages. Sometimes Cheri is able to assist the doctor when she cares for the animals during treatments.

One day, Cheri's neighbor's dog is brought into the office with a broken leg and a bruised stomach. When the doctor asks what happened, its owner says that the dog got out of its pen and ran in the road and was hit by a passing motorcycle. The man didn't even stop to see if the dog was OK. The doctor listened to the neighbor's story but questioned whether that was actually what happened.

Cheri knows what really happened: Her neighbor's son has been kicking the dog. The boy is very mean. She has seen him take insects and rip their legs off their bodies. Once he found a frog and threw it against the ground and then stomped on it. The boy is only 12 years old. Cheri thinks, "If this is what he does now, then when he gets older he may do something even worse."

What should Cheri say or do?

1. Should Cheri tell the veterinarian what she knows and thinks?

   ☐ no, shouldn't tell   ☐ yes, should tell   ☐ can't decide *(check one)*

2. Should Cheri tell the boy's parents what he has been doing to animals?

   ☐ no, shouldn't tell   ☐ yes, should tell   ☐ can't decide *(check one)*

3. What if Cheri tells the boy's parents and they say they know what their son does but that she shouldn't be interfering in their family's business. Should Cheri then tell the police?

   ☐ yes, should tell   ☐ no, shouldn't tell   ☐ can't decide *(check one)*

4. What if you were the boy's parents? Should you tell the veterinarian the truth about what happened, even if your son gets in trouble as a result?

   ☐ yes, should tell   ☐ no, shouldn't tell   ☐ can't decide *(check one)*

5. Should the boy's parents be held responsible for the boy's action and have to go to court for animal cruelty?

   ☐ yes, should be held responsible   ☐ no, should not be held responsible   ☐ can't decide *(check one)*

 From *Aggression Replacement Training®: A Comprehensive Intervention for Aggressive Youth* (3rd ed.), by B. Glick & J. C. Gibbs, © 2011, Champaign, IL: Research Press (800-519-2707, www.researchpress.com).

BIG BEAR'S PROBLEM SITUATION addresses the familiar theme of dealing with an irresponsible friend, one who at least initially won't admit a theft. The responsible position is that Big Bear shouldn't start off by accusing Little Hawk but should attempt to find out what happened and who is responsible and should rely on the elders of the community for help. Mature reasoners do not let Little Hawk minimize his stealing problem as "just trading" or drop the matter if the stolen items are returned; it is not possible to have a close, trusting relationship as long as one's friend has a stealing problem. Although the problem deals with stealing, it also takes into account the skill Dealing with an Accusation. By the seventh week, group members should have enough experiences with moral reasoning processes to engage issues relating to this different culture and set of community principles.

Moral Reasoning—Week 7: Big Bear's Problem Situation

Name _____ Date _____

Big Bear and Little Hawk are part of the Tlingit Alaskan Native American population. They are good friends and hunt, fish, and gather food for their village and families. Little Hawk was named by his family because he was so tiny when he was born and did not grow as tall or strong as others his age. Big Bear can sometimes get Little Hawk angry by teasing him about his size. Sometimes Little Hawk takes the fish Big Bear catches and claims it as his own. Big Bear knows what Little Hawk does but has never confronted him about it, believing it is more important to keep a friend than argue over a few fish.

One day, Big Bear decides to go to the sweat lodge to participate in the clan's purification ceremony. He leaves his clothes outside, as do the others attending the sacred ritual. When he comes out hours later, he finds all his clothes, along with his necklace given to him by his grandfather, are missing. In their place are five fish. Big Bear immediately goes to find Little Hawk, thinking that Little Hawk was the one who exchanged Big Bear's clothes for the fish.

What should Big Bear say or do?

1. Should Big Bear accuse Little Hawk of taking the clothes and necklace his grandfather gave to him?

   ☐ yes, should accuse   ☐ no, should not accuse   ☐ can't decide *(check one)*

2. What if Little Hawk tells Big Bear he didn't take his clothes but knows who did. Should Little Hawk tell his friend who has his possessions?

   ☐ yes, should tell   ☐ no, should not tell   ☐ can't decide *(check one)*

3. Should Big Bear go to the tribal council and let them handle the matter for the community?

   ☐ yes, should go   ☐ no, should not go   ☐ can't decide *(check one)*

4. What if Big Bear's clothes and grandfather's necklace are returned? Should Big Bear continue to try to find out who took his possessions?

   ☐ yes, should continue   ☐ no, should not continue   ☐ can't decide *(check one)*

5. In truth, it was Little Hawk who stole the clothes and left the fish. What if Little Hawk explains that all he did was a little trade, exchanging the clothes for the fish? Does that make what Little Hawk did OK?

   ☐ yes, OK   ☐ no, not OK   ☐ can't decide *(check one)*

6. Is it possible to have a close, trusting relationship with someone who has a stealing problem?

   ☐ yes, possible   ☐ no, not possible   ☐ can't decide *(check one)*

 From *Aggression Replacement Training®: A Comprehensive Intervention for Aggressive Youth* (3rd ed.), by B. Glick & J. C. Gibbs, © 2011, Champaign, IL: Research Press (800-519-2707, www.researchpress.com).

TARA AND LASHONDA'S PROBLEM SITUATION deals with relationships and group pressure. Issues include the friendship between Tara and Lashonda, friendship and loyalty among the members of the basketball team, and the relationships between Parker and Tara and Parker and Lashonda. Those with more mature levels of moral reasoning will identify the attributes of friendship, emphasize the importance of ensuring loyalty in friendship, and will support the need to uphold mutual respect. The problem situation gives participants the opportunity to discuss the effect of group pressure brought upon both Tara and Lashonda and to share different perspectives about self-interest versus doing the "noble" thing for Parker.

Name _____ Date _____

Tara and Lashonda are seniors in high school and looking forward to going to their prom. Both are popular and have dated members of the football and basketball teams. Tara knows that Lashonda likes Parker, the captain of the basketball team. Tara also likes Parker. Both would like Parker to go with them to the prom.

Parker has let it be known to his team members that he has a problem because both Lashonda and Tara want him to ask them to the prom and he doesn't want to hurt or disappoint either of them. Two of Parker's team members decide to help Parker out by going to Lashonda and Tara to try to convince each of them to back off and not pressure Parker to take them to the prom since there is a big game coming up and Parker needs to concentrate on playing well. The team members tell Lashonda and Tara that college scouts will be observing Parker and he must impress the scouts if he is going to get the scholarship he needs to go to college.

What should Tara and Lashonda say or do?

1. Should Tara and Lashonda do what the team asked—that is, back off and not pressure Parker to take them to the prom?

   ☐ yes, should back off   ☐ no, should not back off   ☐ can't decide *(check one)*

2. Should Tara and Lashonda agree between themselves which one should go with Parker to the prom in order to reduce the pressure on Parker?

   ☐ yes, should agree   ☐ no, should not agree   ☐ can't decide *(check one)*

3. What if Parker's team members never approached Tara and Lashonda. Then should they back off and not pressure Parker to take them to the prom?

   ☐ yes, should back off   ☐ no, should not back off   ☐ can't decide *(check one)*

4. What if there are no college scouts observing the game. Then should Tara and Lashonda back off and not pressure Parker to take them to the prom?

   ☐ yes, should back off   ☐ no, should not back off   ☐ can't decide *(check one)*

LIN'S PROBLEM SITUATION again deals with differing cultural values, authority, and protection of friends. While it might be argued by those with less mature reasoning that Kwai is trying to protect his friend by offering him an opportunity to run from the immigration authorities to avoid deportation, it is illegal at the very least. Those reasoning at higher levels will take the position that the laws were made to protect the entire society from illegal activity and that by running away Lin creates additional problems for himself as well as others who have been granted legal immigration status. Even though Kwai attempts to express affection for his friend through his suggestions, he creates a dilemma for Lin by encouraging him to engage in illegal activities.

Name _____ Date _____

Lin and Kwai have been friends ever since they arrived from their home country in Asia. They have lived in the same neighborhood, gone to the same schools, and played on the same after-school sports teams. They have been inseparable.

Kwai tells Lin that he has been denied permanent residence and will have to return to Asia within 60 days. Lin knows he has good feelings toward Kwai and would like to show him in some way how much he cares about him. Lin tells Kwai that he doesn't have to go back—that he can run away and hide and get another identity. Lin says that he has friends who can get Kwai a new identity and help him get to a different part of the country and no one would ever know.

Kwai considers the idea and thinks that it may be possible to do what Lin suggests. However, Kwai doesn't want to do this alone. Kwai tells Lin that if he were a really good friend, he would do the same. They would run away and get a new life together.

What should Lin say or do?

1. Should Lin do what Kwai suggests and run away with him to get a new identity?

   ☐ yes, should run away   ☐ no, shouldn't run away   ☐ can't decide *(check one)*

2. What if Lin is caught? Should Kwai tell the authorities that it was Kwai's idea for Lin to run away and hide?

   ☐ yes, should tell   ☐ no, should keep quiet   ☐ can't decide *(check one)*

3. Was it right for Kwai to suggest something illegal to Lin?

   ☐ yes, right   ☐ no, wrong   ☐ can't decide

4. Was it right for Lin to ask Kwai to run away together with him and get a new life?

   ☐ yes, right   ☐ no, wrong   ☐ can't decide *(check one)*

EMMA'S PROBLEM SITUATION addresses the issue of trust among friends and how to respond when someone has used a confidence to his own advantage at the expense of the confider. The mature and responsible position is that Michael has violated a trust and that he should decline the job offer so that Emma can get the job. The facilitator should promote the dominance of this position over the less mature arguments of some group members that Emma shouldn't complain because "might makes right," "finders keepers," or that Emma has only her big mouth to blame. The issues of work, economics, livelihood, and survival all are critical in this situation, as well as matters relating to honesty and honor among friends and using information unfairly for one's own advantage.

Moral Reasoning—Week 10: Emma's Problem Situation

Name _____ Date _____

Emma has a job interview with a large company that provides a good salary and great health and retirement benefits. She goes for the interview, which includes a face-to-face conversation with the division director and a test that requires Emma to apply her knowledge of the job and basic reading and mathematics skills. Last week, Emma told her neighbor Michael about the job opportunity and that she was going to apply for the job. Emma is good friends with Michael, who has always supported Emma in her activities.

Emma thinks she did well on the interview. On her way home, she meets Michael, who tells her that he also had an interview with the same company applying for the same job. It occurs to Emma that Michael must have found out about the job through her. A few days later, Michael tells Emma he just received a letter offering him the job, which he is accepting.

What should Emma say or do?

1. Should Emma complain to Michael about applying for the same job she did?

   ☐ yes, should complain   ☐ no, should not complain   ☐ can't decide *(check one)*

2. Was it right for Michael to apply for the job—which he found out about thanks to Emma—knowing that Emma was applying for that job as well?

   ☐ yes, right   ☐ no, not right   ☐ can't decide *(check one)*

3. What if Michael found out about the job on his own but knows that Emma is applying for the job? Should Michael inform Emma that he is applying for the same job?

   ☐ yes, should inform   ☐ no, should not inform   ☐ can't decide *(check one)*

4. What if Michael goes to the company and explains the situation? The company tells Michael that Emma is in fact next in line and that if Michael turns down the offer they will offer the job to Emma. Should Michael reject the job offer so that Emma can get the job?

   ☐ yes, should reject   ☐ no, should not reject   ☐ can't decide *(check one)*

Additional Forms

Community Behavior Report

Group member _____ Date _____

Rater _____

Instructions: Please check whether or not, to the best of your knowledge, the youth exhibited each behavior during the past month.

1. Damaged property	☐ yes	☐ no	☐ don't know
2. Helped someone	☐ yes	☐ no	☐ don't know
3. Cursed someone	☐ yes	☐ no	☐ don't know
4. Kept cool when someone provoked him/her	☐ yes	☐ no	☐ don't know
5. Upset he/she couldn't do something right away	☐ yes	☐ no	☐ don't know
6. Showed understanding of someone's feelings	☐ yes	☐ no	☐ don't know
7. Was verbally abusive	☐ yes	☐ no	☐ don't know
8. Resisted negative pressure from others	☐ yes	☐ no	☐ don't know
9. Involved in a physical fight	☐ yes	☐ no	☐ don't know
10. Cooperated with others	☐ yes	☐ no	☐ don't know
11. Slammed doors, punched walls	☐ yes	☐ no	☐ don't know
12. Had to be restrained	☐ yes	☐ no	☐ don't know
13. Expressed affection in appropriate manner	☐ yes	☐ no	☐ don't know
14. Started an argument or fight	☐ yes	☐ no	☐ don't know
15. Complimented someone	☐ yes	☐ no	☐ don't know
16. Complained in an angry manner	☐ yes	☐ no	☐ don't know
17. Complained in appropriate manner	☐ yes	☐ no	☐ don't know
18. Pushed or shoved someone	☐ yes	☐ no	☐ don't know
19. Followed instructions	☐ yes	☐ no	☐ don't know
20. Used an offensive gesture	☐ yes	☐ no	☐ don't know
21. Expressed feelings appropriately	☐ yes	☐ no	☐ don't know
22. Threw something (e.g., chair, food, etc.)	☐ yes	☐ no	☐ don't know
23. Had a pleasant conversation with others	☐ yes	☐ no	☐ don't know
24. Threatened or harassed someone	☐ yes	☐ no	☐ don't know
25. Shared something with others	☐ yes	☐ no	☐ don't know
26. Failed to calm down when requested	☐ yes	☐ no	☐ don't know
27. Negotiated or compomised a disagreement	☐ yes	☐ no	☐ don't know
28. Bickered or argued with someone	☐ yes	☐ no	☐ don't know

 From *Aggression Replacement Training®: A Comprehensive Intervention for Aggressive Youth* (3rd ed.), by B. Glick & J. C. Gibbs, © 2011, Champaign, IL: Research Press (800-519-2707, www.researchpress.com).

Community Adjustment Rating Scale

Group member _____ Date _____

Rater _____

Instructions: Please rate the youth's adjustment at the present time. In addition to each of your ratings, please provide a brief comment explaining the reason for your rating.

1. Home and family adjustment:

☐	☐	☐	☐
Excellent (3)	Good (2)	Fair (1)	Poor (0)

   Comment:

   _____

2. School adjustment:

☐	☐	☐	☐
Excellent (3)	Good (2)	Fair (1)	Poor (0)

   Comment:

   _____

3. Work adjustment:

☐	☐	☐	☐
Excellent (3)	Good (2)	Fair (1)	Poor (0)

   Comment:

   _____

4. Peer adjustment:

☐	☐	☐	☐
Excellent (3)	Good (2)	Fair (1)	Poor (0)

   Comment:

   _____

5. Legal adjustment:

☐	☐	☐	☐
Excellent (3)	Good (2)	Fair (1)	Poor (0)

   Comment:

   _____

Sociomoral Reflection Measure–Short Form

Name _____ Date _____

1. Think about when you've made a promise to a friend of yours. How important is it for people to keep their promises, if they can, to friends?

   ☐ very important   ☐ important   ☐ not important *(check one)*

   Why is that very important/important/not important (whichever one you checked)?

   _____

   _____

2. What about keeping a promise to anyone? How important is it for people to keep promises, if they can, even to someone they hardly know?

   ☐ very important   ☐ important   ☐ not important *(check one)*

   Why is that very important/important/not important (whichever one you checked)?

   _____

   _____

3. What about keeping a promise to a child? How important is it for parents to keep their promises to their children?

   ☐ very important   ☐ important   ☐ not important *(check one)*

   Why is that very important/important/not important (whichever one you checked)?

   _____

   _____

4. In general, how important is it for people to tell the truth?

   ☐ very important   ☐ important   ☐ not important *(check one)*

   Why is that very important/important/not important (whichever one you checked)?

   _____

   _____

5. Think about when you've helped your mother or father. How important is it for children to help their parents?

   ☐ very important   ☐ important   ☐ not important *(check one)*

   Why is that very important/important/not important (whichever one you checked)?

   _____

   _____

From *Aggression Replacement Training®: A Comprehensive Intervention for Aggressive Youth* (3rd ed.), by B. Glick & J. C. Gibbs, © 2011, Champaign, IL: Research Press (800-519-2707, www.researchpress.com). *(Original source: Gibbs, Basinger, & Fuller, 1992.)*

6. Let's say a friend of yours needs help and may even die, and you're the only person who can save him or her. How important is it for a person to save the life of a friend?

   ☐ very important   ☐ important   ☐ not important *(check one)*

   Why is that very important/important/not important (whichever one you checked)?

   _____

   _____

7. What about saving the life of anyone? How important is it for a person (without losing his or her own life) to save the life of a stranger?

   ☐ very important   ☐ important   ☐ not important *(check one)*

   Why is that very important/important/not important (whichever one you checked)?

   _____

   _____

8. How important is it for a person to live even if that person doesn't want to?

   ☐ very important   ☐ important   ☐ not important *(check one)*

   Why is that very important/important/not important (whichever one you checked)?

   _____

   _____

9. How important is it for people not to take things that belong to other people?

   ☐ very important   ☐ important   ☐ not important *(check one)*

   Why is that very important/important/not important (whichever one you checked)?

   _____

   _____

10. How important is it for people to obey the law?

    ☐ very important   ☐ important   ☐ not important *(check one)*

    Why is that very important/important/not important (whichever one you checked)?

    _____

    _____

11. How important is it for judges to send people who break the law to jail?

    ☐ very important   ☐ important   ☐ not important *(check one)*

    Why is that very important/important/not important (whichever one you checked)?

    _____

    _____

Skill Homework Report 1

Name _____ Date _____

FILL IN DURING THE SESSION

What skill will you use? _____

What are the steps for the skill?

Where will you try the skill? _____

With whom will you try the skill? _____

When will you try the skill? _____

FILL IN AFTER YOU PRACTICE THE SKILL

What happened when you tried the skill?

Which steps did you really follow?

How good a job did you do in using the skill *(check one)* ☐ excellent   ☐ good   ☐ fair   ☐ poor

Skill Homework Report 2

Name _____ Date _____

FILL IN BEFORE PRACTICING THE SKILL

What skill will you use? _____

What are the steps for the skill?

Where will you try the skill? _____

With whom will you try the skill? _____

When will you try the skill? _____

If you do an excellent job, how will you reward yourself? _____

If you do a good job, how will you reward yourself? _____

If you do a fair job, how will you reward yourself? _____

FILL IN AFTER YOU PRACTICE THE SKILL

What happened when you tried the skill?

Which steps did you really follow?

How good a job did you do in using the skill *(check one)* ☐ excellent   ☐ good   ☐ fair   ☐ poor

What do you think should be your next homework assignment?

 From *Aggression Replacement Training®: A Comprehensive Intervention for Aggressive Youth* (3rd ed.), by B. Glick & J. C. Gibbs, © 2011, Champaign, IL: Research Press (800-519-2707, www.researchpress.com).

Moral Reasoning Social Decisions Chart

Name	QUESTION NUMBER						
	1	2	3	4	5	6	7
Group decision							

FINAL GROUP DECISION OUTCOMES

Group decision		

References

Adler, A. (1924). *The practice and theory of individual psychology.* New York: Harcourt Brace Jovanovich.

Ahlborn, H. H. (1986). *Dilemma session intervention with adult female offenders: behavioral and attitudinal correlates.* Unpublished manuscript, Ohio Department of Rehabilitation and Correction, Columbus.

Alberto, P. A., & Troutman, A. C. (1982). *Applied behavior analysis for teachers: Influencing student performance.* Columbus, OH: Charles E. Merrill.

American Psychiatric Association. (2000). *Diagnostic and statistical manual of mental disorders* (4th ed., Rev.): Washington, DC: Author.

Andrews, D., & Bonta, J. (2003). *Psychology of criminal conduct* (3rd ed.). Cincinnati: Anderson.

Ayllon, T., & Azrin, N. H. (1968). *The token economy: A motivational system for therapy rehabilitation.* New York: Appleton Century Crofts.

Azrin, N. H., & Holz, W. C. (1966). Punishment. In W. K. Honig (Ed.), *Operant behavior: Areas of research and application.* New York: Appleton Century Crofts.

Bandura, A. (1969). *Principles of behavior modification.* New York: Holt, Rinehart & Winston.

Bandura, A. (1973). *Aggression: A social learning analysis.* Englewood Cliffs, NJ: Prentice Hall.

Barnoski, R. (1994). *Comparative outcomes and costs for JCAA programs.* Olympia: Washington State Institute of Public Policy.

Barnoski, R. (2004, September 17). Benefits and costs of prevention and early intervention programs for youth. *Public Policy Report.* Olympia: Washington State Institute for Public Policy.

Barriga, A. Q., Gibbs, J. C., Potter, G. B., & Liau, A. K. (2001). *How I Think (HIT) Questionnaire manual.* Champaign, IL: Research Press.

Beck, A. T. (1976). *Cognitive therapy and emotional disorders.* New York: International Universities Press.

Beck, A. T. (1999). *Prisoners of hate: The cognitive basis of anger, hostility, and violence.* New York: HarperCollins.

Bronfenbrenner, U. (1979). *The ecology of human development: Experiments by nature and design.* Cambridge, MA: Harvard University Press.

Bush, J., & Bilodeau, B. (1993). *Options: A cognitive change program.* Washington, DC: U. S. Department of Justice, National Institute of Corrections.

Bush, J., Glick, B., & Taymans, J. (1997). *Thinking for a Change:Integrated cognitive behavior change program.* Washington, DC: National Institute of Corrections, U. S. Department of Justice.

Carr, E. G. (1981). Contingency management. In A. P. Goldstein, E. G. Carr, W. Davidson, & P. Wehr (Eds.), *In response to aggression.* New York: Pergamon.

Colby, A., Kohlberg, L., Speicher, B., Hewer, A., Candee, D., Gibbs, J., & Power, C. (1987). *The measurement of moral judgment* (Vol. 2). Cambridge, England: Cambridge University Press.

Colby, A., & Speicher, B. (1973). *Dilemmas for applied use.* Unpublished manuscript, Harvard University, Cambridge, Massachusetts.

Coleman, M., Pfeiffer, S., & Oakland, T. (1991). *Aggression Replacement Training with behavior disordered adolescents.* Unpublished manuscript, University of Texas.

Comstock, G. A., & Paik, H. (1994). The effects of television on antisocial behavior: A meta-analysis. *Communication Research, 21,* 516–546.

Comstock G. A., & Strasburger, V. C. (1990). Deceptive appearances: Television violence and aggressive behavior. *Journal of Adolescent Health Care, 11,* 31–44.

Csikszentmihalyi, M., & Larson, R. (1984). *Being adolescent.* New York: Basic Books.

Curulla, V. L. (1990). *Aggression Replacement Training in the community for adult learning disabled offenders.* Unpublished manuscript, University of Washington, Seattle.

Deffenbacher, J. L. (1996). Cognitive-behavioral approaches to anger reduction. In K. S. Dobson & K. D. Craig (Eds.), *Advances in cognitive-behavior therapy.* Thousand Oaks, CA: Sage.

DiBiase, A. M., Gibbs, J. C., & Potter, G. B. (2005). *EQUIP for educators: Teaching youth (grades 5–8) to think and act responsibly.* Champaign, IL: Research Press.

Donnerstein, E., Slaby, R. G., & Eron, L. D. (1994). The mass media and youth aggression. In L. D. Eron, J. H. Gentry, & P. Schlegel (Eds.), *Reason to hope: A psychosocial perspective on violence and youth.* Washington, DC: American Psychological Association.

Ellis, A. (1962). *Reasoning and emotion in psychotherapy.* Seacaucus, NJ: Lyle Stuart.

Ellis, A. (1997). *The practice of Rational Emotive Behavior Therapy.* New York: Springer.

Ellis, H. (1965). *The transfer of learning.* New York: Macmillan.

Epps, S., Thompson, B. J., & Lane, M. P. (1985). *Procedures for incorporating generalization programming into interventions for behaviorally disordered students.* Unpublished manuscript, Iowa State University, Ames.

Feindler, E. L. (1979). *Cognitive and behavioral approaches to anger control training in explosive adolescents.* Unpublished doctoral dissertation, West Virginia University, Morgantown.

Feindler, E. L. (1981). *The art of self-control.* Unpublished manuscript, Adelphi University, Garden City, NY.

Feindler, E. L., & Ecton, R. B. (1986). *Adolescent anger control: Cognitive-behavioral techniques.* New York: Pergamon.

Feindler, E. L., & Fremouw, W. J. (1983). Stress inoculation training for adolescent anger problems. In D. Meichenbaum & M. E. Jaremko (Eds.), *Stress reduction and prevention.* New York: Plenum.

Feindler, E. L., Latini, J., Nape, K., Romano, J., & Doyle, J. (1980, November). *Anger reduction methods for child-care workers at a residential delinquent facility.* Paper presented at the meeting of the Association for the Advancement of Behavior Therapy, New York.

Feindler, E. L., Marriott, S. A., & Iwata, M. (1984). Group anger control training for junior high school delinquents. *Cognitive Therapy and Research, 8,* 299–311.

Ford, D. H., & Urban, H. B. (1963). *Systems of psychotherapy.* New York: Wiley.

Frances, A., & Ross, R. (2001). *DSM-IV-TR case studies: A clinical guide to differential diagnosis.* Arlington, VA: American Psychiatric Publishing.

Foxx, R. M., & Azrin, N. H. (1973). Restitution: A method of eliminating aggressive-disruptive behavior for retarded and brain damaged patients. *Behaviour Research and Therapy, 10,* 15–27.

Freedman, B. J. (1974). *An analysis of social behavioral skill deficits in delinquent and nondelinquent adolescent boys.* Unpublished doctoral dissertation, University of Wisconsin, Madison.

Gendreau, P. (1996). The principles of effective intervention with offenders. In A. T. Harland (Ed.), *Choosing correctional options that work: Defining the demand and evaluating the supply* (pp. 117–130). Thousand Oaks, CA: Sage.

Gendreau, P., & Andrews, D. A. (1992). Correctional Program Assessment Inventory (CPAI; 5th ed.). St. John, Canada: University of New Brunswick.

Gibbs, J. C. (2010). *Moral development and reality: Beyond the theories of Kohlberg and Hoffman* (2nd ed.). Boston: Pearson Allyn & Bacon.

Gibbs, J. C., Barriga, A. Q., & Potter, G. B. (2001). *How I Think (HIT) Questionnaire.* Champaign, IL: Research Press.

Gibbs, J. C., Basinger, K. S., & Fuller, D. (1992). *Moral maturity: Measuring the development of sociomoral reflection.* Hillsdale, NJ: Erlbaum.

Gibbs, J. C., Basinger, K. S., Grime, R. L., & Snarey, J. R. (2007). Moral judgment development across cultures: Revisiting Kohlberg's universality claims. *Developmental Review, 27,* 443–500.

Gibbs, J. C., Potter, G. B., & Goldstein, A. P. (1995). *The EQUIP Program: Teaching youth to think and act responsibly through a peer-helping approach.* Champaign, IL: Research Press.

Glick, B. (1978). Training aggressive adolescents. *Journal of Adolescence and Youth* 7(1), 73–91.

Glick, B. (1979). Youth between the cracks. *Behavioral Disorders, 4*(4), 227–230.

Glick, B. (1995). *Managing delinquency: Programs that work.* Laurel, MD: American Correctional Association Press.

Glick, B. (2006). *Cognitive behavioral interventions for at-risk youth* (Vol. 1). Kingston, NJ: Civic Research Institute.

Glick, B. (2009). *Cognitive behavioral interventions for at-risk youth* (Vol. 2). Kingston, NJ: Civic Research Institute.

Glick, B., Taymans, J., & Bush, J. (2010). *Thinking for a Change: Integrated cognitive behavior change program* (Rev. ed.). Washington, DC: National Institute of Corrections, U. S. Department of Justice.

Goldstein, A. P., Apter, S. J., & Harootunian, B. (1984). *School violence.* Englewood Cliffs, NJ: Prentice-Hall.

Goldstein, A. P., & Glick, B. (1987). *Aggression Replacement Training: A comprehensive intervention for aggressive youth.* Champaign, IL: Research Press.

Goldstein, A. P., & Glick, B. (1994). *The prosocial gang: Implementing Aggression Replacement Training.* Thousand Oaks, CA: Sage.

Goldstein, A. P., Glick, B., Carthan, W., & Blancero, D. (1994). *The prosocial gang.* Thousand Oaks, CA: Sage.

Goldstein, A. P., Glick, B., & Gibbs, J. C. (1998). *Aggression Replacement Training: A comprehensive intervention for aggressive youth* (Rev. ed.). Champaign, IL: Research Press.

Goldstein, A. P., Glick, B., Irwin, M. J., McCartney, C., & Rubama, I. (1989). *Reducing delinquency: Intervention in the community.* New York: Pergamon.

Goldstein, A. P., & Kanfer, F. H. (1979). *Maximizing treatment gains.* New York: Academic.

Goldstein, A. P., & McGinnis, E. (1997). *Skillstreaming the adolescent: New strategies and perspectives for teaching prosocial skills* (Rev. ed.). Champaign, IL: Research Press.

Goldstein, A. P., Sherman, R. P., Gershaw, N. J., Sprafkin, R. P., & Glick, B. (1978). Training aggressive adolescents in pro-social behavior. *Journal of Adolescence, 7,* 73–92.

Goldstein, A. P., Sprafkin, R. P., & Gershaw, N. J. (1976). *Aggression Replacement Therapy: A trainer's manual.* Syracuse, NY: Syracuse University.

Goldstein, A. P., Sprafkin, R. P., Gershaw, N. J., & Klein, P. (1980). *Skillstreaming the adolescent: A structured learning approach to teaching prosocial skills.* Champaign, IL: Research Press.

Greenwood, C. R., Hops, H., Delquadri, J., & Guild, J. (1974). Group contingencies for group consequences in classroom management: A further analysis. *Journal of Applied Behavior Analysis, 7,* 413–425.

Gregg, V. R., Gibbs, J. C., & Basinger, K. S. (1994). Patterns of developmental delay in moral judgment by male and female delinquents. *Merrill-Palmer Quarterly, 40,* 538–553.

Hoberman, H. M. (1990). Study group report on the impact of television violence on adolescents. *Journal of Adolescent Health Care, 11,* 45–49.

Horney, K. (1939). *New ways in psychoanalysis.* New York: Norton.

Howell, J. C., & Decker, S. H. (1999). The youth gangs, violence, and drug connection. *The Juvenile Justice Bulletin.* Washington, DC: Office of Juvenile Justice and Delinquency Prevention.

Huebner, J., Vloet, T. D., Marx, I., Konrad, K., Fink, G. R., Herpertz, S. C., & Herpertz, D. (2008). Morphometric brain abnormalities in boys with conduct disorders. *Child and Adolescent Psychiatry, 45,* 540–547.

Jones, L. (1993, March). Why are we beating our children? *Ebony,* pp. 17–22.

Jones, Y. (1990). *Aggression Replacement Training in a high school setting.* Unpublished manuscript, Center for Learning and Adjustment Difficulties, Brisbane, Australia.

Kagan, J. (1966). Reflection-impulsivity: The generality and dynamics of conceptual tempo. *Journal of Abnormal Psychology, 71,* 17–24.

Katsiyannis, A., Ryan, J. B., Zhang, D., & Spann, A. (2008). Juvenile delinquency and recidivism: The impact of academic achievement. *Reading and Writing Quarterly, 24,* 177–196.

Kaunitz, C., & Strandberg, C. (2009). Aggression Replacement Training in Sweden: Evidence-based social services in practice. *Socionomen, 6,* 34–62.

Kazdin, A. E. (1975). *Behavior modification in applied settings.* Homewood, IL: Dorsey.

Keeley, S. M., Shemberg, K. M., & Carbonell, J. (1976). Operant clinical intervention: Behavior management or beyond? Where are the data? *Behavior Therapy, 7,* 292–305.

Kennedy, S. M. (1989). *Anger management training with adult prisoners.* Unpublished doctoral dissertation, University of Ottawa, Canada.

Kohlberg, L. (1969). Stage and sequence: The cognitive-developmental approach to socialization. In D. A. Goslin (Ed.), *Handbook of socialization theory and research.* Chicago: Rand McNally.

Kohlberg, L. (Ed.). (1973). *Collected papers on moral development and moral education.* Cambridge, MA: Harvard University, Center for Moral Education.

Kohlberg, L. (1984). *Essays on moral development: Vol. 2. The psychology of moral development.* San Francisco: Harper and Row.

Latessa, E. (2006). Effectiveness of cognitive behavioral interventions for youthful offenders: Review of the research. In B. Glick (Ed.), *Cognitive behavioral interventions for at-risk youth.* Kingston, NJ: Civic Research Institute.

Leeman, L. W., Gibbs, J. C., & Fuller, D. (1993). Evaluation of a multi-component treatment program for juvenile delinquents. *Aggressive Behavior, 19,* 281–292.

Lickona, T. (1983). *Raising good children.* New York: Bantam.

Lipsey, M. (1999). Can intervention rehabilitate serious delinquents? *Annals of the American Academy of Political and Social Science, 564,* 142–166.

Little, V. I., & Kendall, P. C. (1979). Cognitive-behavioral interventions with delinquents: Problem solving, role-taking, and self-control. In P. C. Kendall & S. D. Hollon (Eds.), *Cognitive-behavioral interventions.* Orlando, FL: Academic.

Luria, A. R. (1961). *The role of speech in the regulation of normal and abnormal behavior.* New York: Liveright.

Maltz, D. (1984). *Recidivism.* New York: Academic.

McCrady, F., Kaufman, K., Vasey, M. W., Barriga, A. Q., Devlin, R. S., & Gibbs, J. C. (2008). It's all about me: A brief report of incarcerated adolescent sex offenders' generic and sex-specific cognitive distortions. *Sexual Abuse: A Journal of Research and Treatment, 20,* 261–271.

McGinnis, E., & Goldstein, A. P. (1984). *Skillstreaming the elementary school child: A guide for teaching prosocial skills.* Champaign, IL: Research Press.

McGinnis, E., & Goldstein, A. P. (1990). *Skillstreaming in early childhood: Teaching prosocial skills to the preschool and kindergarten child.* Champaign, IL: Research Press.

McGinnis, E., & Goldstein, A. P. (1997). *Skillstreaming the elementary school child: New strategies and perspectives for teaching prosocial skills* (Rev. ed.). Champaign, IL: Research Press.

McGinnis, E., & Goldstein, A. P. (2003). *Skillstreaming in early childhood: New strategies and perspectives for teaching prosocial skills* (Rev. ed.). Champaign, IL: Research Press.

Meichenbaum, D. H. (1977). *Cognitive-behavior modification: An integrative approach.* New York: Plenum.

Meichenbaum, D. H., & Goodman, J. (1969). The developmental control of operant motor responding by verbal operants. *Journal of Experimental Child Psychology, 7,* 553–565.

Meichenbaum, D. H., & Goodman, J. (1971). Training impulsive children to talk to themselves: A means of developing self-control. *Journal of Abnormal Psychology, 77,* 115–126.

Meyers, D. W. (1982). *Moral dilemmas at Scioto Village.* Unpublished manuscript, Ohio Department of Youth Services, Columbus.

Morawski, J., & Morawski, E. (2009). Strategies for the development of Aggression Replacement Training® in Polish schools and local communities. In B. Glick (Ed.), *Cognitive behavioral interventions for at-risk youth* (Vol. 2.). Kingston, NJ: Civic Research Institute.

National Center for Mental Health Promotion and Youth Violence Prevention. (2007). *Aggression Replacement Training fact sheet.* Retrieved September 10, 2010, from http://www.promoteprevent.org/publications/ebi-factsheets/aggression-replacement-training%C2%AE-art%C2%AE

Novaco, R. W. (1975). *Anger control: The development and evaluation of an experimental treatment.* Lexington, MA: D. C. Heath.

Novaco, R. W. (2004). *Novaco Anger Scale and Provocation Inventory (NAS-PI).* Los Angeles: Western Psychological Association.

Ndrecka, M. K., Bechtel, Lowenkamp, C. T., & Latessa, E. J. (2009). Effectiveness of juvenile cognitive behavioral and family oriented interventions: A meta-analysis. In B.Glick (Ed.), *Cognitive behavioral interventions for at-risk youth.* Kingston, NJ: Civic Research Institute.

Osgood, C. E. (1953). *Method and theory in experimental psychology.* New York: Oxford University Press.

Palmer, E. J., & Hollin, C. R. (1998). A comparison of patterns of moral development in young offenders and non-offenders. *Legal and Criminological Psychology, 3,* 225–235.

Piaget, J. (1965). *Moral judgment of the child* (M. Gabain, Trans.). New York: Free Press. (Original work published 1932)

Piaget, J. (1969). *The mechanisms of perception.* London, England: Routledge and Kegan Paul.

Potter, G. B., Gibbs, J. C., & Goldstein, A. P. (2001). *The EQUIP implementation guide: Teaching youth to think and act responsibly through a peer-helping approach.* Champaign, IL: Research Press.

Preudhomme, G. R., & Dunston, L. G. (1989). *Rites of passage: A program for the New York State Division for Youth.* Albany, NY: Budget Office of the Governor.

Quay, H. (1965). *Juvenile delinquency: Research and theory.* Princeton, NJ: Van Nostrand.

Quay, H., & A. Hogan. (1999). *Handbook of disruptive behavior disorders.* New York: Plenum.

Rank, O. (1945). *Will therapy.* New York: Knopf.

Reno, S. (1997). *Choices.* Madison: Wisconsin Department of Corrections.

Robinson, K., & Little, G. (1988). *Moral Reconation Therapy.* Memphis: Correctional Counseling.

Rogers, C. R. (1951). *Client-centered therapy: Its current practice, implications, and theory.* Boston: Houghton Mifflin.

Ross, R., & Fabiano, E. (1986). *Reasoning and rehabilitation.* Ottawa, Cananda: T3 Associates.

Rudy, S. A. (2009). *Aggression Replacement Training: Recidivism among incarcerated male juveniles with conduct disorder.* Encino, CA: Phillips Graduate Institute.

Ryan, S. (2009). *Aggression Replacement Training: Recidivism among incarcerated male juveniles with Conduct Disorder.* Unpublished doctoral dissertation, Phillips Graduate Institute, Encino, California.

Samenow, S. (1984). *Inside the criminal mind.* New York: Random House.

Samenow, S. (2004). *Inside the criminal mind* (Rev. ed.). New York: Random House.

Sherman, L.W., Farrington, D. P., MacKenzie, D. L., & Welsh, B. C. (2006). *Evidence-based crime prevention* (Rev. ed.). New York: Routledge.

Siegel, J. M. (1986). Multidimensional Anger Inventory. *Journal of Personality and Social Psychology, 51*(1), 191–200.

Sobsey, D. (1990). Modifying the behavior of behavior modification. In A. Repp & N. Singh (Eds.), *Perspectives on the use of nonaversive and aversive interventions for persons with developmental disabilities.* Sycamore, IL: Sycamore Publishing.

Stams, G. J., Brugman, D., Dekovic, M., van Rosmalen, L., van der Laan, P., & Gibbs, J. C. (2006). The moral judgment of juvenile delinquents: A meta-analysis. *Journal of Abnormal Child Psychology, 34,* 697–713.

Stokes, T. F., & Baer, D. M. (1977). An implicit technology of generalization. *Journal of Applied Behavior Analysis, 10,* 349–367.

Straus, M. A. (1994). *Beating the devil out of them: Corporal punishment in American families.* New York: Lexington.

Sullivan, H. S. (1953). *Conceptions of modern psychiatry.* New York: Norton.

Taymans, J. (1997). *Problem solving skills.* Washington, DC: George Washington University.

Tharp, R. G., & Wetzel, R. J. (1969). *Activities and exercises for affective education.* Washington, DC: American Educational Research Association.

Thorndike, E. L., & Woodworth, R. S. (1901). The influence of improvement in one mental function upon the efficiency of other functions. *Psychological Review, 8,* 247–261.

U.S. Department of Education Safe, Disciplined, and Drug-Free Schools Expert Panel (2002). *Exemplary and promising safe, disciplined, and drug-free schools programs, 2001.* Retrieved September 10, 2010, from http://www.ed.gov/admins/lead/safety/exemplary01/exemplary01.pdf

U.S. Justice Department Office of Juvenile Justice and Delinquency Prevention. (1995). *OJJDP models programs guide.* Retrieved September 10, 2010, from http://www.ojjdp.ncjrs.gov/mpg/mpgProgramDetails.aspx?ID = 292

Walker, H. M. (1979). *The acting-out child: Coping with classroom disruption.* Boston: Allyn & Bacon.

Yochelson, S., & Samenow, S. E. (1976). *The criminal personality: Vol. 1. A profile for change.* New York: Jason Aronson.

Yochelson, S., & Samenow, S. E. (1977). *The criminal personality: Vol. 2. The change process.* New York: Jason Aronson.

Zillmann, D. (1999). *Hostility and aggression.* Hillsdale, NJ: Erlbaum.

About the Authors

BARRY GLICK received his PhD from Syracuse University in 1972. Trained as a counseling psychologist, Dr. Glick has devoted his professional career to the development of policies, programs, and services for adolescents. His areas of specialization include juvenile delinquency, aggression and violence, youth gangs, and adolescent emotional disturbance. Dr. Glick has worked in both private child care agencies and state government in the capacity of child care worker, psychologist, administrator, manager, and agency executive staff. Previously Associate Deputy Director for Local Services, New York State Division for Youth, he is currently an international consultant to juvenile and adult correctional systems, educational systems, and mental health systems. He is first author of *Cognitive Behavioral Interventions That Work with At-Risk Youth* (Vols. 1 & 2; Civic Research Institute, 2006, 2009) and two American Correctional Association Press books: *No Time to Play: Youthful Offenders in Adult Systems* (1999), and *Recess Is Over: A Handbook for Managing Youthful Offenders in Adult Systems* (2001). He is coauthor of the first and second editions of *Aggression Replacement Training* (Research Press, 1987, 1998) and *The Prosocial Gang* (Sage, 1994). Dr. Glick also co-developed Thinking for a Change, a multimodal cognitive-behavioral intervention sponsored by the National Institute of Corrections. He serves on several editorial boards; is a member emeritus of the National Gangs Advisory Committee; holds the position of University Scholar at the University of Cincinnati; and is a nationally certified counselor, approved clinical supervisor, and licensed mental health counselor.

JOHN C. GIBBS, PhD (Harvard University, 1972), is a professor of developmental psychology at The Ohio State University. He has been a member of the State of Ohio Governor's Council on Juvenile Justice and is a faculty associate of The Ohio State University Criminal Justice Research Center. His work has focused on developmental theory, assessment of social cognition and moral judgment development, and interventions with conduct-disordered adolescents. A coauthor on the second edition of *Aggression Replacement Training* (Research Press, 1998), he is first author of *The EQUIP Program* (1995) and coauthor of *The EQUIP Program Implementation Guide* (2001). His other books include *EQUIP for Educators* (Research Press, 2005), *Moral Development and Reality: Beyond the Theories of Kohlberg and Hoffman* (2nd ed.; Pearson Allyn & Bacon, 2010) and *Moral Maturity: Measuring the Development of Sociomoral Reflection* (Erlbaum, 1992).

Notes

Notes

Notes

Notes

Notes

Notes

Notes

Notes